MASTERWORKS
OF
CHILDREN'S
LITERATURE

MASTERWORKS

OF

CHILDREN'S

LITERATURE

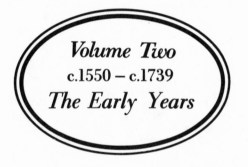

Volume Two
c.1550 – c.1739
The Early Years

EDITED BY *Francelia Butler*

GENERAL EDITOR: *Jonathan Cott*

ASSISTANT EDITOR: *Charity Chang*

THE STONEHILL PUBLISHING COMPANY
IN ASSOCIATION WITH
CHELSEA HOUSE PUBLISHERS
NEW YORK

GENERAL EDITOR: Jonathan Cott
ADVISORY EDITOR: Robert G. Miner, Jr.
VOLUME EDITOR: Francelia Butler
PROJECT DIRECTOR: Esther Mitgang
DESIGNER: Paul Bacon
EDITORIAL STAFF: Philip Minges III, Claire Bottler
PRODUCTION: Coco Dupuy, Heather White, Sandra Su, Susan Lusk, Christopher Newton

First Printing
Printed and Bound in the United States of America
ISBN: 0-87754-376-3
LC: 79-89986

Stonehill Publishing Company
Jeffrey Steinberg, Publisher

Chelsea House Publishers
Harold Steinberg, Chairman and Publisher
Andrew E. Norman, President
Susan Lusk, Vice President
A Division of Chelsea House Educational Communications, Inc.,
133 Christopher Street, New York, NY 10014

ACKNOWLEDGMENTS

Thomas Cogan: *The Haven of Health*, London, 1584. Courtesy of The Armed Forces Medical Library.

John Gerard: *The Herball*, London, 1636. Courtesy of Special Collections Department, University of Connecticut Library.

Thomas Hariot: *A Briefe and True Report of the New Found Land of Virginia*, London, 1590. Courtesy of Dover Publications.

Alex Helm, ed.: *The Seven Champions*, in Chapbook No. 21 of *The Chapbook Mummers' Plays*, Leicester, England, 1969. Courtesy of The Curators of the Bodleian Library, Oxford.

_____: *St. George and the Dragon* from *Five Mumming Plays for Schools*, London, 1965. Courtesy of English Folk Dance and Song Society.

James Janeway: *A Token for Children*/Cotton Mather: *A Token, for the Children of New-England*, Boston, 1700. Courtesy of The American Antiquarian Society, Worcester, Massachusetts.

John Milton: *Comus* from *Works, Volume I*, 1931. Courtesy of Columbia University Press.

Thomas Raynalde: *The Birth of Mankinde*, London, 1598. Courtesy of The Library of Congress.

Henry Sigerist, ed.: *Four Treatises of Theophrastus Von Hohenheim called Paracelsus*, selection from Chapter Four, translated from the German, Baltimore, Maryland, 1941. Courtesy of The Johns Hopkins Press.

Edward Topsell: *The Historie of Foure-Footed Beastes . . .* , London, 1608. Courtesy of The David McCandless McKell Collection, The Ross County Historical Society, Chillicothe, Ohio.

ILLUSTRATIONS

The illustrations by William Blake were done for Milton's *Comus*. Courtesy of the Museum of Fine Arts, Boston. The illustrations from *Orbis Pictus* of John Comenius, London, 1659. Courtesy of The British Museum Library Board. The illustration of St. George from *The Chapbook Mummers' Plays*, edited by Alex Helm, 1969. Courtesy of the Curators of The Bodleian Library, Oxford.

Photography for items reproduced from the Special Collections Department, University of Connecticut Library, is by Richard Akeroyd, a member of The National Commission on Libraries and Information Science, Washington, D.C. Photography for items reproduced from The David McCandless McKell Collection, The Ross County Historical Society, Chillicothe, Ohio, is by Tomastik.

Contents

Part One
Religious
Prose

War With the Devil:

or the Young Man's Conflict
with the Powers of Darkness

In A Dialogue.

Discovering the Corruption and Vanity of Youth;
the Horrible Nature of Sin, and deplorable Condition
of Fallen Man: Also a Definition, Power, and Rule of
Conscience, and the Nature of *True Conversion*

By B. KEACH

SELECTIONS

FIRST PUBLISHED IN *1673, this work was continuously popular for a hundred years, at which time it had gone into its twenty-second edition. It is a young man's conversation with the Devil, with his Conscience, Truth, Companions, a Neighbor who serves as omniscient observer, and Jesus. It descends most notably from medieval debates between personified virtues and vices, which easily turn into morality plays. A similar form appears in Bunyan's* Moral Songs, *No. 17, and Bunyan is believed to have been influenced by it in* The Holy War. *By the time the Youth in Keach's work is converted his Conscience has almost destroyed him. The work is in the iambic couplets popular at the time, with each two lines generally completing a thought—though the couplets are not so "closed" in that respect as those later perfected by Alexander Pope.*

Keach (1640–1704), a Calvinistic Baptist, knew the pillory and imprisonment for his catechism, A Child's Instructor. *On October 20, 1664, this book was burned before his face. He had unorthodox views, one of which was that it was a good idea for a congregation to sing hymns, and he wrote a collection himself. Like many Calvinists, he was narrow in his attitude toward other Protestant sects, criticizing among others the Quakers and the Seventh-Day Baptists. He was a prolific writer, the author of over fifty religious works.*

The portion of War with the Devil *appearing here is reprinted from the twenty-second edition, published in London in 1776, pp. 1–69. The exchange continues for twenty agonizing pages, at the end of which the youth breaks forth into hymns of praise.*

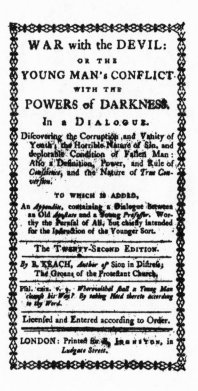

WAR with the DEVIL:
OR THE
YOUNG MAN's CONFLICT
WITH THE
POWERS of DARKNESS.
In a DIALOGUE.

Discovering the Corruption and Vanity of
Youth, the Horrible Nature of Sin, and
deplorable Condition of Fallen Man :
Also a Definition, Power, and Rule of
Conscience, and the Nature of True Con-
version;

TO WHICH IS ADDED,

An Appendix, containing a Dialogue between
an Old Apostate and a Young Professor. Worthy the Perusal of All, but chiefly intended
for the Instruction of the Younger Sort.

The TWENTY-SECOND EDITION.

By B. KEACH, Author of Sion in Distress;
The Groans of the Protestant Church.

Psal. cxix. v. 9. Wherewithal shall a Young Man
cleanse his Way? By taking Heed thereto according
to thy Word.

Licensed and Entered according to Order.

LONDON: Printed for B. Branston, in
Ludgate Street.

TO THE READER,
IN VINDICATION OF THIS BOOK.

ONE OR TWO Lines to thee I'll here commend,
   This honest P O E M briefly to defend
From Calumny, because that at this Day
All Poetry there's many do gainsay,
And very much condemn; as if the same
Did worthily deserve Reproach and Blame.
If any Book in Verse they chance t'espy,
Away, prophane! they presently do cry.
But tho' this kind of Writing some dispraise,
Since Men so captious are in these our Days,
Yet I dare say, howe'er this Scruple 'rose,
Verse has exprest as Sacred Things as Prose:
Tho' some there be that Poetry abuse,
Must we not therefore the same Method use?
Yea, sure; for in my Conscience it is best,
And doth deserve more Honour than the rest;

For, 'tis no human Knowledge gain'd by Art,
But rather, 'tis inspir'd into the Heart
By Means Divine, for true Divinity
Hath with this Science great Affinity.
Tho' some thro' Ignorance do it oppose,
Many do it esteem far more than Prose;
And find also that unto them it brings
Content, and hath been the Delight of Kings.
David, altho' a King, yet was a Poet,
And *Solomon* also, the Scriptures show it.
Then what if for all this some should abase it,
I'm apt to think the Angels do embrace it.
Tho' God doth giv't here but in Part to some,
Saints shall have it perfect in the World to come.

By a Friend, in Praise of these Poems.

M Y MUSE IS DULL; altho' I have a Will
  This Book for to commend, I want the Skill.
I know not how its Worth for to declare;
Few Poems doubtless may with it compare.
The sluggish Soul it strives for to awake
Before it drops into the fiery Lake;
There's very few upon the Earth do live,
But might from hence some Benefit receive:
For tho' it is brought forth in this our Clime,
Yet 'twill agree with every Place and Time.
Its Message is of such a large Extent,
It may in Truth to all the World be sent:
To Male and Female, high and low Degree,
He speaks a Word, to Bond as well as Free;
All in whom *Conscience* dwells, he lets them see

Conscience's great Power and Authority.
When Heav'n's hot Thunderbolt with Fire and Hail,
Made *Egypt's* mighty Monarch's Courage fail,
Conscience steps in, made him cry out amain,
The Lord is just, I and my wicked Train
Have sinn'd: Yea, *Conscience* also brings
Saul Son of *Kish*, the first of *Israel's* Kings
Before the Prophet, humbly to confess
That he had sinn'd and acted Wickedness.
Conscience made *David* to cry out amain,
'Tis I have sinn'd; I have Uriah *slain!*
Although he slew a Lion and a Bear,
And did not the great Giant's Courage fear,
Yet *Conscience* made him stoop and tremble too,
Yea, more than this, you'll find *Conscience* can do.
Here's Counsel for Professors and Prophane,
Choose or refuse, here's Loss and also Gain.
One Reason, Reader, of this Mode or Style,
Is, that it might with honest Craft beguile
Such curious Fancies, who had rather choose
To read ten Lines in Verse, than one in Prose;
For, as the nimble Fly, who lightly springs
Against the Flame, until she burns her Wings,
Is taken Captive with that sulph'rous Flame,
With which the only sought to sport and game;
So, whilst these curious Fancies seem to play
With this small Piece, 'twill secretly betray
Them to their *Conscience;* and if *Conscience* send
Them to God's Word, the Author has his End,
Provided that unto the same they yield,
And *Grace* and *Conscience* do obtain the Field.

    Farewel.   W. B.

THE YOUTH IN HIS UNCONVERTED STATE.

YOUTH.

THE *Naturalists* most aptly do compare
  My Age unto the *Spring* whose Beauty's rare,
  When frightful *Sol* enters the Golden Sign,
Which is call'd *Aries*, his glorious Shrine,
And splendid Rays, do cause the Earth to spring,

And Trees to bud, and quicken every Thing:
All Plants, and Herbs, and Flowers, then do flourish;
The Grass doth sprout, tender *Lambs* to nourish.
These Things in Winter that seem to be dead,
Do now rise up and quickly shew their Head;
And do obtain a natural Resurrection,
By his own Beams, and powerful Reflection.
How in the pleasant fruitful Month of *May*,
Are *Meadows* clad with Flowers rich and gay,
And all Earth's Globe adorn'd in Garments Green,
Mixt with rare Yellow, crowned like a Queen
The *Primrose, Cowslip*, and the *Violet*,
Are curiously with other Flowers set,
And chirping Birds with their melodious Sounds
Delight Man's Heart, whose Pleasures now abounds.
The *Winter's* past, with stormy Snow and Rain,
And long 'twill be ere such Things come again.
Nothing but Joys and sweet Delights appear,
Whilst doth abide the *Spring-time* of the Year;
Thus 'tis with me, who am now in my Prime,
In Merriment and Joy I spend my Time;
And like as Birds do in the lovely Spring,
I so rejoice with my Consorts, and sing,
And spend my Days in Sweet Pastime and Mirth,
And nought shall grieve or trouble me on Earth.
I am resolv'd to search the World about,
And I will suck the Sweetness of it out;
No Stone I'll leave unturn'd, that I may find
Content and Joy unto my troubled Mind;
No Sorrow shall, whilst I do live, come near me,
Nor shall the Preacher with his Fancies scare me;
At *Cards* and *Dice*, and such brave Games I'll play,
And like a Courtier deck myself most gay;
With Perriwig and Muff, and such fine Things,
With Sword and Belt, Goloshoes, and Gold Rings:
Where Bulls and Bears they bait, and Cocks do fight,
I do resort with Speed, there's my Delight;
To drink and sport among the jovial Crew,
I will resolve whatever doth ensue,
And *court Fair Ladies* that I also love,
And of all Things do very well approve,
Which tend my sensual Part to satisfy,
From whence comes all my choice Felicity.
Whate'er mine Ears do hear, or Eyes behold,
Or heart desire, if so that all my Gold
And Silver can for me those Things procure,

I'll spare no Cost, nor Pains, (you may be sure.)
Thus is my Life made very sweet to me,
Whilst others hurried are in Misery,
Whose Minds with strange Conceits troubled remain,
Thinking *by losing all, that Way to gain.*
Such *Riddles* I can't learn, I must them leave;
What's felt and seen I am resolv'd to have.
Let every Man his Mind and Fancy fill,
My Lusts I'll satisfy, and have my Will.
Who dares controul me in my present Way,
Or vex my Mind i'th' least, or me gainsay?
What State of Life can equal this of mine?
Youth's Gallantry so bravely here doth shine.

CONSCIENCE.

   Controul you, Sir? in Truth, and that dare I,
For your Contempt of my Authority;
You tread on me without the least Regard,
As if I worthy were not to be heard.
You strive to stifle me, and therefore I
Am forc'd aloud, Murder, with Speed to cry;
I can't forbear, but must cry out amain,
Such is the Wrong which from you I sustain.

YOUTH.

   What are You, Sir, you dare to be so bold?
I scorn by any He to be controul'd.
Ere I have done with you, I'll make you know,
You shall your Power and Commission show.

CONSCIENCE.

   Be not so hot, and you shall know my Name,
And also learn from whence my Power came;
I'm no Usurper, yet I do command
You for to stop, and make a present Stand;
'Twixt you and I, as will appear anon,
If from these Courses you don't quickly turn.
For all your Courage which you seem to take,
The News I bring's enough to make you quake.

YOUTH.

   Whoe'er thou art, I'll make you by-and-by,
Confess you have accus'd me wrongfully.
From Murder I am clear in Thought and Deed,
Thus to be charg'd, causes my Heart to bleed.
Pray let me crave your Name, if you are free,

If you provoke me, worse 'twill quickly be;
You seek Occasion, and are quarrelsome,
And therefore 'tis I do suppose you're come;
But if your Name you don't declare to me,
I am resolv'd to be reveng'd on thee.

CONSCIENCE.

   What Violence (alas!) can you do more,
Than that which you have done to me before?
Forbear your Threats, be still, and hold your Hand,
And quickly you shall know and understand
My Name, my Pow'r, and Place of Residence,
Which may to you prove of great Consequence.
I am a Servant to a mighty King,
Who rules and reigns, and governs ev'ry Thing;
Who keeps one Court above, and here below
Another he doth keep, as you shall know.
O'er this inferior Court placed am I,
To act and do as his great Deputy.
I truly judge according to my Light;
Yea, and impartially do each Man right:
Those I condemn who vile and guilty are,
And justify the Holy and Sincere.
I order'd am to watch continually
O'er all your Actions with a wary Eye;
And I have found how you have of late Time
Committed many a bold and horrid Crime
Of Murder, Treason, and like Villainy,
Against the Crown and gracious Dignity
Of that great Prince from whence you have your Breath,
Who's *King* and *Ruler* over all the Earth.
I am his Judge, Attorney-General,
And have Commission also, you to call
Unto the Bar, and make you to confess
Your horrid Crimes, and fearful Guiltiness:
A black Indictment I have drawn in Truth,
Against thyself, thou miserable *Youth!*
Thy Pride I shall abate, thy Pleasures mar,
And bring thee to confess with Tears at Bar
Thy Sports and Games, and youthful Lust to be
Nought else but Sin, and cursed Vanity.
And for to put thee also out of Doubt,
My Name is *Conscience*, which you bear about:
No other than th' accusing Faculty
Of that dear Soul which in thy Breast doth lie:
I by that Rule Men's Thoughts and Ways compare,

By which their inward Parts enlightened are,
And as they do accord, or disagree,
I do accuse, or clear immediately:
According to your Light you do not live,
But violate that Rule which God doth give
To you to square your Life and Actions by,
From whence comes all your Woe and Misery.

YOUTH.

   Conscience art thou! Why didst not speak ere now?
To mind what thou dost say, I can't tell how;
Thou melancholy Fancy, fly from me,
My Pleasure I'll not leave, in spite of thee;
Other brave Guests you see to me are come,
And in my House for thee there is no Room.
Dost think I will be check'd by silly Thought,
And into Snares by foolish Fancy brought?
Is't you which cry but Murder? only you?
A Fig (alas) for all that you can do.
For tho' against me you do *prate* and *preach*,
Your very Neck I am resolv'd to stretch.
I'll *swear*, *carouse* and *whore*, do what you will,
Till I have stifled you and made you still
I'll clip your *Wings*, and make you see at length,
I do know how to spoil you of your Strength.
When you do speak I will not lend an Ear,
I'll make in Truth as if I did not hear.
If you speak loud when I am all alone,
I will rise up and straitway will be gone
To the brave Boys who toss the Pot about,
And that's the Way to tire your Patience out.
I'll go to *Plays* and *Games*, and Dancings too,
And ere a while I shall be rid of you.

CONSCIENCE.

   Thou stubborn, foolish Youth, be not so rash,
Lest ere you be aware you feel my Lash;
I have a Sting, a Whip, yea, I can bite;
Before you shall o'ercome I'll stoutly fight;
I'll gripe you sore, and make you howl anon,
If you resolve in Sin still to go on.
I've overcome strong Hearts, and made 'em yield,
And so shall you before I quit the field;
Go where you will, I'll presently come after,
And into Sorrow will turn all your Laughter.
'Twill prove hard Work for you to shake me off,

Though you at me do seem to jeer and scoff,
As if o'er you I had no Jurisdiction,
Or was a Dream, a Fancy, or some Fiction.
For all your Wrath, I yet must you disturb;
Tho' you offended are, I can't but curb
And snub you daily, as I oft' have done,
Till you repent, and from lewd Courses turn.
For till the Cause be taken quite away,
Th' Effect will follow whate'er you do or say;
Unless your Light wholly extinguish'd be,
If Sin remains, Disturbance you will see:
Therefore I do beseech you soberly,
For to submit to my Authority.
Obey my Voice, I pray thee make a Trial,
Before you give another flat Denial.
If more sweet Comfort I don't yield to you,
Than all which doth from sinful Actions flow,
Then me reject; but, otherwise, my Friend,
My Checks receive, and to my Motion bend.
Get Peace within, whatever thou dost do,
And let vain Pleasures, and Corruptions go;
That will be better for thy Soul at last,
Than Gold or Silver, or what else thou hast.
And since we are alone, let you and I
More mildly talk about Supremacy,
Is't best for you that Pride and Folly reign,
Which nothing bring but Sorrow, Shame, and Pain,
And *Conscience* to reject, who perfectly
From Guilt and Bondage strive to set you free?
Have not the Lusts by which you are now led,
Brought many a one to want a Piece of Bread?
What brave *estates* have been consum'd thereby,
And now are forc'd in Barns or Straw to lie?
How has the Wife been ruin'd with the Child,
Besides poor *Conscience* grievously turmoil'd?
Nay, once again give Ear, I pray thee hark,
Hath not many a brave and curious Spark
Been brought in stinking Prisons there to lie,
For yielding to their Lust and Vanity?
How many swing at *Tyburn* ev'ry Year,
For stabbing *Conscience* without Care or Fear!
And some out of their Wits do often run,
And by that Means are utterly undone.
Some Men so stifle me I cannot speak,
And then they sport and play, and merry make;

Resolving that I shall not gripe them more,
But then afresh I quickly make them roar;
Some of them I do drive into Despair,
When in their Face I do begin to stare;
No Rest, nor Peace at all their Souls can find,
I so disturb them, and perplex their Mind.
What say you now, *Young Man?* Will you submit?
Weigh well the Danger and the Benefit.
The Danger on the one Hand will be great,
If me you do oppose and ill intreat.
Sweet Profit comes, you'll see, on th' other Hand,
To such who subject are to my Command.
What dost thou say? Shall I embraced be?
Or wilt thou follow still thy Villainy?

YOUTH.

   Was ever *Young Man* thus perplex'd as I,
Who flourished in sweet Prosperity?
Where'er I go *Conscience* dogs me about,
No Quiet can I have in doors or out.
Conscience, what is the Cause you make such Strife,
I can't enjoy the Comforts of my Life?
I am so grip'd and pinched in my Breast,
I know not where to go, nor where to rest.

CONSCIENCE.

   'Cause you have wronged and offended me,
Loving vain Pleasures and Iniquity.
The Light you have you walk not up unto,
You know, 'tis Evil which you daily do.
My Witness I must bear continually,
For the Great G O D, whose Glorious Majesty
Did in thy Soul give me so large a Place,
As for to stop you in your sinful Race;
I must reprove, accuse, and you condemn,
Whilst you by Sin his Sov'reignty contemn;
I can't betray my Trust, nor hold my Peace,
Till I am stabbed, fear'd, or Light doth cease:
Till you your Life amend, and Sins forsake,
I shall pursue you, though your Heart dothach.

YOUTH.

   How bold and malapert is *Conscience* grown?
Tho' I upon this Fellow daily frown,
And his Advice reject, yet still doth he
Knock at my Door, as if he'd weary me.

Conscience, I'd have you know, in Truth, that I
A Person am of some Authority;
Are you so saucy as to curb and chide
Such a brave Spark, who can't your Ways abide?
'Tis much below my Birth and Parentage,
And it agrees not with my present Age
For to give place to you, or to regard
Those Things from you I have so often heard.

CONSCIENCE.

   Alas! proud Flesh, dost think thyself too high
To be subject to such a one as I?
Thy Betters I continually gainsay,
If they my Motions don't with Care obey;
My Power's great, and my Commission's large,
There's scarce a Man but I with Folly charge;
The King and Peasant are alike to me,
I favour none of high or low Degree;
If they offend, I in their Faces fly,
Without Regard, or Fear of Standers by.

YOUTH.

   Speak not another Word: Don't you perceive
There's scarce a Man or Woman will believe
What you do say, you're grown so out of Date?
Be silent then, and do no longer prate.
In the Country your Credit is but small,
There's few care for your Company at all,
The *Husbandman* the *Land-mark* can't remove,
But you straitway him bitterly reprove;
Nor plough a little of his Neighbour's Land,
But you command him presently to stand.
There's not a Man can go i' th' least awry,
But out against him you do fiercely fly.
The People therefore now so weary are,
They've thrust you almost out of ev'ry Shire:
And in the City you so hated be,
There's very few that care a Rush for thee;
For if they should believe what you do say,
Their Pride and Bravery will soon decay;
Their *Swearing*, *Cursing*, and their *Drunkenness*,
Would vanish quite away, or grow much less.
Our *Craft* of *Profit*, and our *Pleasure* too,
Would soon go down and ruin'd be by you.
The *Whore* and *Bawd*, with the *Play-houses* then
Would be contemned by all Sorts of Men.

You strive to spoil us of our sweet Delight,
Our Pleasures you oppose with all your Might;
The Fabrick of our Joy you would pull down,
And make our Youth like to a Country Clown;
We half *Fanaticks* should be made ('tis clear)
If unto thee we once inclined were.
But this among the rest doth chear my Heart,
There's very few in *London* take thy Part;
Here and there one which we do *Nick-names* give,
Who hated are, and judg'd not fit to live.
'Tis out of Fashion grown, we daily see,
Conscience for to regard i'th' least Degree:
He that can't Whore and Swear without Controul,
We do account to be a timorous Fool.
Therefore, though you so desperately do fall
Upon poor Me, yet I do hope I shall
Get loose from you, and then I'll tear the Ground,
And in all Joy and Pleasure will abound.

CONSCIENCE.
  Ah! poor deceived Soul, Dost thou not know
That most of all Mankind i' th' Broad Way go?
What tho' they do most wickedly abuse me?
Wilt thou also in like Manner use me?
What tho' they will of me no Warning take,
Till they drop down into the *Stygian* Lake;
Wilt thou befriend the cursed Serpent so,
As to go on till comes thy Overthrow?
What though I am in no Request by them,
Don't they likewise God's holy Word contemn?
Don't they the Gospel cast quite out of Sight,
Lest from their Pleasures it should them affright?
What tho' my Friends are toss'd about and hurl'd,
Their inward Peace is more than all the World
Can give to them, or from them take away,
Whilst they with Diligence do me obey;
As I enlight'ned am by God's Precepts,
Which are a Guide and Lanthorn to my Steps,
O come, proud Heart, and longer don't contend,
But leave thy Lusts, and to my Scepter bend;
For I'll not leave thee, but with all my Pow'r,
I'll follow thee unto thy dying Hour.

YOUTH.
  Unto some private Place then I will fly,

Where I may hide myself; and secretly
There I'll enjoy myself in Spite of thee,
And thou shalt not i' th' least know where I be.

CONSCIENCE.

Nay, foolish Youth, how can that Thing be done?
From *Conscience* it is in vain to run.
No secret Place can you find out or 'spy,
To hide yourself from me, such is mine Eye;
I see i'th' Dark as well as in the Light,
No Doors nor Walls can keep thee from my Sight:
Where'er thou art, or go'st, am I not there,
Thy Soul with horrid Guilt to scare and fear?
Could *Cain* and *Judas* get out of my Reach,
When once between us there was the like Breach?
Did I not follow them unto the End,
And make them know what 'twas for to offend
My Glorious Prince, and me his true Viceroy?
Vengeance doth follow those who us annoy.
My Counsel then, I pray thee, take with Speed
For that's the Way alone for to be freed
From Vengeance here, and also Wrath to come,
When thou dost die, and at the Day of Doom.

YOUTH.

What, can't I fly from thee, nor thee subdue?
Then I entreat thee *Conscience*, don't pursue,
Nor follow me so close; forbear a while;
Don't yet my Beauty, nor my Pleasures spoil;
This is the Spring and Flower of my Age,
Oh! pity me, and cease thy bitter Rage.
Don't crop the tender Bud, it is too green,
O let me have those Days others have seen!
Thou hast forborn with some for a long Time,
That which I ask of thee is but the Prime
Of those good Days which are bestow'd on me;
O! that it might but once obtained be
'Tis Time enough for to adhere to thee,
After I've spent my Time in Gallantry;
In earthly Joys, and such transcendent Pleasure,
Young Men do reckon as their chiefest Treasure.

CONSCIENCE.

After all Violence, and Outrage great
Done to poor *Conscience*, you do him entreat,
Thinking for to prevail by Flattery,

But that, in Truth, I utterly defy.
It is against my Nature, you must know,
Unto vile Lust fond Pity for to show:
God hath not given such a Dispensation,
For me to wink at your Abomination:
If God but once doth blow his Candle out,
I shall be quiet then, you need not doubt;
But Woe to you, as ever you was born,
When God doth once his Light to Darkness turn.
But whilst your Soul retains a Legal Light,
Your Sins I can't endure within my Sight;
God, I am sure, no Liberty will give
To any One in horrid Sin to live;
Nor will he give Allowance for a Day,
'Tis very dangerous for to delay
The Work of thy Repentance for an Hour;
What thy Hands find to do, do with all Power.
If me you don't believe, I pray thee, *Youth*,
Go, and resolve thyself of sacred Truth.

YOUTH.

    Well, since that you no Comfort do afford,
I will enquire of GOD's most Holy Word;
So far I will your Counsel take, for I
Am sorely troubled; whither shall I fly?
I will make Trial, I'm resolv'd to see
Whether that *Truth* and *Conscience* do agree.
The Lip of *Truth* can't err, tho' *Conscience* may,
When that misguided is, this goes astray.
If *Truth* and *Conscience* speak the self-same Thing,
It will Amazement to my Spirits bring.
What now I ask, and earnestly do crave,
Is some short Time in Sin longer to have:
Conscience denies it me; *Truth*, what say you?
O that you would a little Favour shew
To a poor Lad, alas! I am but young,
Like to a Flower from the Earth new-sprung;
And as the Frost the tender Bud doth spoil,
So *Conscience* strove to serve me a great while.
Must I reform, and all my Sins forsake?
Some fitter Season, O! pray let me take;
For all Things there's a Time under the Sun,
And when I older am, I will return.

TRUTH.

    Nay, hold, vain *Youth*, you are Mistaken now,

No Time for Sin God doth to thee allow:
If I may speak, attend, and you shall hear;
I with poor *Conscience* must a Witness bear;
I am his Guide, his Rule, 'tis by my Light
He acts and does, and saith the Thing that's right.
Art thou too young thy evil Ways to leave?
And yet hast thou a precious Soul to save?
Art thou too young to leave Iniquity,
When old enough in Hell for Sin to lie?
Some fitter Season dost thou think to find?
The Devil sure darts it into thy Mind.
No Time so fit as when the Lord doth call;
Those who rebellious are, they one Day shall
Smart bitterly for their most horrid Evil,
In yielding to, and siding with the Devil:
But once again; I prithee hark to me;
Don't God, whilst thou art young, call unto thee,
Remember thy Creator? Therefore fly
To him with Speed, and 'fore him prostrate lie;
And thy First-fruits unto th' Almighty give
Of thy best Days, and learn betimes to live
Unto the Praise of his most Holy Name,
And not by Wickedness prophane the same.
This is, young Man, also thy choosing Time,
Whilst thou therefore dost flourish in thy Prime,
Place thou thy Heart upon the Lord above,
And with *Christ Jesus* also fall in Love.
Did not *Jehovah* give to thee thy Breath,
And also place thee here upon the Earth:
And many precious Blessings gave to thee,
That thou to him also should subject be?
God out of Bowels sent his precious Son,
Thy Soul from evil Ways with Speed to turn;
Who, for thy Sake was nailed to a Tree,
To free thy Soul from Hell and Misery:
And while in Sin, vile Wretch, thou dost remain,
Thou dost as 'twere him crucify again.
Thy Sins, O young Man, God doth also hate,
His Soul doth loath, and them abominate;
And wilt thou not, O young Man, be deterr'd
From evil Ways! What, is thy Heart so hard?
Will nothing influence it to repent,
Nor work Convictions in thee to relent?
Give Ear to *Truth*, *Truth* never spoke a Lye,
And fly from Sin, and youthful Vanity.
Those that do seek God's Kingdom first of all,

And do obey his sweet and gracious Call,
They shall find *Christ*, and lie within his breast,
And reap the Comforts of eternal Rest.
But if thou dost this golden Time neglect,
And all good Motions utterly reject,
And slight the Day of this thy Visitation,
That will to God be such a Provocation,
That he'll not wait upon thee any more,
Nor ever knock hereafter at thy Door.
Whilst Terms of Peace he doth to thee afford,
Be subject to him lest he draw his Sword.
If once to anger him you do provoke,
He'll bruize and break your Bones with heavy Stroke.
Who can before his Indignation stand,
Or bear the Weight of his revengeful Hand!
How dar'st thou then a War with him maintain,
And say, O'er thee *Christ Jesus* shall not reign?
Wilt thou combine with his vile Enemy,
And yet presume on his sweet Clemency?
And wilt thou, Traytor-like, contrive the Death
Of that great King from whom thou drawest Breath?
Wilt thou cast Dirt upon the Holy One,
And keep *Christ Jesus* from his rightful Throne?
Is't not his Right thy Conscience for to sway?
Ought he not then to reign, and thou obey?
Durst thou resist, and dread his sov'reign Pow'r,
Yea, or hold Parley with him for an Hour,
To gratify the Devil? who thereby
Renews his Strength; yea, and doth fortify
Himself in thee, and make his Kingdom strong,
By tempting thee to Sin whilst thou art young;
The *Blackmoor* sooner far may change his Skin,
Than canst thou leave and turn away from Sin.
When once a Habit and a Custom's taken,
Then sinful Ways are hard to be forsaken.
Sinner, dare you *Christ's* Government oppose,
And with the Devil and Corruptions close?
Which will be best, dost think, for thee, i'th' End,
The Lord for to please, and Satan to offend?
Or Satan for to please, and so thereby
Declare thyself *Jehovah's* Enemy?
For these who live in Sin, 'tis very clear,
They Enemies to God and *Jesus* are.
And wilt thou yield unto the Devil still,
By greedily accomplishing his Will?
Thinkest, vain *Youth*, he'll prove to thee a Friend,

That thou dost so his cursed Ways commend?
Has Sin, with all its odious Excrement,
So sweet a Smell, yea, and so fragrant Scent?
And dost thou value *Christ* and all he hath,
Not worth vain Pleasure here upon the Earth?
Is there more good in sinful Vanity,
Than is in all the glorious Trinity?
That which Men think is best, that do they choose,
Things of small Value 'tis they do refuse.
What thinkest thou of *Christ*, thou sinful Soul,
That thou his Messengers dost thus controul?
And dost to him so turn a deafned Ear,
His Knocks, his Calls, and Wooings will not hear.
Nor him regard, tho' he stands at the Door,
With Myrrh and Frankincense, yea, and all Store
Of Fruit and precious Spice; as Cinnamon,
Aloes, Spikenard, Camphire, and Saffron;
All costly Things, (O Soul) of Heaven above,
He has with him, yet nothing will thee move
To ope' the Door, for all his Calls and Knocks,
Thou let'st him stand, until his precious Locks
Are wet with Dew, and Drops of the long Night;
Thus dost thou him despise, reject, and slight,
And rather keep thy Lust and Pleasure still,
Than *Jesus* should thy Soul with Heaven fill;
Who makes Grey-headed Winter like a Spring,
And young Men like Cœlestial Angels sing:
The Soul he doth so greatly elevate,
That it disdains, and doth abominate
All sensual Pleasures, in comparison
Of *Jesus Christ*, his dear and only one:
Let me persuade you for to taste and try
How good *Christ* is, and then assuredly
You will admire him, yea, and praise the Lord,
That ever he did to thy Soul afford
Such a dear Saviour, and such good Advice,
To lead thy Soul into sweet Paradise;
For none do know the Nature of that Place,
That inward Joy the which shall never cease,
But he himself, who doth the same possess,
O taste and see, and own the Happiness.
Christ here's the chiefest Good, 'tis only he
In whom alone is true Felicity!
Such is the Nature of Man's panting Breast,
Nothing on Earth can give him perfect Rest;
'Tis not in Honour, that is Vanity;

For such like Beasts and other Mortals die.
Kingdoms and Crowns they tottering do stand,
The Servant may his Master soon command.
Belshazzar, who upon the Throne did sit,
His Knees against each other soon did hit;
Surrounded by his Officers of State,
His scepter'd Arm could scarce endure its Weight:
How was he scar'd when the Hand-writing came
And wrote upon the Wall, even the same
That afterwards befel! his End being come,
Receiv'd his fatal Stroke, which was his Doom.
Great Men are often filled with great Fear,
Being perplext they know not how to steer.
High Cedars fall when little Shrubs abide,
Tho' Winds do blow, and strongly turn the Tide;
For Man in Honour lives but a short Space,
And like a Beast he dies, and ends his Race.
Where's *Nimrod* now, that mighty Man of old,
And Where's the Glory of the Head of Gold?
In highest Place of human Government,
None ever found therein a true Content.
Of *Alexander* 'tis declar'd by some,
How he sat down when he had overcome
The Eastern World; and did weep very sore,
Because there were no Worlds to conquer more.
And to this very Day we find it still,
The World's not big enough Man's Soul to fill.
Riches and Wealth also can't satisfy
That precious Soul which in thy Breast doth lie.
If Store of Gold and Silver thou should'st gain,
'Twould but increase thy Sorrow, Grief and Pain.
Riches, O Young Man! they are empty Things,
And swiftly fly away with Eagle's Wings.

When Riches you do heap, you heap up Sorrow,
They're thine To day, alas! but gone To morrow;
Fires may come, and all thy Treasures burn,
Or Thieves may steal it, as they oft have done.
He that hath Thousands by the Year, this Night,
May be as poor as *Job* by Morning Light.
And as for Pleasure, which thine Age doth prize,
Why should that seem so lovely in thine Eyes?
'Tis but a Moment they with thee will last,
And Sadness surely comes when they are past;
The Brute his Pleasures hath as well as thee,
Man's chiefest Good, surely can't Pleasure be?
And whilst thou striv'st thy evil Lusts to please,
Thy raging Conscience then who shall appease?
With this sweet Meat, I tell thee also, Friend,
Thou sour Sauce shalt have before the End.
And as for Beauty, that also is vain,
Unless you can the inward Beauty gain:
What's outward Beauty but an evil Snare
By which vain Ones often deceived are;
And on a sudden drawn into Temptation,
And do commit most vile Abomination?
That Beauty which the carnal Man doth prize,
Renders not lovely in *Jehovah's* Eyes.
Tho' deck'd with Jewels, Rings, and brave Attire,
The glorious King their Beauty doth admire,
His Heart's not taken with't; but otherwise,
The Beauty of vain Ones he doth despise,
Tho' very fair; but if defil'd with Sin,
They like unto Sepulchres are within;
Loathsome and vile i'th' Sight of God are they,
And soon their seeming Beauty will decay;
It fades and withers, and away doth pass,
Just like unto the Flower of the Grass.
The curled Locks, yea, and the spotted Face,
God ere a while will bring into Disgrace:
Death and the Grave will spoil their Beauty quite,
And none in them shall ever more delight.
As for thy Age, in youthful Days we see
Youth nothing minds but cursed Vanity.
Soon also may the Spring meet with a Blast,
And all the Glory not one Moment last.
The Flower in the Spring which is so gay,
Soon doth it fade, and wither quite away.
Nothing on Earth canst thou find out, or 'spy,

That will content thee long, or satisfy
That soul of thine, if still thou search about,
Till thou dost find the rarest Science out:
For, if on Learning you do place your Mind,
Much Vanity in that you'll also find:
For human Knowledge and Philosophy
Can't bring thy Soul into sweet Unity
With God above, and *Jesus Christ* his Son,
In whom, O *Youth*, is Happiness alone.
Doat not on Honour, then, nor worldly Treasure,
Nor Beauty, Learning, Youth, or other Pleasure;
All is but Vanity that is here below,
Truth and Experience both the same do show.
Come, look to Heav'n, seek thou for higher Joys,
Let Swine take Husks, and Fools all empty Toys.
Come then, and taste of Christ's cœlestial Springs,
To which all outward Joys are trifling Things.
If Heaven's Sweetness thou but once hadst caught.
Thou'lt freely own Earth's best Enjoyments naught.
Honour and Riches too, Christ has great Store,
And at's Right-hand are Pleasures evermore.
Thinkest that he who makes Man's Life so sweet,
Whilst he with many Troubles here doth meet,
And in Believing hath such Sweetness tasted,
Though his own Image greatly is defaced,
Can't give to him much greater Consolation,
When all the Sour's vanish'd of Temptation?
If with the Bitter Saints such Sweetness gain,
What shall they do when they in Glory reign?

YOUTH.

    Be silent, *Truth*, leave off, for I can't bear
Your whining Strains; nor will I longer hear
Such melancholy Whimsies; they're such Stuff
Which suits not with my Age: I have enough
Of it already, and also of you,
Since you my Int'rest strive to overthrow.
When I appeal'd to you, I was perplex'd,
And with sad Melancholy sorely vex'd;
But since I do perceive the Storm is o'er,
You I don't think to trouble any more.
No Liberty to me I see you'll give,
In sweet Delight and Pleasure for to live:
I don't intend Fanatick yet to turn,
Nor after such distracted People run.
An easy Way to Heaven I do know,

And therefore, Sir, Farewel; Farewel to you.
My Pride, my Sports, and my old Company
I will enjoy; and all my Bravery
I will hold fast; yea, wantonly fulfill
My fleshly Mind, say Preachers what they will.

CONSCIENCE.

    Ah, *Youth!* ah, *Youth!* Is't so in very Deed?
Wilt thou no more unto God's *Truth* give heed?
'Twas but my Mouth to stop, I now do find,
That unto *Truth* you seemingly inclin'd.
But this, O Soul, I must assure to thee,
What thou hast heard, has much enlightned me,
And my Compassion too it doth renew,
As must appear by what does next ensue.
Have you from God been called thus upon,
And shall your Heart be hardned like a Stone?
You can't plead Ignorance, O *Youth!* 'tis so;
You've very plainly heard what you should do:
Your Sins will be of grievous Aggravation,
If you don't quickly make a Recantation.
Your Sins will be of a deep Scarlet Dye,
And many Stripes prepared to espy,
With which you must be beat, because that you
Your Master's Will so perfectly do know;
But for to do the same you do refuse,
And your poor *Conscience* wickedly abuse.
You'll shew yourself a cursed Rebel now,
If unto Christ with Speed you do not bow.
Wilt thou thy Sins retain when thou dost hear
How much against the Living God they are?
Wilt thou cast Dirt into his Blessed Face?
O tremble, Soul, and dread thy present Case!

YOUTH.

    Now my good Days I see they will be gone,
My inward Thoughts will ne'er let me alone.
Ah, that I could but sin without Controul,
And *Conscience* never more disturb my Soul!
His bitter Gripes much longer I can't bear;
He's grown so resolute, no Hope is there
But he'll prevail; such Conflicts I do feel,
My Courage now, and Resolutions reel.
However, I'm resolv'd once more to try,
And struggle hard to get the Mastery;
I cowardly will not acquit the Field,

Nor at the second Summons will I yield:
I'll make once more another stout Essay,
Ere unto *Conscience* I will yield the Day.
Ah, how can I my sweet Delights forsake,
Without Resistance to the last I make?
 Conscience, although I sinful am, I see
There's many Thousands worser far than me:
No one can live, and from all Sin be clear,
That I from *Truth* did very lately hear.
My Heart is good, though it is true that I
Am overcome thro' human Frailty.

CONSCIENCE.
 O Reprobate! Dar'st thou thy Heart commend?
Come, tremble, Soul, and it to pieces rend.
Don't I most clearly in thy Heart behold
Such horrid Lust, 'twould shame thee were it told?
Vipers breed there, and many a Cockatrice,
The Spawn of ev'ry Sin and evil Vice.
Like a Sepulchre soul thou art within,
Nothing is there but putrifying Sin:
Out from thy Heart all Evil doth ascend,
And yet wilt thou thy filthy Heart commend?
And dost thou think thy State so good to be,
'Cause you do find many as bad as thee?
You are so bad, if you from Sin don't turn,
You must for Sin in Hell for ever burn.
With haughty *Dives*, and such Wretches lie
In endless Flames to all Eternity.

YOUTH.
 Well, say no more; if this be so, I must
Go unto *Truth* again, or I shall burst;

My Heart will break, I clearly do discern,
I therefore now must yield, and also learn
What is my State by Nature; that I'd know,
Come, *Truth*, I pray, will you this Favour show,
As to explain to me this Thing most clear,
For *Conscience* doth my Soul with Horror scare?
Is he upright, O *Truth*, or is he wrong?
I find Convictions in me very strong.
What is my State? Declare it unto me,
And set my troubled Soul at Liberty.

TRUTH.

  What *Conscience* speaks, O Young Man, is most right,
And vain it is longer with him to fight;
Those he condemns by Light receiv'd from me,
Almighty God condemns eternally:
And God is greater than thy Heart, O Soul,
Who can enough thy grievous State condole!
If *Conscience* does its Testimony give,
And that thou art an unconverted Wretch;
That you in Sin and cursed Ways do live,
If 'tis from hence, between you there's a Breach:
If this be so, as you it can't deny,
What would you do, if you this Night should die?
If in this State you should this Life depart,
Undone for evermore, Young-Man, thou art!
As sure as is the mighty God in Heaven,
Against thy Soul the Sentence will be given;
Conscience from God his Power did receive,
And if you don't obey and him believe,
And do reject his Motions, 'tis all one
As if Christ Jesus you did tread upon:
Whilst he doth rule by Laws that are Divine,
'Tis Treason him to stop, or undermine.
And once again; to shew thee thy Estate,
You being, Young-Man, not Regenerate,
No God, nor Christ have you; 'tis even so;
And this indeed's the Sum of all thy Woe.
God since the Fall became thine Enemy;
His angry Face is set most dreadfully
Against thy Soul; and that's a fearful Thing,
Enough thy Pride with Vengeance down to bring.
Each Attribute against thy Soul is set,
And all of them also together met
To make you ev'ry Way most miserable,
Which Wrath for to resist, what Man is able?

He'll suddenly thy Soul to Pieces tear,
And his Eternal Vengeance make thee bear:
His Wrath it will upon thy Soul remain,
'Till you by Faith are truly born again.

YOUTH.

   This Doctrine which to me you do declare,
It is enough to make a Man despair,
And, *Spira* like, fear hard his flinty Breast,
Till the poor Soul has lost Eternal Rest;
O *Spira! Spira!* Is my Case like thine!
Forbid it, ye Immortal Powers Divine!
For if 'tis so, I grant I am undone;
But God is gracious, and has sent his Son:
He's full of Bowels; therefore hope do I
He'll not on me his Justice magnify.
He dy'd for all Mankind, and therefore He
Surely won't act with such Severity,
As to condemn unto eternal Flame
Mankind, for whose Salvation here He came.
Thro' Nature's Weakness we're misled to sin,
By trivial Faults, when there's no Guilt within;
Which God, who is all merciful and mild,
O'erlooks, as Parents do their only Child;
And so I trust he'll gracious be to me,
In overlooking my Iniquity.

TRUTH.

   'Tis true, God's gracious, yet he will not clear
Those guilty Souls who don't his Justice fear.
He's very gracious, yet is full of Ire;
And is to such like a consuming Fire.
And tho' you please yourself with Hopes that He
Will veil his Eyes from thy Iniquity,
God is more pure, and of diviner Flame,
To see Man sin, and not consume the same.
Not the least Evil shall escape his Eye,
Justice must punish with Severity:

Fruitless and vain, poor *Youth's* thy woeful State,
Since little Sins are punish'd as the great.
He sent his Son, 'tis true, for Souls to die,
But many miss, and falsly do apply
His precious Blood, therefore my Counsel take,
Don't you too soon an Application make
Of God's sweet Grace, nor our Redeemer's Blood,
Until by you the Gospel's understood.
Those who are whole, need no Physician have;
The sick and wounded Soul Christ came to save;
What dost thou judge thy present State to be?
How does it stand, and is it now with thee?

YOUTH.

   I am a Sinner, and my Heart doth bleed,
My sin-sick Soul doth a sweet Saviour need;
My Conscience tells me that I am most vile,
And grievously for Sin doth me turmoil.

TRUTH.

   No Saviour can you have unless you do
Resolve to leave your Sins, and let them go;
Not for your Wounds can there be any Cure,
Till th' Causes are remov'd, which do procure
And bring on you that Pain and bitter Smart,
Which you cry out has seiz'd upon your Heart.

YOUTH.

   My trembling Soul's amaz'd, and fill'd with Fear;
Another Way, O *Truth*, my Course I'll steer:
For Ruin doth attend the Way I'm in,
Whilst I do keep and hug my cursed Sin.
There's scarce a Night which passes o'er my Head,
But I dread much the making of my Bed:
'Fore Morning comes, in the sad Depths of Hell,
My Conscience therefore now doth me compel
To bid adieu to all sweet Joy and Pleasure,
To Lies and Fraud, and all unlawful Treasure.
In Sport and Games I'll take no more Delight,
But otherwise, I'll pray both Day and Night.
Conscience has overcome me with his Gripes,
Truth follows him also with threat'ning Stripes.
The Wall's broke down, the Old Man's run away,
And *Conscience* follows close to cut and stay:
He threatens too, he will no Quarter give,
And ev'ry Thing before him seems to drive.

Lust forced is in Corners for to fly,
Where it doth hide itself most secretly:
And watches also, thinking for to get
An Opportunity, once more to set
And fall on *Conscience*, which it doth disdain,
'Cause *Conscience* says, Corruptions must be slain.
I side with him, because I would have Peace,
But still 'tis doubtful when these Wars will cease.

DEVIL.

   What Pity 'tis thy Sun shou'd set so soon,
Or should be clouded thus before 'tis Noon!
Shall Winter come before the Spring is past,
And all its Fruits be spoil'd with one sad Blast?
Shall that brave Flower which doth seem so gay,
So quickly fade, and wither quite away?
What Pity is't, that one so Young as thee,
Should'st thus be brought into Captivity!
Hark not to Conscience; for I dare maintain
'Tis better for to hug thy Sins again.
Consider well, advise, and thou shalt see
My Ways are best; come, hearken unto me:
I'll give thee Honour, Pleasure, Wealth, and Things
Which prized are by Noblemen and Kings.
Let not this Make-bait, with an angry Frown,
Throw all thy Glory and thy Pleasures down.
Let not sad Thoughts distress thy troubled Mind:
What Satisfaction can you have, or find,
But that which floweth from this World alone?
'Tis I must raise thee to a sublime Throne.
The Hell thou fearest may but be a Story,
And Heaven also but a feigned Glory.
If this don't startle thee, then speedily

I will stir up some other Enemy.
Old-man, rouze up, I charge you to awake,
And swiftly too; your Life and all's at Stake:
And Mistress Heart, stir up your wilful Will:
Is this a Season for him to sit still?
If unto *Truth* and *Conscience* he gives Place,
Our Int'rest will, you see, go down apace.
Judgment is gone already, and doth yield;
And Courage too, I fear, will quit the Field.
Some Sins are slain, and in their Blood do lie,
And others to strong Holds are forc'd to fly.
As for Affection, he doth hold his own,
Tho' *Conscience* doth upon him sadly frown.
Remembrance will unto him trait'rous prove,
If I his Thoughts from Sermons can't remove;
I'll make his Mind run after Things below,
And raise up Trouble which he did not know:
And will forget what lately he did hear,
And then will cease his former Dread and Fear.
If I can please his sensual Appetite,
There is no Danger of a sudden Flight.
His Breast is tender, apt to entertain
The Sparks of Lust, which long he can't restrain;
I'll blow them up, and kindle them anew,
Then to Conviction soon he'll bid Adieu.
New Objects I'll present unto his Sight,
In which, I'm sure he can't but take Delight;
I have such hold of him, there is no Doubt,
But I once more can turn him quite about.
His old Companions also I'll provoke
At's Doors again to give another Stroke;
Their strong Enticements hardly he'll withstand,
They can, you see, his Spirit soon command.

YOUTH'S OLD COMPANIONS.

How do you do Sir? What's the Reason we
Can't here of late enjoy your Company?
It seems to us as if you were grown strange,
As if in *Youth* there were some sudden Change.

YOUTH.

I have not had the Opportunity;
Besides, on me there doth a Burden lie,
Which doth depress my Spirits like a Load,
So that I very seldom go Abroad.

COMPANIONS.

   I war'nt, Sirs, 'tis Sin afflicts his Soul,
And he is just now going to turn Fool.
Come, come away; to Age such Grief belongs,
Brave Mirth to Youth, and fine melodious Songs;
Come, drive away these Thoughts with Pipe and Pot
Sing and carouze till they are quite forgot.
The lovely Strains of the well-tuned Lute,
Where Plays are acted, with thy Nature suit;
Come, go with us upon a brave Design,
Which soon will chear that drooping Heart of thine.
Come, gen'rous Soul, let thy ambitious Eye
Such foolish Fancies and vain Dreams defy.
Shall thy heroick Spirit thus give Place
To silly Dotage, to thy great Disgrace?

UITINUS.

   The young man yields, being possest with Fears,
Or they'd reproach him else with Scoffs and Jeers;
Till *Conscience* 'wakes, and stings in bitter Sort,
Putting a Period to his jovial Sport.
The Thoughts of Death, which Sickness does presage,
Doth trouble him, he cannot bear the Rage.
Nor inward Gripes of his enlightned Breast;
And therefore now again he thinks it best
To hark to *Conscience*, whom he did refuse,
And grievously did many Times abuse.

CONSCIENCE.

   Go mourn, thou Wretch, for sad is thy Condition;
Pour fourth amain the Water of Contrition;
Wilt thou appear to Men Godly to be,
When all is nothing but Hypocrisy?

Wilt thou to *Truth* so often lend an Ear,
And yet to Satan also thus adhere?
You had as good have kept your former Station,
As thus to yield afresh unto Temptation:
Go unto *Truth*, if God give space and Room,
Before I do pronounce your final Doom.

TRUTH.

Come, come, Young man, don't thy Convictions lose,
But cherish them, and timely also choose
The one Thing needful, which alone is Good,
That God may wash thy Soul in Christ his Blood.
Thy Soul is precious, and of greater Worth
Than all Things else that are upon the Earth;
For were it possible the World to gain,
And could you all its Pleasure here obtain;
And in Exchange your Soul should lose thereby,
What would your Profit be, when you must die?
When once thy Soul is lost, thou losest all;
Oh! that will be a very dismal Fall.
Dost thou not know what I of Hell declare,
What hideous Howlings of the Damned's there?
How can'st thou with devouring Fire dwell,
Or lie with Devils in the lowest Hell?
Those who do in their nat'ral State remain,
Must live for ever in that restless Pain.
All Fornicators, Drunkards, and the Lyar,
Must have their Portion in the Lake of Fire,
With Thieves, Revilers, and Extortioners,
And such who are most vile Idolators:
The Proud, the Swearer, and the Covetous,
God doth pronounce on them the self-same curse.
And those who live in vile Hypocrisy,
Or do backslide unto Apostacy;
Let such unto my present Words give Heed;
Their Pain and Torment shall all Mens exceed.
What wilt thou do, or whither canst thou fly?
Where can'st thou hide from the great Majesty,
Who tries the Reins, and searches every Heart?
Since *Conscience* says that thou most guilty art.
Condemned Soul, thou know'st that this is so,
And this moreover, I will plainly show
Will come to pass as sure as God's above,
If from all Sin with Speed you don't remove,
So sure as you do live, when you do die,
To Hell you go to all Eternity;

Except Repentance in your Soul be wrought,
With Vengeance thither you'll at last be brought.
In *Tophet*, that's exceeding large and deep,
What damned Wretches Company must keep.
O call to Mind what *Conscience* doth this Day
Charge you withal, before you're swept away;
Lest you from him do hear no more at all,
Till you into those scorching Flames do fall.
What Mercy is't that *Conscience* strives so long,
And his Convictions still in you are strong!
O fear, lest Sin do sear your Conscience quite,
And God also put out your Candle-Light!
He'll give you up unto a Heart of Stone,
As he in Wrath hath served many a one;
Then to repent it will be much too late;
Such is the Danger of a lapsed State.
Therefore take Heed, and don't this Work delay,
Nor put it off until another Day:
Thy Days on Earth, alas! will be but few;
They fly away like to the Morning Dew:
Like as the Clouds and Shadows swiftly flies,
Or Dew doth pass so soon as Sun does rise,
So fly thy Days, thy golden Months and Years,
Much like the Blossom which most gay appears,
It on a sudden fades, and does decay;
So Youth does often wither quite away:
Thy Age unto the Spring thou dost compare,
And to the Flowers that appear so rare.
The Flower withers, and hangs down his Head,
Which curiously of late so flourished;
The Meadows, clad in glorious Array,
Are soon cut down, and turned into Hay;
Like *Jonah's* Gourd, which sprung up in a Night,
And perished as soon as it was Light;
Or like a Ghost, which quickly passeth by,
Or Weaver's Shuttle, which he maketh fly;
Or as a Ship, when she is under Sail,
Most swiftly runs her Course with a full Gale.
So are thy Days; they in like Manner fly.
How many little Graves may'st thou espy!
Come, measure now thy Days, and see their Length;
Number 'em not by Years, by Health nor Strength;
O! these uncertain Rules you must refuse,
Tho' 'tis the general Way which most Men use:
They think to live till they old aged are,
'Cause their Progenitors long-lived were.

This Rule from Truth, you see does greatly vary;
And sound Experience sheweth the contrary.
You hear the Things which you should reckon by;
Things swift in Motion, gone most speedily.
Thy Life's uncertain, *Youth*, 'tis but a Blast;
Thy Sand is little, long it will not last:
Thy House, tho' new, yet it is very old;
Gone to Decay, and turning into Mould.
You're born to die, and dead also you were,
Before you liv'd, or breathed in the Air;
And die you must, before that live you do,
Except you die to live, as I do show.
Thy dreadful Ruin, Soul, is very nigh,
Unless thy Tears prevent it speedily.
What is thy Purpose now? What's in thy Mind?
Which Way dost think to take, how art inclin'd?

YOUTH.

Thy Ways, O *Truth!* I am resolv'd to run,
And never more to Sin and Folly turn.
I tremble at the Thoughts of Death and Hell;
My Soul is wounded, and my Wounds do swell.
I'll beg of Jesus Christ I may obtain
Some healing Med'cine to remove my Pain.
No rest can I, save in my Duty find,
I unto Pray'r am very much inclin'd.
God will, I hope, these latter Sins forgive,
Since I more Godly do intend to live;
And so resolve to watch, and take such Care,
That Satan shall no more my Soul ensnare.

UITINUS.

He from this Day becomes a great Professor,

Though far from being yet a true Possessor:
Christ he has got into his Mouth and Head,
And not internally rais'd from the Dead;
But in Old *Adam* still he does remain,
Not knowing what 'tis to be born again.
When Satan sees it is in vain to strive,
The Soul into its former State to drive,
But that it will forsake its Wickedness,
And the sweet Truth of Jesus Christ profess;
He yields thereto, resolving secretly
To blind his Eyes in close Hypocrisy,
And so appear under a new Disguise,
Most subtilly the Soul for to surprize;
Persuading him the War which he doth find
Continues daily in his troubled Mind,
Is saving Grace, against Iniquity,
Which has prevail'd, and got the Victory,
When it is common Grace (we do so call)
And not the Grace that's supernatural.
Here he doth Rest, and seems to be at Ease,
When all is done his Conscience to appease.
But I'll give Place to this Religious Youth,
To hear Discourse between him and the Truth.

YOUTH.

   Oh! happy I, and blessed by the Day
That unto *Truth* and *Conscience* I gave way:
I would not be in my old State again,
Might I thereby a Thousand Worlds obtain.
From Wrath and Hell my Soul is now set free;
For I don't doubt but I converted be.
The Word with Power so to me was brought,
A glorious Change within my Soul was wrought.

TRUTH.

   Young-man, take heed, lest you mistaken are;
Conversion's hard: It is a Thing so rare,
That very few that narrow Passage enter,
Tho' for that Way there's Thousands do adventure.
Yet miss their Mark: For all their inward Strife,
They fall far short of the New Creature, Life.
Come, let me hear your Grounds, or Evidence,
For I don't like your seeming Confidence:
I doubt you're still under the Almighty's Curse,
And that your Case is bad, if not much worse
Than 'twas when you did no Profession make;

But did your Swing in all Profaneness take.
The *Pharisee* was a Religious Man,
Yet nearer Heaven was the *Publican;*
If short in Christ, you fix or fastned grow,
'Twill be your Ruin and your Overthrow.

YOUTH.

   What do you mean? This Doctrine's too severe,
For all may see that I converted are:
But if my Grounds you are resolv'd to weigh,
I'll quickly tell you what I have to say:
And the first Ground which I resolve to bring
On this Behalf, to clear and prove the Thing,
Is from Conviction which I have of Sin,
Which once I hugged, and delighted in.

TRUTH.

   Poor Soul, alas! this Reason soon will fly,
For most do so their vile Iniquity.
They are convinced by their inward Light,
That Sin is odious in *Jehovah's* Sight,
But yet vile Sinners are nevertheless,
They don't one Drachm of Saving Grace possess.
King *Pharaoh*, *Esau*, yea, and *Judas* too,
All were convinced of their Sins you know;
That they were Saints there's no Man doth believe,
For all those Three the Devil did deceive;
And has deceived you, as I do judge;
Unless you do some better Reason urge
To prove Conversion in your Soul is wrought,
I do declare your State is very naught.
How many Men under Conviction lie,
Yet never born again until they die!
What hast thou else to say, or to produce,
Since slight Convictions are of little Use?

YOUTH.

   I do not only see my Sin, but I
Do mourn and grieve for Sin continually:
And those which do so mourn, they blessed are,
Don't you also the self-same Thing declare?

TRUTH.

   Nay, hold a Season; thou may'st weep amain,
Yet still in thee may many Evils reign.
You may lament for Sin, as many do,

Because of Shame, and anxious Pain and Woe,
Which now it brings, and leads unto i' th' End;
And that because thereby you did offend
The Living God, and wound your Saviour, who
Did for your sake such Torments undergo.
Mourn more for th' Evil which doth come thereby,
Than for the Evil which in it doth lie:
This Ground is weak, for *Esau* it appears
Did mourn and weep, and let fall bitter Tears;
And yet you know that *Esau* was prophane,
And far was he from being born again.

YOUTH.

 But I go farther yet; I do confess
My horrid Evils, and my Guiltiness.
If I confess my Sins, as I have done,
God he is Just, and is the faithful One,
Who will my Sins forgive, and pardon quite;
He'll blot them out of his most precious Sight:
This being so, What Cause then can you see,
But that I'm turn'd from my Iniquity?

TRUTH.

 This will not do, 'tis not a certain Ground;
Some do confess their Sins with Hearts unsound;
When *Pharaoh* saw the Judgment of the Hail,
His Heart began then greatly for to fail:
I've sinn'd this Time, the Lord is just, said he,
I and my People also wicked be.
Tho' *Pharaoh*, *Saul*, and *Judas* each of them,
God did reject, and utterly condemn;
Yet these, when under Wrath, are forc'd to cry,
Lord, we have sinn'd, their Conscience so did fly
Into their Faces, that it made them quake,
And unto God Confession strait to make,
Confession also may be made in Part,
And not of ev'ry Sin that's in the Heart.
Men may confess their Sins, and their great Guilt,
Who the dire Nature of it never felt:
Confess their Sins in their Extremity,
When *Conscience* pinches them most bitterly;
Confess their Sins which they committed have,
Yet don't intend those cursed Sins to leave.

YOUTH.

 But I confess, and also do forsake,

Therefore my State you very much mistake.
Those who confess, and do their Sins forego,
God will to them his precious Mercy show:
Therefore don't trouble me, 'tis very plain,
I for my Part am truly born again.

TRUTH.
 In this also you may deceived be,
Men may forsake all gross Iniquity.
Yet in their Souls may some sweet Morsels lie,
Which they may hug, and keep close secretly.
If the least Sin thou dost forsake aright,
All Sins would then be odious to thy Sight.
Judgment and Reason may your Sins oppose,
And utterly with them refuse to close.
Yet may thy Will and thy Affections join
To savour still, and love those Sins of thine.
If Sin's not out of the Affections cast,
Thou wilt appear an Hypocrite at last;
If Sin's i' th' Will and the Affections found,
'Tis a true Sign their Hearts are quite unsound.
Like to the Seamen some Professors do,
Who over-board some goods are forc'd to throw,
When they do meet with Storms and windy Weather,
Lest all their Goods and Ship do sink together.
When in the Soul great Storms and Tempest rise,
The Devil then may subtilly advise
The Soul to throw some of his Sins away,
To make a Calm, that so thereby he may
Persuade the Soul the Danger is quite gone,
And that the Work in him is fully done.
'Tis not enough therefore some Sins to leave,
But ev'ry Sin must of yourself bereave,
And cast o'er board, yea, and that willingly,
Or else you'll sink to all Eternity:
Nor by Constraint, as Conscience doth compel,
As some are forc'd to do, who like it well,
Who leave the Act, but love it to retain,
Such leave their Sins, but yet their Sins remain.

YOUTH.
 These are hard Sayings which you do relate,
And I indeed should question my Estate,
Wer't not for other Grounds, and Reasons clear,
By which I know that I converted were.
Sir, there's in me a very Glorious Change,

Most Men admire it, and do think it strange
That one who lately did but scoff and jeer
Those Men and People which I now do hear,
And follow'd Vice, and ev'ry Vanity,
Should on a sudden thus reformed be;
And utterly myself also deny
Of my sweet Joys, and former Company.

TRUTH.
   From outward Filthiness a Man may turn,
And not be chang'd in Heart when he has done.
An outward Change in Men there may be wrought,
When that their Hearts within are very naught.
The Swine that wallows in the Mire now,
May washed be, and still remain a Sow.
Persons may cleanse the Outside of the Cup,
And Dogs may spue their nasty Vomit up,
But yet do keep their beastly Nature still,
And ere a while they plainly shew it will.
Many Professors fall away, and die,
For want of being changed thoroughly;
The *Pharisee* was chang'd, he did appear
Indeed, as if a precious Saint he were.
He differ'd quite from the poor *Publican;*
He thought himself a far more happy Man:
But all this was in Shew, and not in Heart;
He therefore had in Christ no Share nor Part:
Except your Righteousness does his excel,
You in no wise shall in God's Kingdom dwell.
Old *Herod* will reform in many Things
When once he finds his Conscience bites and stings.
To hear *John* Baptist also was he led,
Yet afterwards depriv'd him of his Head.
So far this seeming Saint was turn'd aside,
That he also our Saviour did deride:
And then his Men of War set him at naught,
Whilst Accusations they against him brought.
   Simon the Sorcerer also you read,
Was hanged so, he gave great Care and Heed
To *Philip's* Preaching; yea and suddenly
He leaves his Witchcrafts and his Society.
But was a cursed Caitiff all the While,
Like a Sepulchre painted, inward vile.
Another Man in Shew, 'tis like thou art,
Yet not made New, and changed in thy Heart;
Men in thy Life may no great Blemish 'spy,

Yet in thy Breast much Rottenness may lie.
Towards all Men thy Conscience may be clear,
Conscience so far for thee may Witness bear,
That you in Morals it may not offend,
Yet unto God it may not you commend;
But otherwise it in your Face may fly,
And you condemn for Sin continually.
Therefore, O Young Man, if you look about,
Of your Conversion you have cause to doubt;
Satan so greatly may your Heart deceive,
That not one Drachm of Grace thy Soul may have,
Which saving is, and of the purer Kind,
For that, alas! there's very few do find.

YOUTH.

    But I am call'd of God, and do obey
The Voice of *Truth* and *Conscience* ev'ry Day,
God's called Ones, I'm sure, you can't deny,
But they are such whom He doth justify.
Wherefore 'tis clear, and very evident,
That Grace alone hath made me penitent.
My Heart is sound, my Graces true also,
My Confidence there's none shall overthrow.

TRUTH.

    Thou seem'st too confident, 'tis a sad Sign:
For Fears attend where saving-Grace doth shine
I tell the, *Youth,* that many called be,
But few are chosen from Eternity.
Judas was call'd, and did obey in part,
And yet he was a Devil in his Heart.
There is an outward and an inward Call,
The latter only is Effectual.

Therefore you must produce some better Ground,
For this don't prove that your Conversion's sound;
But that thou may'st stick fast still in the Birth,
Or prove Abortive when thou art brought forth.
'Tis rare, O *Youth*, for to be born anew,
And hard to find out when the Work is true.

YOUTH.
  Though it be so, what Cause have I to fear,
When that my Evidences are so clear?
I do believe, and trust in God through Faith,
And he which doeth so, the Witness hath
Within himself, and shall assuredly
Be saved also when he comes to die.

CONSCIENCE.
  Thou may'st believe, as most of People do,
And yet to Hell at last thy Soul may go.
The Faith of Credence it is like you have,
Which cannot quicken, purify, or save.
Some *Jews* believ'd in Christ, you also find,
Yet to their Lusts their Hearts were then inclin'd,
And out of Satan's Kingdom were not freed,
Nor made Disciples of the Lord indeed.
Simon the Sorcerer, he did believe,
Yet did his Soul no saving Grace receive.
The stony Ground with Joy receiv'd the Seed,
And for a Time brought forth, as you may read,
And yet their Hearts they were but Hearts of Stone,
Their Faith 'twas temporary, soon 'twas gone.
The Devils do believe as well as you,
Yea, and confess that Jesus they do know:
They tremble also, when some Men can't say
They ever did unto this present Day.
Such Faith as Devils have, most Men obtain,
Which only serves to aggravate their Pain.
If on a Death-bed Conscience do awake,
'Twill cause 'em then to tremble and to quake,
And roar like Devils, when they do espy
The dreadful Wrath of that great Majesty
Whom they offend, and against purest Light
And Knowledge too most wickedly did slight.
This Faith will serve their Grief to aggravate,
But not to help them out of that Estate;
'Tis easy to believe that Christ did die,

But hard his Blood in Truth for to apply.
Men may raise up the Dead to Life again,
As easy as true saving Faith obtain,
By their own Power and inherent Skill?
Nothing obstructs it more than Man's own Will:
Until Almighty Power makes it bend,
'Twill not to Grace nor Jesus condescend.
That Pow'r which rais'd up Jesus from the Dead
Works Faith in Saints, whereby they're quickened.
The precious Faith, the Faith of God's Elect,
As 'tis a Grace, and gloriously bedeckt
With other Graces, so 'twill never grow
But in the honest Heart, where God doth sow
This blessed Seed, which like a Garden pure
Doth yield its Fruits to th'last, you may be sure;
And when this Faith is wrought in any Soul,
It throws down Self, and wholly then doth roll
On Jesus Christ, that most beloved One,
On whom it rests and doth depend alone:
If God hath wrought this precious Grace in thee,
Sin thou dost hate, yea, all Iniquity;
And Lust doth not predominate and reign,
If thou by Faith are truly born again.
Christ thou exaltest as he's Priest and King,
And as a Prophet too in ev'ry Thing;
He does in thee wholly the Scepter sway,
And thou art govern'd by him ev'ry Day,
Sin can't prevail, such is thy happy Case;
If thou hast gotten this victorious Grace;
It purges and doth purify the Heart,
Wholly renewing thee in ev'ry Part.
Men by its Fruits true Faith may come to know,
And by their Works the same also do show.
What Faith is thine? what think'st thou now of it?
I greatly fear 'twill prove a Counterfeit.
Examine thy Estate, and take good Heed
To close with Jesus Christ, and that with Speed;
For as the Body without the Spirit's dead,
The same of Faith you know is also said;
Without Obedience doth thy Faith attend,
You'll not withstanding perish in the End.

YOUTH.

  I am obedient, and I am free to join
In Fellowship with Saints, such Faith is mine:

I willing am to do, as to believe,
The Devil therefore can't my Soul deceive.
The many Pray'rs I make both Day and Night,
Do doubtless prove that my Conversion's right.

TRUTH.

   I tell thee, Soul, Men may do more than this,
And yet they may of true Conversion miss;
God's Ordinances many do obey,
And Members of his holy Church are they,
And Privileges of it seem to share,
As if that they converted truly were;
They may discourse, and seem to be devout,
And may not be discerned, nor found out;
They with the Flock may walk, lie down and feed,
And so remain till many Years succeed:
Nay, not discover'd be until they stand
Among the Goats, at Jesus Christ's Left hand.
The Foolish Virgins join'd themselves with Wise,
And for to meet the Bridegroom did arise
When their Profession was but meer Out side,
Who did no Oil, or saving Grace provide.
Many great Preachers, and Disputers too,
Christ will not own, or any Favour shew,
Tho' in his Name they mighty Works have done,
He'll say to them, Ye wicked ones be gone.
I know you not; therefore be gone from me,
All you vile Workers of Iniquity.
You often say you seek the Lord in Pray'r,
That you may do, and let fall many a Tear,
And yet not be in a converted State,
For many seek with Tears when 'tis too late.
Others, like Seamen in a Storm do cry,

When Conscience doth rebuke them bitterly.
And some under Afflictions cry and howl,
And grievously their State do then condole;
They Promises and Resolutions make,
That they such Courses will no longer take:
But when the Storm and the Affliction's o'er,
They are as bad, nay, worser than before.
Some pray in Form, and others pray by Art,
And some to mend the Badness of their Heart:
Their Hearts are wounded, and then speedily,
Their Pray'rs to heal it they do strait apply.
They sin by Day, but pray when it is Night,
Then sin again, but Pray'r doth heal it quite;
And so that Way poor *Conscience* they beguile,
They silence him, yet Sinners all the while.
Their Pray'rs, alas! can't wash their Filth away,
Tho' they do nothing else both Night and Day.
'Tis on their Pray'rs they rest and do depend,
Which, like a broken Staff, will fall i' th' End.
A Saint at Pray'r no Ease nor Rest can gain,
Unless Christ's Blood thereby he doth obtain;
And Grace also his Sins to mortify,
For Christ, as well as Pardon he doth cry:
But otherwise it is with most of Men,
They cry for Pardon, and do also then
In their vile Hearts regard Iniquity;
And for this Cause God doth their Suit deny.
Their Prayers are to God Abomination,
Whilst they do hide and cover their Transgression.
Some out of Custom do perform their Pray'r,
Not out of Conscience, nor from Godly Care:
And others also for Vain-glory sake,
Like *Pharisees* they many Prayers make.
In Sight of Men, in Publick such will pray,
But in the Closet little have to say.
They with their Mouths and Tongues much Kindness show,
Fixing their Hearts on earthly Things below.
'Tis for the Heart that Christ doth chiefly call,
And it is Reason he should have it all;
For he the same did purchase very dear;
Yet Satan has the chief Possession there.
God at the Door, and in the Porch doth stand,
While Satan may the bravest Room command.
They'll ope' to him, and keep *Jehovah* out,
And yet in Pray'r they seem to be devout.

Some kneel to pray as soon as they arise,
And think such Pray'rs for Sin a Sacrifice;
Rise up, and to their Looking glass repair,
And pride themselves in Dress and Fashion there.
Whoever prays, and prays not fervently,
In Faith, in Truth, and in Sincerity,
Their Pray'rs are Sin, and God will not them hear,
Nor mind their cry when they to him draw near:
'Tis not enough a Duty for to know,
But how also each Duty you shou'd do.
For Men may Pray, Read, Hear, and Meditate,
And yet be in an unconverted State.
They outwardly may many Truths profess:
But not in Heart the Pow'r of them possess;
The Letter of the Law keep as the Shell,
Yet feed on Husks, and want the true Kernel.
The Young-Man which to Jesus Christ did run,
He many Things as well as you had done,
And yet fell short, as you now plainly see,
Of the chief Part of true Christianity.
What say you now, O *Youth!* Do you not fear,
That you by Satan much deceived are?
Have you no *Delilah*, which secretly
Doth in your Heart, or in your Bosom lie;
Which will at last thy precious Soul betray,
And leave thee to thine Enemy a Prey?
So *Sampson* was of old entic'd aside
To his own Ruin by his treach'rous Bride.
Don't you to Sin some secret Love retain?
If it be so, you are not born again.
Conscience, I fear, and God's restraining Grace,
Has only stopt you in your former Race
Like to a Dog that's kept up by a Chain,

So *Conscience*, often does from Sin restrain;
But if the Chain should slip, then loose he goes,
And presently his churlish Nature shows.
To your own Righteousness O do not trust,
I fear you do; come, speak, or *Conscience* must.
Don't you conclude, God is oblig'd to you,
Since you have let so many Evils go,
And are so holy here of late become?
Are not your Duties set up in the room
And place of Christ? O see you do not make
A Saviour of your own for Jesus' sake!
Did ever Sin sinful to you appear,
And, as 'tis Sin, to it great Hatred bear?
Would you not sin, were there no Hell of Pain;
Because you know the Lord doth it disdain?
Rather, is't not thro' Fear of Punishment,
You thus begin of late for to relent?
Or, doth there not some carnal, base Design
Move thee so far unto God's Truth to join?
Is not thy End to get a Name thereby,
Or only done *Conscience* to satisfy?
Or done to free thee from Reproach and Shame,
Which Sin doth bring upon a Person's Name?
Hast not it done, and wisely cast about
Such Ways for to prevent a Bankrupt?
Or done for to augment thy outward Store?
Or save thy Stock, and add unto it more?
For riotous living, which attends thy Age,
Consumes apace, and Want it doth presage.
Come, speak, O *Youth!* and be thou not unfree
To let me understand how 'tis with thee,
Come, call to mind, what thou hast heard of late,
And thereby judge of this thy present State.

YOUTH.

   I do not see but my Condition's good,
I have such Hope and Faith in Christ's dear Blood,
Tho' many Imperfections I do see,
Yet God is gracious, and will pardon me;
For there are many Failings in the best,
What is amiss I'll mend; and so I rest.

TRUTH.

   Thy Hope will fail, like to a Spider's Web,
Thy Flood of Confidence will have its Ebb;
If you prove guilty of those Things that I

Did unto thee so lately signify,
Thy Sports will not be like the Sports of those
Which God for Children to himself hath chose.
And since you are so loth for to be try'd,
Fearing you should also some Evils hide;
To *Conscience*, I'll appeal, you have done Wrong
To stop his Mouth, and hinder him so long;
He's so enlightned now, he can declare
As much as we at present need to hear.
He'll speak the Truth, and his Opinion too,
And nothing will he hide which he does know.
If unto him you do attend with Care,
No other Need of Witnesses is there:
If he, O Young Man, be but on your Side,
And is your Friend, you need none else provide;
But if against you, and does prove your Foe,
With Vengeance then be sure down will you go:
But if you will not hear what he shall say,
He'll make you tremble at the Judgment Day.
Conscience, I do, i'th' Name of the great King
Require you forth your Evidence to bring
Against this Man; accuse, or set him free,
According as you find his State to be.
Stand up for Jesus Christ, your Sovereign Lord,
And judge for him as he doth Light afford.
Be not deceiv'd by Lust a Bride to take,
But judge by Law, Christ's Honour lies at Stake.
For to speak home and loud have you forgot?
Is he converted now? or, is he not?
What do you say, your Testimony give;
Is all Sin dead, or doth there any live?
Is he new born, and chang'd in every Part,
Or is't in Shew only, and not in Heart?
Come, speak your Mind, you are oblig'd thereto,
For 'tis an Office, Heaven's appointed you;
That Sinners may have nothing left to say,
When God shall try each soul i'th' Judgment Day.

CONSCIENCE.

Sir, say no more, I am at your Command,
And you shall hear how Things at present stand.
He hath, O *Truth*, almost deceived me,
By's late Pretences unto Sanctity;
But having now afresh receiv'd more Light,
I must declare he was a Hypocrite.

He's not renew'd or truly born again,
Which I to you shall clearly now explain.
For, first of all, his Faculty call'd Will,
That is perverse, and very wicked still;
Though I stir up to Goodness ev'ry Hour,
Will doth oppose it with his greatest Pow'r.
He'll never pray in private Day or Night
But I must force him to't with all my Might;
The old Man is not slain, I do espy,
But has much Favour shewn him secretly.
Although I force him into Holes to run,
Yet he doth nourish him when all is done.
His Love and his Affections are for Sin,
And so in Truth they ever yet have been.
He's troubled more at Sin because of Guilt,
Than at the Odium of its cursed Filth.
When he's Abroad among Religious Men,
Precise and zealous he is always then;
But when amongst such who Ungodly be,
He suits himself to their vile Company.
Some Sins are left which Men condemn as gross,
Yet one he hugs, and keeps it very close:
Lust doth bear Rule, and much predominate,
And he on it doth love to ruminate.
Pleasant to him is all it's secret Charms,
And Thoughts of private Lusts his Spirits warms:
Tho' he may others outwardly rebuke,
And like a Saint most gravely seem to look;
'Tis Shame and outward Fear doth him restrain,
Or else the Act he would commit again.
If he from outward Blots can keep his Name,
That Saints can't him accuse, or justly blame,
He's satisfy'd, and very well content,
Tho' to his Peace I never gave Consent,
Speak he doth oft times unto his poor Soul,
And scarce will suffer me him to controul.
When I sometimes do catch him in a Lie,
And do reprove him for Hypocrisy,
To stop my Mouth, he vows he will with Speed
Amend what is amiss, and take more Heed:
Nay, more than this of him I cou'd relate,
Shewing you how you've hit his present State,
But that he will not suffer me to speak;
He blinds my Eyes, and so I might not rake
Into his Heart and Life, lest he thereby
Meet with great Shame for his Iniquity.

TRUTH.

    Conscience, forbear, you need not to enlarge,
If you do lay these Things unto his Charge,
His Soul's undone. The Gospel he'll profess,
But still remain i'th' Land of Bitterness.
Is this the Saint that seemed so precise,
And did appear God's Statutes much to prize?
A Saint in Shew, a Devil in his Heart,
And must with Devils also have a Part:
The Day is coming, and is very near,
When Hypocrites shall be surpriz'd with Fear;
The everlasting, burning, fiery Lake
Is made more hot on purpose for his Sake.
But since you are not seal'd, nor I yet gone,
Before we leave him quite, do you go on;
Let us pursue him still, for who doth know,
What God may yet upon his Spirit do?
If God grant him one Dram of saving Grace,
That will yet do, though 'tis a doubtful Case
Whether or not God will his Grace afford
To such as he, who thus offends the Lord;
For such whom Satan doth this Way deceive,
'Tis hard to bring them truly to believe.
He never was convinced thoroughly
Of Sin, and of his nat'ral Misery:
His lost Estate he truly never saw,
Nor what it is for to transgress God's Law;
Now he's undone thereby: he never knew
Not what for Sin Original was ever due.
He never saw the great Necessity
Of Jesus Christ; he never did espy,
But on false Bottoms he has built, 'tis clear;
I do conjure you therefore to declare
Him utterly unclean from *Top to Toe,*
And let him understand you are his Foe.
The Plague is in his Head, and no Place free,
But in his Heart it rages desperately.
Launce him then to the quick, and make him feel
Such heavy Blows, as may cause him to reel.

CONSCIENCE.

    Come, come, O Young Man, listen unto me,
I will no longer thus deceived be.
I from God's Word Commission have anew,
To tell thee what is like for to ensue;

For all thy Hopes and seeming godly Show,
Thou art a wretched Sinner, thou dost know.
Dost think on *Conscience* to commit a Rape,
And yet God's dreadful Vengeance to escape?
Dar'st thou again, under a new Disguise,
Encounter with those former Enemies?
You are the same, I'm sure, although you have
Changed your Coat poor Mortals to deceive.
Ungodly Wretch, dost thou not dread my Name!
I'm come once more against thee to proclaim
A second War; and to declare also
God's still thy Enemy, and bitter Foe
His Sword is whet, his Bow he'll also bend,
To cut down those that do like thee offend.
Nought he hates more than vile Hypocrisy,
And from his Presence, *Youth*, thou canst not fly.

YOUTH.

   Conscience be still, tho' I a Sinner be,
There's none doth know it now, but only thee.

CONSCIENCE.

   Deceived Soul! Doth none know it but I?
Where's the Great GOD? Is he not also nigh?
Dost think, vain *Youth*, the interposing Cloud,
From God's all-searching Eye, can be a Shroud?
Or dost thou think God's Seat is so on high,
That he cannot thy inward Thoughts espy?
None knows but me! Know'st thou not who I am?
Have I not power to accuse and damn?
Should I be still, it would be a sad day,
Unless thy Sins were purged clean away.
And whilst I speak, and thou dost stop thine Ear,
Nothing but Wars and Tumults thou wilt hear.
I'll never side with thee, nor take thy Part,
Whilst horrid Guilt remains in thy base Heart.
Nor would I mind thy Flattery or Frown,
Were thou the highest Prince of great Renown
That ever did on Earth a Scepter sway,
Before thy Face I would thy Evils lay:
For where I am an Enemy indeed,
I'll plague that Heart until I make it bleed.
Whate'er you think, or speak, or act, or do,
Of it, poor Soul, I very well do know:

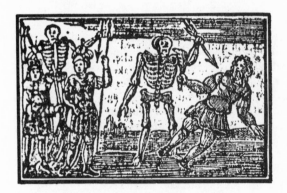

Thy secret Lust, and what is done i'th' Night,
Which thou ashamed art should come to Light:
I then am nigh, and know it very well;
Nay, more than this, I am resolv'd to tell:
I unto thee shall prove an Enemy,
When thou art brought into Adversity;
When painful Sickness comes, then thou shalt see
Death flying swift to make an End of thee.
All-conqu'ring Death will not regard thy Strength,
But will convey thee to the Grave at length;
   So *Sampson* stout he brought unto the Ground,
And *Alexander* great his Dart did wound.
Then my black Bill against thee will be large,
For then against thee I will bring a Charge.
Which will like Ashes make thy Visage look,
And wound thy Soul as if a Knife was struck
Into thy very Heart, and make thee mourn,
And curse the Day that ever thou wast born.
I'll make thee clearly understand i'th' End,
What 'tis, vile Sinner, *Conscience* to offend.
Hearken again, for I have more to say;
When this Life's ended, there's another Day.
Look now about thee, *Youth*, for there's to come
The black, the dark, the dreadful Day of *Doom*.
When thou dost die, I'll bite and sting thy Soul,
Whilst burning in the Flames it doth condole
Its damned State for yielding unto Sin,
Which has alone the Ruin of it been.
And also when i'th' Judgment-Day you stand
Among the Goats at Jesus Christ's Left-hand,
Thy dreadful State and Trial there to hear,
Then I against thee straitway must appear;
Yea, and shall speak more plain than now I can,

Because I'm clouded by the Fall of Man;
And am by Satan oftentimes misled,
So that I'm quite unable rendered
A true and right Decision to make,
He so beguile's me that I do mistake,
And a wrong Judgment oftentimes retain
'Till *Truth* sets me into the Light again.
But Satan then shall no more Power have,
Man's wretched sinful Heart for to deceive;
I in that Day shall you provoke and urge,
For to confess with Shame before the Judge.
Thy evil Lust and close Hypocrisy,
Unto thy own eternal Misery;
I shall accuse thee so in that Great Day;
Young-Man, thou shalt not have one Word to say.
Thy inward Parts so open'd then shall be,
That nothing shall be hid i'th' least from me;
And I before the dreadful Judge shall shew
All secret Things that ever you did do.
And in your Face so fiercely also fly,
That you with Horror shall be forc'd to cry,
Guilty, Guilty, O Lord; then you must hear
The dreadful Sentence which no one can bear,
Go, Go, ye Cursed; that's a Word of Ire;
And you must down into eternal Fire,
Where Hypocrites and Unbelievers lie,
Broiling in Pain to all Eternity.
And as the Fire evermore will burn,
And thou from thence shall never more return,
So also I shall then afflict your Soul,
Whilst thou in scalding Sulphur Flames dost roll;
I, like a Worm, or Serpent then will bite,
And gnaw thy Soul, thou cursed Hypocrite.
Those inward Stings which always thou wilt find,
Or cruel Gnawings in thy tortur'd Mind,
Will then increase, and aggravate thy Woe,
In such a Sort, there is no Tongue can show.
You then will think how you did me abuse,
And my good Counsel utterly refuse;
Your base Delays, and put-offs you'll repent,
And that your Time so foolishly you spent;
That you for Love which unto Lust you bore,
Should loose your Soul, and that for evermore.
To think how near you were to your Salvation,
Will prove another grievous Aggravation,

To bid so fair for Heaven, yet to miss,
What greater Trouble can there be than this?
To see the Ship i'th' Mouth o'th' Haven lost,
That doth, ye know, perplex the Merchant most.
I'll tell you also how you wilfully
Brought on yourself that dreadful Misery;
And how I did to you oft-times declare
The bitter Torments which you then must bear;
And what your Pride and Lust will bring you to,
If you did not resolve to let them go.
Ah! thou wilt see that thou art quite undone,
And how all Hopes for evermore are gone.
Thoughts of these golden Seasons once you had,
And vainly lost, will then be very sad.
Thou might'st, had'st thou improv'd the Means of Grace,
Beheld with Saints God's reconciled Face;
And enter'd Paradise, where Angels sing
Anthems of Joy to their Eternal King.
Thou might'st have sung to him melodious Psalms,
With those, whose Hands shall bear triumphant Palms;
Who with Eternal Love shall ravish'd be,
Reigning with Christ to all Eternity.
Heav'n is a Place whose Glory doth excel,
The Thousandth Part of it no Tongue can tell;
For who'd lose Christ, and his immortal Treasure,
For one base Lust, and Moment's Time of Pleasure?
But if what's said of Heav'n will not invite thee,
Then let Hell's Torments with its Vengeance fright thee,
And make thee yield to Truth without Delays,
Before God puts a Period to thy Days.
As Eye can never see, nor Tongue express
The Glory which God's Saints in Heav'n possess,
So there's no Man which can conceive the Woe
That Souls shut up in Hell do undergo.
If Men could number all the Stars in Heaven,
Or count the Dust which with the Wind is driven,
Or tell the Drops of Water in the Seas,
Or count the Sands; then might a Man with Ease
Declare the Nature of that dreadful Pain,
Which damned Souls for ever must sustain:
But Stars, nor Dust, nor Drops, nor Sands can be
Number'd by any one; neither can he
Express the Nature of God's dreadful Ire,
Which Souls lie under in Eternal Fire.
In Hell all's Death and yet there is no dying,

Nought there is heard but a most hidious Crying,
There Pains end not, from it there's no Exemption;
Their Cries admit no Hell, there's no Redemption.
Nor none to pity them, nor hear their Groans,
Whilst they do make their lamentable Moans.
The Lord who dy'd, will then rejoice to see
Vengeance pour'd forth upon those Souls that be
Vessels of Wrath; who for rejecting grace,
Must have their Portion in that doleful Place:
No earthly Pains or Torments can declare
The woful Anguish which the Damned bear!
For if those Plagues could be defin'd by Men,
Infinite Punishments 'twould not be then,
Infinite Wrath it is to satisfy:
And God, be sure, will Justice magnify.
Didst thou but hear the Groans and hideous Cry
Of Souls condemned to Eternity,
How it would scare, and cause thy Heart to ach,
And ev'ry Limb to tremble and to quake:
Think, think on this, before the Time doth come,
That God doth pass on thee the final Doom.

TRUTH.

What say'st thou now? How can'st thou sleep in Peace
Until these inward Gripes of *Conscience* cease?
How canst thou think i'th' least thy State is good,
When *Conscience* swells, and makes so great a Flood;
Or raises Storms and Tempests in thy Breast,
Because of Sin, he will not let thee rest.
Come, make a Search, *Conscience* is not misled,
The very Truth before you he has spread.
What will you do at Death and Judgment Day,
If *Conscience* thus you slight and disobey?
Make Peace with God, for worser are his Cries
Then if Ten Thousand Witnesses arise
Against thy Soul: 'Twill be a dreadful Thing,
To have thy *Conscience* then to bite and sting.

YOUTH.

Some Comfort, *Truth*, alas! my Soul doth melt;
Such Gripes as these what Man has ever felt?
I have some Doubt my Cause is very naught,
And that Conversion is not truly wrought.
My Heart condemns me, and doth me reprove,
'Tis thou alone which canst my Grief remove.

TRUTH.

   Before you have a Plaister for your Sore,
Your Wound must yet be search'd a little more:
If slightly heal'd, only for present Ease,
The Remedy's as bad as the Disease.
Dost know what Time thou didst this Wound receive?
'Tis worser far I fear, than you believe:
'Tis deep, it stinks: yea, and is venomous,
And doth expose thee to God's dreadful Curse.
Thy State is bad; thou hast thy mortal Wound;
No Limb nor any Part of thee is sound:
If thou could'st live, and never more offend,
Yet, by the Law, thy Soul is quite condemn'd.
If from all actual Sin you might be clear,
Yet by the Law you still more guilty are
Of former Crimes, Treason and Felony,
And Justice doth aloud for Vengeance cry:
Nor will the Pardon or Reprieve give forth
To any Sinner living on the Earth.
Against thee for the Sentence is forth gone,
And th' Day of Execution drawing on:
Nought is between thee and eternal Death,
But some short Hours of uncertain Breath.
Sin is so vile, and Justice so severe,
That in the least 'twould not Christ Jesus spare;
But Justice he must fully satisfy,
Who came to be Man's blest Security.
And since in Christ thou hast no Share or Part,
See what a Self condemned Soul thou art.

YOUTH.

   O cursed Sin! is this my sad Condition!
Truth, I believe, has made a right Decision:
I have my Soul deceived all along,
Tho' in my Heart Convictions oft were strong.
Oh! horrid Lust, and base deceitful Devil,
Is this the Fruit of your sweet pleasing Evil?
And thou false World too, what art thou to me?
For I, alas! am ruined by thee.
Oh! whither shall I fly! what Path untrod,
For to escape th' incensed Wrath of God?
Will none for me some secret Place provide,
Where I from flaming Vengeance close may hide?

TRUTH.

   Vain is all this; for none can find a Place

To hide from God, such is thy bitter Case;
If to the End of all the Earth you fly,
Vengeance will you pursue with Hue and Cry.
If you should take some sudden hasty Flight,
To seek some Shelter in the Shade of Night,
'Twould also fail thee, though it should be done;
For unto God Darkness and Light are one.
Can Rocks, dost think, prevent, yea, or restrain
The Stroke of Justice, and not fly in twain?
There is no Sea, nor Shade, nor Rock, nor Cave,
Which can from Vengeance shelter thee, or save;
The Sea would part, the hardned Rock will split,
Where Justice aims, her fiery Darts must hit.
Canst thou escape? alas! what Place is there
To hide from him who's present ev'ry where?

YOUTH.

   Oh! *Truth*, what shall I do? how can I stand,
Or bear those Tortures of God's heavy Hand?
My Spirit may Infirmities sustain,
But who can help this inward cutting Pain?
Is there no Help, no Salve to heal my Wound?
What! no Physician for me to be found?
Will Tears nor Pray'rs no Help at all afford,
Nor Watchings, Feastings, Hearing of the Word?
Or if that I could live, and sin no more?
O what is Sin! and what's my gangrene Sore!
O what's the Nature of Iniquity,
If nought my Soul can cleanse or purify,
Ah! I am lost, the Case is truly so;
I am undone, and know not what to do;
Have you no Word of Comfort now for me?
Oh! must I die in this Extremity?

TRUTH.

   Dost find thyself sick at the very Heart?
And doth my Searching make thy Wounds to smart?
Doth Sin, as Sin, upon thy Spirits lie?
And doth its Weight and Burden make thee cry?
Dost know thy Wound is epidemical,
And that for thee there is no help at all,
By Law or *Levite?* Dost thou see thy Loss,
And thy own Righteousness to be but Dross?

YOUTH.

   I know not what to say, I am in Doubt,

Some Sin is hid, which yet I can't find out;
My Heart is deep, and very traiterous,
Every Day I find it worse and worse
I grieve for Sin, and yet I am in dread,
That I in Sin am greatly hardened.
Yet this, O *Truth*, I hope is wrought in me.
Sin I do hate, as 'tis Iniquity.
I would not Christ offend, nor grieve again,
Were there no Hell, or Place of future Pain:
O that e'er I against the Lord should sin,
Who has to me so good and gracious been!
Against the Lord, against the Lord alone,
Have I this horrid Evil often done.
Oh! I do see that I in Sin am dead,
And my Iniquity's gone o'er my Head,
As a great Burden, which I cannot bear;
Oh! that I might but of a Saviour hear.

TRUTH.

  Come *Youth*, chear up, if this be so indeed,
I tell thee then, Christ for thy Soul did bleed:
Glad Tidings now I unto thee do bring,
There's Mercy for thee in the Heavenly King.
Christ, to appease God's Wrath, did hither come,
And I am sent by him to call thee home.
Rise up, rise up, his Blood for to apply,
And thou shall soon be healed perfectly.

Milk for Babes, And Meat for Men

Or Principles necessary, to bee known and learned of such as would know Christ here, or be known of him hereafter.

By HUGH PETERS

F IRST PUBLISHED IN *1630, this little book is a good example of a Puritan catechism. It is especially good because through the strange and moving life of its author the circulation of it or the ideas in it covered two continents.*

Hugh Peters, also spelled Peter *(1598–1660), was an almost incredibly active person, highly motivated by his interest in Puritanism. A graduate of Cambridge University, he was connected by marriage with the family of John Winthrop. First a preacher at St. Sepulchre's in London, and a very effective one, he decided as a nonconformist to go to Holland, where he became minister of the English church at Rotterdam. Tired of religious disputes engendered in Holland by Archbishop Laud, Peters went to New England—to Boston, in 1635. He became minister of the church at Salem. He was narrow in his treatment of those who did not share his independent views, and urged the excommunication of Roger Williams, who nevertheless respected him. He also played a prominent role in the founding of a new colony at the mouth of the Connecticut River.*

When the colony was economically disturbed by the difficulties of Charles I in 1641, Peters was sent as one of three agents to negotiate trade. He stayed on as Chaplain for a Roundhead army in Ireland, attacked the behavior of Archbishop Laud, went on various missions to Holland and elsewhere, and generally dabbled in politics as well as preaching, to such an extent that after Cromwell died and Richard Cromwell was overthrown, Peters, accused by the Royalists of being instrumental in the trial and execution of Charles I, was confined in the Tower and condemned to death. He was first forced to witness the hanging and quartering of his friend, John Cook. By then, Peters had become so unpopular that, according to an official report, no one who witnessed his execution pitied him.

He seemed to be a complex character, in some respects extremely narrow and in some ways tolerant and kindly. Vigorous and helpful with social and economic problems of the people, he also was personally ambitious and self-seeking. His enemies claimed that he told bawdy stories, some of which were published after his death, but this claim could easily be anti-Puritan propaganda. Had he been "loose," Roger Williams and the Winthrops would hardly have respected him.

Milk for Babes *was published while Peters was a preacher in Holland. It is addressed* to friends in England as a token: "Not that you want Catechismes, but that you may still know much Water cannot quench my love." The small book contains simple questions and answers in the Calvinist framework: "What must you know concerning sin?"—"That the nature of man is stained from his byrth." Job 14:4 (p. 7); "How is it manifest that the Pope is Antichrist?" (p. 26); auricular confession is "utterly without warrant" (p. 30); there is no ground to believe in transubstantiation (p. 32); and ministers can marry—"The contrary is the Doctrine of Devilis" (p. 34).

Milk for Babes is reproduced from a late nineteenth-century facsimile based on the first edition of 1630, published in Rotterdam.

MILK for BABES,
And
MEAT for MEN.

OR

Principles necessary, to bee known and learned, of such as would know Christ here, or be known of him hereafter.

2. THESS. 1. 8.

In flaming Fire, taking vengeance on them that know not God: & that obey not the Gospel of our Lord IESVS CHRIST.

Rom. 10. 15
How beautifull are the feet of them that preach the Gospell of peace, &c.

Imprinted Anno 1630.

MILK for BABES,
And
MEAT for MEN.

OR

*Principles necessary, to bee known
and learned, of such as would know
Christ here, or be known of him
hereafter.*

2. THESS. 1. 8.

In flaming Fire, taking vengeance
on them that know not *God*: & that
obey not the *Gospel* of our *Lord*
IESVS CHRIST.

Rom. 10. 15
*How beautifull are the feet of them that
preach the Gospell of peace, &c.*

Imprinted Anno 1630.

EPISTLE.

*To those, whom I have reason to
hold deere in Sepulchers* London, *&
elswhere in* England, *where I have spent
the poore Talent, the Lord hath
lent mee.*

BELOVED FREINDS.

IT often falls out whilst some have
thought it nothing to quit the out-
works, and have blamed the watch
that guarded them, the enemy hath got-
en within the ports, & the chiefe Citta-
dell hath beene endangered.

Give mee leave to tell you, that the
cause of all uneven walking, carnall fearing, & painted profession amongst you,
ariseth from a hart either *unbroken* or
unbottomd.

For the former of these, you have had
amongst you my poore endevours, I wish
they had beene more spirituall, more prevalent.

You had my liberty, and I wish my
life had gone with it, could that have accomplished the end of my labours, the
salvation of your soules in the day of the

A 2   LORD.

EPISTEL.

LORD. I complaine not of unan
swerable love from you.

For the second, I send you this toké,
not that you want *Catechismes*, but that
you may still know much Water cannot
quench my love.

Commend mee to your Children
and Servants and give them this. And,
know, that good things, if they bee not
esteemd in the abundance of them, will
bee better valued by their want.

Oh walke worthy of the Gospell,
lest with some desolate Churches you
once say : *Wee had the Gospell.*

I commend you all to his grace, who
is able to keepe you in the Fellowship
of the Gospel and rest.

Yours in him

H. P.

To

Epistle.

*To those, whom my Ministry may
concerne in the* Netherlands, *especially these of* Rotterdam, *who
have had most of my Labours.*

Loving Freinds.

I Know what meanes, what mercies
you injoy in these parts, & yet I am
not ignorant, what disadvantages
Godlines in the power of it hath, by errour in judgment, and loosenes in life ;
Look well, and you will finde, it is not
all gold that glistereth : Beleeve it, *A
compleate Christian,* is allmost as dainty as
the man the Lord lookt for, *Ezech.* 22.
Wherfore as you meet with my labours
in publicke, so accept of this for you, &
yours in private.

You have many other helps ; but having resolved to pitch upon something
of this kind, and finding all said before
that could bee sayd, I pitcht upon this
ground-worke, which I put into this
order, for your *Furtherance.*

Never dreame of building without
foundations, when you have well disge-

A 3   sted

Epistle.

sted this *Milke*, you must then bee fit for stronger *Meat*.

The *Lord* make us wise with *Ioseph*, it is a getting time*, there will come a spending. And remember that if ever your poore Infants bee driven to wildernesses, to hollow caves, to Fagot and Fire, or to sorrowes of any Kinde, they will thanke God & you, they were well catechized.

The comfort of these principles hee wisheth you who is

Yours in the

Rock Christ.

H . P .

What

 Hat is the end and *scope of Catechizing*?

To procure & increase knowledge.

What is the originall and fountain of knowledge ?

The Scripture , that is : The Bookes of the Old and New Testament.

What is necessary to bee knowne concerning them ?

Two things. The *first* is : That they are the very word of God , or they flow from God, by Divine inspiration, 2.*Tim*. 3.16.

What is the second thing ?

That they are perfect without defect or errour, every way sufficient of themselves alone, to guide

Wee must beleeve Two things concerning the Word.

A 4 us

---

us in all things needfull to salvation , without adding ought to them, or diminishing ought from them. *Psal*.19.7.

What is the subject of knowledge ?

God : who must be considered first in his Nature, secondly in his workes.

What is necessary to be knowne in the Nature of God?

Foure things. First: That there is a God. Secondly : That hee is glorious in nature. Thirdly: That he is three in persons, Fourthly : That hee is one in essence.

How doe you prove there is a God ?

Every line in Scripture proves it , and every Creature speakes it , and every conscience in horrour knowes it &c.

Concerning the Nature of God. Foure things.

How

How prove you hee is glorious ?

As many Scriptures prove it : so it may bee seene in these particulars. 1. he is a incorporeall. 2. b eternall. 3. c incomprehensible. 4. d immutable. 5. e omnipotent. 6. f omniscient. 7. most g holy. 8. h allsufficient. 9. most i mercifull. 10. k immortall.

How doe you prove hee is three in persons, and one in essence ?

Many Scriptures give testimony to the Trinity, as Matth. 28. 19. 1.Ioh. 5. 7. And that there is but one, is cleere, Isa.44.6.8. Mark.12. 29. 1.Cor. 8.4.

What are the workes of God?

They bee either of Creation or providence.

What is necessary for you to beleeve concerning the Creation?

These five things. First: That the

a Ioh. 4.24
b Psal.90.2
c 1.Kings 8. 27
d Iam. 1.17
e Psl.115.3.
f Psl. 147.5
g Psal.5.4.
h Gen.17.1
i Exod.34. 5.7
k 1.Tim.1. 17.

A 5 the

4   M I L K for B A B E S,

the World had a beginning , and was not eternall. *Genef.*1.1. *Second-ly.* That the World and all things were made by God. *Act.*17. 24.
What are the reft?
Thirdly. That all was made of nothing. *Rom.*4. 17. *Fourthly.* That God made all things by his Word only. *Genef.*1.
Fiftly, That all things in their Creation were made good. *Genef.* 2. 1.
What muft you know concerning his Providence?
Seven things.
Concerning Gods pro vidence. Seven things.   *Firft.* That God ftill knowes and takes continuall notice of all things. *Prov.*15.3. *Secondly.* That God upholds & governs and difpofeth of the World, fo as all things continue through him. *Pfal.* 119. 91.
What are the other?
Thirdly. That this Providence

of God

And M E A T for M E N   5

ofGod reacheth to all things,even the fmalleft things are governed and upheld by God. *Rom.* 11.36.
Fourthly.
That of all Creatures God hath moft care and refpect of Men. *Prov.* 8. 31.
What are the reft?
Fiftly.
That the good or evill, which befalleth Man , is not without Gods Providence. *Amos* 3.6.
Sixtly.
That hee doth whatfoever plea-feth him in Heaven or in Earth. *Pfal.*115.3   *Laftly.*
That Gods dominion is ever-lafting. *Pfal.* 146. 10.
What muft you know, concerning his particular Providence, touching Man?
The things , concerning Man, have refpect unto his fourefold Eftate. The *firft.* Of Innocency, the

fecond

6   M I L K for B A B E S,

fecond of corruption or mifery, the third of grace , the fourth of glory.
Concerning mans firft eftate, what muft you know?
Concerning Mans firft Eftate. Two things.   Two things. *Firft :* God made man after his owne image. *Gen.*1. 26. *Secondly :* This image of God chiefly côfifted in knowledge, ho-lines,and righteoufnes. *Eccl.*7.29.
What muft you know concerning mans fecond eftate of mifery?
It muft bee confidered two wayes. *Firft :* In the caufe of it. *Secondly :* in the parts of it.
The caufe of it was the fall of our firft parents.
In their fall what muft you know?
In the Fall. Three things.   Three things.
What is the firft?
That our parents Adam & Eve fell and loft fpeedily the happines

in

And M E A T for M E N.   7

in which they were created: as ap-pears *Gen.*3.7. And there they did loofe God, Paradice , and Gods Image.
What are the other two ?
Secondly : This loffe befell them only for their owne finne. *Rom.* 5. 12. *Thirdly :* By their fin wee are defiled, and deprived of the glory of God. *Rom.* 3. 23.
What be the parts of mans mifery?
They are two, namely fin , and punifhment.
What muft you know concer-ning fin?
Thefe foure things. *Firft :* That all men have finned. *Pfal.* 14.1.2. 3. *Secondly :* That the nature of man is ftained from his byrth. *Iob* 14. 4.
What are the other two?
Thirdly : That this infection hath over-fpread the whole nature of

man,

8 — MILK for BABES

man, and tainted it many waies.

Fourthly : Besides this , every man is guilty of horrible and vile actuall sins, and that very many.

What must you know concerning the punishment of sin ?

That all Men in their naturall Estate are extreamly miserable in respect of the punishmēt to which they are lyable for their sins. *Nahum.* 1.2.3.6. And the forts of mpunishments are many and grievous, the last, whereof is eternall paine and damnation.

Is this all you are to beleeve concerning sin ?

To this must bee added, that the least transgression of the Law , is sin.

1 1. *Extream darknes*. 2. *insensiblenes*. 3. *Impotency*. 4. *Enmity to good*. 5. *Impunity*. 6. *abundance of false principles*. 7 *pronenes to all evill*. 8. *Want of all righteousnes*. 9. *The mēbers servants of sin*. 10. *A servile will*. 11. *a naturall aptnes to be scandalized*. 12. *a relishing of the things of Satan*. 13. *corruptiō of memory*. 14. A naturall disunion one from another. 15. 1. The losse of paradice. 2. the curse of the creatures. 3. an impure and painfull birth. 4. the displeasure of God. 5. a privation of the knowledge of God. 6 bondage to Satan. 7. spiritual death. 8. miserable bodyes. 9. judgments in our outward estates: 10. the retayning good things from us. 11. the cursing of blessings. 12. scourging of sin with sin. 13. hellish horrour. 14. feare of death. 15. A miserable departure, 16. A terrible generall judgement. 17. & lastly Hell.

Now

And MEAT for MEN. 9

Now, for the third estate of man, which is of grace. How must that bee considered ?

Three wayes. First. in respect of the meanes of the foundation of it. *Secondly*. In respect of the subject of the possession of it , which is the Church. *Thirdly*. In respect of Application.

What is the meanes of Foundation ?

Twofold. *First.* Election in God. *Secondly*. Redemption in Christ.

What are you to know concerning Election ?

These *five* things. *First.* That there was a Choise and Election, made by God. *Ephes.* 1.4. *Secondly*. That this Choise was before the foundation of the World. *Rom*. 9. 11. *Thirdly*. That some Men are chosen , not all Men , for if all were taken, how could there bee Election? *Matth.* 20.16.

Concerning Election. five things.

What

10 — MILK for BABES

What is the fourth ?

The cause of our election is the only free grace of God , and not our works. *Ephes.* 1. 5. And *fiftly*. Gods Election is unchangeable : all the Elect shall be saved. *Rom*. 8. 30.

What is the second foundamentall meanes of grace ?

Redemptiō in Christ; in whom wee must consider his person , & his office, and in his person, his divine , and humane nature.

What ought you to know concerning his divine nature ?

That Jesus Christ was very God, *Isai*. 9. 6. *Ioh*. 1. 1. and divers other wayes it may bee proved. And it was needfull hee should bee God. *First.* For the greatnes of our evill. *Secondly*. For the greatnes of our good.

What must you know, concerning his humane nature ?

Foure

And MEAT for MEN — 11

Foure things. The *first*, about the matter, namely, that the *Son* of *God* was incarnate , did assume the true nature of man , and was a very man among us. *Ioh*. 1. 1.

The other three concerne the manner.

What are they ?

First, that he was not conceived as other Men , but by the Holy Ghost. *Luke* 1. 35. *Secondly*. That he was borne of a virgin. *Esai*. 7. 14. *Thirdly*. That his humane nature did subsist in the divine, and so both made but one person. *Col*. 2. 9.

Having done with his person, how consider you his office ?

Either in the whole , or in the parts of it. The whole office of Christ being this, namely : To bee a Mediator; wherin I must observe five things.

Concerning Christs humane nature, foure things.

Concerning the Mediator, five things.

B   What

What are they?

First: There is but one Mediator betweene God and man even Iesus Chriſt. 1.*Tim.*2. 5. *Secondly:* That the cauſe of our ſalvation in his mediation is not merit in man but grace in God & Chriſt *.

* 2.Tim, 1.9.

What are the reſt?

Thirdly: That this mediation was from the beginning of the world, and ſhall bee to the end. *Heb.* 13.8. *Fourthly.*

That without the mediation of Chriſt no fleſh can be ſaved. *Act.* 4.12. *Fiſtly.*

By the mediator a new contract or covenant was made with God. *Ierem.* 31.33.

How many ſorts or parts of Chriſts offices are there?

Three. His Propheticall, Prieſtly, & Kingly office. Concerning his Propheticall office, theſe things muſt bee knowne. *Firſt.* That in

Seve things about Chriſts Prophe- ticall Office.

Chriſt

Chriſt are all the treaſures of wiſdome and knowledge. *Coloſ.* 2. 3.

What elſe?

Secondly. That it is Chriſt only that revealed the truth out of the boſom of his Father. *Matth.*11.27.

Thirdly. That Chriſt himſelfe taught doctrine amongſt men. *Heb.*1.2. *Fourthly.* That hee hath revealed the whole counſell of God. *Ioh.*15.15.

What are the reſt?

Fiftly. The miniſtery in the church is by authority frō Chriſt, *Matth.*23.34.

Sixtly. The whole efficacy of Doctrine, either recorded in Scripture, or taught by men from thence, depends upon Chriſt. 2.*Pet.*1.20.21. *Laſtly.* The prophecy of Chriſt, belongs generally to all Nations. *Iſai.* 49. 6.

What is his Prieſtly office?

It is that part of his Function,

B 2 wher.

wherby hee maketh Satisfaction unto God for Men.

What is required of Chriſt as the Prieſt of his Church?

Firſt. Hee muſt obey the Law of God perfectly. *Secondly.* Hee muſt make expiation for our ſins by ſacrificing to God. *Thirdly.* Hee muſt make interceſſion for us.

For the firſt of theſe, namely his obedience: What muſt you beleeve?

Firſt. I muſt beleeve that hee was without ſin in his nature. *Ioh.* 8.46. *Secondly.* Hee fulfilled the Law of God perfectly in all his Actions: hence is hee called the holy one, & the holy Child Ieſus. *Act.* 2. 27.

What more?

Thirdly. That hee fulfild the Law not only for himſelfe, but for us, and for our ſakes. *Rom.* 8. 3. 4.

Fourthly. This righteouſnes of

In Chriſts obedience foure things

his

his is an everlaſting righteouſnes, and ſuch, as ſerves for the Elect of all ages, and a righteouſnes, that cannot bee loſt. *Dan.* 9. 24.

For his expiation of ſin, what muſt you beleeve?

That it was made by the Paſſiō of Chriſt, wherin divers things muſt bee knowne: as *firſt*, that the paſſion of Chriſt was by the decree and everlaſting fore-appointment of God. *Act.* 2. 23.

For the expiation of ſins, ſix things.

What more?

Secondly. The ſuffrings of Chriſt were for our ſins & for our ſakes, ſo as hee bare all our iniquities, 1.*Pet.* 2,24. *Thirdly.* That by his paſſion hee did pacifye God, and make expiation for all our ſins. *Matth.*17.5.

Proceede to the reſt.

Fourthly. In his owne perſon hee fullfilled and finiſhed all ſuffrings, needfull for our ſalvation

B 3 hee

16   MILK for BABES,

hee did it once for all. 1.Pet.3.18.
What more?

Fiftly. That the Paſſion of Chriſt
is a ſufficient price for the ſins of
the whole World, *Ioh.*1.29. *Sixtly.*
that Chriſt ſuffred extreme things
for us, even the moſt grievous
things could bee imagined, *Iſai.*
63.1.2.7.8.
*What muſt you know about his
Interceſſion?*

*About his
Intercef-
ſion,
foure
things.*

Firſt. That Chriſt at the right
hand of God maketh Interceſſion
for us, *Rom.* 8.34. *Secondly.* That
wee have no Interceſſor in Heaven but Chriſt, 1.*Tim.* 2.5.6.
What more?

Thirdly. The Interceſſion of
Chriſt is perpetuall, hee doth it
once, that hee will never faile to
doe it in all ages, *Heb.*7,25.28.

Fourthly. That hee maketh Interceſſion only for the Elect, *Ioh.*
17.9.

What

And MEAT for MEN   1-?

*What are you bound to beleeve.
concerning his Regall office?*

Many things. And *frſt*: That hee
overcame Sin, Death, the Grave,
and Hell, and roſe again from the
dead, and aſcended into Heaven,
& ſitteth at the right hand of God
in Majeſty, *Rom.* 1.4. *Mar,* 16.19.
Proceede to the reſt?

Secondly. That Chriſt, who pur-
chaſed the Church by his blood, is
appointed of God, to bee the King,
and head of his Church, & Prince
over the People of God, having
all power in his owne hands, *Pſal.*
2.6.*Toirdly.*Hee is appointed Law-
giver to the Church, & the judge
of the whole world, *Iam.* 4.12.
What are the reſt?

Fourthly. That his governemēt ex-
tēds to all nations*.*Fiftly.*His kingdome is not of this world, but ſpi-
ritual & celeſtialt. *sixtly.*He wil be
with his to the end of the world†

*Concerning
his Regall
office.ſevē
things.*

* *Pſal.2.8*
† *John 18.
36.*
‡ *Matth.
28.22.*

B 4   *Laſtly.*

---

18   MILK for BABES,

Laſtly. His Kingdome is everla-
ſting, *Luke* 1.33.
*So much of the meanes of Grace.
What is the ſubject of Grace?*

The*Church*, which is the whole
multitude of Men and Women,
elected to eternall life by God in
Chriſt.
*What muſt you know concerning
the Church?*

*Concerning
the*Church
ſeven
things.*

Many things. And *firſt*, that it
is a Company ſeparate from the
world, gathered by the voice of
Chriſt: The Scripture ſtill maketh
difference betwixt the World and
the Church: And the Word ſig-
nifyes ſuch, as are gathered by the
voice of Gods Cryers, *Ioh.*17.9.

Secondly, Shee is one, *Epheſ.*4.4.
What more?

*Thirdly,*Shee is Knit unto Chriſt,
her head by an indiſſoluble union
*Col.*1.18.Shee is one with Chriſt,
not in nature, but in ſpirit.*Ioh.*4.13

Fourthly,

And MEAT for MEN.   19

Fourthly, Shee is holy, *Epheſ.*5.27.
What are the reſt?

Fiftly, Shee is Catholike, *firſt*, in
reſpect of time. *Secondly,* in regard
of place. And *thirdy,* Perſons.

Sixtly, Shee is militant, that is,
expoſed to many evills in this life
2.*Tim.* 4.7,8. *Seventhly,* Shee is
invincible, *Matth.*16.18.
*So much for the ſubject of Grace.
What is the Application?*

For the calling of us to God in
Chriſt for our juſtification, adoption, and ſanctification.
*Concerning Iuſtification, what
muſt you beleeve?*

Many things. *Firſt,* That by
mans owne works no Fleſh can
bee juſtifyed, *Rom.* 3.20. *Secondly.*
The righteouſnes, that maketh us
juſt, is in Ieſus Chriſt being made
ours by Imputation, 2.*Cor.*5.21.
What more?

Thirdly, That this righteouſnes

*In Iuſtifi-
cation.
Sixe things*

B 5   is made

20 MILK for BABES,

is made ours only by faith, so wee are justified only by Faith, as it layes hold upon the righteousnes of Christ, *Rom.* 3, 28.

Fourthly. This Faith is the gift of God, *Ioh.* 6. 29.

Are these all ?

No. *Fiftly.* All men have not Faith, *Isai.* 53.1. *Sixtly.* There is but one Kind of Faith, by which all the Elect of God are justified, *Ephes.* 4. 5. *Lastly.* Being justified by Faith, wee have peace with God, and forgivenes of all our sins *Rom.* 3. 25.

What are you to beleeve about Adoption ?

That so many as beleeve have this honor to be called the Sons and Heires of God, for the sealing, wherof, hee giveth the Spirit of Adoption, wherby they cry: *Abba Father,* 1. *Iohn* 3. 1.

What

21

What must you know and beleeve concerning Sanctification ?

First. That whom God justifieth, hee sanctifieth, *Rom.* 8. 30.

Secondly. To bee truly sanctified, is in unfained repentance to dye to sin and to rise againe to newnes of life and obedience. *Rom.* 6. 1. 2. 3.

Thirdly. Except wee be borne againe, wee cannot enter into the Kingdome of God, *Iohn* 3. 5.

What else must you know herein ?

Fourthly. That Sanctification is Gods gift, and worke in *Iesus Christ,* wee can no more convert ourselves, then wee can beget ourselves at first, wee can no more create ourselves new men, then wee can create ourselves men. *Acts* 5. 31.

Lastly. Our Sanctification is imperfect in this life. 1. *Iohn* 1, 8.

Sanctification, five things.

What

22 MILK for BABES,

What are the ordinances of God for procuring and furthering this grace ?

Chiefly *five.* The Word preached. *Secondly,* The administratiō of Sacraments. *Thirdly.* Prayer. *Fourthly,* Discipline. *Lastly,* Christian Communion.

Now, for the fourth and last estate of man, what must you beleeve.

Wee must consider the three degrees of it, which are the Resurrection of the Body, the last judgment, and the glory of Heaven.

What concerning the Resurrection ?

Resurrection, three things.

First, That the Bodyes of the dead shall rise out of the earth, and their owne Soules shall enter into them againe, *Iob.* 19. 23, 26. The Sea, Fier, Beasts, Ayre, Foules, &c. shall give up their dead, *Revel.* 20. 12, 13. *What else ?*

Secondly, That the same Bodies,

which

23

which men carry about with them in this World, shall rise againe, *Iob* 19. 26, 27. *Thirdly,* This Resurrection shall bee at the end of the World, even the last day of the World, *Iob.* 6. 44.

For the last Iudgment, what must you know ?

Many things. *First,* There shallbe a generall judgment. *Iude* 14. 15. *Secōdly,* that Christ shall bee judge, and that in the humane nature, *Act.* 10. 42. *Thirdly,* all men shall be then judged, just and unjust, quick and dead, small and great, *Rom.* 14. 9.

Goe on with the rest.

Fourthly, All the secret things of mens natures and workes shall bee brought to light, *Luk.* 8. 17. *Fiftly,* It shall bee at the last day, but the precise day & houre is not knowne to any Men or Angells, *Matth.* 24. 36.

About the last judgment, seven things.

Is

24 MILK for BABES,

Is this all ?

No. *Sixth.* The judgment shall bee moſt righteous & juſt, all shall confeſſe it, *Rom.*14.10. *Laſtly.* The Iudgment shall bee according to mens works. 2.Cor. 5. 10.

Concerning the Glory of Heaven, what ought you to beleeve ?

The glory of heavē Foure things.

Firſt. For the greatnes of it, it is unſpeakeable , and in reſpect of us here on earth incomprehenſible, 1.*Cor.*2.9. The *ſecond* concerns the continuance of it, & ſo it is eternal, & therefore is this life called eternall life,and immortality.*Mat.* 25. 46. *What more ?*

The *third* concernes the cauſes of it. Heaven is the gift of God, & proceeds only frō his free grace,& not frō any merit in us.*Luk.*12.32.

The *fourth* and *laſt*,concerns the perſons , that shall injoy it : The Elect of God only obtaine this glory. 1.*Cor.* 15. 50.

The

The hart being Poſſeſt with the former Poſitive Truths, may thus bee eſtabliſhed againſt Gainſayers.

NOw, let me know how you are furniſhed againſt the Adverſaries : And which are they , that moſt trouble you ?

They are either the Romiſh Catholikes, or their neere neighbors,the Revived Pelagians.

What Weapon have you to encounter them ?

That

---

26 MILK for BABES,

That which Chriſt uſed againſt Satan , their leader and maiſter, namely : The Scripture.

Can you confute the Papiſt by the word in all things wee lay to his charge ?

Clearly, as shall appeare, if you will take tryall.

How is is manifeſt that the Pope is Antichriſt ?

By theſe Scriptures.

1. Point. Of Popery confuted.

Revel. 13. 18.	Matth. 24.24.
Revel. 17. 3.5.	1. Ioh. 2. 18.
1.Tim. 4.1.2.3.	2.Theſ. 2.3.4.

Are the Scriptures ſufficient to debate all controverſies and doubts?

Yea. Read and conſider theſe Scriptures.

2.

Pſal.119.105.	Act.10.43.
Iſai.8.19.20.21.	2.Tim.3.16.
Luk.16.29.30.	Heb.4.12.

How

How prove you that all ſorts ought to know and reade the Scriptures ?

By theſe places.

Deut. 6.6.7.8.	Acts 17.11.	
Pſal. 1. 2.	Col. 3. 16.	*3.*
Iohn 5. 39.	Revel. 1. 3.	

Can you prove, the Scriptures eaſy to bee underſtood of the ſimple ?

Yea. Read

Deut.30.11.12.	Ierem.31.34.	
Pſal.119.130.	Matth. 11.25.	*4.*
Prov.14.6.	Matth 13. 11.	

May wee not bee ignorant of the Scriptures without any danger ?

No. As you may perceive by theſe Texts.

Pſal. 95.10.11.	Ier.4.22.	
Prov.1.28.29. &c.	Matth.15.14.	*5.*
Iſai. 1.3.4.	1.Cor. 15.34.	

Doth the word of God then containe in it , all things neceſſary for our ſalvation ?

C *Yea.*

28 MILK for BABES,

Yea. As you may fee

6.

Ifai. 8.20.	Rom. 1.16.
Ioh.20. 31.	Heb. 4. 12.
Acts 20.32.	Iames 1. 21.

May nothing bee added to , nor ta-ken from the word of God ?

No. See

7.

Deut. 5.22.	Mat.15.3.
Iof. 1.7.	Gal. 1.8.
Prov.30.5.6.	Revel.22.18.19.

So much for the Scriptures. How prove you, that Faith only doth justi-fie ?

From thefe places.

8.

Gen.15.6.	Rom.3.25.&c.
Mark.5.36.	Gal.2.16. &c.
Act. 10.43.	Ephef.2.8.

Have wee then no merits nor righ-teoufnes of our owne ?

Nonc.

And MEAT for MEN. 29

Nonc. As you may fee

Deut.9.4,5.	Rom 30.10.11.&c.	9.
Iob 9.30.31.	1.Cor.4.4.7.	
Ifai.6 4.6.	Ephef.2.8.9.	

What is the heynoufnes of originall fin ?

Great. As thefe Texts fhew.

Genef. 5.6.7.	Prov.20.9.	10.
Iob 14.4.	Ioh.3.6.	
Pfal. 51.5.	Rom.5.12.	

Is it not poffible for us to fullfill the Law ?

No. As you may perceive by

Deut.27.16.	Rom.8.3.	
Mat.5.21.22.	1.Cor,2.14.	11.
Acts 15.10.	Iames 2.10.	

Cannot the Pope or a Prieft for-give fins ?

C 2 No.

30 MILK for BABES,

No. Only God. See

12.

Pfal.3. 8.	Acts 14.14.
Ifai.43.25.	Iames 5 21.
Mat. 1.21.	1.Tim.1.15.

What fay you then to Auricular Confeffion ?

It is utterly without warrant. See

13.

Pfal.32.5.	Dan. 9.15.
1.Kings 8. 47.	Mat.15.18.
Ier.14.20.	1.Ioh.1.9.

May wee not pray for the dead ?

No. As you may read.

14.

2. Sam. 12.22.23.	Mar.8.36.37.
Pfal.49.7.8.	Luk.16.27.28
Exod. 20.7.	1.Thef. 4.13.14

What fay you of Purgatory, and the Popes pardons ?

That

And MEAT for MEN 31

That they are unwarranted by the Word. See

Ifai.57. 1.2.3.	Matth.7.13.14.	15.
Pfal. 51. 7.	Ioh. 3.18.	
Ecclef.9.5.6.	Revel.14.13.	

Have wee no Mediator or Intercef-for in Heaven but only Chrift ?

None elfe. As appeares

Mat. 11.28.	Rom.5.10.	
Mark. 1.11.	1.Tim.2.5.	16.
Acts 20.28.	Heb.7.25.	

May wee not pray to the Saints de-parted ?

No. As is eafy to gather from

Ifai.63.16.	Matt.11.28.	
Ierem.15.1.	Ioh. 14.6.	17.
Ezech. 14.14.	Rom.10.14.	

May wee not pray in a ftrange tongue, that wee underftand not ?

C 3 No.

32   MILK for BABES,

No. See

18.

Act. 2. 1. 2. 3. &c.
1. Cor. 14. 14. 15. &c.

May not Saincts and Angells have Divine Worship?

No. As it is cleere in

19.

Iudg. 13. 15. 16.   Mat. 4. 10.
Pſal. 29. 2.   Act. 10. 25. 26.
Iſai. 42. 8.   1. Cor. 1. 13.

What ſay you to Tranſubſtantia-tion? Is not the very Fleſh and blood of Chriſt in the Sacrament, even the ſame Body that was crucifyed?

There is no ground to thinke ſo. See

20.

Mat. 26. 26. 27. &c. 1. Cor. 10. 16. 17
Luk. 22. 15. 16. &c. 1. Cor. 11. 26.
Ioh. 6. 53.   Ioh. 16. 7.

How doe wee eate the Body and Blood of Chriſt then?

Only

And MEAT for MEN   33

Only by Faith, as is cleere.

Ioh. 6. 47. 58.   1. Cor. 10. 1, 4. 5.
Ioh. 11. 26.   Epheſ. 3. 17.
Ioh 15. 5.   2. Cor. 5. 7.

21.

Cannot Chriſts Body bee here by his Allmighty power?

It can bee but in one place at one time, as you may ſee by theſe Scriptures.

Mat. 24. 23.   Phil. 3. 20.
Mark. 16 19.   Heb. 8. 1.
Act. 1. 9. 10. 11. Heb. 10. 12.

22.

What can you ſay againſt their choiſe of meats?

The Spirit of God ſaith thus.

Mat. 15. 11.   Col. 2. 16. 17. 21.
Act. 10. 13. 14. 15. Tit. 1. 15.
1. Cor. 8. 8.   Heb. 13. 9.

23.

What have you againſt their ſett Faſtings?

D 4   Theſe

---

34   MILK for BABES,

Theſe Scriptures.

24.

Iſai. 58. 4 5. 6.   Luk. 18. 11. 12. &c.
Mat. 15. 11. 20.   Mat. 6. 17, 18.

May wee not warrantably receive and practiſe the Ceremonies and Tra-ditions of men?

You may bee pleaſed to con-ſider theſe Scriptures.

25.

Deut. 5. 32. 33.   Hoſ. 9. 15.
Levit. 10. 2.   Mat. 23. 4.
Iſai. 1. 12 13. 14.   Gal. 4. 10.

May Miniſters or Biſhops marry as lawfully as other men?

The contrary is the Doctrine of Devills. See

26.

1. Cor. 7. 2. 9.   1. Tim. 2, 4, 5,
1. Cor. 9. 5.   Heb. 13. 4.
1. Theſ. 4. 3. 4.   1. Tim. 4. 2. 3.

Is

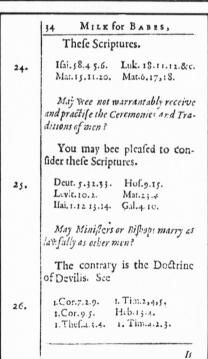

And MEAT for MEN.   25

Is not Maſſe the Sacrifice of the New Teſtament?

Prayer is, but we have no ground for Maſſe.

Pſal. 4. 5.   Phil. 4. 18.
Pſal. 51. 17. 18. 19. Heb. 13. 15. 16.
Mat. 12. 7.   1. Pet. 2. 5.

27.

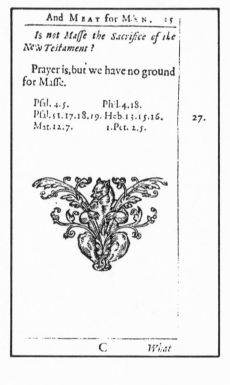

C   What

Panel 1 (page 36)

WHat Strength have you now againſt your other Adverſaries, the Pelagians or Armi?

Such as the Holy Ghoſt affords out of the former Treaſury.

Then tell mee. Are there ſome elected, and ſome reprobated of Gods free Decree?

Yea certainly : Which theſe Scriptures make manifeſt.

1. Point of Arm. confuted.

Exod.33.19.	Rom.9.11.23.
Pſal. 33. 12.	Rom.8.28.
Prov.16.4.	Epheſ. 1.4.5.11.
Ioh.12.39.40.	1.Pet.1.1.2.
Acts 13.48.	Revel.13.8.

Can

Panel 2 (page 37)

Can any man bee certaine of his faith and ſalvation , and ought wee earneſtly to looke therunto?

You may conſider theſe Scriptures.

Ioh.19.25.	Gal 4.5.
Ioh. 10.9.	Heb.10.12.23.
Rom. 8.1.17.	Iames 5.8.
1.Pet. 1,10.	

2.

Hath not man free will after his fall in ſpirituall things, and can hee not of him ſelfe move God-ward?

No. Which may bee proved by theſe truths.

Geneſ.6.5.	Ioh.1.13.
Pſal. 14.3.	Rom.7.14.
Prov. 20.9.	1.Cor.3.7.
Ierem.10.23.	Phil.2.13.
Ezech.36.26.27.	Iames 1.17.
Mat. 10.20.	Epheſ.2.3.

3.

What

Panel 3 (page 38)

What thinke you of univerſall Grace , or whether did not Chriſt dye for all?

Hee did not. Theſe Scriptures well weighed, may ſatiſfye.

4.

Mat.25.32.	2.Cor.5.15.
Ioh.7.11.15.27.28.	Epheſ.5.25.
Ioh.17.24.	Tit.2.14.
Ioh.17.9.19.20.21.	Heb.1.14.
Rom.3.22.	Heb.5.9.
Rom.8.3.4.	Heb.10.14.
Ioh.1.12.	

When wee have gotten Grace, cannot wee looſe it all againe , and fall away finally and totally?

No. Theſe Scriptures are plaine.

5.

Ierem.31.33.34.	Rom.14.4.
Iſai.54.10.	Rom.11,7.
Iſai,57.15.&c.	Rom.8.35.37.38
Hoſ. 2.18.	Epheſ.5.23.
Pſal.125.	2.Tim.1.12.

Ioh.6.

Panel 4 (page 39)

Ioh.6.37.	1.Pet.1.5.
Ioh.14.16.	Mat.16,18.
Luk.8.15.	Ioh. 5. 25.
Ioh. 6.35.	

Other points and other proofs might be added, but this ſwells too big allready.

Paſſe by literall faults : And give *God* praiſe for this lime,& haire, amongſt the other rich ſtuffe for *Gods* Houſe.

Vive ut diſcas,
Diſce ut vivas.

F I N I S.

A Token for Children

Being An Exact Account of the Conversion, Holy
And Exemplary Lives and Joyful Deaths of several
Young Children.

By JAMES JANEWAY

TO WHICH IS ADDED,

A Token, for the Children of New-England.

By COTTON MATHER

SOMBER AS THESE deathbed testimonials to the greatness of God may seem, children who heard them and were awed by them at least believed in something. These children believed themselves to be important in the eyes of an all-seeing God. Life and death had meaning.

Of special interest beyond Janeway's famous case histories of dying children in England are the comparable accounts of the behavior of dying American children, in this unique volume published precisely at the turn of the seventeenth century (1700), reproduced here by courtesy of the American Antiquarian Society, Worcester, Massachusetts. This is the first American edition.

Here one reads of little Ann Greenough (Example IV), who, dying of tuberculosis at the age of five, was asked "Whether she were willing to Dye." And "She would still chearfully Reply, Ay, by all means, that I may go the Lord Jesus Christ."

By such examples, children were prepared to face the inevitable—a preparation which demanded faith in God and a godly life.

James Janeway (1636?–1674) was only thirty-eight when he died of tuberculosis. Though a graduate of Christ Church, Oxford, he did not conform with the Anglican teachings, and his somber and rigid interpretations of the Bible are evident in his sermons, one of which was the "Joyful Death" sermon later printed and reprinted as a book to instill righteous conduct in children. It was first printed in 1671–72, and it was to this sermon that Cotton Mather's accounts of Joyful Deaths were added in the rare book published in 1700.

Cotton Mather, a Puritan clergyman in Boston (1662?–1728?), was graduated from Harvard in 1678 at the age of sixteen. He was not very popular in school since he was always trying to correct the moral behavior of his classmates and also, perhaps, because he had an irritating stammer. Almost one hundred years before the Revolution, Mather showed opposition to English domination. He was less courageous in defending those in

Salem accused of witchcraft, even when he doubted their guilt. His best known work is Wonders of the Invisible World *(1693) in which he defended the verdicts at the witchcraft trials. Though obviously derivative from the English work of Janeway, Cotton's dying children are in an American setting.*

An irascible, arrogant, generally unlovable man, he was left alone enough to write 450 books. Both professionally and personally, his life dissatisfied him. He failed to become President of Harvard, two of his wives died and the third became insane, and most of his children died early. He did a number of good things, however. In medical histories, he is remembered for having urged smallpox inoculation, and so having assisted in saving lives. He also began and supported a school for the education of slaves. Since children liked to be around him and he liked to spend time with them, a core of simplicity and kindness must have existed beneath the troubled image he presented to many adults.

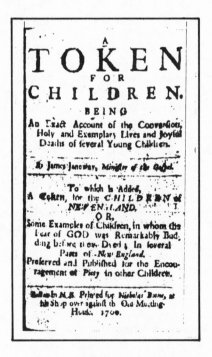

To all Parents, School Masters and School-Mistresses, or any that have any hand in the Education of Children.

Dear Friends,

I HAVE *oft thought that* Christ *speaks to you, as* Pharaoh's *Daughter did to* Moses's *Mother, Take this Child and Nurse it for me O Sirs, consider what a precious Jewel is committed to your charge*

what an advantage you have to shew your love to
Christ, *to stock the next generation with Noble*
Plants, and what a joyful account you may make, if
you be faithful: Remember, Souls, Christ & Grace
cannot be over-valued, I confess you have some disad-
vantages, but let that only excite your diligence;
the Salvation of Souls, the commendation of your
Master, the greatness of your reward, and everlasting
Glory will pay for all. Remember the Devil is at
work hard, wicked ones are industrious, and a cor-
rupt nature is a rugged, knotty piece to hew: But
be not discouraged, I am almost as much afraid of
your laziness and unfaithfulness, as anything Do
but fall to work lustily, & who knows but that rough
stone may prove a Pillar in the Temple of God? In
the Name of the living God, as you will answer it
shortly at his Bar, I command you to be faithful in
Instructing and Catechizing your young ones; if you
think I am too peremptory, I pray read the command
from my Master himself, Deu: 6.7 Is not the duty
clear? and dare you neglect so direct a Command?
Are the souls of your Children of no value? Are you
willing that they should be Brands of Hell? Are you
indifferent whether they be Damned or saved? shall
the Devil run away with them without controul?
will not you use your utmost endeavour to deliver
them from the wrath to come? You see that they are
not subjects uncapable of the Grace of God; what
ever you think of them, Christ doth not slight them;
they are not too little to die, they are not too little
to go to Hell, they are not too little to serve their
great Master, too little to go to Heaven; For of
such is the Kingdom of God: And will not a pos-
sibility of their Conversion and Salvation, put you
upon the greatest diligence to teach them? Or are
Christ and Heaven, and Salvation, small things with
you? If they be, then indeed I have done with you:
But if they be not, I beseech you lay about you with
all your might; the Devil knows your time is going
apace, it will shortly be too late: O therefore what
you do, do quickly, and do it, I say, with all your
might; O pray, pray, pray, and live holily before
them, and take some time daily to speak a little to
your Children, one by one, about their miserable
Condition by Nature; I knew a Child that was
converted by this sentence, from a godly School Mi-

stress in the Country, Every Mothers Child of
you are by Nature Children of wrath. *Put
your Children upon learning their Catechism, and
Scriptures, and getting to pray and weep by
themselves after* Christ: *take heed of their company; take heed of pardoning a* lye; *take heed of
letting them mispend the Sabbath, put them I
beseech you, upon imitating these sweet Children;
let them read this Book over an hundred times, and
observe how they are* affected, *and ask them what
they think of those Children, and whether they
would not be such? and follow what you do with
earnest cries to God, and be in travel to see Christ
formed in their Souls. I have prayed for you, I
have oft prayed for your Children, and I love them
dearly; and I have prayed over these papers; that
God would strike in with them, and make them effectual to the good of their Souls. Incourage your
Children to read this Book, and lead them to improve it. What is presented, is faithfully taken from
experienced solid Christians, some of them no way
related to the Children, who themselves were Eye
and Ear witnesses of God's works of Wonder, or
from my own knowledge, or from Reverend Godly
Ministers, and from persons that are of unspotted
reputation, for Holiness, Integrity and Wisdom;
and* several *passages are taken* verbatim *in writing from their dying Lips.* I may add many
other excellent Examples, if I have any encouragement in this Piece. That the Young Generation may be far more excellent than this,
is the Prayer of one that dearly loves little
Children.

James Janeway

A PREFACE

*Containing Directions to
Children.*

Y̲OU MAY NOW HEAR (my dear Lambs) what
other good Children have done, and remember how they wept and prayed by them-

selves; how earnestly they cried out for an interest in the Lord Jesus Christ: May you not
read how dutiful they were to their Parents?
How diligent at their Books? how ready to
learn the Scripture, and their Catechisms? Can
you forget what Questions they were wont to
ask? How much they feared a lye, how much
they abhorred naughty company, how holy
they lived, how dearly they were loved, how
joyfully they died?

But tell me my dear Children, and tell me
truly, Do you do as these Children did? Did
you ever see your miserable state by Nature? Did
you ever get by your self and weep for Sin, and
pray for grace and pardon? Did you ever go to
your Father and Mother, Master, or Mistress, &
beg of them to pity you, & pray for you, & to
teach you what you shall do to be saved, what
you shall do to get Christ, Heaven and Glory?
Dost thou love to be taught good things?
Come tell me truly, my dear Child,
for I would fain do what I can possibly to
keep thee from falling into everlasting
Fire. I would fain have one of those little ones,
which Christ will take into his arms & bless. How
dost thou spend thy time? is it in play & Idleness,
& with wicked Children? Dare you take Gods
Name in vain, or swear, or tell a lye? Dare you
do any thing which your Parents forbid you, &
neglect to do what they command you? Do you
dare to run up and down upon the Lords-day?
or do you keep in to read your Book, & to learn
what your good Parents command you? what
do you say, Child? Which of these two sorts are
you of? Let me talk a little with you, and ask
you a few Questions.

1. Were not these Children sweet Children,
which feared God & were dutiful to their Parents?
Did not their Fathers & Mothers, & every body
that fears God, love them & praise them? What
do you think is become of them, now they are
dead and gone? Why, they are gone to Heaven,
& are singing Hallelujahs with the Angels: they
see Glorious things, and having nothing but joy
& pleasure, they shall never sin any more, they

shall never be beat any more, they shall never be sick, or in pain any more.

2. And would not you have your Fathers love, your Mothers commendation; your Masters good word? Would not you have God & Christ love you? & would not you fain go to Heaven, when you die? And live with your godly Parents in Glory, and be happy for ever.

3. Whither do you think those Children go when they die, that will not do what they are bid but play the Truant, and lye, and speak naughty words, and break the Sabbath? whither do such Children go do you think? why, I will tell you, they which Lie, must to their Father the Devil into everlasting burning; they which never pray, God will pour out his wrath upon them; and when they beg and pray in Hell-Fire, God will not forgive them; but there they must lie for ever.

4. And are you willing to go to Hell to be burned with the Devil and his Angels? Would you be in the same condition as naughty Children? O Hell is a terrible place, that's worse a thousand times than whipping, Gods anger is worse than your Fathers anger; and are you willing to anger God? O Child, this is most certainly true that all that be wicked, and die so, must be turned into Hell; and if any be once there, there is no coming out again.

5. Would you not do any thing in the world rather than be thrown into Hell Fire? Would you not do any thing in the world to get Christ, and grace and glory.

6. Well now, what will you do? Will you read this book a little, because your good Mother will make you do it, and because it is a little new Book, but as soon as ever you have done, run away to play, and never think of it?

7. How art thou now affected, poor Child, in the Reading of this Book? Have you shed ever a tear since you begun reading? Have you been by your self upon your knees; and begging that God would make you like these blessed Children? or are you as you use to be, as careless & foolish and disobedient and wicked as ever?

8. Did you never hear of a little Child that died? & if other Children die, why may not you

be sick & die? and what will you do then,
Child, if you should have no grace in your
heart, and be found like other naughty Children.

9. How do you know but that you may be
the next Child that may die? and where are
you then if you be not God's Child.

10. Wilt thou tarry any longer my dear Child,
before thou run into thy Chamber, & beg to God
to give thee a Christ for thy Soul, that thou mayst
not be undone forever,? Wilt thou get presently
into a corner to weep and pray? Methinks I see
that pretty Lamb begin to weep, & think of getting by himself, & will as well as he can cry unto
the Lord, to make them one of these little ones that
go into the Kingdom of Heaven; Methinks there
stands a sweet Child, & there another, that are
resolved for Christ & for Heaven: Methinks that
little Boy looks as if he had a mind to learn good
things: Methinks I hear one say, Well, I will never tell a lye more, I will never keep any naughty Boy company more, they will teach me to
swear, and they will speak naughty words, they
do not love God. I'le learn my Catechism, &
get my Mother to teach us to pray, and I will
go to weep and cry to Christ, and will not be
quiet till the Lord hath given me Grace. O
that's my brave Child indeed!

11. But will you not quickly forget your
promise? are you resolved by the strength of
Christ to be a good Child? Are you indeed?
nay, but are you indeed? Consider, dear Child,
God calls you to remember your Creator in the
days of your youth; & he takes it kindly when
little ones comes to him, and loves them dearly;
and godly people, especially Parents, & Masters
and Mistresses, they have no greater joy, than
to see their Children walk in the way of truth.

Now tell me, my pretty dear Child, what
will you do? Shall I make you a Book? Shall I
pray for you, and entreat you? Shall your good
Mother weep over you? And will not you
make us all glad, by your turning quickly to
the Lord? Shall Christ tell you that he will
love you? And will not you love him? Will
you strive to be like those Children? I am per-

suaded, that God intends to do good to the
souls of some little Children by these papers, be
cause he hath laid it so much upon my heart to
pray for them and over these papers, & through
mercy I have already experienced, that something
of this nature hath not been in vain: I shall
give a word of direction, and so leave you.

1. Take heed of what you know is naught;
as lying, O that is a grievous fault indeed, and
naughty words, and taking the Lords name in
vain, and playing upon the Lords day, & keeping bad company, and playing with ungodly
Children: But if you go to School with such, tell
them that God will not love them, but that the
Devil will have them, if they continue to be so
naught.

2. Do what your Father and Mother bids
you, chearfully; and take heed of doing any
thing that they forbid you.

3. Be diligent in reading the Scripture, and
learning your Catechism; and what you do not
understand, to be sure ask the meaning of.

4. Think a little sometimes by your self about
God and Heaven, and your Soul, and what
Christ came into the world for.

5. And if you have no great mind to do thus
but had rather be at play, then think, what is it
that makes me that I do not care for good things;
is this like one of God's dear Children? I am a-
fraid I am none of God's Child, I feel, I do not
love to come unto him: O! What shall I do?
Either I will be Gods Child or the Devils; O!
what shall I do? I would not be the Devils
Child for any thing in the World.

6. Then go to your Father or Mother, or
some Good Body, and ask them what thou shalt
do to be God's Child; and tell them that thou
art afraid, and that thou canst not be contented,
till thou hast got the love of God.

7. Get by thy self, into the Chamber or Gar-
ret, and fall upon thy knees, and weep and
mourn, and tell Christ thou art afraid that he
doth not love thee, but thou would fain have his
love; beg of him to give thee his Grace and
pardon for thy sins, and that he would make

thee his Child: Tell God thou dost not care
who don't love thee, if God will but love thee:
Say to him, Father, hast thou not a blessing for
me thy poor little Child! Father, hast thou not
a blessing for me, even for me? O give a Christ!
O give me a Christ! O let me not be undone
for ever! Thus beg, as for your lives, and be
not contented till you have an answer; and do
thus every day, with as much earnestness as you
can, twice a day at least.

8. Give your self up to Christ: say, dear Jesus,
thou didst bid that little Children should be suffered to come unto thee; and Lord I am come
as well as I can, would fain be thy Child;
take my heart and make it humble, and meek,
and sensible and obedient, I give my self unto thee dear Jesus, do what thou wilt with
me so that thou wilt but love me, and give me
thy Grace and Glory.

9. Get acquainted with Godly people
and ask them good questions, and endeavour
to love their talk.

10. Labour to get a dear love for Christ;
read the History of Christ's sufferings; and
ask the reason of his sufferings, and never be
content till you see your need of Christ, and
the excellency and use of Christ.

11. Hear the most powerful Ministers; &
read the most searching books and get your
Father to buy you Mr. *White*'s Book for
little Children, and *A Guide to Heaven*.

12. Resolve to continue in well-doing all your
days; then thou shalt be one of those sweet
little ones that Christ will take into his arms
and bless and give a Kingdom, Crown and
Glory too. And now dear Children I have
done, I have written to you, I have prayed
for you; but what you will do I can't tell.
O Children, if you love me, if you love
your Parents, if you love your Souls,
you would scape Hell Fire, and if you
would live in Heaven when you die, do you
go and do as these good Children, and that
you may be your Parents joy, your Countreys
honour, and live in Gods fear, and die

in his love, is the prayer of your dear Friend.

J. Janeway

EXAMPLE I

Of one eminently Converted between Eight and
Nine years Old, with an account of her
Life and Death.

1. Mrs. *Sarah Howley,* when she
was between Eight and Nine
years Old, was carried by her
Friends to hear a Sermon,
where the Minister Preached upon Matt.
11.13. *My Yoke is easy, and my Burden is*
light: in the applying of which Scripture,
this Child was mightily awakned, and
made deeply sensible of the Condition
of her Soul, and her need of a Christ,
she wept bitterly to think what a case she
was in; and went home and got by her
self into a Chamber, and upon her knees
she wept and cryed to the Lord, as well as
she could, which might easily be perceived
by her eyes and countenance

2. She was not contented at this, but
she got her little Brother and Sister into
a Chamber with her, and told them of
their condition by Nature, and wept over
them, and prayed with them and for
them.

3. After this she heard another Ser-
mon upon *Prov.* 29.1. *He that being often re-*
proved, hardneth his heart, shall suddenly be de-
stroyed & that without remedy: At which she
was more affected than before, and was
so exceeding solicitous about her Soul, that
she spent a great part of the night in
weeping and praying, and could scarce
take any rest day or night for some time
together; desiring with all her Soul to
escape from everlasting flames, and to get

an interest in the Lord Jesus; *O what
should she do for a Christ! what should she
do to be Saved!*

4. She gave her self much to attend-
ing upon the Word preached, and still
continued very tender under it, greatly
favouring what she heard.

5. She was very much in secret Prayer, as might easily be perceived by those
who listened at the Chamber door, and
was usually very importunate, and full of
tears.

6. She could scarce speak of sin, or be
spoke to, but her heart was ready to
melt.

7. She spent much time in reading the
Scripture, and a Book called, *The best friend
in the worst of Times;* by which the Work
of God was much promoted upon her
Soul, and was much directed by it how
to get acquaintance with God, especially
toward the end of that Book. Another
Book that she was much delighted with,
was Mr. *Swinnock's Christian Mans Calling,*
and by this she was taught in this measure
to make Religion her business. The
Spiritual Bee was a great companion of
hers.

8. She was exceeding dutiful to her
Parents, very loath to grieve them in
the least: and if she had at any time
(which was very rare) offended them, she
would weep bitterly.

9. She abhorred lying, and allowed her
self in no known sin.

10. She was very Conscientious in
spending of time, and hated Idleness,
and spent her whole time either in praying, reading instructing at her Needle, at
which she was very ingenious.

11. When she was at School, she was
eminent for her diligence, teachableness,
meekness and modesty. Speaking little;
but when she did speak it was usually
spiritual.

12. She continued in this course of Religious duties for some years together.

13. When she was about fourteen years old, she brake a Vein in her Lungs (as is supposed) and oft did spit blood, yet did a little recover again, but had several dangerous relapses.

14. At the beginning of *January* last, she was taken very bad again, in which sickness she was in great distress of Soul. When she was first taken, she said, O Mother, pray, pray, pray for me, for Satan is so busy that I cannot pray for my self; I see I am undone without a Christ, and a Pardon! O I am undone unto all Eternity.

15. Her Mother knowing how serious she had been formerly, did a little wonder that she should be in such agonies; upon which her Mother asked her what sin it was, that was so burdensome to her Spirit: O Mother, said she, it is not any particular sin of Omission or Commission, that sticks so close to my Conscience, as the sin of my Nature; with out the Blood of Christ, that will damn me.

16. Her Mother asked her what she should pray for, for her; she answered That I may have a saving knowledge of Sin and Christ: and that I may have an assurance of Gods love to my Soul. Her Mother asked her why she did speak so little to the Minister that came to her? She answered that it was her duty with patience and silence to learn of them: and it was exceeding painful to her, to speak to any.

17. One time when she fell into a fit, she cried out, *O I am a going, I am a going: But what shall I do to be Saved?* Sweet Lord Jesus; I will lye at thy feet; and if I perish, it shall be at the Fountain of thy mercy.

18. She was much afraid of persumpti-

on, and dreaded a mistake in the matters of her Soul, and would be often
putting up ejaculations to God, to deliver
her from deceiving her self. To instance
in one: *Great and Mighty God, give me
Faith and true Faith, Lord, that I may not
be a foolish Virgin, having a Lamp and not
Oyl.*

19. She would many times be laying
hold upon the promises, and plead them
in prayer. That in *Matt.* 11.28, 29. was
much in her tongue, and no small relief
to her Spirit. How many times would
she cry out, Lord, hast not thou said,
*Come unto me all ye that are weary, and
heavy laden, and I will give you rest.*

20. Another time her Father bid her
be of good cheer, because she was going to
a better Father; at which she fell into
a great passion, and said, but how do
I know that? I am a poor sinner that
wants assurance *O, for assurance!* It was
still her note, *O, for assurance!* This was
her great, earnest, and constant request,
to all that came to her, to beg assurance
for her; and, poor heart, she would look
with so much eagerness upon them, as if
she desired nothing in the world so much,
as that they would pitty her, and help
her with their prayers; never was poor
creature more earnest for any thing, than
she was for an assurance; and the Might
of Gods Countenance: O the piteous
moan that she would make! O the Agonies
that her Soul was in!

21. Her mother ask'd her, if God
would spare her Life, how she would live?
Truly Mother, said she, we have such base
hearts that I can't tell, we are apt to
promise great things when we are sick,
but when we are recovered, we are already to forget our selves and to turn
again unto folly; but I hope I should be
more careful of my Time and my Soul,
than I have been.

22. She was full of natural affection to
her Parents, and very careful least her
Mother should be tired out with much
watching: Her Mother said, *how shall I bear
parting with thee, when I have scarce dryed
my eyes for thy Brother?* she answered, the
God of love, support and comfort you;
it is but a little while and we shall meet
in Glory, I hope. She being very weak,
could speak but little, therefore her
Mother said, *Child, if thou hast any comfort
lift up thy hand;* which she did.

23. The Lords day before that, in which
she died, a Kinsman of hers came to see
her, and asking of her, whether she knew
him? She answered, *Yes, I know you, and
I desire you would learn to know Christ: you
are young, but you know not how soon you may
die; and O to die without a Christ, it is a
fearful thing: O redeem Time! O Time,
Time, Time, precious Time!* Being requested
by him not to spend herself, she said, she
would fain do all the good she could while
she lived, and when she was dead too,
if possile; [sic], upon which account, she desired that a Sermon might be Preached
at the Funeral, concerning the precious-
ness of Time. O that young ones would
now remember their Creator!

24. Some Minister that came to her,
did with earnestness beg that the Lord
would please to give her some token for
good, that she might go off triumphing,
and Bills of the same nature were sent to
several Churches.

25. After she had long waited for an
answer of their prayers, she said, *Well,
I will venture my Soul upon Christ.*

26. She carried it with wonderful patience, and yet would often pray that
the Lord would give her more patience,
which the Lord answered to astonishment; for considering the pains and
agonies that she was in, her patience was
next to a wonder; *Lord, Lord, give me*

patience, said she, *that I may not dishonour thee.*

27.   Upon *Thursday,* after long waiting, great Fears, and many Prayers, when all her Friends thought she had been past speaking, to the astonishment of her Friends, she broke forth thus with a very Audible Voice, and Cheerful Countenance; *Lord, thou hast promised, that whosoever comes unto thee, thou wilt in no wise cast out; Lord I come unto thee, and surely thou wilt not cast me out. O so sweet! O so glorious is Jesus! O I have the sweet and glorious Jesus; he is sweet, he is sweet, he is sweet! O the admirable love of God in sending Christ! O free Grace to a poor lost Creature.* And thus she ran on repeating many of these things an hundred times over; but her Friends were so astonished to see her in this Divine Rapture, and to hear such Gracious Words, and her Prayers and Desires satisfied, that they could not write a quarter of what she spoke.

28.   When her Soul was thus ravished with the love of Christ, and her tongue so highly engaged in the magnifying of God; her Father, Brethren, and Sisters, with others of the Family, were called, to whom she spake particularly, as her strength would give leave. She gave her Bible as a Legacy to one of her Brothers, and desired him to use that well for her sake, & added, to him & the rest O make use of time to get a Christ for your Souls; spend no time in running up and down, in playing: O get a Christ for your Souls while you are young; remember now your Creator before you come to a sick bed: put not off this great work till then, for then you will find it a hard work indeed. I know by experience, the Devil will tell you it is time enough; and you are young, what need you to be in such hast? You will have

time enough when you are old. But
there stands one (meaning her Grand-
mother) that stayes behind, and I that
am but young, am going before her. O
therefore make your Calling and Election
sure, while you are in health: But I
am afraid this will be but one nights
trouble to your thoughts; but remember,
these are the words of a dying Sister. O
if you knew how good Christ were! O if
you had but one taste of his sweetness, you
would rather go to him a thousand times
than stay in this wicked world. I would
not for ten thousand, and ten thousand
worlds part with my interest in Christ.
O how happy am I, that I am going to
everlasting Joys! I would not go back
again for twenty thousand worlds; and
will you not strive to get an Interest in
Christ?

29. After this, looking upon one of
her Fathers Servants, she said, *What shall
I do? What shall I do at the great Day,*
when Christ shall say to me, *Come, thou
Blessed of my Father, inherit the Kingdom
prepared for thee.* And shall say to the
wicked, *Go, thou Cursed unto the Lake that
burns for ever.* What a grief is it for me
to think, that I shall see any of my friends
that I knew upon Earth, turned into that
Lake that burns forever! O that word,
For Ever, remember that *For Ever!* I
speak these words to you, but they are
nothing, except God speak to you too:
O pray, pray, pray, that God would give
you Grace! And then she prayed, *O Lord
finish thy work upon their Souls.* It will be
my comfort to see you in Glory, but it
will be your Everlasting happiness.

30. Her Grand-mother told her she
spent her self too-much; she said; I care
not for that, if I could do any Soul good,
O with what vehemency did she speak,
as if her heart were in every word she
spoke.

31. She was full of Divine Sentences,
and almost all her discourse, from the
first to the last, in the time of her sickness, was about her soul, Christs sweetness, and the Souls of others, in a word
like a continued Sermon.

32. Upon *Fryday*, after she had had
such lively discoveries of Gods love, she
was exceeding desirous to dye, and cryed
out, *Come Lord Jesus, come quickly, conduct
me to thy Tabernacle, I am a poor Creature
without thee: but Lord Jesus, my Soul longs
to be with thee: O when shall it be? Why
not now, dear Jesus? Come Lord Jesus, come
quickly;* but why do I speak thus? *Thy
time, dear Lord, is the best; give me patience!*

33. Upon *Saturday* she spoke very little
(being very drowsie) yet now and then
dropt these words: *How long sweet Jesus?
Finish thy work Sweet Jesus, Come away sweet
dear Lord Jesus, come quickly,; sweet Lord
help, come away, now, now, dear Jesus come
quickly; Good Lord give patience to me to
wait thy appointed time; Lord Jesus help me,
help me, help me.* Thus at several times
(when out of her sleep) for she was asleep
the greatest part of the day.

34. Upon the Lord's day, she scarce
spoke anything, but much desired that
Bills of thanksgiving might be sent to
those who had formerly been praying for
her, that they might help her to praise
God for that full assurance that he had
given her of His love; and seemed to be
much swallowed up with the thoughts of
God's free love to her Soul. She oft
commended her Spirit into the Lords
hands; and the last words which she was
heard to speak, were these, *Lord help
Lord Jesus help; Dear Jesus, Blessed Jesus.* — — — —
And thus upon the Lords Day, between
Nine and Ten of the Clock in the fore-
noon, she slept sweetly in Jesus, and began
an everlasting Sabbath, *February* 19, 1670.

EXAMPLE II

*Of a Child that was admirably affected with
the things of God, when he was between
Two and Three years Old; with a brief
account of his Life and Death.*

1. A CERTAIN little Child, whose Mother
had dedicated him to the Lord in
her womb when he could not speak
plain, would be crying after God, and
was greatly desirous to be taught good
things!

2. He could not endure to be put to
Bed without Family duty, but would put
his Parents upon duty, and would with
much devotion kneel down, & with great
patience and delight, continue till duty
was at an end, without the least expression of being weary; and he seemed
never so well pleased, as when he was
engaged in duty.

3. He could not be satisfied with Family duty, but he would be oft upon
his knees by himself in one corner or
other.

4. He was much delighted in hearing
the Word of God, either Read or Preached.

5. He loved to go to School, that he
might learn something of God and would
observe and take great notice of what he
had read, and come home and speak of
it with much affection; and he would
rejoyce in his book, and say to his Mother,
O Mother! I have had a sweet lesson to-
day, will you please to give me leave to
fetch my book that you may hear it?

6. As he grew up, he was more and
more affected with the things of another
world; so that if we had not received our
information from one that is of undoubted
fidelity, it would seem incredible.

7. He quickly learned to read the

Scripture, and would, with great Reverence, Tenderness and Groans, read till tears and sobs were ready to hinder him.

8. When he was at secret prayer, he would weep bitterly.

9. He was wont oftentimes to complain of the naughtiness of his heart, and seemed to be more grieved for the Corruption of his Nature, than for Actual Sin.

10. He had a vast Understanding in the things of God, even next to a wonder, for one of his age.

11. He was much troubled for the wandring of his thought in duty, and that he could not keep his heart alway fixed upon God, and the work he was about, and his affections constantly raised.

12. He kept a watch over his heart, and observed the workings of his Soul, and would complain that they were so vain and foolish, and so little busied about Spiritual things.

13. As he grew up, he grew daily in knowledge and experience, and his carriage was so heavenly, and his discourse so excellent and experimental, that it made those which heard it, even astonished.

14. He was exceeding importunate with God in duty,; and would plead with God at a strange rate, and use such arguments in prayer, that one would think it were impossible should ever enter into the heart of a Child; he would beg, and expostulate, and weep so, that sometimes it could not be kept from the ears of Neighbours; so that one of the next house was forced to cry out, The prayers and tears of that Child in the next house will sink me to Hell, because by it he did condemn his neglect of prayer, and his slight performance of it.

15. He was very fearful of wicked company, and would oft beg of God to

keep him from it, and that he might never
be pleased in them that took delight in
displeasing of God: And when he was at
any time in the hearing of their wicked
words, taking the Lords Name in vain, or
Swearing, or any filthy words, it would
even make him tremble, and ready to go
home and weep.

16.   He abhorred lying, with his Soul.

17.   When he had committed any fault,
he was easily convinced of it, and would
get in some corner and secret place, and
with tears beg pardon of God, & strength
against such a sin. He had a friend that
oft watched him, and listned at his Cham-
ber-door, from whom I received this
Narrative.

18.   When he had been asked, whether
he would commit such a sin again, he
would never promise absolutely, because
he said his heart was naught; but he would
weep and say, he hoped by the Grace of
God he should not.

19.   When he was left at home alone upon the Sabbath days, he would be sure not to
spend any part of the day in idleness & Play,
but be busied in praying, reading in the
Bible, and getting of his Catechism.

20.   When other Children were playing,
he would many a time and oft be praying.

21.   One day a certain person was discoursing with him, about the Nature, Offices, and Excellency of Christ, and that
He alone can satisfie for our Sins, and
merit Everlasting life for us; and about
other of the great Mysteries of Redemption: he seemed savingly to understand
them & was greatly delighted with the discourse.

22.   One speaking concerning the Resurrection of the body, he did acknowledge it; but that the same weak body that
was buried in the Church-yard, should be
raised again, he thought very strange, but
with admiration yielded, that nothing was

impossible to God; and that very day
he was taken sick unto death.

23. A Friend of his asked him whether
he were willing to dye, when he was first
taken sick; he answered, *No; because he
was afraid of his state as to another world:*
Why Child, said the other, thou didst pray
for a new Heart, for an humble, and sincere Heart, and I have heard thee; didst
thou not pray with thy heart? *I hope I did,*
said he.

24. Not long after, the same person
asked him again, whether he were willing
to dye? He answered, *Now I am willing,
for I shall go to Christ.*

25. One asked him what should become of his Sister, if he should dye and
leave her? He answered, *The will of the
Lord must be done.*

26. He still grew weaker and weaker,
but carried it with a great deal of sweetness and patience, waiting for his change,
and at last did cheerfully commit his Spirit
unto the Lord; and calling upon the
Name of the Lord, and sayd, *Lord Jesus, Lord Jesus,* — — — — — in whose bosome
he sweetly slept, Dying as I remember,
when he was about Five or Six years old.

EXAMPLE III

*Of a little Girl that was wrought upon,
when she was between Four and Five years
Old, with some account of her
holy Life and triumphant Death.*

1. **M**ARY A. When she was between
Four and Five years old, was
greatly affected in hearing the Word of
God, and became very solicitous about
her Soul, and everlasting Condition, weeping bitterly, to think what would become
of her in another World, asking strange

Questions concerning God and Christ, and
her own Soul. So that this little *Mary*
before she was full five years old, seemed
to mind *The one thing needful,* and to
choose *The better part,* and sate at the
Feet of Christ many a time, and oft with
Tears.

2. She was wont to be much in secret
Duty, and many times come off from her
knees with Tears.

3. She wou'd chuse such times & places
for secret Duty, as might render her less
observed by others, and did endeavour
what possibly she could to conceal what
she was doing, when she was engaged in
secret Duty.

4. She was greatly afraid of Hypocrisie,
and of doing any thing to be seen of men,
and to get commendation and praise; and
when she had heard one of her Brothers
saying, *That he had been by himself at prayer,*
she rebuked him sharply, and told him how
little such prayers were like to profit him,
and that, was little to his praise, to pray
like a Hypocrite, and to be glad that any
should know what he had been doing.

5. Her Mother being full of sorrow after the Death of her Husband, this Child
came to her Mother, and ask'd her why
she wept so exceedingly? Her Mother answered, She had cause enough to weep, because her Father was dead: *No dear Mother,
said the Child, you have no cause to weep so
much; for God is a Good God still to you.*

6. She was a dear lover of faithful
Ministers. One time after, she had been
learning of Mr. *Whitaker,* she said I love
that man dearly, for the sweet words that
he speaks concerning Christ.

7. Her Book was her delight and what
she did read, she loved to make her own
and cared not for passing over what she
learned, without extraordinary observation and understanding; and many times
she was so strangely affected in reading

of the Scriptures, that she would burst out
into Tears, and would hardly be pacified;
so greatly was she taken with Christs Sufferings, the zeal of Gods Servants, the
danger of a Natural State.

8. She would complain oftentimes of the
corruption of her Nature, of the hardness
of her Heart, that she could Repent no
more throughly, and be no more Humble
and Grieved for her Sins against a good
God; and when she did thus complain,
it was with abundance of Tears.

9. She was greatly concerned for the
Souls of others, and grieved to think of
the miserable Condition that they were
in upon this account; when she could
handsomely, she would be putting in some
pretty sweet word of Christ; but above
all, she would do what she could to draw
the hearts of her Brethren and Sisters
after Christ and there was no small hopes,
that her example and good Counsel did
prevail with some of them when they
were very young, to get into corners to
pray, & to ask very gracious Questions a-
bout the things of God.

10. She was very Conscientious in keeping the Sabbath, spending the whole time
either in Reading or Praising, or learning
her Catechism, or teaching her Brethren
and Sisters. One time when she was
left at home upon the Lords Day, she
got some other little Children together, with her Brothers and Sisters, and
instead of Playing (as other naughty
Children use to do) she told them, That
that was the Lords Day, and that they
ought to remember that Day to keep it
holy; and then she told them, how it was
to be spent in Religious Exercises all the
day long, except so much as was to be
taken up in the Works of necessity and
mercy; then she prayed with them herself, and among other things begged, that
the Lord would give Grace and Wisdom

to them little Children, That they might
know how to serve him, as one of the little
ones in the company with her, told afterwards.

11. She was a Child of a strange tenderness and compassion to all, full of bowels
and pity; whom she could not help, she
would be ready to weep over; especially
if she saw her Mother at any time troubled,
she would quickly make her sorrows her
own, and weep for her, and with her.

12. When her Mother had been somewhat solicitous about any worldly thing,
she would, if she could possibly, put her
off from her care one way or other. One
time she told her, *O Mother, Grace is better
than that,* (meaning something her Mother
wanted,) *I had rather have Grace and thy
Love of Christ, than any thing in the world.*

13. This Child was often musing and
busied in the thoughts of her Everlasting
Work; witness that strange question, *O
what are they doing, which are already in
Heaven?* And she seemed to be hugely
desirous to be among them that were
praising, loving, delighting in God, and
serving of Him without Sin. Her Language
was so strange about Spiritual matters
that she made many excellent Christians
to stand amazed, as judging it scarce to be
parallell'd.

14. She took great Delight in reading
of the Scripture and some part of it
was more sweet to her than her appointed
food; she would get several choice Scriptures by heart, and discourse of them favour-
ly, and apply them suitably.

15. She was not altogether a stranger
to other good Books, but would be reading
of them with much affection; and where she
might, she noted the Books particularly,
observing what in the reading did most
warm her heart, and she was ready upon
occasion to improve it.

16. One time a woman coming into

the House in a great Passion, spoke of her
Condition, as if none were like hers, and
it would never be otherwise; the Child said,
it were a strange thing to say when it is
night, it will never be day again.

17. At another time a near Relation of
hers being in some streights made some
complaint, to whom she said, I have heard
Mr. *Carter* say a Man may go to heaven
without a Penny in his Purse, but not without Grace in his Heart.

18. She had an extraordinary Love for
the People of God; and when she saw any
that she thought feared the Lord, her Heart
would e'en leap for joy.

19. She loved to be much by her self, &
would be greatly grieved if she were at any
time deprived of a conveniency for secret
Duty; she could not live without constant
Address to God in secret; and was not
a little pleased when she could go into a
corner to pray and weep.

20. She was much in praising God, &
seldom or never complained of any thing
but Sin.

21. She continued in this course of
praying and praising of God, and great dutifulness and sweetness to her Parents, and
those that taught her any thing, yet she
did greatly encourage her Mother while
she was a Widow, and desired that the absence of a Husband, might in some measure be made up by the dutifulness and
holiness of a Child. She studied all the
wayes that could be to make her Mothers
Life sweet.

22. When she was between eleven and
twelve years old, she sickned, in which
she carried it with admirable patience and
sweetness, and did what she could with
Scripture Arguments, to support and encourage her Relations to part with her,
that was going to Glory, and to prepare
themselves to meet her in a Blessed Eternity.

23. She was not many days sick before
she was marked; which she first saw herself, and was greatly rejoyced to think that
she was marked out for the Lord, and was
now going apace to Christ. She called to
her Friends, and said, *I am marked, but
be not troubled, for I know I am marked for
one of the Lords own.* One asked her, How
she knew that? She answered, *The Lord
hath told me, that I am one of His dear Children.* And thus she spake with a holy
Confidence in the Lords Love to her Soul,
and was not in the least daunted when
she spake of her death; but seemed greatly
delighted in the apprehension of her near-
ness to her Fathers House. And it was not
long before she was filled with joy unspeakable in believing.

24. When she just lay a Dying, her
Mother came to her, and told her, She
was sorry that she had reproyed, and corrected so good a Child so oft. O Mother,
said she, *Speak not thus, I bless God, now I
am Dying, for your Reproofs and Corrections
too; for it may be, I might have gone to Hell,
if it had not been for your Reproofs and Corrections.*

25. Some of her Neighbours coming
to visit her, asked her, if she would leave
them? She answered them, *If you serve the
Lord, you shall come after me to Glory.*

26. A little before she died, she had a
great conflict with Satan, and Cryed out,
I am none of his; her Mother seeing her in
trouble, asked her what was the matter?
She answered, *Satan did trouble me, but now
I thank God all is well, I know, I am none of
his, but Christs.*

27. After this, she had a great sence
of Gods Love, and a Glorious sight, as
if she had seen the very Heavens open,
and the Angels come to receive her;
by which her Heart was filled with joy, and
her Tongue with praise.

28. Being desired by the standers by,

to give them a particular account of what
she saw. She answered, *You shall know
hereafter;* and so in an extasie of Joy
and holy Triumph, she went to Heaven
when she was about Twelve years old.

Hallelujah

EXAMPLE IV

Of a Child that began to look towards Heaven,
when she was about Four years old, with
some observable Passages in her Life,
and at her Death.

1. A CERTAIN LITTLE Child, when she was
about Four years old, had a Conscientious sence of her Duty towards her
Parents, because the Commandment saith
Honour thy Father and thy Mother. And
though she had little advantage of Education, she carried it with the greatest Reverence to her Parents imaginable, so that
she was no small Credit as well as Comfort
to them.

2. It was no usual thing for her to weep,
if she saw her Parents troubled, though
her self had not been the occasion of it.

3. When she came from school, she
would with grief and abhorrency say that
other Children had sinned against God by
speaking grievous words, which were so
bad, that she durst not speak them again.

4. She would be oftentimes admiring
of Gods mercy, for so much goodness to
her rather than to others; that she saw
some begging, others blind, some crooked,
and that she wanted nothing that was good
for her.

5. She was many a time, and often, in
one hole or another, in Tears upon her
knees.

6. This poor little thing would be ready

to counsel other little Children, how they
ought to serve God; and putting them
upon getting by themselves to pray; &
hath been known when her friends have
been abroad, to have been teaching Children to pray, especially upon the Lords
Day.

7. She very seriously begged the prayers of others, that they would remember
her, that the Lord would give her Grace.

8. When this Child saw some that were
laughing, who she judged to be very wicked; *She told them, that she feared that they
had little reason to be merry.* They asked
whether one might not laugh? She answered, *No indeed, till you have Grace;
they who are wicked, have more need to Cry,
than to Laugh.*

9. She would say, that it was the Duty
of Parents, Masters and Mistresses, to reprove (those under their charge) for sin,
or else God will meet with them.

10. She would be very attentive when
she read the Scriptures, and be much affected with them.

11. She would by no means be perswaded to prophane the Lords Day, but would
spend it in some good Duties.

12. When she went to School, it was
willingly and joyfully, and she was very
teachable & exemplary to other Children.

13. When she was taken sick, one asked
her *Whether she were willing to Dye?* She answered, *Yes, if God would Pardon her Sins.*
Being asked how her Sins should be Pardoned? she answered, *Through the Blood of
Christ.*

14. *She said; she did believe in Christ, &
desired, and longed to be with Him,* and did
with a great deal of chearfulness give up
her Soul.

There were very many observable passages, in the Life & Death of this Child, but
the hurry and grief that her Friends were
in, buried them.

EXAMPLE V

Of the Pious Life, and Joyful Death, of a Child which Dyed when he was about Twelve years Old, 1632.

1. CHARLES BRIDGMAN had no sooner
learned to speak, but he betook
himself to Prayer.

2. He was very prone to learn the things
of God.

3. He would be sometimes teaching them
their Duty that waited upon him.

4. He learned by heart many good
things, before he was well fit to go to
School: & when he was sent to School, he
carried it so, that all that observed him,
either did or might admire him. O the
sweet Nature, the good Disposition, the
sincere Religion which was in this Child!

5. When he was at School, what was it
that he desired to learn, but Christ and
Him Crucified.

6. So Religious and Savoury were his
Words, his Actions so upright, his Devotion so hearty, his Fear of God so great,
that many were ready to say, as they did
of *John; What manner of Child shall this be?*

7. He would be much in reading the
Holy Scriptures.

8. He was desirous of more Spiritual
knowledge, and would be oft asking very
serious & admirable Questions.

9. He would not stir out of doors before
he had poured out his Soul to the Lord.

10. When he eat any thing, he would
be sure to lift up his Heart unto the Lord
for a Blessing upon it; and when he had
moderately refreshed himself by eating, he
would not forget to acknowledge Gods
goodness in feeding of him.

11. He would not lye down in his Bed,

til he had been upon his knees; and when
sometimes he had forgotten his Duty, he
would quickly get out of his Bed, and
kneeling down upon his bare knees, covered with no Garment but his linnings, ask
God forgiveness for that sin.

12. He would rebuke his Brethren if they
were at any time too hasty at their Meals,
and did eat without asking a Blessing, his
check was usually this; *Dare you do thus?*
God be merciful to us, this bit of Bread might
choak us.

13. His Sentences were wise & weighty,
and well might become some ancient
Christian.

14. His sickness was a lingring Disease
against which, to comfort him, one tells
him of possessions that must fall to his Portion, *And what are they?* said he, *I had*
rather have the Kingdom of Heaven, than a
thousand such Inheritances

15. When he was sick, he seemed much
taken up with Heaven, and asked very serious Questions about the Nature of his
Soul.

16. After he was pretty well satisfied
about that, *he enquired how his Soul might*
be Saved; the answer being made *by the*
applying of Christs Merits by Faith; he was
pleased with the answer, and was ready to
give any one that should desire it, an account of his Hope.

17. Being asked, whether he had rather
Live or Dye? He answered, *I desire to Dye,*
that I may go to my Saviour.

18. His Pains encreasing up him, one
asked him, Whether he would rather still
endure those Pains, or forsake Christ?
Alas, said he, *I know not what to say, being*
but a Child, for these pains may stagger a
strong Man; but I will strive to endure the
best that I can. Upon this he called to
mind that Martyr *Thomas Bilney;* who
being in Prison, the Night before his burning, put his Finger into the Candle, to

know how he could endure the Fire.
O (said the Child) *had I Lived then, I would
have run through the Fire to have gone to
Christ.*

19. His sickness lasted long, and at least
three dayes before his Death, he Prophesied
his Departure, and not only that he must
dye, but the very Day. *On the Lords Day,*
said he, *look to me;* neither was this a
word of course, which you may guess by
his often repetition, every day asking till
the day came indeed, *What, is Sunday come?*
At last, the lookt for day came on; and
no sooner had the Sun beautified that
morning with its light but he falls into
a Trance; his Eyes were fixed, his Face
chearful, his Lips smiling, his Hands and
Feet clasped in a Bow, as if he would have
received some Blessed Angel that were at
hand to receive his Soul. But he comes to
himself, and tells them how he saw the
sweetest Body that ever Eyes beheld, who
bid him be of good cheer, for he must presently go with Him.

20. One that stood near him, as now
suspecting the time of his Dissolution nigh,
bid him say, Lord, into thy hands I commend my Spirit, which is thy due; for
why thou hast redeemed it, 'O Lord my
God most true.

21. The last Words which he spake
were exactly these: *Pray, pray, pray, nay,
yet pray; and the more Prayers, the better
all prospers; God is the best Physician; Into
His Hands I commend my Spirit. O Lord
Jesus receive my Soul: Now close mine
Eyes: Forgive me Father, Mother, Brother,
Sister, all the world. Now I am well, my Pain
is almost gone my Joy is at hand. Lord have
mercy on me, O Lord receive my Soul unto thee.*
And thus he yielded his spirit up unto the
Lord, when he was about Twelve years old.

This Narrative was taken out of
Mr. Ambrose his Lifes Lease.

EXAMPLE VI

Of a poor Child that was awakened when she was about Five years Old.

1. A CERTAIN very poor Child, that had a very bad Father, but it was to be hoped a very good Mother, was by the Providence of God, brought to the sight of a Godly Friend of mine, who upon the first sight of the Child, had a great pitty for him, and took an affection to him, & had a mind to bring him up for Christ.

2. At the first, he did with great sweetness and kindness allure the Child, by which means it was not long before he got a deep interest in the Heart of the Child, and he began to obey him with more readiness than Children usually to their Parents.

3. By this a Door was opened for a farther Work, & he had a greater advantage to instil Spiritual principles into the Soul of the Child, which he was not wanting in, as the Lord gave opportunity, and the Child was capable of.

4. It was not long before the Lord was pleased to strike in with the Spiritual Exhortations of this good Man, so that the Child was brought to a liking to the things of God.

5. He quickly learnt a great part of the Assemblies Catechism by heart, and that before he could read his Primer within Book; and he took a great delight in learning his Catechism.

6. He was not only able to give a very good account of his Catechism, but he would answer such Questions as are not in the Catechism, with greater understanding than could be expected of one of his Age.

7. He took great delight in discoursing about the things of God; and when my friend had been either praying or reading,

expounding or repeating Sermons, he seemed very attentive, and ready to receive
the truths of God, and would with incredible gravity, diligence and affection,
wait till duties were ended, to the not
small joy and admiration of them which
observed him.

8. He would ask very excellent questions and discourse about the condition
of his Soul and Heavenly things, and
seemed mightily concerned what should
become of his Soul when he should dye:
so that his discourse made some Christians
even to stand astonished.

9. He was greatly taken with the great
kindness of Christ in dying for sinners,
and would be in tears at the mention of
them: and seemed at a strange rate to be
affected with the unspeakable *Love* of Christ.

10. When no body hath been speaking
to him, he would burst out into tears,
and being asked the reason, he would say,
that the very thoughts of Christs love to
sinners in suffering for them, made him
that he could not but Cry.

11. Before he was Six years old, he
made Conscience of a secret Duty, and
when he prayed, it was with such extraordinary meltings, that his eyes have looked
red and sore, with weeping by himself for
his sin.

12. He would be putting of Christians
upon Spiritual discourse when he saw them,
and seemed little satisfied, unless they
were talking of good things.

13. It is evident, that this poor Childs
thoughts were very much busied about the
things of another World, for he would oftentimes be speaking to his Bed-fellow at
mid-night, about the matter of his Soul;
and when he could not sleep, he would
take Heavenly conference to be sweeter
than his appointed rest. This was his usual custome, and thus he would provoke
and put forward an experienced Christian,

to spend waking hours in talk of God and
the everlasting rest.

14. Not long after this his good
Mother dyed, which went very near his
heart, for he greatly honoured his Mother.

15. After the Death of his Mother, he
would often repeat some of the Promises
that are made to Fatherless Children, especially that in Exod. 22.22. *Ye shall not afflict*
any Wife or the Fatherless Child; if thou
do afflict them in any wise, and they Cry at all
unto me, I will surely hear their Cry————
These words he would often repeat with
tears and say, *I am Fatherless and Mother-*
less upon Earth, yet if any wrong me, I have
a Father in Heaven who will take my part;
to Him I commit my self, and in Him is all
my trust.

16. Thus he continued in a course of
Holy Duties, living in the fear of God
& shewed wonderful Grace for a Child, &
died sweetly in the Faith of Jesus.

My Friend, is a judicious Christian of
many years experience, who was no ways
related to him, but a constant eye and ear
witness of his Godly life, and honourable
and cheerful death, from which I received
this Information.

EXAMPLE VII

Of a Notorious Wicked Child, who was taken
up from Begging, and admirably Converted;
with an account of his holy Life and
joyful Death, when he was Nine Years Old.

1. A VERY POOR Child, of the Parish
of *Newington-Butts,* came begging,
to the door of a dear Christian Friend of
mine, in a very lamentable case, so filthy
and nasty, that he would even have turned
ones stomack to have looked on him: But
it pleased God to raise in the heart of my

Friend a great pitty & tenderness towards
this poor Child, so that in Charity he took him
out of the streets, whose Parents were unknown, who had nothing at all in him to
commend him to any ones Charity, but his
misery. My Friend eyeing the Glory of
God, and the good of the Immortal Soul
of this wretched Creature, discharged the
Parish of the Child, and took him as his
own, designing to bring him up for the
Lord Christ. A Noble piece of Charity!
And that which did make the kindness far
the greater, was, that there seemed to be
very little hopes of doing any good upon
this Child, for he was a very Monster of
wickedness, and a thousand times more
miserable and vile by his Sin, than by his
Poverty. He was running to Hell as soon
as he could go, and was old in naughtiness when he was young in years; and
one shall scarce hear of one so like the Devil
in his Infancy, as this poor Child was.
What Sin was there (that his age was capable of) that he did not commit? What
by the Corruption of his Nature, and the
abominable Example of little Begger-boys,
he was arrived to a strange pitch of Im-
piety. He would call filthy Names, take
Gods Name in vain; Curse and Swear,
and do almost all kind of Mischief; and
as to any thing of God, worse than an
Heathen.

2. But this Sin and Misery was but a
stronger Motive to the Gracious man to
pity him, & to do all that possibly he could
to pluck this Fire-brand out of the Fire, &
it was not long before the Lord was pleased
to let him understand, that He had a design
of everlasting kindness upon the Soul of
this poor Child; for no sooner had this
good Man taken this Creature into his
house, but he prays for him; and labours
with all his might to convince him of his
miserable condition by Nature, and to teach
him something of God, the worth of his

own Soul, and that Eternity of Glory or
Misery that he was born to: And Blessed
be Free Grace; it was not long before the
Lord was pleased to let him understand
that it was Himself which put it into his
heart to take in this Child that he might
bring him up for Christ. The Lord soon
struck in with his Godly Instructions so
that an amazing Change was seen in the
Child, in a few weeks space he was soon
convinced of the evil of his ways; no more
News now of his calling of Names, Swearing, or Cursing; no more taking of the
Lords Name in vain; now he is civil and
respective; and such a strange alteration
was wrought in the Child, that all the
Parish that rung of his Villany before, was
now ready to talk of his Reformation;
his company, his talk, his imployment
is now changed, and he is like another
Creature; so that the Glory of Gods Free
Grace began already to shine in him.

3. And this Change was not only an
external one, and to be discerned abroad,
but he would get by himself, and weep and
mourn bitterly, for his horrible wicked
life, as might easily be perceived by them
that lived in the house with him.

4. It was the great care of his Godly
master, to strike in with those Convictions
which the Lord had made, and to improve
them all he could; and he was not a little
glad to see that his labour was not in vain
in the Lord; he still experiences that the
Lord doth carry on his own work mightily on the heart of the Child; he is still
more and more broken under a sence of his
undone state by Nature; he is oft in tears
and bemoaning his lost and miserable Condition. When his Master did speak of the
things of God, he listned earnestly, and
took in with much greediness and affection
what he was taught. Seldom was there
any discourse about Soul-matters in his
hearing, but he heard it as if it were for

his life, and would weep greatly.

5. He would after his Master had been
speaking to him, or others, of the things
of God, go to him, and question with him
about them, and beg of him to instruct &
teach him further, and to tell him those
things again, that he might remember and
understand them better.

6. Thus he continued seeking after the
knowledge of God and Christ, and practi-
cing holy Duties, till the sickness came into
the house, with which the Child was smitten; at his first sickning, the poor Child
was greatly amazed and afraid, and though
his pains were great, and the distemper
very tedious, yet the sence of his sin, and
the thought of the miserable condition
that he feared his Soul was still in, made
his trouble ten times greater; he was in
grievous agonies of Spirit, and his former
sins stared him in the face, and made him
tremble; the poyson of Gods Arrows did
even drink up his Spirits; the sence of Sin
and Wrath was so great, that he could not
tell what in the world to do; the weight
of Gods Displeasure, and the thoughts of
lying under it to all Eternity, did even
break him to pieces, and he did Cry out
very bitterly, *What should he do? He was a
miserable Sinner, and he feared that he should
go to Hell; his Sins had been so great and so
many, that there was no hopes for him.* He
was not by far so much concerned for his
Life, as for his Soul, what should become
of that forever. Now the plague upon his
Body seemed nothing to that which was in
his Soul.

7. But in this great Distress the Lord
was pleased to send one to take care for
his Soul, who urged to him the great and
precious Promises which were made to one
in his condition, telling him that there was
enough in Christ for the Chiefest of Sinners
and that He came to seek and save such a
lost Creature as he was. But this poor

Child found it a very difficult thing for
him to believe that there was any mercy
for such a Dreadful Sinner as he had
been.

8. He was made to Cry out of himself
not only for his Swearing and Lying, and
other outwardly notorious Sins; but he
was in great Horrour for the Sin of his Nature, for the Vileness of his Heart, and O-
riginal Corruption; under it he was in so
great anguish, that the trouble of his Spirit,
made him in a great measure to forget the
pains of his body.

9. He did very particularly confess and
bewail his sins with tears; and some sins
so secret, that none in the world could
charge him with.

10. He would Condemn himself for sin, as
deserving to have no Mercy, & thought that
there was not a greater Sinner in all *London*
than himself, and he abhorred himself as
the vilest creature he knew.

11. He did not only pray much with
strong Cryes and Tears himself, but he
begged the prayers of Christians for
him.

12. He would ask Christians, whether
they thought there were any hopes for him,
and would beg of them to deal plainly with
him, for he was greatly afraid of being deceived.

13. Being informed how willing and
ready the Lord Christ was to accept of
poor Sinners, upon their Repentance and
Turning, and being counselled to venture
himself upon Christ, for Mercy and Salvation, he said he would fain cast himself upon Christ, but he could not but wonder
how Christ should be willing to dye for such
a vile wretch as he was, and he found it
one of the hardest things in the world
to Believe.

14. But at last, it pleased the Lord to
give him some small hopes that there
might be Mercy for him. for he had been

the Chiefest of Sinners; and he was made
to lay a little hold upon such promises, as
that, *Come unto me, all ye that are weary and*
heavy laden, and I will give you rest. But
O! how did this poor Boy admire and Bless
God for the least *Hopes!* How highly did
he advance Rich and Free Grace, that
should pity and pardon him! *And at last*
he was full of Praise, and admiring of God,
so that, (to speak in the words of a Precious
man, that was an eye and ear witness) to the
Praise and Glory of God be it spoken, the house
at that day, for all the sickness in it, was a
little lower Heaven, so full of Joy and
Praise.

15. The Child grew exceedingly in
Knowledge, Experiences, Patience, Humility
and *Self-abhorrency*; & he thought he could
never speak bad enough of himself, the
Name that he would call himself by, was a
Toad.

16. And though he prayed before, yet
now the Lord poured out upon him the
Spirit of Prayer, in an extraordinary manner for one of his age; so that now he
prayed more frequently, more earnestly,
more spiritually than ever. O how eagerly
would he beg to be washed in the Blood
of Jesus! and that the King of Kings, and
Lord of Lords, that was over Heaven and
Earth, and Sea, would pardon and forgive
him all his Sins, and receive his Soul into
his Kingdom. And what he spoke, it was
with so much life and fervour of Spirit,
as that it filled the Hearers with astonishment and joy.

17. He had no small sense of the use
and excellency of Christ, and such longings
and breathings of his Soul after him, that
when mention hath been made of Christ, he
hath been ready almost to leap out of his
bed for joy.

18. When he was told, that if he should
recover, he must not live as he list, but he
must give up himself to Christ, and to be

his Child and Servant, to bear his Yoke and
be obedient to his Laws, and live a holy
life and take his Cross, and suffer mocking
and reproach, it may be, persecution for
His Name sake. Now, Child, (said one
to him,) are you willing to have Christ upon such terms? He signified his willingness
by the earnestness of his looks and words,
and the casting up of his Eyes to Heaven,
saying, *Yes, with all my Soul, the Lord helping me, I will do this.*

19. Yet he had many doubts and fears,
and was ever and anon harping upon that,
*That though he were willing, yet Christ he
feared was not willing to accept of him, because
of the greatness of his Sin*; yet his hopes
were greater than his fears.

20. The *Wednesday* before he Died, the
Child lay as it were in a Trance for about
half an hour, in which time he thought he
saw a Vision of Angels: When he was out
of his Trance, he was in a little pett, and
asked his Nurse, Why she did not let him
go? Go, whether Child said she: Why a-
long with those brave Gentlemen (said
he:) but they told me they would come
and fetch me away for all you, upon *Fryday*
next. And he doubled his words many
times, upon *Fryday* next, those brave Gentlemen will come for me; and upon that
day, the Child died joyfully.

21. He was very thankful to his Master
and very sensible of his great kindness in
taking him out of the streets, when he was
a begging, and he admired at the goodness
of God, which put it into the mind of
a stranger to look upon, and to take such
Fatherly care of such a pittyful sorry
Creature as he was. O my dear Mother,
(said he) and Child of God, I hope to
see you in Heaven, for I am sure you will
go thither. O Blessed, Blessed be God,
that made you take pitty upon me, for I
might have Dyed, and have gone to the
Devil, and have been Damned for ever,

if it had not been for you.

22. The *Thursday* before he Dyed, he
asked a very Godly friend of mine, what
he thought of his condition, and whether
his Soul was now going? For he said, he
could not still but fear, lest he should deceive himself with false hopes, at which
my Friend spoke to him thus; Child, for
all that I have endeavoured to hold forth
the Grace of God in Christ to thy Soul,
and given you a warrant from the Word
of God, that Christ is as freely offered
to you, as to any sinner in the world; if thou
art but willing to accept of Him, thou
mayest have Christ and all that thou dost
want, with Him; and yet thou givest
way to these thy doubtings and fears, as
though I told you nothing but lies. Thou
sayest, thou fearest that Christ will not
accept of thee; I fear thou art not heartily
willing to accept of Him. The Child answered, *Indeed I am;* Why then, Child,
if thou art unfeignedly willing to have
Christ, I tell the, He is a thousand times more
willing to have thee, & wash thee, & save thee,
than thou art to desire it. And now at this
time Christ offers Himself to thee again;
therefore receive Him humbly by Faith freely into thy heart, & bid Him welcome, for
He deserveth it. Upon which words the
Lord discovered His love to the Child,
and he gave a kind of a leap in his bed, and
snapt his fingers and thumb together with
abundance of joy, as much as to say, *Well,
yea all is well, the Match is made, Christ is
willing, and I am willing too; and now Christ
is mine, and I am His forever.* And from
that time forward, in full Joy & assurance
of God's love, he continued earnestly
praising God, with desiring to dye, and
be with Christ. And on *Fryday-morning* he
Sweetly went to rest, using that very expression, *Into thy hands, Lord I commit
my Spirit.* He Died punctually at that
time which he had spoke of, and in which

he expected those Angels to come to him;
he was not much above Nine years old
when he Died.

This Narrative I had from a Judicious
Holy man, unrelated to him, who was
an Eye and Ear-witness to all these
things.

THE END OF THE FIRST PART

The Second Part

Being A farther Account of
the CONVERSION,
Holy and Exemplary Lives,
and Joyful Deaths, *of several other*
Young Children, *not Published in The First Part.*

PSAL. 2.
Out of the Mouth of Babes and Sucklings,
hast thou Ordained Strength.

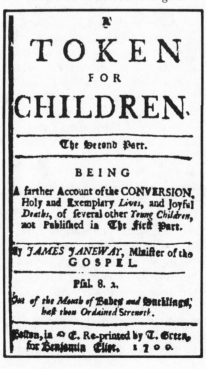

A PREFACE
TO THE READER,

Christian READER,

1. IN THE FORMER *Part of my Token for Children, I did in part Promise,* That if that
Piece met with kind entertainment,
it might be followed with a Second of the
same Nature. *If it did not seem a little to
savour of Vanity, I might tell the World what
encouragement I have met with in this Work;
but this I will only say,* That I have met with
so much as hath perswaded me to give this
Little Book leave to go abroad into the
World. *I am not also Ignorant, what Dis-
couragements I may meet with, from some, but
as long as I am sure I shall not meet with this,*
That it's Improbable, if not Impossible, that
it should Save a Soul; *I think the rest may
easily be answered, or warrantable slighted.
But because I am perswaded by some, that one
Example in the former, (viz. that of a Child
that began to be serious between Two and Three
Years old) was scarce credible, and they did
fear might somewhat prejudice the authority of
the rest, I shall say something to answer that.*
They which make this Objection are either
Good or Bad; *If Bad,* I expect never to satisfy them, except I should tell them of a
Romance or Play, or somewhat that might
suit a Cardinal Mind; it is like Holiness in
older Persons; it is a matter of Contempt and Scorn to them, much more in
such as these I mention. The truth of it is,
it is no wonder at all to me, that the Subjects of Satan should not be very well pleased
with that, whose design is to undermine
the interest of their great Masters: Nothing will satisfie some, except Christ and
Holiness may be degraded and vilified.
But hold Sinner, hold, never hope it, Heaven shall never be turned into Hell for thy

sake, and as for all thy Atheistical Objecti-
ons, Scoffs and Jeers, they shall e're long
be fully answered, and the Hosannah's &
Hallelujah's of these Babes shall Condemn
thy Oaths, Blasphemies, and Jeers, and
then thou wilt be silenced, and except Con-
verting Grace turn thy heart quickly, thou
wilt forever rue thy Madness and Folly
when it is too late to remedy it.

*But if the persons that make this Objection
be Godly, I question not, but that I may give
them reasonable satisfaction.*

First, Consider who it is that I had that
Example from. It was one *Mrs. Jeofries* in
Long-Lane in *Mary Magdalen Bermondsey
Parish,* in the County of *Surry,* a Woman
of that fame in the Church of Christ, for
her Exemplary Piety, Wisdom, Experience,
& singular Watchfulness over every Puncti-
lio that she speaks; that I question not,
but that her name is precious to most of the
Ministers of *London,* at least in the *Burrough;*
& as a Reverend Divine said, Such a Mother
in *Israel,* her single Testimony about *London,*
is as much Authority almost as any one
single Ministers: And having since discoursed this matter with her, she calls God to
Witness, that she hath spoken nothing but
Truth; only in this she failed, in that she
spake not by far so much as she might have
done concerning that sweet Babe. *I might
add, that I have since seen a Godly Gentleman
out of the Country, that did profess to me, that he
had seen as much as that in a little one of the
same Age, who since that time, I hear, went
sweetly to Heaven.* Doth not the Reverend
Mr. *Clark,* in his Works, quote a Child of
two years old, that looked towards Heaven?
Doth not credible History acquaint us with
a Martyr at seven years old, that was whip-
ped almost to Death, and never shed one
tear, nor complained, & at last had his Head
struck off? *I do not speak of these as common
matters, but record them amongst these stupen-
dious Acts of Him that can as easily work Won-*

ders as not. What is too hard for the Almighty?
Hath God said, He will Work no more Wonders?
I think most of Gods Works in the business of
Conversion call for Admiration: And I believe
that Silence, or rather Praise, would better be-
come Saints, than questioning the truth of such
things, especially where an apparent Injury
thereby done to the interest of Christ, the Honour
of Gods Grace, and the Reputation of so eminent
a Saint. I judge this sufficient to satisfie
most, as for others I trouble not my self;
if I may but promote the Interest of Christ,
& the Good of Souls, and give up my Account with Joy, it's enough. *That the Lord*
would Bless my endeavours to these ends, I beg
the Prayers of all Saints, & yours also sweet Chil-
dren that fear the Lord; and that Parents and
Masters would assist me with their warm appli-
cation of these things, & that Children may be
their Crown and their Joy, is the Prayer of all
that desires to Love Christ and little Children
dearly.

James Janeway

EXAMPLE VIII

Of a Child that was very Serious at Four Years
Old, with an Account of his Comfortable Death,
when he was Twelve Years, and Three Weeks Old.

1. J OHN SUDLOW, was Born of Religious
Parents, in the County of *Middle-*
sex, whose great care was to instil
Spiritual Principles into him, as soon as he
was capable of understanding of them;
whose Endeavours the Lord was pleased to
Crown with the desired success: So that
(to use the Expression of a Holy Man concerning him) *Scarce more could be expected*
or desired from so little a one.

2. When he was scarce able to speak
plain, he seemed to have a very great awe
and reverence of God upon his Spirit, and

a strange sence of the things of another
world, as might easily be perceived by
those serious and admirable questions which
he would be oft asking of those Christians
that he thought he might be bold with.

3. The first thing that did most affect
him, and made him endeavour to escape
from the wrath to come, and to enquire
what he should do to be Saved, was the
Death of a little Brother; when he saw
him without breath, and not able to stir,
and then carried out of doors, and put into a Pit-hole, he was greatly concerned,
and asked notable questions about him;
but that which was most affecting of himself and others, was, *Whether he must Dye
too*, which being answered, it made such
a deep impression upon him, that from
that time forward, he was exceeding Serious, & this was when he was about four
Years old.

4. Now he is desirous to know what
he might do that he might live in another
World, and what he must avoid, that he
might not Dye for ever, and being instructed by his Godly Parents, he soon labours to avoid whatsoever might displease
God; now tell him that any thing was
Sinful, and that God would not have him
to do it, and he is easily kept from it, and
even at this time of day, the apprehensions
of God, and Death and Eternity laid such
a restraint upon him, that he would not
for a World have told a lye.

5. He quickly learned to read exactly,
and took such pleasure in reading of the
Scriptures and his Catechism, and other
good Books, that it is scarce to be parallell'd;
he would naturally run to his Book without bidding, when he came home from
School, and when other Children of his age
and acquaintance were playing, he reckon'd
it his Recreation to be doing that which
was good.

6. When he was in Coats, he would

be still asking his Maid serious questions;
and praying her to teach him his Catechism, or Scriptures, or some good thing;
common Discourse he took no delight in,
but did most eagerly desire to be sucking
in of the knowledge of the things of God,
Christ, his Soul, and another World.

7. He was hugely taken with the reading of the Book of *Martyrs* and would
be ready to leave his Dinner to go to his
Book.

8. He was exceeding careful of redeem-
ing and improving of Time; scarce a moment of it, but he would give an excellent
account of the expence of it; so that this
Child might have taught elder Persons, and
will questionless Condemn their idle and
unaccountable wasting of those Precious
hours in which they should (as this sweet
Child,) have been laying in provision for
Eternity.

9. He could not endure to read any
thing over slightly, but whatsoever he read
he dwelt upon it, laboured to understand
it throughly, and remember it; and what
he could not understand, he would oft
ask his Father or Mother the meaning of
it.

10. When any Christian Friends have
been discoursing with his Father, if they
began to talk any thing about Religion,
to be sure they should have his company,
and of his own accord, he would leave all
to hear any thing of Christ, and crept as
close to them as he could, and listen affectionately though it were for an hour or
two: He was scarce ever known to express the least token of weariness while he
was hearing any thing that was good, and
sometimes, when Neighbours Children
would come and call him out, and entice
him, and beg of him to go with them, he
could by no means be perswaded, though
he might have had the leave of his Parents,
if he had any hopes that any good Body

would come into his Fathers House.

11. He was very modest whilst any
stranger was present, and was loth to
ask them any questions: but as soon as they
were gone, he would let his Father know
that there was little said or done, but he
observed it, and would reflect upon what
was past in their discourse, and desire satisfaction in what he could not understand
at present.

12. He was a Boy of almost prodigious
parts for his age, as will appear for his
solid and rational questions; I shall but
mention but two of many.

13. The first was this, when he was
reading by himself, in *Draiton's* Poems a-
bout *Noah's* Flood and the Ark, he asked,
Who Built the Ark? It being answered, that
it was likely that *Noah* hired men to help
him to Build it: *And would they (said he)
Build an Ark to Save another, and not go into
it themselves?*

14. Another question he put was this:
Whether had a greater Glory, Saints or Angels?
It being answered, that Angels were the
most Excellent of Creatures, and it's to be
thought, their Nature is made capable of
greater Glory than Mans. *He said, he was
of another mind, and his reason was, because
Angels was Servants, and Saints are Children;
and that Christ never took upon him the Nature of Angels, but he took upon him the Nature of Saints, and by his being MAN, he
hath advanced humane Nature above the Nature of Angels.*

15. By this you may perceive the greatness of his parts, and the bent of his
thoughts; and thus he continued for several Years together, labouring to get
more and more Spiritual knowledge, and to
prepare for an endless Life.

16. He was a Child of an excellent
sweet Temper, wonderfully Dutiful to his
Parents, ready and joyful to do what he
was bid, and by no means would do any

thing to displease them, and if they
were at any time seemingly angry, he
would not stir from them till they were
thorowly reconciled to him.

17. He was not only good himself,
but would do what he could to make o-
thers so too, especially those that were
nearest to him; he was very watchful
over his Brethren and Sisters, and would
not suffer them to use any unhandsome
words, or to do any unhandsome action,
but he would be putting them upon that
which was good, and when he did
at any time rebuke them, it was not
Childishly and Slightly, but with great
Gravity and Seriousness, as one that was
not a little concerned for Gods Honour, &
the Eternal welfare of their Souls.

18. He would go to his Father and
Mother with great tenderness & compassion, (being far from telling of Tales) and
beg of them, to take more care of the Souls
of his Brethren and Sisters, and to take heed
lest they should go on in a Sinful Christless
state, and prove their sorrow and shame,
and go to Hell when they dye, & be ruined
for ever,

19. He was exceedingly affected with
hearing of the Word of God Preached, and
could not be satisfied, except he could
carry home much of the substance of what
he heard; to this end he quickly got to
learn Short-hand, and would give a very
pretty account of any Sermon that he
heard.

20. He was much engaged in secret
duty, and in reading the Scriptures; to be
sure morning and evening he would be by
himself, & was no question, wrestling with
God.

21. He would get choice Scriptures by
heart, and was very perfect at his Catechism.

22. The Providences of God were not

passed by, without considerable observation
by him.

23. In the time of the Plague, he was
exceedingly concerned about his Soul and
Everlasting state; very much by himself
upon his knees.

This Prayer was found written in Short-
hand after his Death.

*O Lord God and Merciful Father, take pitty
upon me, a miserable Sinner, and strengthen me,
O Lord, in thy Faith, and make me one of thy
Glorious Saints in Heaven. O Lord keep me
from this Poisonus Infection; however, not
my will, but thy Will be done, O Lord, on Earth
as it is in Heaven; but O Lord, if thou hast
appointed me to Dye by it, O Lord, fit me
for Death, and give me a good heart to
bear up under my afflictions: O Lord God
and Merciful Father, take pitty on me, thy
Child, teach me O Lord thy Word, make me
strong in Faith. O Lord I have sinned against
thee, Lord Pardon my Sins; I had been in Hell
long ago if it had not been for thy Mercy. O
Lord, I pray thee to keep my Parents in thy
Truth, and save them from this Infection, if
it be thy Will, that they may live to bring me
up in thy Truth: O Lord, I pray thee stay this
Infection that rageth in this City, and Pardon
their Sins, and Try them once more, and see if
they will turn unto thee. Save me O Lord
from this Infection, that I may Live to Praise
and Glorify thy Name; but O Lord, if thou
hast appointed me to dye of it, fit me for Death,
that I may dye with comfort; and O Lord,
I pray thee to help me to bear up under all
afflictions, for Christ His sake. Amen*

24. He was not a little concerned for
the whole Nation, and begged that God
would pardon the Sins of this Land, and
bring it nearer to himself.

25. About the beginning of *November*
1665, this sweet Child was smote with the
Distemper but he carried it with admirable
patience under the hand of God.

26. These are some of his Dying Expres-

sions——*The Lord shall be my Physician, for He will cure both Soul and Body——Heaven is the best Hospital,——It is the Lord, Let Him do what seemeth good in His Eyes. A-gain,——It is the Lord that taketh away my Health, but I will say as* Job *did, Blessed be the Name of the Lord——If I should live longer, I shall but Sin against God.* Looking upon his Father, he said, *If the Lord would but lend me the least Finger of his Hand, to lead me through the dark entry of Death, I will rejoyce in him.*

27. When a Minister came to him, a-mong other things, he spoke somewhat of Life. He said, *This is a wicked world, yet it is good to Live with my Parents, but it is better to Live in Heaven,——*

28. An hour & an half before his Death, the same Minister came again to visit him and asked him, *John, Art thou not afraid to die?* He answered, *No, if the Lord will but comfort me in that hour.* But said the Mi-nister, *How canst thou expect comfort, seeing we deserve none?* He answered, *No, if I had my deserts I had been in Hell long ago.* But replied the Minister, *Which way dost thou expect Comfort and Salvation, seeing thou art a Sinner?* He answered, *in Christ alone——* In whom, about an hour an half after, he fell asleep, saying, *He would take a long sleep, Charging them that were about him not to wake him.*

He Died when he was Twelve Years Three Weeks and One Day old.

EXAMPLE IX

Of a Child that was very Eminent, when she was between Five and Six Years Old, with some Memorable Passages of her Life, who Died about 1640.

1. ANNE LANE was Born of honest Pa-

rents in Colebrook, in the County
of Bucks, who was no sooner able to speak
plain, and express any thing considerable
of reason, but she began to act as if she
were Sanctified from the very Womb.

2. She was very Solicitous about her
Soul, what would become of it when she
should die, and where she should live forever, and what she should do to be saved
when she was about Five Years old.

3. She was wont to be oft ingaged in
secret Prayer, and pouring out of her Soul
in such a manner, as is rarely to be heard
of from one of her years.

4. I having occasion to lie at *Colebrook*,
sent for her Father, an old Disciple, an *Is-
raelite* indeed, and desired him to give
me some account of his Experiences, and
how the Lord first wrought upon him?

5. He gave me this answer, *That he
was of a Child somewhat Civil; Honest and
as to man Harmless, but he was little acquainted with the Power of Religion, till this sweet
Child put him upon a thorow enquiry into the
state of his Soul, and would still be begging
of him and pleading with him to redeem in
Time, and to all with life and vigour in the
things of God, which was no small demonstration to him of the reality of Invisibles, that
a very Babe and Suckling should speak so feel-
ingly about the things of God, and be so greatly
concerned not only about her own Soul, but about
her Fathers too, which was the occasion of his
Conversion, and the very thought of it was a
quickning to him for Thirty Years, and he
hopes never to wear off the Impressions of it from
his Spirit.*

6. After this she (as I remember) put
her Father upon Family Duties, and if at
any time he were for any time out of his
shop, she would find him out, with so
much sweetness and humility beg of him
to come home, and to remember the pre-
ciousness of time, for which we must all
give an account.

7. She was grieved if she saw any that
conversed with her Father if they were
unprofitable, unsavoury, or long in their
Discourse of common things.

8. Her own Language was the Language
of *Canaan*. How Solidly, Profitably, and
Spiritually would she talk? So that she
made good people take great delight in
her company, and justly draw the admiration of all that knew her.

9. She could not endure the company
of common Children, nor play, but was
quite above all those things which most
Children are taken with; her business was
to be reading, praying, discoursing about
the things of God, and any kind of business that her age and strength was capable of, idle she would not be by any
means.

10. It was the greatest Recreation to her
to hear any good People talking about God,
Christ, their Souls, the Scriptures, or any
thing that concerned another Life.

11. She had a strange Contempt of
the world, and scorned those things which
most are too much pleased with. She could
not be brought to wear any Laces, or any
thing that she thought superfluous.

12. She would be complaining to her
Parents, if she saw any thing in them that
she judged would not be for the honour of
Religion, or suitable to that condition
which the Providence of God had set them
in, in the World.

13. This Child was the joy and delight
of all the Christians there-abouts, in those
cities, who was still quickning and raising
of the Spirits of those that talked with her.
This poor Babe was a great help to both
Father and Mother, and her memory is
sweet to this day.

14. She continued thus to walk as a
stranger in the World, and one that was
making haste to a better place. And after she had done a great deal of work for

God and her own Soul, and others too,
she was called home to rest, and received
into the Arms of Jesus before she was ten
Years old; she departed about 1640.

EXAMPLE X

*Of a Child that was awakened when She was
between Seven and Eight Years Old, with
some Account of her last Hours, and
Triumphant Death.*

1. TABITHA ALDER was the Daughter of
a Holy and Reverend Minister in
Kent, who lived near *Gravesend.* She was
much instructed in the Holy Scriptures and
her Catechism, by her Father and Mother,
but there appeared nothing extraordinary
in her, till she was between Seven and Eight
Years old.

2. About which time, when she was
sick, one asked her, *what she thought would
become of her if she should Dye?* She answered *That she was greatly afraid that she should
go to Hell.*

3. Being asked *why she was afraid she
should go to Hell?* She answered, *Because
she feared she did not love God.*

4. Again, being asked *how she did know she
did not love God?* She replied, *What have
I done for God ever since I was born?* And
besids this, I have been taught *That he that
loves God keeps His Commandments, but I have
kept none of them all.*

5. Being further demanded, *if she
would not fain love God,* She answered, *Yes
with all her heart, if she could, but she found
it a hard thing to love one she did not see.*

6. She was advised to beg of God a heart
to love Him: She answered, *She was afraid
it was too late.*

7. Being asked again, whether she was
not sorry that she could not love God: She

answered *Yes,* but was still afraid it was
too late.

8. Upon this, seeing her in such a despond-
ing condition, a dear Friend of hers spent
the next day in Fasting and Prayer for her.

9. After this, the Christian Friend
askt her how she did now? She answered
with a great deal of joy, that now she
blessed the Lord, she loved the Lord Jesus
dearly, she felt she did love Him. *Oh, said she,*
I love Him dearly.

10. Why said her Friend, did you not
say yesterday, that you did not love the
Lord, and that you could not? What did
you mean to speak so strangely? *Sure* (said
she) *it was Satan that did put into my mind:*
But now I love Him, O blessed be God for the
Lord Jesus Christ.

11. After this, she had a discovery of
her approaching Dissolution, which was no
small comfort to her: *Amen* (said she, with
a holy Triumph) *I shall be with Jesus, I am*
Married to Him, He is my Husband, I am
His Bride, I have given my self to Him, and
He hath given Himself to me, and I shall live
with Him for ever.

12. This strange language made the
Hearers even stand astonished: But thus
she continued for some little time, in a
kind of extasie of joy, admiring the excellency of Christ, rejoycing in her Interest
in Him, and longing to be with Him.

13. After a while some of her friends
standing by her, observed a more than ordinary earnestness and fixedness in her
countenance; they said one to another,
Look how earnestly she looks, sure she seeth
something.

14. One asked what it was she fixed her
Eyes upon so eagerly: I warrant (saith
one that was by) she seeth Death a coming.

15. No (said she) it is Glory that I
see, tis that I fix my Eye upon.

16. One askt her what was Glory like?

She answered, *I can't speak what, but I am
going to it; will you go with me? I am going
to Glory, O that all of you were to go with me
to that Glory?* With which words her Soul
took wing, and went to the possession of
that Glory which she had some believing
sight of before.

She Died when she was between
Eight and Nine Years old,
about 1644.

EXAMPLE XI

*Of a Child that was greatly affected with the
things of God, when She was very Young;
with an exact Account of her admirable
Carriage upon her Death-Bed.*

1. SUSANNE BICKS was Born at *Leiden* in
Holland, Jan. 24, 1650. of very
Religious Parents, whose great care was
to instruct and Catechise this their Child,
and to present her to the Ministers of
the place, to be publickly instructed and
Catechised.

2. It pleased the Lord to bless Holy
Education, the good Example of her Parents, and Catechising, to the good of her
Soul, so that she soon had a true savour
and relish of what she was taught, and
made an admirable use of it in a time of
need, as you shall hear afterwards.

3. She was a Child of great Dutifulness to her Parents, and of very sweet,
humble, spiritual Nature, and not only
the truth, but the power and eminency of
Religion did shine in her so clearly, that
she did not only comfort the hearts of her
Parents, but drew the admiration of all
that were witnesses of Gods works of love
upon her, and may well be proposed as a
pattern not only to Children, but to Persons of riper years.

4. She continued in a course of Religious Duties for some considerable time,
so that her life was more excellent than
most Christians, but in her last sickness
she excelled her self, and her deportment
was so admirable, that partly through
wonder and astonishment, and partly
through sorrow, many observable things
were pass'd by without commiting to Pa-
per, which deserved to have been written
in Letters of Gold: But take these which
follow, as some of many which were taken
from her dying Lips, and first published
by Religious and Judicious Christians in
Dutch, afterward translated into *Scotch*,
and with a little alteration of the stile,
(for the benefit of *English* Children)
brought into this form by me.

5. In the Month of *August*, 1664, when
the Pestilence raged so much in *Holland*
this sweet Child was smitten, and as soon
as she felt her self very ill, she was said
to break forth with abundance of sense
and feeling, in these following words: *If
thy Law were not my delight, I should perish
in my affliction.*

6. Her Father coming to her to encourage her in her sickness, said to her, be of
good comfort my Child, for the Lord
will be near to thee and us, under this
heavy and sore Trial, He will not forsake
us though He chasten us. Yea farther
(said she) our Heavenly Father doth chasten us for our profit, that we may be par-
takers of His Holiness; no chastisement
seemeth for the present to be joyous, but
grievous, but afterwards it yieldeth the
peaceable fruit of righteousness to them
which are exercised thereby. The Lord
is now chastning of me upon this sick bed,
but I hope He will bless it so to me, as
to use it to yield to me that blessed fruit, according to the riches of His mercies which
fail not.

7. After this, she spake to God with

her Eyes lift up to Heaven; saying, *Be merciful to me, O Father, be merciful to me a sinner,
according to thy Word.*

8. Then looking upon her sorrowful
Parents, she said; It is said, *Cast thy burden upon the Lord, and He shall sustain the,
and He will never suffer the Righteous to be
moved.* Therefore, my dear Father and
Mother, cast all your care are upon Him who
causes all things to go well that do concern you.

9. Her Mother said unto her, O my
dear Child, I have no small comfort from
the Lord in thee, and the fruit of His
Grace whereby thou hast been so much exercised unto Godliness in reading the Word,
in Prayer and gracious Discourse, to the
edification of thy self and us. The Lord
Himself who gave thee to us, make up the
loss, if it be His pleasure to take thee away
from us.

10. Dear Mother (said she) though I
leave you, and you me, yet God will never
leave us; for it is said, *Can a Woman forget
her sucking Child, that she should not have
compassion on the pride of her Womb, yet will
not I forget thee, behold I have graven thee
upon the palms of my hands.* O comfortable
words, both for Mothers and Children!
Mark, dear Mother, how fast the Lord
keeps and holdeth His people, that He
doth even grave them upon the palms of
His hands. Though I must part with
you, and you with me, yet Blessed be God,
He will never part either from you or
me.

11. Being weary with much speaking,
she desired to rest a while, but after a
little time awaking again, her Father asked
her how it was with her? She made no
direct answer, but asked what day it was?
Her Father said, it was the Lords Day.
Well then, said she, have you given up
my name to be remembred in the publick
Prayers of the Church: Her Father told

her he had. I have learnt, said she, *That
the effectual fervent Prayer of the Righteous
availeth much.*

12. She had a very high esteem for the
faithful Ministers of Christ, and much desired their company where she was, but
knowing the hazard that such a visit might
expose them and the Church too, she
would by no means suffer that the Ministers
would come near her person, but chose rather to throw her self upon the Arms of
the Lord, and to improve that knowledge
she had in the Word, and her former experience, and the visits of private Christians, & those which the Church had appointed in such cases, to visit and comfort the
sick.

13. One of those which came to visit
her, was a very great use to her to comfort her, and lift her up in some measure
above the fears of Death.

14. Though young, she was very much
concerned for the interest of God and Religion, for Gospel-Ministers, and for
the Sins and the Decay of the power of
Godliness in her own Countrey, which
will further appear, by what may follow.

15. Her Father coming in to her, found
her in an extraordinary passion of weeping, and asked her what was the cause of
her great sorrow; She answered, have I
not cause to weep, when I hear that *Domine
de Wit* was taken sick this day in his Pul-
pit, and went home very ill; Is not this
a sad sign of Gods displeasure to our
Countrey, when God smiteth such a faithful Pastor?

16. She had a high valuation of God,
and could speak in *David's* Language, *Whom
have I in Heaven but thee, and there is none
on Earth that I can desire in comparison with
thee.* She was much lifted up above the
fears of Death; what else was the meaning of such expressions as these? *O how*

do I long!—even as the heart panteth after the
water-brooks, so my Soul panteth after thee,
O God, for the loving God, when shall I come
and appear before God.

17. She was a great hater of Sin, and
did with much grief and self-abhorrency
reflect upon it; but that which lay most
upon her heart, was the Corruption of
her Nature and Original Sin. How oft
would she Cry out in the words of the
Psalmist, *Behold I was Shapen in Iniquity,*
and in Sin did my Mother Conceive me: and
I was altogether Born in Sin. She could
never lay her self low enough under a
sense of that Original Sin which she brought
with her into the world.

18. She spake many things very judi-
ciously of the Old Man, and putting it off,
and of the New Man, and putting that
on; which showed that she was no stranger
to Conversion, and that she in some measure understood what Mortification, Self-
denial, and taking up of her Cross, and
following of Christ meant. That Scripture was much in her mouth, *The Sacri-*
fices of God are a Contrite Heart; a Broken
and a Contrite Spirit, O God, thou wilt not
despise. That brokenness of heart (said
she) which is built upon & flows from Faith,
and that Faith which is built upon Christ,
who is the proper and alone Sacrifice for
Sin.

These are her own words.

19. Afterwards she desired to rest, and
when she had slumbered a while, she said,
O dear Father and Mother, how weak do
I feel my self! My dear Child (said her
Father) God will in His tender Mercy
strengthen thee in thy weakness. Yea
Father (said she) that is my Confidence:
For it is said, *The Bruised Reed He will not*
break, and the Smoking Flax He will not
quench.

20. Then she discoursed excellently of
the Nature of Faith, and desired that the

Eleventh of the *Hebrews* should be read
unto her; at the reading of which, she
Cryed out, O what a stedfast loyal Faith
was that of *Abraham,* which made him
willing to offer up his own and only Son.
Faith, is the substance of things hoped for,
the evidence of things not seen.

21. Her Father and her Mother hearing
her excellent discourse, and seeing her admirable carridge, burst out into abundance
of tears: Upon which, she pleaded with
them to be patient, and content with the
hand of God. O (said she) why do
you weep at this rate over me, seeing I
hope, you have no reason to question, but
if the Lord take me out of this miserable
world, it shall be well with me to all E-
ternity. You ought to be well satisfied,
seeing it is said, *God is in Heaven, and doth
whatsoever pleaseth Him:* And do you not
pray every day, that the Will of God may
be done upon Earth as it is in Heaven?
Now Father, this is Gods Will that I
should lie upon this sick bed, and of this
disease; shall we not be content when
our prayers are answered? Would not
your extream sorrow be murmuring against
God, without whose good pleasure nothing comes to pass. Although I am struck
with this sad disease, yet because it is the
Will of God, that doth silence me, and I
will as long as I live, pray that Gods Will
may be done, and not mine.

22. Seeing her Parents still very much
moved, she further argued with them from
the Providence of God, which had a special hand in every common thing, much
more is the disposal of the lives of Men
and Women: *Are not two Sparrows sold for
a farthing, and not one of them falls to the
ground without our Heavenly Father?* Yea,
*the hairs of our Head are all numbred: there-
fore fear not: you are of more value than
many Sparrows.* Adversity and Prosperity they are both good: Some things seem

evil in our Eyes, but the Lord turns all
to the good of them which are His.

23. She came then to speak particularly
concerning the Plague. Doth not (said
she) the Pestilence come from God?
Why else doth the Scripture say, *Shall
there be evil in the City which I have not sent?*
What do those people mean, which say,
the Pestilence come from the Air? Is not
the Lord the Creator and Ruler of the
Air, and are not the Elements under His
Government? Or if they say it comes
from the Earth, hath He not the same
Power and Influence upon that too? What
talk they of a Ship that came from *Africa.*
have we not read long ago, together out
of Lev. 26.25. *I shall bring a Sword upon
you, and avenge the quarrel of my Covenant,
and when you are assembled in the Cities
then will I bring the Pestilence in the midst of
you.*

24. After this, having taken some little rest, she said, O now is the day for
opening of the first question of the Catechism, and if we were there, we should
hear, that whether in Death or Life a
Believer is Christs, who hath Redeemed
us by His own precious Blood from the
power of the Devil: and then she quoted, Rom. 14. 7,8. *For none of us Liveth
unto himself, and none of us Dieth to himself.
For whether we Live we Live unto the Lord,
and whether we Die we Die unto the Lord,
whether then we Live or Die, we are the
Lords.* Then be comforted, for whether
I live or die, I am the Lords. O why do
you afflict your selves thus! But what
shall I say? With weeping I came into
the World, and with weeping I must go out
again. O my dear Parents, better is
the Day of my Death, than the Day of
my Birth.

25. When she had thus encouraged her
Father and Mother, she desired her Father
to pray with her, and to request of the

Lord that she might have a quiet & peaceable passage into another World.

26.   After her Father had prayed for her, he asked her, whether he should send for the Physician; she answered, by no means, for I am now beyond the help of Doctors. But said he, my Child, we are to use the ordinary means appointed by the Lord for our help, as long as we live, and let the Lord do as seemeth good in His Eyes. But said she, give me the Heavenly Physician, He is the only helper. Doth not He say, *Come unto me all ye that are weary and heavy laden, and I will give you rest;* and doth not He bid us call upon Him in the day of distress, and He will deliver us, and we shall glorifie Him: Therefore, dear Father, call upon Him yet again for me.

27.   About this time a Christian friend came in to visit her, who was not a little comforted when he heard and saw so much of the Grace of God living in a poor young thing which could not but so far affect him as to draw tears of joy and admiration from him, and her deportment was so teaching that he could not but acknowledge himself greatly Edified and Improved by her Carriage and Language.

28.   That which was not the least observable in her, was the ardent affection she had for the Holy Scriptures and her Catechism, in which she was throughly Instructed by the Divines of the place where she lived, which she could not but own as one of the greatest mercies next the Lord Christ. O how did she bless God for her Catechism, and beg of her Father to go particularly to those Ministers that had taken so much pains with her to instruct her in her Catechism, and to thank them from her, a Dying Child for their good instructions, and to let them understand, for their encouragement to go on in that

work of Catechising, how refreshing those
truths were now to her in the hour of her
distress. O that sweet Catechising, said
she, onto which I did always resort with
gladness, and attended without weariness.

29. She was much above the vanities of the
World, and took no pleasure at all in those
things which usually take up the heart and
time of young ones. She would say that
she was grieved and ashamed both for
young and old to see how glad and mad
they were upon vanity, and how foolishly they spent their time.

30. She was not forgetful of the care
and love of her Master and Mistress which
taught her to read and work, but she desired that thanks might also be particularly
given to them. Indeed she thought she
could never be thankful enough both to
God and Man for that kindness that she
had experience of: But again and again,
she desired to be sure to thank the Ministers that instructed her, either by Catechising or Preaching.

31. After some rest, her Father ask'd
her again how she did, and began to express somewhat of that satisfaction and
joy that he had taken in her former diligence, in her reading the Scriptures and
writing, and her dutifulness, and that
great progress that she had made in the
things of God, upon which she humbly
and sweetly desired to own God and His
kindness in her Godly Education, and
said, that she esteemed her Holy Education under such Parents and Ministers as
a greater portion than ten thousand Gild-
ers, for thereby I have learned to comfort my self out of the Word of God,
which the world besides could never have
afforded.

32. Her Father perceiving her to grow
very weak, said, I perceive Child thou art
very weak; It is true Sir *(said she)* I feel

my weakness increaseth, and I see your
sorrow increasing too, which is a piece of
my affliction; be content, I Pray you, it
is the Lord which doth it, and let you and
I say with *David, Let us fall into the Lords
hands, for His Mercies are great.*

33. She laid a great Charge upon her
Parents not to be over-grieved for her
after her Death, urging that of *David* upon them, while the Child was sick, he
fasted and wept, but when it died, he
washed his face, and sat up and eat, and
said, *Can I bring him back again from Death,
I shall go to him, but he shall not return to me.*
So ought you to say after my Death, *Our
Child is well, for we know it shall be well with
them that trust in the Lord.* She did lay a
more particular and straight Charge upon
her Mother; saying to her, dear Mother,
who have done so much for me, you must
promise me one thing before I Dye; and
that is, that you will not sorrow overmuch for me; I speak thus to you, because
I am afraid of your great affliction; Consider other Losses what they have been;
remember *Job;* forget not what *Christ*
foretold: *in the World you shall have Tribulation, but be of good Cheer, in me you
shall have Peace;* and must the *Apostles* suffer
so great tribulation, and must we suffer
for none? Did not Jesus Christ my only
Life and Savior, sweat drops of Blood?
Was He not in a bitter agony, mocked,
spit at, nailed to the Cross, and a spear
thrust thorow His Blessed side, and all
this for my sake, for my stinking Sins sake?
Did not He Cry out, *My God, my God,
why hast thou forsaken me?* Did not Christ
hang naked upon the Cross to purchase for
me the garments of Salvation, & to cloath
me with His Righteousness, for there is
Salvation in no other name.

34. Being very feeble and weak, she
said, O if I might quietly sleep in the bosome of Jesus! and that till then He would

strengthen me! O that He would take me
into His arms as He did those little ones,
where He said, *Suffer little Children to come
unto me, for of such is the Kingdom of Heaven, and He took them into His arms, and
laid His hands on them and blessed them.* I
lye hear as a Child, O Lord I am thy
Child, receive me into thy gracious Arms.
O Lord, Grace! Grace! and not Justice!
for if thou shouldest enter into Judgment
with me, I cannot stand, yea, none living
should be just in thy sight.

35. After this, she Cryed O how faint
am I! But fearing lest she should dis-
hearten her Mother, she said, while there
is life, there is hope: if it should please
the Lord to recover me, how careful would
I be to please you in my work and learning, and whatsoever you should require of
me!

36. After this, the Lord did again send
her strength, and she laboured to spend
it all for Christ in the awakening, edifying and comforting of those that were
about her; but her chiefest endeavour was
to support her dear Parents from extraordinary sorrow, and to comfort them out
of the Scriptures, telling them, *That she
knew all things did work together for the good
of them that did love God, even to those
which are Called according to His purpose;
O God establish me with thy Free Spirit! Who
shall separate us from the Love of Christ, I
am persuaded that neither Life, nor Death,
nor Angels, nor Principalities, nor Powers,
nor things Present, nor things to Come, nor
Heighth, nor Depth, nor any other Creature
shall separate us from the Love of God, which
is towards us in Christ Jesus our Lord. My
Sheep* (saith Christ) *hear my voice, and I
know them, and they follow me, and I give
unto them Eternal Life, and they shall never
Perish, and no man shall Pluck them out of
my hands. My Father who gave them me
is Greater than all, and none shall Pluck them*

out of my Fathers hand. Thus she seemed
to attain a Holy Confidence in God, and
an assurance of her State as to another
World.

37. When she had a little refreshed
her self with rest, she burst forth with a-
bundance of joy, and gladness of Heart,
with a Holy Triumph of Faith, saying
out, Death is swallowed up of Victory,
O Death where is thy Sting; O Grave where
is thy Victory? The Sting of Death is Sin,
and the Strength of Sin is the Law; but
Thanks be to God who hath given us the
Victory through our Lord and Saviour Jesus
Christ.

38. That she might the better support
her Friends, she still insisted upon that
which might take off some of their burthen, by urging the necessity of Death:
We are from the Earth, and to the Earth
we must return: Dust is the Mother of us all,
the Dust shall turn to Dust, from where he
is; and the Spirit to God which gave it.

39. Then she discoursed of the short-
ness of Mans Life. O what is the life of
man! *The days of man upon the Earth are*
as the grass, and the flowers of the Field, So
he flourisheth, the wind passeth over it, and
it is no more, and his place knows him no
more.

40. She further urged the sin and sorrow that did attend us in this life, and
the longer we Live, the more we Sin;
now the Lord will free me from that sin
and sorrow. We know not the thoughts
of God, yet do we know so much, that
they are mercy and peace, and do give an
expected end. But what shall I say, my
life shall not continue long, I feel much
weakness, O Lord, look upon me graciously, have pitty upon my weak distres-
sed heart. I am oppressed, undertake for
me, that I may stand fast and overcome.

41. She was very frequent in Spiritual
ejaculations, and it was no small comfort

to her, that the Lord Christ did pray for
her, and promise to send His Spirit to
comfort her. Its said, (said she) *I will
Pray the Father, and He shall give you another
Comforter.* O let not Him leave me! O
Lord, continue with me till my battle and
work be finished.

42. She had very low and undervaluing
thoughts of her self, and her own Righteousness; what meant she else to Cry out
in such Langauge as that, None but Christ!
without thee I can do nothing? Christ is
the true Vine! O let me be a Branch of
that Vine! What poor worms are we! O
dear Father, how lame and halting do we
go in the ways of God and Salvation?
We know but in part, but when that
which is perfect is come, then that which
is imperfect shall be done away. O that
I had attained to that now: But what
are we our selves; Not only weakness and
nothingness, but wickedness. For all the
thoughts and imaginations of mans heart,
are only evil, and that continually, we are
by Nature Children of wrath, and are
Conceived and Born in Sin and Unrighteousness. Oh! Oh! this wretched and vile
thing SIN! But thanks to God who
hath redeemed me from it.

43. She comforted her self and her
Father, in that great Scripture, Rom. 8.15,
16, 17. *Ye have not received the Spirit of
Bondage again to fear, but ye have received
the Spirit of Adoption, by which ye Cry* Abba
Father. *It is the Spirit that witnesseth with
our Spirits, that we are the Children of God;
and if Children, then are we Heirs, Heirs of
God, and Joynt-Heirs with Christ.* You see
thence Father, that I shall be a fellow-heir
with Christ, who hath said, *In my Fathers
house are many mansions, if it were not so, I
would have told you, I go to prepare a place
for you, I will come again, and take you to my
self, that where I am there ye may be also.*
O Lord, take me to thy self. Behold dear

Mother, He hath prepared a place and
dwelling for me,

44. Yea, my dear Child, said her Mother, He shall strengthen you with His
Holy Spirit, until He hath fitted and prepared you fully for that place which He
hath prepared for you.

45. Yea Mother, it is said in the Eighty-
fourth Psalm, *How lovely are thy Tabernacles,
O Lord of Hosts, my Soul doth thirst, and
longeth for the Courts of the Lord; One day
in thy Courts is better than a thousand; yea, I
had rather be a Door-keeper in the House of
God, than dwell in the Tents of the Wicked.*
Read that Psalm, dear Mother, wherewith
we may comfort one another. As for me,
I am more and more spent, and draw near
my last hour.

46. Then she desired to be pray'd with,
and begged that the Lord would give her
an easie passage.

47. After this, she turned to her Mother, with much affection, she said, Ah my
dear & loving Mother; that which cometh
from the heart, doth ordinarily go to the
heart, once more come and kiss me before
I leave you.

48. She was not a little concerned about
the Souls of the rest of her Relations, & did
particularly charge it upon her Father, to
do what he could possibly to bring them up
in the ways of God. O let my Sister be
trained up in the Scriptures, and Catechising, as I have been.

49. I formerly wept for my Sister,
thinking that she would dye before me,
and now she weepeth for me, and then she
kissed her weeping Sister. Also she took
her young little Sister in her Arms, a Child
of Six Months old, and she kissed it with
much affection, as if her very bowels had
moved within her, and spoke with many
Heart-breaking words, both to her Parents
and the Children.

50. Her Father spake to one that was

by, to take the poor little Child away from
her, from the hazard of that fiery distemper, and bid his Daughter to give her from
her, for he had already too much to bear.
Well Father, said she, did not God preserve the three Children in the Fiery Fur-
nace: And did you not teach me that
Scripture, *When thou passeth through the Fire,
thou shalt not be Burnt, neither shall the Flame
kindle upon thee.*

51. She had a very strong Faith in the
Doctrine of the Resurrection, and did
greatly solace her Soul with excellent Scriptures, which do speak the happy state of
Believers, as soon as their Souls are sepa-
rated from their Bodies, and what she
quoted out of the Scripture, she did excellently and suitably apply to her own use,
incomparibly above the common reach of
her Sex and Age. That in *I Cor. 15.42.*
was a good support to her, *The Body is
sown in Corruption, but it shall be raised incor-
ruptible; It is sown in dishonour, but it shall be
raised in glory; It is sown in weakness, but it
shall be raised in power.* And then she sweetly applyes it, and takes in this Cordial.
Behold thus it is, and thus it shall be with
my poor mortal flesh: *Blessed are the dead which
die in the Lord, because they rest from their
labours, and their marks do follow them. The
Righteous perish, and no man layeth it to
heart, and the Upright are taken away, and
no man regardeth it that they are taken away
from the evil to come, they shall enter into peace,
they shall rest in their beds, every one who
walked in their uprightness.* Behold now
Father, I shall rest and sleep in that Bed-
chamber.

52. Then she quoted Job 19.25, 26, 27.
*I know that my Redemer liveth, and that He
shall stand at the latter end upon the Earth;
and though after my skin worms destroy this
body, yet in my flesh shall I see God; whom I
shall see for my self, and my eyes shall behold,
and not another, though my veins be consumed*

within me. Behold now Father, this very
skin which you see, and this very flesh
which you see, shall be raised up again;
and these very eyes which now are so
dim, shall on that day see, and behold my
dear and precious Redeemer; albeit the
worms eat up my flesh, yet with these
eyes shall I behold God, even I my self,
and not another for me.

53. Then she quoted Joh. 5.28. *Mar-*
vel not at this, for the hour is coming on which
all that are in their Graves shall hear His voice,
and come forth; those that have done good un-
to the Resurrection of Life. See Father, I
shall rise in that day, and then I shall behold my Redeemer; then shall He say,
Come ye Blessed of my Father, inherit the King-
dom prepared for you before the beginning of the
World.

54. *Behold now I live, yet not I, but Christ*
liveth in me, and the life that I now live in the
flesh, is by the Faith of the Son of God, who
loved me, and gave Himself for me. I am
saved, and that not of my self, it is the Gift
of God, not of Works, that no man should
boast.

55. My dear Parents, now we must
shortly part, my speech faileth me, pray
the Lord for a quiet close to my combat.

56. Her Parents replied, Ah our dear
Child! how sad is that to us, that we must
part? She answered, I go to Heaven, and
there we shall find one another again; I go
to Jesus Christ.

57. Then she comforted her self to
think of her seeing her precious Brother
and Sister again in Glory. I go to my
Brother *Jacob,* who did so much Cry and
Call upon God to the last moment of his
breath: And to my little Sister who was
but three years old when she died: Who,
when we asked her whether she would
Dye? Answered, Yes, if it be the Lord's
will. I will go to my little Brother, if it
be the Lord's will, or I will stay with my

Mother, if it be the Lord's will. But I
know that I shall Dye, and go to Heaven
and to God. O see, how so small a Babe
had so much give it to behave it self every
way, and in all things so submissively to
the will of God, as if it had no will of its
own; but if it be the will of God, if it
please God; nothing for her, but what
the Will and Pleasure of God: And therefore, dear Father and Mother, give the
Lord thanks for this His free & rich Grace,
and then I shall the more gladly be gone.
Be Gracious then, O Lord, unto me also,
be Gracious to me. Wash me thorowly from
my Unrighteousness, and cleanse me from
my Sin.

58. After this, her Spirit was refreshed
with the sense of the Pardon of her Sins,
which made her to Cry out, Behold God
hath washed away my sins, O how do I
long to die! The Apostle said, *In this Body*
we earnestly sigh and groan, longing for our
House which is in Heaven, that we may be
Cloathed therewith. Now I also lie here
sighing and longing for that Dwelling
which is above. In the last Sermon which
I heard; or ever shall hear, I heard this in
the New-Church, which is matter of great
comfort unto me.

59. Then she repeated several notable
Scriptures which were quoted in that Sermon, afterward she desired to be pray'd
with, and put Petitions into their Mouths,
viz. That all her Sins might be forgiven,
That she might have more abundant Faith,
and the assurance of it; and the comfort
of that assurance, and the continuation and
strength of that comfort, according as her
necessity should require. Afterwards she
prayed her self, and continued a pretty
space.

60. When Prayers was ended, she called to her Father and Mother, and demanded of them, whether she had any time
angered or grieved them, or done any-

thing that did not become her? And begged of them to forgive her.

61. They answered her, that if all
Children had carried themselves so to their
Parents as she had done, there would be
less grief and sorrow on all hands than
there is; and if any such thing hath escaped
thee, we would forgive it withal our
hearts, you have done as became a good
Child.

62. Her heart being quieted with her
peace with God and her Parents, she began
to dispose of her Books; particularly she
intreated her Mother, to keep Mr. DeWits
Catechise Lectures, as long as she lived
for her sake, and let my little Sister have
my other Book as my remembrance.

63. Then (said she) she felt her breath
exceedingly pained, by which she knew
that her end was very nigh. Her Father
spake to her as he was able, telling her the
Lord would be her strength in the hour of
her necessity.

64. Yea said she, *The Lord is my Sheperd
although I pass through the Valley of the Shadow
of Death, I will not fear, for thou art with
me, thy Rod and thy Staff, they comfort me:*
And it is said, *The sufferings of this present
life are not worthy to be compared with the
glory that shall be revealed in us.* Shall I not
suffer and endure, seeing my Glorious Redeemer was pleased to suffer so much for
me? O how was He mocked and crowned with Thorns, that He might purchase
a Crown of Righteousness for us: And
that is the Crown of which *Paul* spoke,
when he said, *I have fought the good fight,
I have finishing my Course, I have kept the
Faith, henceforth is laid up for me a Crown
of Righteousness, which the Lord the Righteous
Judge, shall give unto me in that day; and
not only unto me, but to all that love His Appearing.*

65. *Ye are bought with a Price, therefore
Glorify God with your Souls and Bodies, which*

are His. Must I not then Exalt and Bless
Him while I have a being, who hath bought
me, yea, bought me with His Blood?
Surely He hath born our griefs and took our
infirmities, and we esteemed Him smitten and
stricken of God; But He was wounded for
transgressions, and bruised for our sins: the
chastisment of our peace was upon Him, and
by His stripes are we healed, and the Lord
laid upon Him the iniquity of us all. Behold
the Lamb of God that taketh away the sins of
the World: That Lamb is Jesus Christ,
who hath satisfied for my Sins. So saith
Paul, *Ye are washed, ye are sanctified, ye are*
justified in the Name of our Lord Jesus, and
through the Spirit of our God.

66.   My end is now very near, now I
shall put on white Raiment, & be cloathed
before the Lamb, that spotless Lamb, and
with His spotless Righteousness. Now
are the Angels making ready to carry
my Soul before the Throne of God. *These*
are they who are come out of great Tribulation,
who have washed their Robes, and made them
white in the Blood of the Lamb.

67.   She spoke this with a Dying voice,
but full of Spirit, and of the Power of
Faith.

68.   Her lively assurance she further
uttered in the words of the Apostle, *We*
know that if this earthly house of our Taber-
nacle be dissolved, we have one which is built
of God, which is Eternal in the Heavens;
for in this, we sigh for our house, which is
in Heaven, that we may be Cloathed there-
with.

69.   There Father, you see that my
Body is this Tabernacle, which now shall
be broken down; my Soul shall now part
from it, and shall be taken up into that
Heavenly Paradise, into that Heavenly *Je-*
rusalem. There shall I dwell and go no
more out, but sit and sing, *Holy, holy, holy,*
is the Lord God of Hosts, the Lord of Sab-
bath! Her last words were these: *O Lord*

God, into thy Hands I commit my Spirit, O
Lord be Gracious, be Merciful to me a poor
Sinner.——

And here she fell asleep.

70. She Died the First of *September*,
1664 betwixt Seven and Eight in the
Evening; in the Fourteenth Year of her
Age; having obtain'd that which she so
oft intreated of the Lord a quiet and
easie departure, and the End of her Faith,
the Salvation of her Soul.

EXAMPLE XII

Of the excellent Carriage of a Child upon his Death-Bed, when but Seven Years Old.

1. Jacob Bicks, the Brother of *Susanna Bicks*, was Born in *Leiden*, in the
Year 1657. and had Religious Education,
under his Godly Parents, the which the
Lord was pleased to sanctify to his Conversion, and by it lay in excellent Provisi-
ons to live upon in an hour of distress.

2. This sweet little Child was visited of the
Lord of a very sore sickness, upon the
sixth of *August* 1664. three or four weeks
before his Sister, of whose life and death
we have given you some account already:
In his distemper he was for the most part
very sleepy and drousie, till near his Death,
but when he did awake, he was wont still
to fall a praying.

3. Once when his Parents had prayed
with him, they asked him if they should
once more send for the Physician? No
(saith he) *I will have the Doctor no more*
the Lord will help me; I know He will take
me to Himself, and then He shall help
all.

4. Ah my dear Child, said his Father,
that grieveth my heart: *Well,* (said the
Child) *Father let us pray, and the Lord shall be
near for my helper.*

5. When his Parents had Prayed with
him again, he said, *Come now dear Father
and Mother, and kiss me, I know that I shall
Dye.*

6. Farwel dear Father and Mother,
farewel dear Sister, Farewel all. Now
shall I go to Heaven unto God & Jesus Christ,
and the Holy Angels: Father know you
not what is said by *Jeremiah: Blessed is he
who trusteth in the Lord.* Now I trust in
Him, and He will bless me. And in I *Joh.*
2. it is said, *Little Children love not the
World, for the World passeth away.*

7. Away then all that is to the World,
away with all my pleasent things in the world:
away with my Dagger; for where I go,
there is nothing to do with Daggers and
Swords: men shall not fight there, but praise
God. Away with all my Books; there
shall I know sufficiently, and be learned
in all things of true Wisdom, without
Books.

8. His Father being touched to hear
his Child speak at this rate, could not
well tell what to say; but my dear Child,
the Lord will be near thee, & uphold thee.

9. Yea Father *(said he)* the Apostle
Peter saith, *God Resisteth the Proud, but
He giveth Grace to the Humble.* I shall humble my self under the mighty hand of God,
and He shall help and lift me up.

10. O my dear Child, said his Father,
hast thou so strong a Faith?

11. Yes, said the Child, God hath given
me so strong a Faith upon Himself through
Jesus Christ, that the Devil himself shall
flee from me, for it is said, *He who Be-
lieveth in the Son hath Everlasting Life, and
he hath overcome the wicked One.* Now I
Believe in Jesus Christ my Redeemer, and
He will not leave or forsake me, but shall

give unto me Eternal Life, and then shall
I Sing, *Holy, holy, holy is the Lord of
Sabbath.*

12. Then with a short word of Prayer,
Lord be Merciful to me a poor Sinner,
he quietly breathed out his Soul, and
sweetly slept in Jesus, when he was about
Seven Years old. He died *August* 8, 1664.

Hallelujah.

EXAMPLE XIII

*Of one that began to look toward Heaven,
when he was very Young, with many
Eminent Passages of his Life, and his
joyful Death, when he was Eleven Years
and Three Quarters Old.*

1. J OHN HARVY was Born in *London,*
in the Year 1654. his Father was
a Dutch Merchant, he was piously
Educated under his virtuous Mother, and
soon began to suck in Divine Things with
no small delight.

2. The first thing very observable in
him was, that when he was two years
and eight months old, he could speak as
well as other Children do usually at five
years old!

3. His Parents judging, that he was
then a little too young to send out to
School, let him have his liberty to Play
a little about their Yard. But instead of
playing, he found out a School of his own
accord hard by home, and went to the
School-Mistress, and intreated her to teach
him to read, and so he went for some time
to School without the knowledge of his
Parents, and made a very strange progress
to his Learning, & was able to read distinctly, before most Children are able to know
their Letters.

4. He was wont to ask many serious &
weighty Questions, about matters which
concerned his Soul and Eternity.

5. His Mother being greatly troubled
upon the Death of one of his Uncles, this
Child came to his Mother and said, *Mother,*
though my Uncle be Dead, doth not the Scrip-
ture say, he must Rise again: Yea, and I must
Dye, & so must every Body, & it will not be long
before Christ will come to Judge the World,
and then we shall see one another again, I
pray Mother do not weep so much. This
grave Counsel he gave his Mother, when
he was not quite five years old, by which
the sorrow for her Brother was turned into
admiration at her Child, & she was made
to sit silent and quiet under that smarting
stroke.

6. After this, his Parents removed to
Aberdeen in Scotland, and settled their Child
under an able & painful School-Master there,
whose custome was upon the Lord's day
in the Morning, to examine his Scholars
concerning the Sermons that they had
heard the former Lords day, and to add
some other Questions which might try the
Understanding & Knowledge of his Scholars;
the Question that was once proposed to
his Forme was, *Whether God had a Mother?*
None of all the Scholars could answer it,
till it came to *John Harvy,* who being
asked, *Whether God had a Mother?* Answered *No, as He was God, He could not*
have a Mother, but as He was Man He had;
this was before he was quite Six Years
old His Master was somewhat amazed
at the Childs answer, and took the first
opportunity to go to his Mother, to
thank her for instructing her Son so well;
but she replied, that he was never taught
that from her, but that he understood
it by Reading, and his own Observation.

7. He was a Child that was Extraordinary inquisitive, & full of good questions,

and very careful to observe and remember
what he heard.

8. He had a great Hatred of whatsoever he knew to be displeasing to God,
and was so greatly Concerned for the
Honour of God, that he would take on
bitterly, if that any gross Sins were committed before him. And he had a deep
sense of the worth of Souls, and was
not a little grieved when he saw any do
that which he knew was dangerous to their
Souls.

9. One day seeing one of his near
Relations come into his Fathers House
distempered with Drink as he thought,
he quickly went very Seriously to him
and Wept over him, that he should so
Offend God, and Hazard his Soul, and
begged of him to spend his Time better
than in Drinking and Gaming; and this
he did, without any instruction from his
Parents, but from an inward Principle
of Grace, and love to God and Souls, as it
is verily believed.

10. When he was at play with other
Children, he would be oftentimes putting
in some word to keep them from nagh-
ty talk, or wicked actions; and if any
did take the Lords Name in vain, or do
any thing that was not becoming of a
good Child, they should soon hear of it
with a witness; nay, once hearing a
Boy speak very prophanely, and that
after two or three admonitions, he would
not forbear, nor go out of his Company
neither, he was so transported with Zeal;
that he could not forbear falling upon
him, to beat him, but his Mother chiding
him for it, he said, that he could not
endure to hear the Name of God so abused
by a wretched Boy.

> *This is observed not to Vindicate the*
> *Act, but to take notice of his Zeal.*

11. He was a Child that took great

delight in the Company of Good men,
and: especially Ministers and Scholars;
and if he had any leisure time, he would
improve it by visiting of such, whose discourse might make him wiser and better;
and when he was in their Society, to be
sure, his talk was more like a Christian &
Scholar, than a Child.

12. One day after School time was over,
he gave Mr. *Andrew Kent* (one of the Ministers of *Aberdeen*) a visit, & asked him several
solid Questions, but the Good man asked
him some questions out of his Catechism:
And finding him not so ready in the answers as he should have been, did a little
reprove him and told him, that he must
be sure to get his Catechism perfectly
by heart; the Child took the reproof very
well, and went home, and fell very hot
upon his Catechism, and never left, till
he got it by heart; and not only so,
but he would be enquiring into the sense
and meaning of it.

13. He was so greatly taken with
his Catechism, that he was not content
to learn it himself, but he would be putting others upon learning their Catechism,
especially, those that were nearest to him;
he could not be satisfied, till he had perswaded his Mothers Maids to learn it,
and when they were at work, he would
be still following them with some good
questions or other; so that the Child seemed to be taken up with the thoughts of
his Soul, and Gods Honour, & the good
of other Souls.

14. He was a Conscientious observer
of the Lord's day, spending all the time
either in secret Prayer, or reading the
Scriptures, and Good Books; Learning
of his Catechism, and Hearing of the Word
of God, and publick Duties; and was
not only careful in the performance of
these Duties himself, but was ready to
put all that he knew upon a strict ob-

servation of the Lor'ds day, and was exceedingly grieved at the Prophanation
of it; one Lords day, a Servant of his
Fathers going out of the house upon extraordinary occasion, to fetch some Beer,
he took on so bitterly, that he could
scarce be pacified, because that Holy Day
was so abused (as he judged) in his
Fathers house.

15. When he was betwixt Six and
Seven Years old; It pleased God to Afflict
him with sore eyes, which was no small
grief unto him, because it kept him from
School, which he loved as well as many
Boys do their play; and that which was
worse, he was Commanded by the Doctor
not to read any Book whatsoever at home.
But, O how was this poor Child grieved, that
he might not have liberty to Read the Holy
Scriptures! And for all their Charge, he
would get by himself, and stand by the
window, and read the Bible and good
Books; yea, he was so greedy of reading
the Scripture, and took so much delight in
it, that he would scarce allow himself
time to dress himself; for reading the
Word of God was his great delight.
Yea, though he had been beat for studying
so much, yet judging it Gods Command
that he should give himself up to reading, he could not be beat off from it, till
he was so bad, that he had like never to
have recovered his sight more.

16. It was his practice to be much
by himself in Secret Prayer, and he was
careful to manage that work, so as that
it might be as secret as possible it might be,
but his frequency and constancy made it
to be so easily observed, upon which, *One
time one having a great mind to know
what this sweet Babe Prayed for, got into
a place near him, and heard him very earnestly Praying for the Church of God, desiring
that the Kingdom of the Gospel might be
spread over the whole World, and that the*

*Kingdom of Grace might more and more
come unto the Hearts of God's People, and
that the Kingdom of Glory might be hastened.*
He was wont to continue half an hour,
sometimes an hour, upon his knees together.

17. He was much above the vanities
that most Children are taken with, and
was indeed too much a man to live long.

18. He was very humble and modest,
and did by no means affect fineness in apparel, but hated any thing more than necessaries, either in cloaths or diet.

19. When he perceived either his
Brother or Sisters pleased with their new
Cloathes, he would with a great deal
of Gravity reprove their Folly, and
when his reproof signified little, he would
bewail their vanity.

20. Once he had a New Suit brought
from the Taylors, which when he looked on, he found some Ribbons at the
knees, at which he was grieved; asking
his Mother, *Whether those things would
keep him warm?* No, Child, said his
Mother; *Why then* (said he) *do you suffer
them to be put here, you are mistaken, if
you think such things please me; and I doubt,
some that are better than us, may want
the Money that this Cost you, to buy them
Bread.*

21. He would intreat his Mother to
have a care of gratifying a proud humour in his Brother and Sisters, he did
tell them of the danger of Pride, and
how little reason they had to be Proud
of that which was their Shame; for
said he, *If it had not been for Sin, we should
have had no need of Cloathes.*

22. At leisure times, he would be talking to his School-fellows about the things
of God, and urge the necessity of a holy
life. That Text he much spoke on to
them, *The Axe is laid on the Root of the
Tree, and every Tree that bringeth not forth*

good Fruit, is hewn down and cast into the
Fire. Every Mothers Child of us that
doth not bring forth the fruit of good
Works, shall shortly be cut down with
the Axe of Gods wrath, and cast into
the Fire of Hell; and this he spake like
one that believed and felt the power
of what he spake, and not with the least
visibility of a Childish levity of Spirit.
This was, when he was between Seven
and Eight years old, and if he perceived
any Children unconcerned about their
Souls, he would be greatly troubled at
it.

23. After this, his Parents removed
not far from *London,* where he continued
till that dreadful year, Sixty Five; he
was then sent to the *Latin* School, where
he soon made a very considerable Progress,
and was greatly beloved of his Master,
the School was his beloved place, and
Learning his recreation. He was never
taught to write, but took it of his own
ingenuity.

24. He was exceeding Dutiful to his
Parents, and never did in the least dispute their Command, except, when he
thought they might cross the Command
of God, (as in the forementioned business
of reading the Scriptures when his eyes
were so bad.)

25. He was exceeding contented with
any mean Diet, and to be sure he would
not touch a bit of any thing, till he had
begged Gods Blessing upon it.

26. He would put his Brother and
Sisters upon their Duties, and observe them
whether they performed it or no, and
when he saw any neglect, he would soon
warn them; if he saw any of them take
a spoon into their hands before they had
craved a Blessing, he said that is just
like a Hog indeed.

27. His Sister was afraid of the darkness, and would sometimes Cry, upon

this account; he told her, she must fear
God more, and she need then be afraid
of nothing.

28. He would humbly put his near
Relations upon their Duty, and minding
the Concerns of their Souls and Eternity,
with more Seriousness and Life, and to
have a care of doing that which was for
the dishonour of God, and the hazard
of the Soul.

29. He was of a compassionate and
charitable disposition, and very pitiful to
the poor, or any that were in distress,
but his greatest pity was to poor Souls;
and as well as he could, he would be putting Children, Play-fellows, Servants,
Neighbours, upon minding their poor
Souls.

30. One notable instance of his true
Charity, I cannot omit. *A certain* Turk
*was by the Providence of God, cast into the
place where he Lived, which this sweet Child
hearing of, had a great pity to his Soul, and
studied how he might be any way instrumental to do it good; at last finding a man
that understood the Language of the* Turk,
*he used means to get them together, which
he at last procured; the first thing that he
did, was to put his Friend upon discoursing
with the* Turk *about his Principles, whether
he acknowledge a Deity; which the* Turk
*owning; the next thing he enquired after,
was, What he thought of the Lord Jesus
Christ. At which the* Turk *was troubled and
put off the discourse, and said, he was athirst
and an hungry; which the Child being informed
of, by the Interpreter, immediately went to a
Brew-house near at hand (his own house
being far off) and did intreat the Master of
the Brew-house to give him some Beer for
the* Turk, *and the argument he used was this:
Sir, here is a poor stranger that is athirst,
we know not where we may be cast before we Dye: He went to another place,
and begged Food for him; using the same*

*argument as before, but his Friends hearing
of it, were angry with him, but he told them
he did it for a poor stranger that was far
from home, and he did it that he might think
the better of the Christians, and the Christian
Religion.*

31. He would have a savoury word
to say to every one that he conversed
with, to put them in mind of the worth
of Christ, and their Souls; and their near-
ness to Eternity. Insomuch, that good
People took no small pleasure in his
Company. The Taylor that made his
Cloathes, would keep them the longer
before he brought them home, that he
might have the benefit of his Spiritual
and Christian Society; and more frequent
visits.

32. He bewailed the miserable condition of the generality of man-kind
(when he was about Ten Years old)
that were utterly estranged from God,
though they called Him Father, yet they
were His Children only by Creation,
and not by any likeness they had to God,
or interest in Him.

33. Thus he continued walking in the
ways of God, ingaged in reading, praying, hearing the Word of God, and Spiritual discourse, discovering thereby his
serious thoughts of Eternity.

34. He had an earnest desire if it
might be the Lords good pleasure, to
give himself up to the Lord in the work
of the Ministry, if he should live; and
this out of a dear love to Christ, and
Souls.

35. He was next to the Bible most,
taken with reading of Reverend Mr. *Bax-
ter's* works, especially his *Saints Everlasting Rest*; and truly, the thoughts of that
Rest, and Eternity, seemed to swallow up
all other thoughts; and he lived in a
constant preparation for it, and looked
more like one that was ripe for Glory,

than an inhabitant of this lower World.

36. When he was about Eleven years and Three quarters old, his Mothers house was visited with the Plague; his eldest Sister was the first that was visited with this distemper, and when they were praying for her, he would Sob and Weep bitterly.

37. As soon as he perceived that his Sister was Dead, he said, *The Will of the Lord be done: Blessed be the Lord.* Dear Mother, said he, you must do as *David* did, after the Child was Dead, he went and refreshed himself, and quietly submitted to the Will of God.

38. The rest of the Family held well for about Fourteen Days, which time he spent in Religious Duties, and preparing for his Death; but still his great Book was, *The Saints Rest;* which he read with exceeding curiosity, gathering many observations out of it in writing, for his own use. He wrote several Divine meditations of his own, upon several Subjects, but that which seemed most admirable, was a meditation upon the Excellency of Christ; he was never well but when he was more immediately engaged in the Service of God.

39. At Fourteen Days end, he was taken sick at which he seemed very Patient and Chearful; yet sometimes he would say that his Pain was great.

40. His Mother looking upon his Brother, shaked her head, at which he asked, if his Brother were marked; she answered, Yes Child; he asked again, whether he were marked; she answered nothing; well, says he, I know I shall be marked; I pray let me have Mr. *Baxters* Book, that I may read a little more of Eternity, before I go into it. His Mother told him that he was not able to read; he said that he was; however, then pray by me, and for me; his Mother answered, that she was

so full of grief, that she could not pray
now; but she desired to hear him pray
his last prayer.

41. His Mother asked him, whether
he were willing to Die, and leave her?
He answered, *Yes, I am willing to leave
you, and go to my Heavenly Father.* His
Mother answered, Child, if thou hadst
but an assurance of Gods Love, I should
not be so much troubled.

42.   He answered, & said to his Mother,
*I am assured, dear Mother, that my Sins are
Forgiven, and that I shall go to Heaven,* for
said he, *here stood an Angel by me, that told
me, I should quickly be in Glory.*

43. At this his Mother burst forth into tears. O Mother, said he, did you
but know what joy I feel, you would not
weep, but rejoyce. I tell you I am so
full of comfort, that I can't tell you how
I am; O Mother I shall presently have
my head in my Fathers bosome, and
shall be there, where the *Four and Twenty
Elders cast down their Crowns, and Sing
Hallelujah, Glory and Praise, to Him that
sits upon the Throne, & unto the Lamb for ever.*

44. Upon this, his Speech began to
fail him, but his Soul seemed still to be
taken up with Glory, and nothing now
grieved him but the sorrow that he saw
his Mother to be in for his Death; a
little to divert his Mother, he asked her,
What she had to Supper; but presently in
a kind of Divine Rapture, he Cryed out,
*O what Sweet Supper have I making ready for
me in Glory!*

45. But seeing all this did rather increase, than allay his Mother's grief, he
was more troubled, and asked her, what
she meant, thus to offend God; know you
not, that it is the Hand of the Almighty.
*Humble your self under the mighty hand of God,
Lay your self in the Dust, and kiss the Rod
of God, and let me see you do it, in token of
your submission to the Will of God, and bow
before Him.* Upon which, raising up him-

self a little, he gave a lowly bow, and
spake no more; but went Chearfully and
Triumphingly to rest, in the bosome of
J E S U S.

Hallelujah.

A Token, For The Children Of New-England.

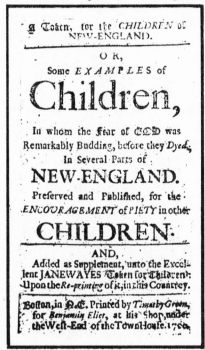

If the Children of *New-England*
should not with an *Early Piety*, set
themselves to *Know* and *Serve* the
Lord JESUS CHRIST, *the God
of their Fathers,* they will be Condemned, not only by the *Examples* of *Pious Children* in other parts of the world,
the Published and Printed Accounts whereof have been brought over hither; but
there have been *Exemplary Children* in the
midst of *New-England* it self, that will
Rise up against them for their Condemn-

ation. It would be a very profitable
thing to our *Children,* and highly Accep-
table to all the Godly *Parents* of the
Children, if, in Imitation of the Excellent
Janeway's, Token for Children, there
were made a true Collection of Notable
Things, Exemplified in the *Lives* and
Deaths of many among us, whose *Child-
hood* hath been Signalized for what is
Vertuous and Laudable.

No doubt, when the *Church-history*
of *New-England* comes abroad, there will
be found in it, the *Lives* of many, Eminent persons, among whose Eminencies,
not the least was, *Their fearing of the Lord
from their Youth,* and their being *Loved by
the Lord, when they were Children.*

But among the many other Instances,
of a *Child-hood and Youth* delivered from
Vanity, by Serious *Religion,* which *New-
England* has afforded, these few have particularly been preserved.

EXAMPLE I

LITTLE more than Thirteen years
old, was JOHN CLAP of *Scituate,* when he Dy'd; but it
might very Truly be said of him,
*That while he was yet Young, he began to seek
after the God of his Father.* From his very
Infancy he discovered a Singular Delight
in the Holy Scripture, whereby he was
made *Wise unto Salvation;* and he also
made himself yet further Amiable, by his
Obedience to his Parents, and his *Courtesy*
to all his Neighbours. As he grew up,
he signalized his Concern for Eternity,
not only by his diligent attendance upon
both Publick and Private *Cathechising,* but
also by the like attendance on the *Ministry*
of the Word, which he would Ponder
and Apply, and Confer about, with much
Discretion of Soul, and *Pray* for the Good
effect thereof upon his own Soul. Yea,

'twas even from his Childhood observable
in him, that ever after he began to speak
Reasonably, he would both affectionately
regard the *Family-Prayers*, and likewise,
both Morning and Evening, with a most
unwearied constancy recommend himself
by his own *Prayers* unto the Mercies of
God.

Arriving higher in his Age, he was
very Conscientious of his Duty, both
to God, and Man; and particularly careful of his Fathers *Business,* which now
became his own *Calling.* At Work with his
Father in the Field, he would frequently be
propounding of *Questions,* by the Answers
whereof he might be promoted in the
knowledge of God: and at the seasons
which others usually imploy to vain pur-
poses, he would be abounding in the exercises of Devotion. But of all the Imitable
things to be seen in him, he was exemplary for nothing more, than his endeavours
in *Preparation* for, and *Sanctification* of, the
Lords Day. Yea, his Parents have affirmed, that for a Year or two before he
Dy'd, *They never heard an Unprofitable Word
come out of his Mouth;* but he would often bewayl the Idle, Tryfling, Vain Dis-
courses of other People.

About a Year and a half before he
Dyed, the Good Spirit of God, Blessed
him, with yet a more thorow Conviction of his Misery by reason of *Sin* both *Original, & Actual:* whence tho he had been
such a *Pattern* of *Innocency,* yet he would aggravate his own *Sinfulness,* with Lamentati-
ons truly extraordinary. And for his Relief against the *Terrors* of God, wherewith
he was now *Distracted,* he was brought
unto an utter Despair of his own Righte-
ousnesses and Abilities; but in this Condition, he came to Adore the Grace of
God, offering a JESUS who is *Able to Save
unto the Uttermost*: In his Longings to
enjoy the Love of God, through *Jesus,*

he was like the *Hart panting after the Water-brooks!*

The Wounds of his *Spirit,* were accompanyed with a Languishing and Consuming of his *Flesh;* yet with great Patience he endured the Hand of God, & he followed the Lord with *Prayers,* with *Cries,* with *Tears,* for the manifestation of the Divine Love unto him.

It was also Observed and Admired, that when he was abroad at the Publick Worship, in the time of his Weakness, he would *stand* the whole time of the Long exercises, and be so affectionately attentive, that one might see every Sentence uttered in those Exercises, make some impression upon him. The best *Christians* in the place professed themselves, made ashamed by the Fervency of this *Young Disciple.* And in Days of Publick *Humiliations,* or *Thanksgivings,* kept with regard unto the general Circumstances of the Countrey, he would bear his part, with such sense of the Publick *Troubles* or *Mercies,* as argued more than a common measure of a Publick *Spirit* in him.

The Minister of the Place, visiting of him, after Sickness had confined him, found him, in an extreme dejection of Soul; his very Body Shook, through his Fear, lest the *Day of Grace* were over with him; yet justifying of God, though he should be forever cast among the Damned. But yet his *Fears* were accompanyed with *Hopes* in the Alsufficient merits of the Blessed *Jesus;* in which *Hopes* he continued using all the *Means of Grace,* according to his Capacity, and Lamenting after those whereof he was not Capable.

A Month before he Dy'd he kept his Bed; the *First Fortnight* whereof he was very Comfortless, and yet very *Patient;* abounding all this while in Gracious Admonitions unto other Young

People, that they would be concerned for
their own Eternal Salvation. And you
should not now have heard him complain,
that he wanted *Health* and *Ease*, though
he did *so;* but that he wanted *Faith,* and
Peace, and *Christ;* yet Expressing a pro-
found Submission to the Will of God.
But in the *Last Fortnight* of his Life, this
poor Child of God, had his weary Soul
more comfortably Satiated with the *Promises* of the *New-Covenant.* God filled
him with a marvellous Assurance of His
love, and so *Sealed* him with His own
Spirit, that he *Rejoyced with Joy Unspeakable and full of Glory.* He would often be
saying, *Whom have I in Heaven but thee?
and there is none on Earth, that I desire besides thee: My Flesh and my Heart faleth,
but God is the Strength of my Heart, and my
Portion for ever.* And, *I know that my
Redeemer Lives, and that He shall Stand at
the Latter Day upon the Earth.* And, *If
I Live, I shall Live unto the Lord; if I Dye
I shall Dy unto the Lord; and whether I Live
or Dy, I am the Lords.* And, *When Christ,
who is my Life, shall appear, then shall I also
appear with Him in Glory.* He would profess,
that his Communion with the Lord Jesus
Christ, was *Inexpressible*; and the Specta-
ters judg'd his Consolations, to be as
Great, as could be born, in a mortal Body.
Being now asked, *Whether the Thought of
Dying Troubled him not?* He replyed, *No,
Death is no Terror to me, because Christ has
taken away my Sin, which is the Sting of Death.*
But being asked, *Whether he was willing to
Live?* He answered, *I am willing to submit
unto the Will of God; but if God have ap-
pointed me to Life, I desire I may Live to His
Glory.* And being asked, Whether God
had put out of Doubt, his Interest in a
Dying and Rising *Jesus?* He returned,
*Yes; and God has fully answered my Desires;
I am now going to a thousand times better
World.* He told his Mother, *I Love you

as dearly as my own Life, yet I had rather Dy,
and be with Christ.

He continued *Six Days*, with his
Teeth so shut, as that they could not
be opened; and for the first *Three Days*
and Nights, he took no Sustenance; afterwards, though this but seldome, he
Sucked in between his Teeth, nothing
but a little *Cold Water:* in which Time,
they that Laid their Ears to his Lips
could over-hear him continually Expressing his Comfort in God. But just before
his Death, his Teeth were opened; when
he would often say, *Oh! how precious is*
the Blood of Christ, it is worth more than a
Thousand Worlds! and often pray, *Come,*
Lord Jesus, Come quickly! and at Last, he
gave up himself to God, in those words,
Lord Jesus, receive my Spirit. He desired
his Mother to turn his *Face unto the Wall;*
whereupon she said, *John, Dost thou now*
Remember Hezekiah's *Turning his Face unto*
the Wall? He said, *Yes, I do Remember it:*
and as she Turned him in her Arms, he
so quietly breathed his Soul into the Arms
of his Blessed Saviour.

[Extracted out of the Account, Written
and Printed, by Mr. *Witheril,* & Mr. *Baker,*
Ministers of *Scituate;* and Prefaced by
Mr. *Urian Oakes,* who takes that Occasion to say, of this *John Clap, He was a*
Young Old Man, full of Grace, though not
full of Dayes.]

EXAMPLE II

MR. THOMAS THORNTON, the aged and
faithful Pastor of *Yarmouth,* was
blessed with a Daughter, named *Priscilla,*
which at the Age of Eleven, left this
world, having first given demonstrations of
an Exemplary Piety.

She was one remarkably grave, devout,
serious,; very inquisitive about the mat-

ters of Eternity; and in her particular
Calling very diligent. She was nevertheless troubled with sore *Temptations* and
Exercises about the state of her own Soul:
the Anguish of her Spirit, about her *Body
of Death*, caused her to pour out many
tears and prayers; and she pressed, That
some other pious Children of her acquaintance, might with her keep a Day of Hu-
miliation together, *That* (as she expressed
it) *they might get power against their sinful
Natures.* But it pleased God at length to
bless the words of her Godly Mother, for
the quieting of her mind. It was her
singular Happiness, that she had such Godly Parents; but it was her Opinion and
Expression, *We trust too much to the Prayers
of our Parents, whereas we should Pray for our
selves.*

At last, she fell Mortally Sick. In the
beginning of her Sickness, she was afraid
of Dying; *For,* said she, *I know of no Promise to encourage me.* She could not but
own that she had in some measure walked
with God; yet she complain'd, *That she
had not found God meeting her in her Prayers,
and making her Heart willing to be at His
Dispose*; and that the *Pride* of her heart,
now lay as a *Load* upon it. She own'd,
That she had many Thoughts of Jesus
Christ, and that *it grieved her that she had
Sinned against Him, who had* Done & Dy'd
for her.

But many dayes were not past, before
she could profess her self *Willing to Dye*
with some Assurance of her then going to
Eternal Blessedness. Many Thanks and
Loves did she now render to one of her
Superiors, declaring, *'Twas because they
had curb'd her, and restrain'd her from sinful
vanities.* And she said, *Were I now to
choose my Company, it should be among the
People of God; I see plainly that they are
the only Company.* She was not without
her Conflicts in this time, wherein one of
her Speeches was, *Damnation, that is the*

worst thing of all, but Christ is of all the best;
I find it so; Christ is to me, Wisdom, Righte-
ousness, Sanctification, and Redemption. She
told her Father, she knew she was made
up of all manner of Sin; but said she, *I*
hope God has Humbled me, and Pardoned
me, in the Merits of the Lord Jesus Christ.
Unto her affectionate Mother she said,
Mother, why do you Weep, when I am well
in my Soul? Will you Mourn, when I am
so full of Joy? I pray Rejoyce with me.

When she was extreamly spent, she
said unto her Parent, *O my Father, I have*
been much troubled by Satan, but I find Christ
is too hard for him, and Sin, and all. She
now said, *I know now that I shall Dye;*
and being asked, Whether she were afraid
of Death; with a sweet smile she replied,
No, not I, Christ is better than Life!
And so she continued in a most joyful
frame, till she Dyed: a little before
which, it being the *Lords-day*, she asked,
What time of the day 'twas, and when
they told her, 'Twas Three of the Clock;
she replied, What? *Is the Sabbath almost*
done? Well, my Eternal Sabbath is going
to begin, wherein I shall enjoy all Felicity,
and sing Hallelujahs to all ETERNITY.
And hereupon she quickly fell asleep in
the Lord.

EXAMPLE III

MR. NATHANAEL MATHER,
dyed Oct. 17. 1688. at the Age of
Nineteen, an instance of more than common Learning and Vertue. On his Grave-
stone, at *Salem*, there are these words
deservedly inscribed, *The Ashes of an*
Hard-Student, a Good Scholar, and a
Great Christian.

He was one, who used an Extraordinary diligence, to obtain skill in the several *Arts*, that make an Accomplished
Scholar; but he was more diligent in his

Endeavours to become an Experienced
Christian.
He did with much Solemnity enter into Covenant with God, when he was
about Fourteen years old. And afterwards he Renewed that solemn Action, in
such a Form as this.

'I do Renounce all the *Vanities* and
Wretched Idols and Evil Courses of the
World.

'I do Choose, and will ever Have, the
Great God, for my Best Good, my
Last End, my Only Lord. He shall be
the Only One, in the Glorifying and
Enjoying of whom shall be my Welfare;
and in the Serving of whom shall be my
Work.

'I will ever be Rendring unto the Lord
Jesus Christ my proper Acknowledgments, as unto my Priest, my Prophet,
and my King; and the physician of my
Soul.

'I will ever be studying what is my Duty in these Things; and wherein I find
my self to fall short, I will ever count it
my Grief, and Shame; and betake my
self to the Blood of the Everlasting
Covenant.

'Now, Humbly Imploring the Grace
of the Mediator to be sufficient for me,
I do as a further Solemnity, hereunto
Subscribe my Name, with both Heart and
Hand.

Having done This, he did for the rest of
his Life, walk with much Watchfulness, &
Exactness.

One of the *Directories*, which he drew
up, for himself, was This.

'O that I might lead a *Spiritual Life!*
'Wherefore let me regulate my Life by
the *Word* of God and by such Scriptures
as these.

'1.   For regulating my *Thoughts, Jer.* 4.
14. *Isa.* 55-7. *Mal.* 3.17. *Psal.* 104.34.
Phil. 4.8. *Prov.* 23.26. *Deut.* 15-9. *Eccles.*

10.20. *Prov.* 24.9. *Mat.* 9.4. *Zech.* 8.17.

'2. For regulating my *Affections, Col.* 3.
2, 5. *Gal.* 5.24. For my *Delight, Psal.* 1.2.
Psal. 37.5. For my *Joy, Phil.* 4.4. *Psal.* 43.
4. My *Desire, Isa.* 26.8,9. *Ezek.* 17.16. My
Love, Mat. 22.37. *Psal.* 119.97. My *Ha-
tred, Psal.* 97.10. My *Fear, Luk.* 12.4,5.
My *Hope, Psal.* 39.7. My *Trust, Psal.* 62.18.
Isa. 26.4.

'3. For regulating my *Speech, Eph.* 4.29.
Col. 4.6. *Deut.* 6.6,7. *Psal.* 119.46.
Psal. 71. 8, 24. *Prov.* 31.26.

'4. For regulating my *Work, Tit.* 3.8.
2 *Tim.* 2.12. 1 *Tim.* 5.10. *Tit.* 2.14.
Mat 5.47. 1 *Tim.* 6.8. *Rev.* 3.2. *Rom.* 13.
12. *At.* 20.20.

Another of his *Directories* was found
into an *Hymn.*
'*Lord,* what shall I return unto
Him from whom all my mercies flow?

' (I.) To me to *Live,* it *Christ* shall be,
For all I do I'le do for *Thee.*

' (II.) My Question shall be oft beside,
How thou mayst most be Glorify'd?

' (III.) I will not any Creature Love;
But in the *Love* of Thee above.

' (IV.) Thy *Will* I will embrace for mine,
And every management of thine
Shall please me. (V.) A *Conformity*
To Thee shall be my *Aim* and *Eye.*

' (VI.) *Ejaculations* shall ascend
Not seldom from me. (VII.) I'le attend
Occasional Reflections, and
Turn all to *Gold* that comes to hand.

' (VIII.) And in particular among
My Cares, I'le try to make my *Tongue*
A Tree of Life, by speaking all
As be accountable who shall.

' (IX.) But *last,* nay *first* of all, I will
Thy *Son* my *Surety* make and still
Implore Him, that He would me bless
With *Strength* as well as *Righteousness.*

He would also keep *whole Days of Prayer,*
and *Praise,* by himself: And he would set

himself to Consider much on that Question,
What shall I do for God?

He was much in *Meditation*, and often
wrote the chief Heads of his *Meditation*.
He would Read the Scripture, with a *Note*,
and a *Wish* fetched out of every verse.
And at Night, he would ask.

I. *What has Gods mercy to me been this day?*

II. *What has my Carriage to God been this
day?*

III. *If I Dy this night, is my Immortal
Spirit safe?*

Many more such imitable things, are in
the History of his Life: (Diverse times
Printed at *London*,) reported of him.

EXAMPLE IV

Ann Greenough, the Daughter
of Mr. *William Greenough*, left the
world, when she was but about five years
old, and yet gave astonishing Discoveries
of a Regard unto God and Christ, and her
own Soul, before she went away. When she
heard any thing about the Lord *Jesus Christ*,
she would be strangely transported, and
ravished in her Spirit at it; and had an
unspeakable Delight in *Cathechising*. She
would put strange *Questions* about Eternal things, and make *Answers* her self
that were extreamly pertinent. Once
particluarly, she asked, *Are not we dead in
Sin?* and presently added, *But I will take
this way, the Lord Jesus Christ shall make
me alive.* She was very frequent and constant in *Secret prayer*, and could not with
any patience be interrupted in it. She
told her Gracious Mother, *That she there
prayed for her!* And was covetous of being
with her Mother, when she imagined such
Duties to be going forward. When she
fell sick at last of a Consumption, she would
not by any sports be diverted from the

Thoughts of *Death*, wherein she took such
pleasure, that she did not care to hear of
any thing else. And if she were asked,
Whether she were willing to Dye? She would
still chearfully Reply, *Ay, by all means,*
that I may go the Lord Jesus Christ.

EXAMPLE V

A<small>T</small> B<small>OSTON</small>, *12d. 3m.* 1694. there
dyed one DANIEL WILLIAMS,
in the Eighteenth year of his Age.

There was a Collection made of some
of his Dying Speeches.

Being asked, *Whether he Loved God?*
He replied, *Yes, I Love Him dearly; for,*
Lord, whom have I in Heaven, but thee?

He said, 'God has promised, *They that*
seek Him Early shall find Him: Ever since
I was a Child, I Dedicated my self to
seek and serve the Lord. Though I have
not had so much Time, as some others,
yet that little Time which I had, I spent
in waiting on, and wrestling with, God by
prayer: and I said, *I will not let thee go,*
till thou hast blessed me.

Seeing some of his Relations weep, he
said, *why do you Cry, when I am ready to*
Sing for Joy?

They saying, They knew not how to
part with him, he replyed, *Why? Are you*
not willing I should go to my Heavenly Father?
I shall quickly be with my Heavenly Father,
& with His Holy Angels, where they are singing
of Hallelujahs. Its better being there than
here. When I am there, I shan't wish my
self here, in this Troublesome world again.
I have a desire to depart, and to be with
Christ, which is best of all.

He was much Concerned for poor pe-
rishing Souls. He would say, 'Oh, that
I had but Strength! How would I Pray,
and Sigh, and Cry to God, for the
poor world, that lives in Sin and Pride!

He Expressed himself, most pathetically
to his Relations, when he took his leave
of them.

At last, he asked, *What Angel that was,
that he saw before him? well,* said he, *I shall
quickly be with him: Come, Lord Jesus, come
quickly!*

A Friend asking him how he did, he
said, *'I am one bound for Heaven.* I would
not have you pray for my Life; I am
afraid you do!

On the day of his Death, being full
of Pain, he said, 'Jesus Christ bore more
than this, and He Dyed for me; and
shall I be afraid to Dy, and go to Him:
No, I am not.

Then said he, *O Death where is thy Sting?
O Grave where is thy Victory?*

EXAMPLE VI

An Extract of a Letter from Southold, *23 d. 4 m. 1698.*

I HAVE BEEN REQUESTED, to give you
this Account, from the Parents of a
Gracious Child, who in all her Life did
comport her self, to walk in the Lords
Holy Fear, and gave a great Attention
in Hearing the Word of God, and the
Lord was pleased to ripen her for Himself, though she was but fifteen years,
and four months old. Though she was
Young, it pleased the Lord, to put a
great fear and awe upon her Heart, of
breaking the *fifth Commandment.* And
when she was under the Dispensation of
God in Sickness, it pleased the Lord for
to endue her with patience, to be willing
to bear His Hand, with all meekness.
She Confessed herself to be a great Sinner,
and to have sinned against a Gracious
God But the Lord vouchsafed her a
strong Faith, to Believe, that He is a

merciful God, & willing to Forgive Sins,
and that He had Forgiven her Sins, in the
Blood of our Blessed Saviour Jesus Christ.
And, therefore she was very willing to
leave the world, and her Father and
Mother, having Faith, that she was *going to Christ*. These were her own Expressions. When her Mother did ask
her, if she was *willing to Dy*, for she was
too young to Dy : She sometime before
she dyed, said, she was not *fit to Dye*,
but prayed unto the Lord, that He would
please to *fit* her & *make* her, willing to Dy.
Oh, said she, *Death comes unawares, it comes
like a Thief in the Night!* The Lord granted
her desire: For afterwards, when her
Mother asked her, *My Child are you willing to Dy?* Her answer was, That now
she was *willing* to Dy, and to leave a
thousand worlds, and Father and Mother,
and all to go to Christ. She desired, That
the *Curtains* might be drawn, that the
light of this world might not deprive her
from beholding the Brightness and the
Glory of the other World. And when
she see her Father and Mother weeping
for her, she said, *My dear Father and
Mother, don't mourn for me; you might
well mourn for me, if I were to go into
utter Darkness; but I am going to God in
Heaven. I long to be in the New Jerusalem, with the Lord Jesus Christ: And
now I can Dye.* And lying a while in an
Agony, when she came out of that Agony, she said, *Mother, did you not hear
me Sing? I thought, I was in Heaven with
the Lord Jesus Christ, & my Grand-Parents,
and the Holy Angels, and heard such melodious Praises of God, as I never heard; and
I was very sorry that I could not Sing like
them.* She said unto her Relations, *Oh,
don't set your Hearts upon the world, nor
look for the Honours and Riches of this
world, but seek first the Kingdom of Heaven!*

She would call upon her Father to go to
Prayer at the Evening, and say, *I cannot,
I dare not go to sleep without it.* She
wished, That some Young People might
come to her, to put 'em in mind, to
Consider their Latter End, and leave off
their Pride. There came a Young maid
to see her, and she said to her, with
Tears in her Eyes, That she should not
follow the Fashions of the world, and not
put off Repentance to a sick-bed. Yea,
she spake to all them that were about
her, *That they would not mind this world,
but the other World.* Her Mother asked
her, If she was not afraid to ly in the
Dust? But she was not thoughtful, what
should become of her *Body,* believing her
Soul should go to God. *Mother,* said she,
*I could not Sing here, but now I am going
to Sing the Praises of God in Heaven.*
Looking on her Father, she said, *Oh,
Father, there is no God like our God, for
He is a God Pardoning Iniquity, Transgressi-
on, and Sin.* She said, *I wonder how you
do, to love to live in such a Troublesome,
Evil, and Sinful world: Don't you see how
the Judgments of God, are all over the Earth.*
She often Cried out, *O Lord Jesus, Come:
Let thine Angels come, and carry me to the
Bosome of Abraham!*

This is a true Relation of this Graci-
ous Flower of the Lord Jesus Christ.
She was an only Child; her Name was
Bethiah, the Daughter of *Thomas* and
Mary, Longworth.

'The Lord raise up your Heart, to
declare His wonderful mercies, in working so Graciously upon the Heart of such
a young Flower; that the Lord may raise
up more such Gracious Souls, in our Rising Generation.

I remain, your affectionate Brother.
I. S.

EXAMPLE VII

A Notable passage, transcribed from the
Life *of Mr.* John Baily, *as it was Related
in a Sermon Preached on the Day of his Funeral,
at* Boston, N.E. 16.d. 10.m. 1697.
By Mr. Cotton Mather; *and afterwards Printed.*

FROM A CHILD *he did know the Holy Scrip-tures*: Yea, *From a Child he was wise
unto Salvation.* In his very *Childhood* he
discovered the *Fear of God,* upon his young
Heart, and Prayer to God, was one of his
Early Exercises.

There was one very Remarkable effect
of it. His *Father* was a man of a very Li-centious Conversation; a Gamester, a
Dancer, a very Lewd Company-keeper.
The Mother of this *Elect-Vessel,* one day
took him, while he was yet a *Child,* and
calling the Family together, made him to
Pray with them. His *Father* coming to
understand, at what a rate the *Child* had
Pray'd with his Family, it smote the Soul
of him, with a great Conviction, & proved
the Beginning of his Conversion unto God.
God left not off work on his Heart,
until he proved One of the most *Eminent
Christians* in all that Neighbour-hood.
So he *Lived,* so he *Dyed;* a man of more
than Ordinary Piety. And it was his
manner sometimes to Retire unto those
very places of his Lewdnesses, where,
having that his little Son in his Company,
he would pour out Floods of Tears, in
Repenting Prayers before the Lord.

Some Scriptural Hymns For Children.

[I.] Little Children
Brought unto the Lord JESUS CHRIST.
On Mat. XIX. 14.

WHEN LITTLE CHILDREN once were brought
To our most Gracious Lord,

Them that Oppos'd, He better Taught,
    By this most precious Word:

'*Suffer* Your *Little Children*, so,
    '*Forbid* them not, I say,
'*Their* Saviour to *come* unto;
    'I'm *He*, and *come* they may.

'Acknowledge me a mighty *King*
    'That *Heavenly Graces* give,
'*Infants* to me for *Subjects* bring;
    'My *Heaven* does *them* receive.'

Thus does our Blessed *Shepherd* call,
    Our *Lambs* into His *Fold:*
Lord pour thy *Blessings* on them all.
    Blessings richer than Gold.

Oh! What a Glorious *Grace* is This,
    Which God through Christ will grant,
That HE *ours* and *our Childrens* is,
    In His Best *Covenant.*

[II.] Early Religion
King. XVIII.12.

O That while I am *Young* I might
    Fear the most Glorious One;
And not my Great *Redeemer* Slight:
    Thine, Lord, I'm THINE *alone.*
        2 *Chron.* 34. 3.
May I while I am very *Young,*
    Seek unto God by *Prayer:*
And those *Lov'd* Ones be found among
    That *Early Seekers are:*
        Psal. 119.9.
May I, while I am *Young,* give Heed
    Unto thy *Holy* Word;
Call'd, there to *Cleanse* my wayes with Speed,
    By the most *Holy Lord.*
        2 Joh. 4.
Though I am yet a *Child,* I wou'd
    In my most Forward *Youth,*
Walk, by the conduct of my God,
    In the *pure* paths of *Truth.*
        2 *Tim.* 2. 22.
Those *Lusts* that *Youthful* are, to me
    May they most *Hateful* prove;

And may the *Laws* of JESUS be
   My Sweetest Joy and Love.
      Eccl. 12. 1.
Lord, THEE, my Maker, *Thee,* To-Day,
   God, *Father, Son,* and *Spirit,*
I would *Remember,* that I may
   Eternal Life Inherit.

[III.] The Consent of the Believer
unto the Ten Commandments.

LORD, I should have no *Lord,* beside
   Thee, to be Lov'd, Serv'd, *Glorify'd.*
I should the *Glory* due to Thee,
In *Wayes,* pay, that *Appointed* be.

Thy *Names,* Thy *Words,* Thy *Works,* I should,
Sacred for *proper Uses,* hold
The *Dayes* which thou made *Sacred* hast,
I should not in *Diversions* wast.

In their *Fit places,* every one,
I should with all *Fit Honours* own.
That *Life* none may unjustly Loose,
Means I should with all kindness use.

Chast I should be in every *part,*
Yea, *Chast* in every *Thought* of Heart.
To *Get* and *Keep* my Worldly *Wealth,*
I should commit no sort of *Stealth.*

Truth I should utter, and *maintain,*
And no *Good Name* with *Slander* stain.
With sweet *Content* I should Receive
All the *Wise God* will please to give.

Lord, By the *Blood of* CHRIST, I pray,
Save me, who do not thus obey;
And by the *Strength* of CHRIST, fromhence,
Sav'd, Let me yield Obedience.

[IV.] The Lords Prayer.

OUR *Father,* in the Heavenly Throne,
   Inclin'd from thence to Help us all,
Tiny *Children* thus upon Thee Call.
For the Sake of thy Blessed *Son.*

We would thy Ever-glorious *Name,*
As *Holy,* with Great Fear Adore:
And with that All may in the same,
Thy *Holy One Praise* Evermore.

May thy Just *Kingdom Come,* we Pray;
That thou art *the Worlds King,* we know:
But, Oh! bring on that Happy Day,
When all *the World* shall own Thee so.

May we thy Righteous *Will* approve,
And it all Things commanding see,
As it in the *New Heaven* above,
And the *New Earth* below, shall be

Lord, Give us a *Convenient Food;*
What may be *Such,* to *Thee* we leave,
And let us not want *any Good;*
All we Rely on *Thee* to give.

Our *Faults,* by which we are in *Debt*
To Thy dread Justice, Lord, Release:
Christ Payes our *Debt;* And we Forget,
For *this,* our Neighbours Injuries.

We're Frail; Us from Temptation Save;
Sins, Oh! *Sins,* The *worst Evils* are:
Us Let not *Evil Tempters* have,
And hold in any Sinful *Snare.*

Thou hast the *Rule* of All; A Word
Of thine can *Do* All: To Thee then
All *Honour's* due: We Shout, O Lord,
AMEN, in *Faith* of thy, AMEN!

[V.] The Lords-Day.
On Rev. I 10.

THIS is the *Day of Rest,* whereon
  Our Lord *Rose* from the Dead;
The Price of mans *Redemption,*
  This Day was fully paid.

This is to us, the *Joyful Day,*
  Which our *Lord* made His *own,*

By His most *Wonderful* Display
    Of *Pow'r* and *Grace* thereon.

The *Jewish Sabbath* Laid *Asleep*
    With our *Lord* under Earth,
Directs us Now *This Day* to keep
    Of our Lords *Second Birth*.

This is the *Day*, our *Lord* now chose
    Thereon still to *Appear;*
The *Day*, for Him *preferr'd* by Those
    That His *Apostles* were.

It is Declar'd, *The Lords-Day*, Now,
    Holy unto the *Lord*
It will no *Worldly Thought* allow,
    No Worldly *Work* or *Word*.

Now, *Lord*, on this *Thy Day*, dispence,
    Thy *Spirit* unto me:
And by thy *Spirits* Influence
    Let me now *Acted* be.

This Day, Oh! *Spirit*, from on High,
    Make thou a *Mean* and *Sign*,
Of that *Great Sabbatism*, when I
    Shall in thy *Glory* shine!

[VI.]   Prayer Encouraged.
Matth. 7.7.—11. with *Luk.* 11.9.13.

THAT Lord. on whose Account alone
    Our *Pray'rs* prevail with God,
Bids us Address that Glorious One,
    With *Prayers* For Ev'ry Good.

Ask now, and ye shall *have,* (Saith He)
    '*Seek* now, and ye *shall find.*
Heav'ns Doors, at which you *Knocking* be.
    Shall *Open* to your Mind.

What *Father*, to a *Sons* Request
    For *Bread* or *Fish*, will throw
A *Stone* or *Snake?* His very best
    He'l on a *Son* bestow.

God is your *Better Father;* You
   In me, *His Children* are;
You'l Gain, with His *Good Spirit* now.
   All Good Things else, by Pray'r.

Job. 16.23.

Children, Then to the *Father* Go;
   Go, in my Name, I say:
Rich *Blessings* He will give unto
   Them, in that Name, who *Pray.*

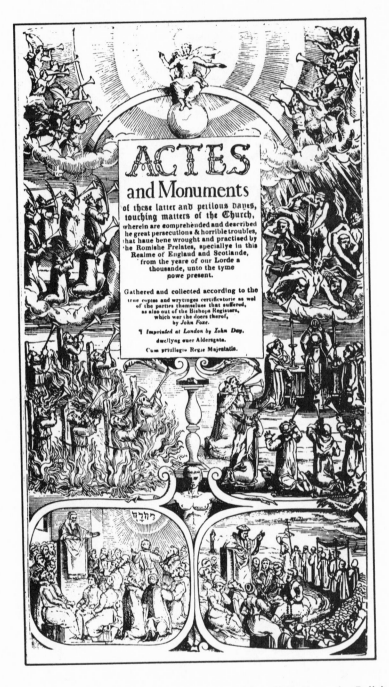

Reduced copy of the title page of the first English Edition, 1563. From the Religious Tract Society Edition (London, 1877), Volume I, p. 34.

Actes and Monuments
of the Church
(Book of Martyrs)
By JOHN FOXE

SELECTIONS

ALONG WITH TALES *of the persecutions for their faith of early saints, John Foxe (1517–1587) gave an account of the persecutions of Protestants during the reign of Queen Mary (1553–1558). At that time, alternate persecutions of Protestants or Catholics were common, depending on the faith of the ruler. These horrifying stories caught the public imagination. Copies appeared in homes along with the Bible, and even small churches had copies. More terrible than those in any television show except the live telecasts of battles and bombings of civilians, the accounts were familiar to children in the seventeenth century. (See Bibliography, p. 346). They are believed to have been influential in bringing on revolutions in seventeenth-century England. Such horror, depicted either in prose or on the screen, has an effect on the human psyche.*

The excerpts printed here are from the fourth edition of Foxe's book published in London in 1877 in eight volumes by The Religious Tract Society. The Lady Jane excerpt is from Vol. 6, pp. 423–24. The Dr. Ridley and Master Latimer excerpt is from Vol. 7, pp. 541–547. The text in each case parallels that of the 1563 edition.

The Words And Behaviour Of
The Lady Jane Upon The Scaffold.

THESE ARE THE words that the lady Jane spake upon the scaffold, at the hour of her death. First, when she mounted upon the scaffold, she said to the people standing thereabout, "Good people, I am come hither to die, and by a law I am condemned to the same. The fact against the queen's highness was unlawful, and the consenting thereunto by me: but, touching the procurement and desire thereof by me, or on my behalf, I do wash my hands thereof in innocency before God, and the face of you, good christian people, this day:" and therewith she wrung her hands, wherein she had her book. Then said she, "I pray you all, good christian people, to bear me witness that I die a true christian woman, and that I do look to be saved by no other mean, but only by the mercy of God, in the blood

Mary.

A. D.
1554.

of his only Son Jesus Christ: and I confess, that when I did know the word of God, I neglected the same, loved myself and the world; and therefore this plague and punishment is happily and worthily happened unto me for my sins; and yet I thank God, that of his goodness he hath thus given me a time and respite to repent. And now, good people, while I am alive, I pray you assist me with your prayers." And then, kneeling down, she turned her to Fecknam, saying: "Shall I say this psalm?" And he said, "Yea." Then said she the psalm of "Miserere mei Deus" in English, in most devout manner, throughout to the end; and then she stood up, and gave her maiden, mistress Ellen, her gloves and handkerchief, and her book to master Bruges. And then she untied her gown, and the hangman pressed upon her to help her off with it; but she, desiring him to let her alone, turned towards her two gentlewomen, who helped her off therewith, and also with her frowes paste and neckerchief, giving to her a fair handkerchief to knit about her eyes.

Then the hangman kneeled down and asked her forgiveness, whom she forgave most willingly. Then he willed her to stand upon the straw; which doing, she saw the block. Then she said, "I pray you dispatch me quickly." Then she kneeled down, saying, "Will you take it off, before I lay me down?" And the hangman said, "No, madam." Then tied she the handkerchief about her eyes, and feeling for the block, she said, "What shall I do? Where is it? Where is it?" One of the standers-by guiding her thereunto she laid her head down upon the block, and then stretched forth her body, and said, "Lord, into thy hands I commend my spirit;" and so finished her life, in the year of our Lord God 1554, the 12th day of February.

The Behaviour Of Dr. Ridley And Master Latimer, At The Time Of Their Death, Which Was The 16th Of October, 1555.

UPON THE NORTH-SIDE of the town, in the ditch over against Balliol-college,[1] the place of execution was appointed: and for fear of any tumult that might arise, to let the burning of them, the lord Williams was commanded, by the queen's letters, and the householders of the city, to be there assistant, sufficiently appointed. And when every thing was in a readiness, the prisoners were brought forth by the mayor and the bailiffs.

Master Ridley had a fair black gown furred, and faced with foins, such as he was wont to wear being bishop, and a tippet of velvet furred[2] likewise about his neck, a velvet night-cap upon his head, and a corner cap upon the same, going in a pair of slippers to the stake, and going between the mayor and an alderman, etc.

After him came master Latimer in a poor Bristol frieze frock all worn, with his buttoned cap, and a kerchief on his head, all ready to the fire, a new long shroud hanging over his hose, down to the feet: which at the first sight stirred men's hearts to rue upon them, beholding on the one side, the honour they sometime had, and on the other, the calamity whereunto they were fallen.

Ridley
and Lati-
mer
brought
together
to the
stake.

Master doctor Ridley, as he passed toward Bocardo, looked up where master Cranmer did lie, hoping belike to have seen him at the glass-window, and to have spoken unto him. But then master Cranmer was busy with friar Soto and his fellows, disputing together, so that he could not see him, through that occasion. Then master Ridley, looking back, espied master Latimer coming after,

Beha-
viour of
Ridley
and Lati-
mer at
the stake.

unto whom he said, "Oh, be ye there?" "Yea," said master Latimer, "have after as fast as I can follow." So he, following a pretty way off, at length they came both to the stake, the one after the other, where first Dr. Ridley entering the place, marvellous earnestly holding up both his hands, looked towards heaven. Then shortly after espying master Latimer, with a wondrous cheerful look he ran to him, embraced, and kissed him; and, as they that stood near reported, comforted him, saying, "Be of good heart, brother, for God will either assuage the fury of the flame, or else strengthen us to abide it."

With that went he to the stake, kneeled down by it, kissed it, and most effectuously prayed, and behind him master Latimer kneeled, as earnestly calling upon God as he. After they arose, the one talked with the other a little while, till they which were appointed to see the execution, removed themselves out of the sun. What they said I can learn of no man.

Dr. Smith
preaching
at the
burning
of Ridley
and Lati-
mer.

Then Dr. Smith, of whose recantation in king Edward's time ye heard before, began his sermon to them upon this text of St. Paul, "If I yield my body to the fire to be burnt, and have not charity, I shall gain nothing thereby."[1] Wherein he alleged that the goodness of the cause, and not the order of death, maketh the holiness of the person; which he confirmed by the examples of Judas, and of a woman in Oxford that of late hanged herself, for that they, and such like as he recited, might then be adjudged righteous, which desperately sundered their lives from their bodies, as he feared that those men that stood before him would

Dr. Smith
raileth
against
the mar-
tyrs.

do. But he cried still to the people to beware of them, for they were heretics, and died out of the church. And on the other side, he declared their diversity in opinions, as Lutherans, Œcolampadians, Zuinglians, of which sect they were, he said, and that was the worst: but the old church of Christ, and the catholic

Christ's
congrega-
tion bur-
dened
with di-
versity of
opinions.

faith believed far otherwise. At which place they lifted up both their hands and eyes to heaven, as it were calling God to witness of the truth: the which countenance they made in many other places of his sermon, where as they thought he spake amiss. He ended with a very short exhortation to them to recant, and come home again to the church, and save their lives and souls, which else were condemned. His sermon was scant; in all, a quarter of an hour.

Dr. Ridley said to master Latimer, "Will you begin to answer the sermon, or shall I?" Master Latimer said, "Begin you first, I pray you." "I will," said master Ridley.

Then, the wicked sermon being ended, Dr. Ridley and master Latimer kneeled down upon their knees towards my lord Williams of Thame, the vice-chancellor

Mary.

A. D.
1555.

of Oxford, and divers other commissioners appointed for that purpose, who sat upon a form thereby; unto whom master Ridley said, "I beseech you, my lord, even for Christ's sake, that I may speak but two or three words." And whilst my lord bent his head to the mayor and vice-chancellor, to know (as it appeared) whether he might give him leave to speak, the bailiffs and Dr. Marshall, vice-chancellor, ran hastily unto him, and with their hands stopped his mouth, and said, "Master Ridley, if you will revoke your erroneous opinions, and recant the same, you shall not only have liberty so to do, but also the benefit of a subject; that is, have your life." "Not otherwise?" said master Ridley. "No," quoth Dr. Marshal. "Therefore if you will not so do, then there is no remedy but you must suffer for your deserts." "Well," quoth master Ridley, "so long as the breath is in my body, I will never deny my Lord Christ, and his known truth: God's will be done in me!" And with that he rose up, and said with a loud voice, "Well then, I commit our cause to Almighty God, which shall indifferently judge all." To whose saying, master Latimer added his old posy, "Well! there is nothing hid but it shall be opened." And he said, he could answer Smith well enough, if he might be suffered.

Incontinently they were commanded to make them ready, which they with all meekness obeyed. Master Ridley took his gown and his tippet,[1] and gave it to his brother-in-law master Shipside, who all his time of imprisonment, although he might not be suffered to come to him, lay there at his own charges to provide him necessaries, which from time to time he sent him by the serjeant that kept him. Some other of his apparel that was little worth, he gave away; other the bailiffs took.

He gave away besides, divers other small things to gentlemen standing by, and divers of them pitifully weeping, as to sir Henry Lea he gave a new groat; and to divers of my lord Williams's gentlemen some napkins, some nutmegs, and rases of ginger; his dial, and such other things as he had about him, to every one that stood next him. Some plucked the points off his hose. Happy was he that might get any rag of him.

Master Latimer gave nothing, but very quietly suffered his keeper to pull off his hose, and his other array, which to look unto was very simple: and being stripped into his shroud, he seemed as comely a person to them that were there present, as one should lightly see; and whereas in his clothes he appeared a withered and crooked silly old man, he now stood bolt upright, as comely a father as one might lightly behold.

Then master Ridley, standing as yet in his truss, said to his brother, "It were best for me to go in my truss still." "No," quoth his brother, "it will put you to more pain: and the truss will do a poor man good." Whereunto master Ridley said, "Be it, in the name of God;" and so unlaced himself. Then, being in his shirt, he stood upon the foresaid stone, and held up his hand and said, "O heavenly Father, I give unto thee most hearty thanks, for that thou hast called me to be a professor of thee, even unto death. I beseech thee, Lord God, take mercy upon this realm of England, and deliver the same from all her enemies."

Then the smith took a chain of iron, and brought the same about both Dr.

Ridley ready to answer Smith's sermon, but not suffered. Marshal, vice-chancellor of Oxford, stoppeth Ridley.

Ridley committeth his cause to God. Latimer's words when he could not be suffered to answer Dr. Smith.

Ridley giveth away his apparel and other gifts to the people.

Latimer at the stake in his shirt.

Ridley thanketh God for his martyrdom, and prayeth for England.

Mary.

A. D.
1555.

Gunpow-
der given
to the
martyrs.

Ridley's, and master Latimer's middles: and, as he was knocking in a staple, Dr. Ridley took the chain in his hand, and shaked the same, for it did gird in his belly, and looking aside to the smith, said, "Good fellow, knock it in hard, for the flesh will have his course." Then his brother did bring him gunpowder in a bag, and would have tied the same about his neck. Master Ridley asked, what it was. His brother said, "Gunpowder." "Then," said he, "I take it to be sent of God; therefore I will receive it as sent of him. And have you any," said he, "for my brother;" meaning master Latimer. "Yea sir, that I have," quoth his brother. "Then give it unto him," said he, "betime; lest ye come too late." So his brother went, and carried of the same gunpowder unto master Latimer.

Ridley's
suit to the
lord of
Thame,
for leases
of poor
men.

Bonner
taketh
away the
leases
from poor
men,
granted
before by
Ridley.

In the mean time Dr. Ridley spake unto my lord Williams, and said, "My lord, I must be a suitor unto your lordship in the behalf of divers poor men, and especially in the cause of my poor sister: I have made a supplication to the queen's majesty in their behalfs. I beseech your lordship for Christ's sake, to be a mean to her grace for them. My brother here hath the supplication, and will resort to your lordship to certify you hereof. There is nothing in all the world that troubleth my conscience, I praise God, this only excepted. Whilst I was in the see of London, divers poor men took leases of me, and agreed with me for the same. Now I hear say the bishop that now occupieth the same room, will not allow my grants unto them made, but, contrary unto all law and conscience, hath taken from them their livings, and will not suffer them to enjoy the same. I beseech you, my lord, be a mean for them: you shall do a good deed, and God will reward you."

The
church
lightened
by the
martyr-
dom of
saints.

Then they brought a faggot, kindled with fire, and laid the same down at Dr. Ridley's feet. To whom master Latimer spake in this manner: "Be of good comfort, master Ridley, and play the man. We shall this day light such a candle, by God's grace, in England, as I trust shall never be put out."

And so the fire being given unto them, when Dr. Ridley saw the fire flaming up towards him, he cried with a wonderful loud voice, "In manus tuas, Domine, commendo spiritum meum: Domine recipe spiritum meum." And after, repeated this latter part often in English, "Lord, Lord, receive my spirit;" master Latimer

Latimer's
prayer
and mar-
tyrdom.

crying as vehemently on the other side, "O Father of heaven, receive my soul!" who received the flame as it were embracing of it. After that he had stroked his face with his hands, and as it were bathed them a little in the fire, he soon died (as it appeareth) with very little pain or none. And thus much concerning the end of this old and blessed servant of God, master Latimer, for whose laborious travails, fruitful life, and constant death, the whole realm hath cause to give great thanks to Almighty God.

Mary.

A. D.
1555.

But master Ridley, by reason of the evil making of the fire unto him, because the wooden faggots were laid about the gorse, and over-high built, the fire burned first beneath, being kept down by the wood; which when he felt, he desired them for Christ's sake to let the fire come unto him. Which when his brother-in-law heard, but not well understood, intending to rid him out of his pain (for the which cause he gave attendance), as one in such sorrow not well advised what he did, heaped faggots upon him, so that he clean covered him, which made

Ridley long in burning.

the fire more vehement beneath, that it burned clean all his nether parts, before it once touched the upper; and that made him leap up and down under the faggots, and often desire them to let the fire come unto him, saying, "I cannot burn." Which indeed appeared well; for, after his legs were consumed by reason of his struggling through the pain (whereof he had no release, but only his contentation in God), he showed that side toward us clean, shirt and all untouched with flame. Yet in all this torment he forgot not to call unto God still, having in his mouth, "Lord have mercy upon me," intermingling his cry, "Let the fire come unto me, I cannot burn." In which pangs he laboured till one of the standers by with his bill pulled off the faggots above, and where he saw the fire

The death and martyrdom of Ridley.

flame up, he wrested himself unto that side. And when the flame touched the gunpowder, he was seen to stir no more, but burned on the other side, falling down at master Latimer's feet; which, some said, happened by reason that the chain loosed; others said, that he fell over the chain by reason of the poise of his body, and the weakness of the nether limbs.

This illustration appears opposite p. 550 in Volume VII of the Religious Tract Society Edition of 1877. The illustration is identical to that used in the 1563 edition.

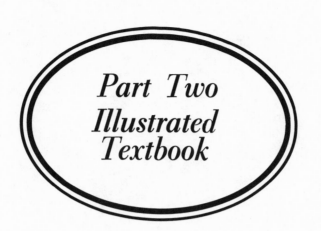

Part Two
Illustrated
Textbook

5

Orbis Pictus
By JOHN AMOS COMENIUS

SELECTIONS

COMENIUS WAS A *Czech priest of the seventeenth century whose aim of attaining more knowledge of this world was influenced by the ideas of Francis Bacon. He felt that the sense experience of children should be guided—that they should be enticed into learning in a practical way. Thus, in his* Orbis Pictus, *he depicts plays and various games including tennis. Because he realistically portrayed in words and pictures the life of his time so that it could be seen, felt, heard, smelled, and tasted almost from the printed page, the book he produced is a lively but concentrated one in which pictures serve as lessons in themselves and also as symbols for concepts. It appealed, and still appeals, both to children and to adults. An edition appeared in German in Nuremberg in 1658 and was translated into English and printed in London the following year. The work also serves as a vocabulary book, with words in English on the left and Latin on the right. It was reprinted many times in the seventeenth, eighteenth, and on into the nineteenth century, the first American edition appearing in 1810.*

The pictures and text reproduced here are from the 1968 Oxford University Press facsimile of the first English edition of 1659.

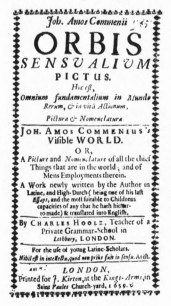

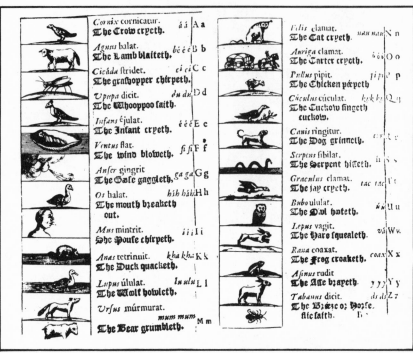

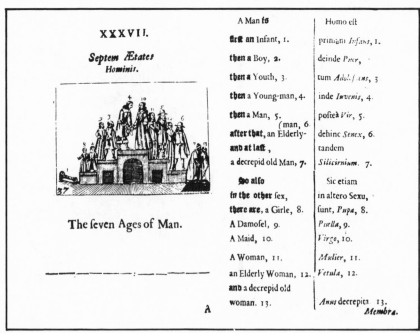

XXXVI J.

Septem Ætates
Hominis.

The seven Ages of Man.

A Man is	Homo eſt
firſt an Infant, 1.	primùm *Infans*, 1.
then a Boy, 2.	deinde *Puer*,
then a Youth, 3.	tum *Adoleſcens*, 3
then a Young-man, 4.	inde *Iuvenis*, 4.
then a Man, 5.	poſteà *Vir*, 5.
after that, an Elderly-(man, 6.	dehinc *Senex*, 6.
and at laſt,	tandem
a decrepid old Man, 7.	*Silicirnium*. 7.
So alſo	Sic etiam
in the other ſex,	in altero Sexu,
there are, a Girle, 8.	ſunt, *Pupa*, 8.
A Damoſel, 9.	*Psella*, 9.
A Maid, 10.	*Virgo*, 10.
A Woman, 11.	*Mulier*, 11.
an Elderly Woman, 12.	*Vetula*, 12.
and a decrepid old woman. 13.	*Anus* decrepita 13.

A

Membra.

CXXIX.

Sepultura.

A Buriall.

Dead Folks (**burned,**
heretofore were
and their ashes
put into
an Urn 1.
We enclose
our dead Folks,
in a Coffin 2.
lay them up a Bier, 3.
and see they be carried
out in a Funeral-pomp
towards ẙ Church-
where they are (yard, 4.
laid into the Grave, 6.
by the Bearers 5.
and are interred ;
this is covered
with a Grave-stone 7.
and is adorned
with Tombs, 8.
and Epitaphs 9.
As the Corps
go along,
Psalms **are sung,**
and the Bells
are rung. 10.

Defuncti
olim cremabantur,
& Cineres
in *Urnâ* 1.
recondebantur.
Nos includimus
nostros *demortuos,*
Loculo (*Capulo*) 2.
imponimus *Feretro,* 3.
& efferri curamus
Pompâ funebri
versus *Cœmeterium,* 4.
ubi
à *Vespillonibus* 5.
inferuntur *Sepulchro,* 6.
& humantur ;
hoc *Cippo* 7.
tegitur,
& *Monumentis* 8
ac *Epitaphiis* 9.
ornatur.
Funere
prodeunte,
cantantur *Hymni,*
& *Campana* 10.
pulsantur.

Dead

S 4   *Ludus*

CXXXI.

Præstigiæ.

Sleights.

The Tumbler 1.
maketh
several Showes,
by the nimbleness
of his body,
walking to and fro
on his hands,
leaping thorow
a Hoop, 2. &c.
Sometimes also
he danceth 4.
having on a Wizzard.
The Jugler 3.
sheweth sleights,
out of a Purse.
The rope-dancer, 5.
goeth and danceth
upon a Rope,
holdeth a Poise, 6.
in his Hand ;
or hangeth himself
by the Hand
or Foot, 7. &c.

Præstigiator 1.
facit
varia *Spectacula,*
volubilitate
corporis,
deambulando
manibus,
saliendo
per *Circulum,* 2. &c.
Interdum etiam
tripudiat 4.
larvatus.
Agyrta 3.
Præstigias facit,
è *marsupio.*
Funabulus, 5.
graditur & saltat
super *funem,*
tenens manu
Halterem ; 6.
aut suspendit se
manu
vel *Pede,* 7. &c.

The

Pr-

CXXXVI.

Ludi Pueriles.

Boyes-Sports.

Boyes	Pueri
use to play either with	ludere folent,
Bowling-ftones ; 1.	vel *globis fictilibus* ; 1.
oz thzowing	vel jactantes
a Bowl 2.	*Globum* 2.
at Nine-pins ; 3.	ad *Conas* ; 3.
oz ftriking a Ball	vel *Spærulam.*
thozow a Ring , 5.	*Clavâ* 4. mittentes
with a Bandy; 4.	per *Annulum* ; 5.
oz fcourging a Top 6,	vel *Turbinem* 6.
with a Whip; 7.	*Flagello* 7.
oz fhoting with	verfantes ;
a Trunck, 8.	vel *Sclopo*, 8.
and a Bow; 9.	& *Arcu* 9.
oz going upon	jaculantes ;
Stilts; 10.	vel *Grallis* 10.
oz toffing	incedentes ;
and fwinging	vel fuper *Petanrum* 11.
themfelves upon	fe agitantes
a Merry-totter. 11.	& ofcillantes.

Boyes

T 3   *Regnum*

CXLIX.

Gods Providence: *Providentia Dei.*

Mens States,	*Humana Sortes,*
are to be attributed	non tribuendæ funt
to Fortune,	*Fortunæ,*
oz Chance,	aut *Cafui,*
oz the influence of the	aut *Siderum Influxui,*
Stars (Comets 1.	(*Comica* 1. quidem
indeed are wont to	folent nihil boni
portend no good)	portendere)
but to the provident	fed provido
Eye of God 2.	*Dei Oculo* 2.
and to his	& ejufdem
Governing Hand ; 3.	*Manni rectrici* ; 3.

even our fights,	etiam .... *Prudentia*
oz overfights,	vel *Impru....ia,*
oz even our Faults.	vel etiam *Nos....*
God	*Deus*
hath his Minifters	habet *Minifor... Dos*
and Angels, 4.	& *Angelos,*
who accompany	*qui comu... 1. 5.*
a Man 5.	a nativitate ; s,
from his Birth,	ie afto rant,
as Guardians,	ut *Cuftodes,* contra
againft wicked Spirits	*Malos s piritus,*
oz the Devil, 6.	feu *Diabolum,* 6.
who every minute	qui nis ratio
layeth wait foz him,	erin.... is fit t,
to tempt	ad te tan lum
and vex him.	vel vexandem.
Woe be to the mad	Væ dementibus
wizzards and witches,	*Magis* & *Lamiis,*
who give themfelves	qui Cacodæmoni
to the Devil (being	fe dedunt
enclofed in a Circle, 7.	(ardua *Circulo*, 7.
calling upon him	enm ad ... ntes
with Charms)	incantamentis)
they daily with him,	cum eo colludunt,
and fall from God !	& à Deo deficiunt !
foz they fhall receive	r iw. cum illo
their reward is him.	mercedem accipient.

even	
	X *Ludi.*

Part Three
Drama

The Seven Champions of Christendom:

A Juvenile Play For Christmas Or Easter-Tide.

MUMMERS' PLAYS ARE *very ancient—at least a thousand years old. Surviving scripts, however, appear not to date earlier than the seventeenth century. Mummers' plays were done by village folk in various parts of the world, the purpose being to promote good fortune and fertility.*

Though The Seven Champions *descends from a still older story, "Bevis of Hampton," in the germ of its play form it probably dates even earlier than Bevis to a struggle between the forces of good and the forces of evil, the "good guys" and the "bad guys"— from the dim days then to the dim days now, an eternal struggle—and that is why the play, even in its early form, still lingers on in folk memory. It is interesting to note that in most of these plays, the evil force can never be permanently put down, but must be fought again and again. The mummers' version used here has a nationalistic ending— St. George of England licks saints from other countries. This does not indicate, however, that the play is recent. Nationalism was strong in England, particularly after the English defeated the Spanish Armada in 1588.*

Mummers, incidentally, are those who go merrymaking in disguise during festivals.

The Seven Champions *is reprinted from* The Chapbook Mummers' Plays, *ed. Alex Helm (Leicester, England: The Guizer Press, 1969), pp. 46–54.*

Characters Represented
With Their Appropriate Dresses:

ST. GEORGE OF ENGLAND: Scale Armour and Sword.
ST. PATRICK OF IRELAND: Green Tunic, with Red Cross on Breast.
ST. JAMES OF SCOTLAND: Highland Dress, Tartan, &c.
ST. DENIS OF FRANCE: Tunic of Fleur-de-lis Pattern.
ST. THULIS OF DENMARK: Red Mantle, Purple Dress, and Helmet.
ST. WANSKI OF RUSSIA: Grey Dress, Visor, &c.
ST. PIETRO OF ITALY: Blue Mantle Edged with White.
GUILLAUME, KING OF GERMANY: Red Double Tippet Edged with Ermine, Crown
of Gold, Sceptre, &c.
ROSALIND, THE KING'S DAUGHTER: Dress of Pure White.
HANS LIGHTHEAD, THE KING'S JESTER: Fool's Dress of Motley Colours.

All have Swords and Bucklers, except, of course, the last three characters.

*(The King of Germany and his Daughter
are seated. Hans Lighthead stands by
their side.)*

HANS.

My Liege, seven loyal knights without
Crave for admittance. There's no doubt
These brave warriors are so indeed;
Each rides a fiery, prancing steed.

GUILLAUME.

What want they, Fool? their errand state:
Though on our pleasure they must wait.
The revels which we hold to-day,
Even for visitors, cannot stay.

ROSALIND.

Good father dear, pray let me see
Who these loyal knights may be.

GUILLAUME.

Thee, daughter! No, remain within
Until the revels shall begin;
When all the knights our land can boast,
Shall strive for thee for lance and joust.
I'll see these braves, and learn their wish.

HANS.

You play the lacquey! Pish, sire, pish!
'Tis not 'the cheese' for Royal Kings
To bother and fuss about such things.
Leave all to me; I'll eye them o'er;
Their aim I'll know you may be sure!

GUILLAUME.

The fool says well,—he'll see, no doubt,
What all these knights have come about.
Perhaps 'tis to join the revels here;
To fight for you, my rosy dear.
Your face doth brighten;—wait a while:
To cheer all hearts, thou need'st but smile.
The stoutest lance, the boldest knight,
Still claim thee as his well-earned right.

HANS.

Saint George of England speaks without,
And asks me if my sire's about;
I answer 'Yes.' The other six
Say 'On we go, then; jolly bricks!'

GUILLAUME.

Well, let them come; we'll welcome give,
'May George of England ever live!'

*(Enter the Seven Champions
of Christendom.)*

ST. GEORGE.

Good morrow, king and maiden fair!
Great Heaven hold you free from care.
We've heard of jousting here to-day,
So to your court have made our way.
I fight for England, home, and beauty,
And always mean to do my duty.
If this fine maid's to be the prize,
I swear I'll win by those fair eyes.

ST. PATRICK.

Sure, I'm the man to lick you all,
The big, the little, small and tall.
St. George, bedad! I'll break his scull,
And give him *sich* a bellyfull;
With my shillelagh cut his nose,
Knock him down, tread on his toes.
In short, I'll make of him mince meat;
(You'll find him rather tough to eat.)
St. Patrick, sure, will spoil your game,
And carry off that lovely dame!

ST. JAMES.

Oh! oh! there's boasting here to-day;
Let *me* put in a word, I pray.
I bear, good sirs, the best of names:
You all know me! I'm great St. James.
From Scotia's land, where brave men live.
I come, a blow to take or give:
I'll lay some low, or else I'm wrong,
For James is daring, brave, and strong.
That lady fair shall sure be mine,
As my bright star o'erhead she'll shine.
Now, then, I long to come to blows,
And at her feet to lay my foes!

ST. DENIS.

Parbleu! here's idle words enough,
From men who do not fear rebuff.
Now, I'm from France, St. Denis too;
I'll make some of you youngsters rue.
My trusty sword will lay you low;
Conqueror here I'll quickly show.
St. George I'll pierce with many holes,
And fire away like Captain Coles!
Come on, St. Patrick, from the land of 'taters,'

I'll grind your bones like nutmeg graters!
Then as for Scotty, all o'er snuff,
Of me he shall have quite enough;
I'll tan his hide, so nice, so well,
That it from calf-skin you won't tell.
And for the three who follow here,
I'll soon make them feel rather queer!

ST. THULIS.

Hold! hold! I'm Thulis, Royal Dane,
I've oft met foes and will again;
For, ever where the Dane makes war,
The nations fly, both near and far.
Shall I then, yield the vantage ground?
Shall I a weakly Dane be found?
A norseman pale! and tremble now?
The coward's crown wear on his brow?
Not I! For now I'll firmly stand
Against the bravest in the land;
While I have breath, I'll still fight on,
Until I've beaten every one.
Lady, betide me good or ill,
For thy fair hand I'll shew my skill!

ST. WANSKI.

From Russia, far off land I come;
The ice-bound north has been my home:
These prating fools shall learn to know
That *I'm* the man to strike a blow!
My dearest friend, my trusty sword,
In all I say maintains my word;
It makes a wound with blade so keen,
That where it entered scarce is seen!
Ere you can speak it lays you low;
Come on, my foes, I'm ready now!

ST. PIETRO.

England, Scotland, Ireland, France,
Have boastings made about their lance.
The Royal Dane and Russian bold
Are doughty foes, so I've been told.
But with my trusty sword of steel,
My prowess they shall quickly feel.
St. Pietro fights; he does not talk,
Nor on such high-flown crutches stalk!
Now, high-born dame, by thy sweet face,
Where every beauty now I trace,
I'll try and win thee, fighting fair;
For thy dear sake all danger dare!

GUILLAUME.

These knights speak well, Hans! Hither, fool!
Although I know 'tis not the rule;
These gentlemen alone shall fight!

HANS.

No one else, sir? Oh, blow me tight!
Why, eighty knights are ready drest,
And waiting here to do their best.

ROSALIND.

Papa, I like the notion well.
Away, Hans!

HANS.

(*Aside*) Lor! now, here's 'a sell!'
Well, well, he has a Royal will;—
To know *him*'s quite beyond my skill.
(*Aloud.*)
Hi! there without! no joust to-day,
The king commissions me to say;
Seven knights alone are picked to fight,
So 'cut your stick' with all your might!
Go 'maul' each other—have it out;
Find out who's the master—have no doubt.
Meet face to face within the ring,
Though not before our gracious King.

GUILLAUME.

Prepare, ye knights; now, one and all
Be ready!—answer to your call.
And he who's victor, by command,
Shall claim our Royal daughter's hand!

HANS.

I beg to say, sir—

GUILLAUME.

Hist! fool, hist!

ST. GEORGE.

I challenge any man to fight;
By my stout heart of arm of might,
I've always vanquished all I've fought,—
The thickest danger ever sought!
The Dragon I have stricken low,
And conquered him with one great blow!
John Bull has never cried 'I am beat;'
Nor have I yet sustained defeat.

ST. PATRICK.

I do accept thy challenge here;
Nor do I think I've ought to fear.

Defend thyself—be on thy guard,
The struggle will be long and hard.

*(They fight some time, and St. Patrick
falls wounded.)*

ST. GEORGE.
Now, rise, St. Patrick and succumb;
For other boasters make thou room,
Who come like thee to meet their doom.
ST. JAMES.
I come, for one, thou proud St. George;
Thy idle words thou soon shalt gorge!
I've fought with ten to one before,
Yes, and would dare to meet a score.
Shall I fear one? Not I, indeed!
Bold England's boasts I will not heed.
Though thou hast laid brave Erin low,
Much tougher mettle I shall show!
Prepare to meet me—let's begin,
And see who will the struggle win!
ST. GEORGE.
Come on, thou coxcomb, lying knave,
And try thy shaking bones to save!
Such men as thee I soon run through;
My sword's then whet for more to do!

(They fight, and St. James falls.)

ST. JAMES.
What! thou triumphant! 's death,
I'll fight again, while I have breath!
HANS.
Nay, friend; I think 't were wiser still
To rest awhile; thou'st had thy fill!
ROSALIND.
I like St. George, he's brave and good.
HANS.
I think he's yours, my royal bud.
Like skittles how he knocks 'em down!
He well deserveth his renown.
GUILLAUME.
Go on, St. George; four knights remain;
To see their prowess I am fain.
So far, thou fightest with an arm
As strong as thy good heart is warm.

My Rosa's eyes oft rest on thee;
She prays that thou may'st conqueror be!
ST. GEORGE.
Most gracious King! much time to save,
And prove to you that I am brave,
With two I'll fight instead of one;
The sport has hardly yet begun!
Now, bold St. Wanski,—Pietro too,
Let swords be crossed 'tween me and you:
If I am vanquished, you must fight.
HANS.
Ha! two to one's a jolly sight!
ST. WANSKI.
Well; I could fight thee with one arm,—
To fight with *one* will make thee warm.
If Pietro helps me we will try
To make thee heave thy dying sigh.
ST. PIETRO.
Agreed! Two swords will surely slay
The braggart we see here to-day:
We'll make him eat his words, I trow.
HANS.
Stop! wait a bit; we'll see just now.
ST. PIETRO.
Now, then, St. George, be on thy guard,
For both will hit thee, quick and hard!

*(St. George fights with both. Soon Wanski
falls; and for some time, Pietro fights with
St. George alone; but he also gives in.)*

HANS.
Well, here's a knight who's really great;
I hope to fight him's not *my* fate!
ST. GEORGE.
The Royal Dane alone remains,
To stain with blood these wide-spread
    plain:
Thy wounded comrades, silent now,
To me each bent his haughty brow.
But as thou say'st—when Danes make war,
The nations tremble near and far.
Shalt thou then yield this vantage ground?
Shalt thou a weakly Dane be found?
ST. THULIS.
I will not fight thee, George the brave,

Nor seek from thee to find a grave.
I will not fight thee; but I yield
To thee this Lady and the field!
Our blood runs in the Royal veins.
On England's throne sit Royal Danes.
No! I'll not fight thee; here's my hand,
Thou champion bold of every land!
(*To Guillaume.*)
Great King! St. George the victor stands,
Give him your daughter and your lands.
(*To St. George.*)
Now, brave St. George, secure thy prize;
She loves thee by her glancing eyes!
HANS.

Well, here's a go. There's no mistake
How Gregory plays at Duck and Drake!
He's master here,—he beats them all,
The big, the little, short or tall.
GUILLAUME.

Great George of England, I proclaim
Thy title to this little Dame.
'Gainst all the world thou hold'st thy own;
I swear it by our Royal Crown!
ST. GEORGE.

I thank thee, King, and take thy gift,
For which to Heaven my eyes I lift:
My foes are beaten as you see;
And more than conquered they can't be.
Good Thulis, here's my hand for thee;
As long as life lasts, friends we'll be.
ROSALIND.

Yet, just a little speech from me.
In which I think you'll all agree:
To keep our revels up to-night,
And re-enact our glorious fight,
Kind people here pray help us now,
And on these Royal Knights bestow
Good bounty, to enable them
To come and see you once again.
HANS.

To all of which 'hear, hear', I say;
Shell out, good friends, without delay!
Still more—I hope your hearts incline
To bring forth cheer, both good and prime.
Your money, too, howe'er so small,
We won't object to—not at all.

St. George
and the Dragon
Lancaster Pace-Egg Play

THIS PLAY WAS OFTEN *performed at Easter, at which time it was known as a "pace egg" (peace egg) play. The play, with ancient origins, is believed to be associated with the death of winter and the revival of spring. Slasher in the following rendition is revived from death. In previous forms, Slasher is an enemy force—a dragon sometimes with scales like iron. (Slasher's head is made of iron, his body made of steel.) After performing a peace egg play, the players would go about collecting eggs from the onlookers— eggs being a symbol of fertility and renewal of life long before Christianity. Today, in the Soviet Union, fragments of egg shells are put on graves during the Easter season to suggest the continued life of the dead, at least in the memory of the living.*

Children performed this play, dressed up in wallpaper which was pinned together with cheap jewelry, and marched about the streets in the hope of being given eggs or money. Later the eggs were hardboiled in colored water. On Easter Monday, outside on

a hill or in a field, the eggs were rolled against each other until they were broken. Easter Monday egg rollings still take place in England and in the United States—even on the White House lawn, where members of the First Family preside over the festivities.

St. George and the Dragon *is reprinted from* Five Mumming Plays for Schools, *ed. Alex Helm (London: English Folk Dance and Song Society, Folk-lore Society, 1965), pp. 37–45.*

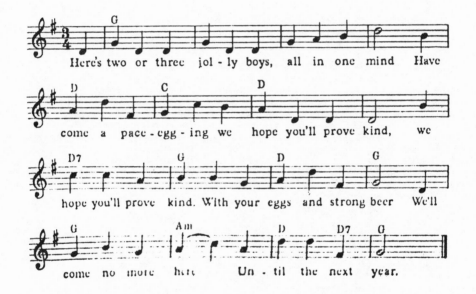

IN CHORUS

Here's two or three jolly boys, all in one mind,
Have come a pace-egging. We hope you'll prove kind,
With your eggs and strong beer.
We'll come no more here,
Until the next year.

LORD NELSON

The first that comes in is Lord Nelson, you see,
With a bunch of blue ribbons tied down to his knee.

The star on his breast like silver doth shine—
We hope you'll remember it's pace-egging time.

LORD COLLINGWOOD
The next that comes in is Lord Collingwood, star
He fought with Lord Nelson all during last war.
He fought with Lord Nelson till he shed his blood,
And that's why we call him the Lord Collingwood.

JACK TAR
The next that comes in is jolly jack tar,
He sailed with Lord Nelson all during last war—
He sailed with Lord Nelson all during last war,
And that's why we call him old jolly jack tar.

MISER
The next that comes in is old Miser you see,
He's a valiant old man in every degree;
He's a valiant old man so valiant and gay,
And all his delight is in drinking all day.

BETTY
The next that comes in is old Betty Brown Bags
She's afraid of her money; she wears her old rags,
She's afraid of her money; she wears her old rags
And that's why we call her old Betty Brown Bags.

MISER
Room, room, brave gallants and give us room to sport
For in this room we wish to resort,
Resort, and repeat our merry rhyme,
For remember good sirs, it is Eastertime.
Time to cut up goose pies now doth appear,
So we are come to act our merry customs here.
To the sound of the trumpet and the beat of the drum,
Make ready gentlemen, and let our merry actors come.

CHORUS
We are the merry actors that traverse the street;
We are the merry actors that fight for our meat;
We are the merry actors that show a pleasant play,
Step in, St. George, thou champion, and clear the way.

ST. GEORGE
I am St. George, who from old England sprung;
My famous name throughout the world hath rung;

Many bloody deeds and wonders have I made known
Made giants tremble upon their throne.
I followed a fair lady to a giant's gate;
Confined in dungeon deep to meet her fate,
When with her true knight I broke open the door,
And set the prisoners free.
When the giant almost struck me dead,
But, by my valour, I cut off his head!
I have searched the world all round and round
But a man to equal me I never found.

SLASHER

I am a valiant soldier and Slasher is my name,
With sword and buckler by my side, I hope to win the game;
And for to fight with me I see thou art not able,
So with my trusty broadsword I soon will thee disable.

ST. GEORGE

Disable? Disable? It lies not in thy power,
For, if I draw my trusty sword, I soon will thee devour.
Stand off Slasher! and let no more be said,
For if I draw my sword I am sure to break thy head.

SLASHER

How canst thou break my head?
Since my head is made of iron,
My body made of steel;
My hands and feet are knuckle bone,
I challenge thee to feel.

They fight. Slasher is slain

MISER

Alas! Alas! My chiefest son is slain,
What must I do to raise him up again?
Here he lies in the presence of you all—
I loudly for a doctor call.

ST. GEORGE

I'll go and fetch a doctor.

DOCTOR

Here am I.

MISER

Are you a doctor?

DOCTOR
Yes, that you can plainly see
By my art and activity.

MISER
What is your fee to cure this man?

DOCTOR
Ten pounds is my fee, but Jack, if you be an honest man
I will take only five of thee.

MISER *(aside)*
You'll be wondrous cunning to get any.
How far have you travelled in your doctorship?

DOCTOR
From Italy to Italy, ay, Germany, France and Spain,
And now I am returned to cure the diseases in old England again.

MISER
So far and no farther?

DOCTOR
Yes, a great deal.

MISER
How far?

DOCTOR
From the fireside to the cupboard door,
And upstairs and into bed.

MISER
What diseases can you cure?

DOCTOR
All sorts.

MISER
What's all sorts?

DOCTOR
The itch, the pitch, the palsy and the gout,
If a man's got nineteen devils in his skin, I'll fetch twenty of them
    out.

I cured Sir Harry of a hangnail almost fifty five yards long,
Surely I can cure this man.
Here, take a little of my bottle,
Let it run down thy throttle;
Thou be not quite slain:—
Rise up, bold Slasher, and fight again.

SLASHER
Oh, my back!

MISER
What's the matter with thy back?

SLASHER
My back is wounded—my heart is confounded,
To be struck out of seven senses into four score,
The like was never seen in old England before.
Oh, hark! hark! I hear that silvery trumpet sound!
Down yonder is the way—
Farewell, St. George, I can no longer stay.

Exit

BLACK PRINCE
I am the black prince of Paradise, born of high renown,
Soon I will fetch St. George's lofty courage down.
Before St. George shall be received by me
St. George shall die to all eternity.

ST. GEORGE
Stand off thou black Morocco dog,
Or by my sword thou'llt die;
I'll pierce thy body full of holes
And make thy buttons fly.
For I will tame thee of thy pride,
And lay thy anger, too, aside.
I'll hinch thee, and pinch thee, and cut thee up as small as flies
And send thee over the sea to make mince pies.
Mince pies hot, mince pies cold,
I'll send thee to the devil before thou'rt three days old.

BLACK PRINCE
How canst thou tame me of my pride
And lay mine anger too, aside?
Hinch me and pinch me and cut me up as small as flies

How canst thou send me over the sea to make mince pies?
Mince pies hot, mince pies cold—
How canst thou send me to Black Sam before I'm three days old.
Since my head is made of iron;
My body made of steel,
My hands and feet are knuckle bone:—
I challenge thee to feel.

ST. GEORGE
Lay down thy sword; take up to me a spear;
Then I will fight thee without dread or fear.

They fight. The Black Prince is slain.

ST. GEORGE
Now the Black Prince of Paradise is dead,
And all his anger is entirely fled.
Take him and give him to the flies,
And never more bring him before mine eyes.

THE KING
I am the King of Egypt as plainly doth appear,
I have come to seek my son—my son and only heir.

ST. GEORGE
He is slain.

THE KING
Who did him slay? Who did him kill?
And on the ground his precious blood did spill?

ST. GEORGE
I did him slay, I did him kill,
And on the ground his precious blood did spill.

THE KING
Oh, Hector, Hector, help me with speed,
For in my life I never stood more in need.
Stand not there with sword in hand,
But rise and fight at my command.

HECTOR
Yes, yes, my liege, I will obey,
And by my sword, I hope to win the day;
If that be he who does stand there

Who slew my master's son and heir,
If he be sprung from royal blood,
I'll make it run like Noah's flood.

ST. GEORGE
Oh, Hector, bold Hector, do not be so hot
For here thou knowest not whom thou hast got—
For I can tame thee of thy pride,
And lay thine anger too, aside.
Lay down thy sword; take up to me a spear
Then I will fight thee without dread or fear.

They fight. Hector is wounded

HECTOR
Many bloody deeds have I made known;
Made giants tremble on their thrones,
But from St. George I received this bloody wound,
Down yonder is the way;—
Farewell, St. George, I can no longer stay.

BIG HEAD
In comes I who never came yet,
With my big head and little wit;
Let my wit be ever so small,
Me and my cudgel'll hammer 'em all.
If you won't believe the words I say,
Enter in, Little Devil Doubt, and clear the way.

LITTLE DEVIL DOUBT
In comes I, Little Devil Doubt,
If you won't give me money, I'll sweep you all out.
Money I want, and money I crave,
If you won't give me money, I'll sweep you all to your grave.

Commences sweeping

Big Head, Big Head, there's war wherever we go.

They fight

BIG HEAD
Where? Where? Where?

LITTLE DEVIL DOUBT
Here! Here! Here!

Knocks Big Head down with his broom

LITTLE DEVIL DOUBT
Here lies the body of old John Dunn,
When he dies,
The Devil cries,
"Come, John, come!"

$\widehat{8}$

Hero and Leander:
A Puppet Show, From Bartholomew Fair

By BEN JONSON

IN THE FINAL ACT OF HIS PLAY Bartholomew Fair *(1614), Shakespeare's scholarly friend Ben Jonson includes a puppet show,* Hero and Leander, *as it might have been acted by a simple showman, Leatherhead, standing outside a booth at Smithfield during the Fair. A mixture of two classical legends familiar to Elizabethans, Hero and Leander and Damon and Pythias, the show presents the legends in a coarse, jesting manner to appeal to common people at the Fair. According to George Speaight in his* Punch and Judy *(London, 1970), "it lifts the story of the English puppet theatre from surmise into literature." (Speaight was very familiar with the show. He played Leatherhead in it at the Old Vic Theatre in 1950.) Many references exist in literature, however, to puppet shows produced in the seventeenth century. In Shakespeare's* Winter's Tale, *for instance, Autolycus speaks of someone who "compassed a motion of the Prodigal Son"—that is, got possession of a puppet show of that title. Later on in the century, Pepys records having enjoyed several puppet shows, including (Dick)* Whittington *at Southwark Fair and* Patient Grizill *(Griselda) at Bartholomew Fair. Sometimes he found the puppet shows to be more fun than the Restoration dramas.*

The first story fused in the puppet show was the Greek legend Hero and Leander. *It had been made into a poem in iambic pentameter couplets by another Elizabethan playwright, Christopher Marlowe (murdered in 1593). The poem was published in London in 1598. Hero lives in Sestos, and Leander in Abydos, and the waters of the Hellespont separate them. Hero is lovely to behold as Marlowe describes her, with golden hair, white skin, wearing light garments of lawn or sheer linen lined with purple silk and decorated with gilt stars. She has a myrtle wreath on her head from which hangs a veil embroidered with flowers and leaves. Strands of pebbles are around her neck. Her boots, which come to the knee, are decorated with silvered shells and coral. No wonder Leander finds her interesting—Leander with his blond hair which he never cuts, dark-eyed, straight-bodied, firm-bellied. Worshipping at Venus' temple, these two beautiful human beings meet and fall in love. Leander begins to woo her. He argues that it is a sin against Love not to perform the rites of love, and these are banquets, music, revels, plays and masques. Hero smiles but stays at a distance. Still, she cannot resist telling Leander to come see her in Sestos. Leander is quick to accept. He climbs the tower in which she has her room. In anticipation of his visit, she has scattered it with roses. They kiss and embrace, but she keeps her chastity. Hungry with love, Leander returns to Abydos. Soon, Leander decides to swim the Hellespont to join Hero. As he swims, the god Neptune himself falls in love with Leander and seeks to detain him, but Leander manages to get to shore and the two lovers are united. The lovers later die tragically, but not in Marlowe's poem. This romantic story has the charm of a fairy tale.*

The story of Damon and Pythias is, like that of David and Jonathan, a demonstration of the qualities of true friendship. On the instigations of a courtier, Carisophus, Damon is arrested as a spy and brought before the Greek king, Dionysius. When Damon is condemned to die, Damon and Pythias quarrel over who should be executed, each wanting to die to spare the other. The King ends up sparing them both and exiling the evil courtier. This play was acted before Queen Elizabeth by the Children of the Queen's Chapel and published in 1571.

In his puppet show, a play within the play Bartholomew Fair, *Ben Jonson fuses the stories of the lovers, Hero and Leander, so that Damon and Pythias come courting Hero, too. All the characters are transferred from ancient Greece to the London slums. Leatherhead, the puppeteer who serves as commentator, charges fairgoers tuppence apiece to see the show, which is full of slapstick and bawdy remarks. Though at times the show is rather difficult to follow, this is somewhat in the tradition of puppet shows, partially perhaps because many of them first were put on by foreigners in England and partly because the holiday spirit of the play is more important than the action and the plot. People are milling around outdoors, and the audience is probably too distracted to follow a consistent story.*

The play was first produced in the Hope Theatre in Southwark, a circular theatre which doubled as a bear-baiting ring. (I have always suspected that these circular theatres actually descended from the circular forts or barbicans, the design for which was brought back from the East by crusaders in the Middle Ages. Several of them were on the outskirts of London, and since they were not churches, would not be banned from play presentation. One such barbican, strikingly like the theoretical plan of the Globe Theatre, both inside and out, still stands in Cracow, Poland.)

This scene is reproduced from The Works of Ben Jonson *(Boston: Phillips, Sampson, and Company, 1855). For interesting comment on the play, see the introduction by E. A. Horsman, ed.,* Bartholomew Fair *(Cambridge, Mass: Harvard University Press, 1960). The edition is part of The Revels Plays, of which Clifford Leech was General Editor.*

SCENE III

Another part of the Fair.
The Puppet-show Booth, as before.

Enter Sharkwell and Filcher, with bills, and Cokes in his doublet and hose, followed by the Boys of the Fair.

COKES.
How now! what's here to do, friend? art thou the master of the monuments?
SHARKWELL.
'Tis a motion, an't please your worship.

Enter Overdo behind.

OVERDO.

My fantastical brother-in-law, master Bartholomew Cokes!

COKES.

A motion! what's that! [*Reads.*] *The ancient modern history of Hero and Leander, otherwise called the Touchstone of true Love, with as true a trial of friendship between Damon and Pythias, two faithful friends o' the Bank-side.* Pretty, i'faith, what's the meaning on't? is't an interlude, or what is't?

FILCHER.

Yes, sir, please you come near, we'll take your money within.

COKES.

Back with these children; they do so follow me up and down!

Enter Littlewit.

LITTLEWIT.

By your leave, friend.

FILCHER.

You must pay, sir, an you go in.

LITTLEWIT.

Who, I! I perceive thou know'st not me; call the master of the motion.

SHARKWELL.

What, do you not know the author, fellow Filcher? You must take no money of him; he must come in gratis: master Littlewit is a voluntary; he is the author.

LITTLEWIT.

Peace, speak not too loud, I would not have any notice taken that I am the author, till we see how it passes.

COKES.

Master Littlewit, how dost thou?

LITTLEWIT.

Master Cokes! you are exceeding well met: what, in your doublet and hose, without a cloke or a hat?

COKES.

I would I might never stir, as I am an honest man, and by that fire; I have lost all in the Fair, and all my acquaintance too: didst thou meet any body that I know, master Littlewit? my man Numps, or my sister Overdo, or mistress Grace? Pray thee, master Littlewit, lend me some money to see the interlude here; I'll pay thee again, as I am a gentleman. If thou'll but carry me home, I have money enough there.

LITTLEWIT.

O, sir, you shall command it; what, will a crown serve you?

COKES.

I think it will; what do we pay for coming in, fellows?

FILCHER.

Two-pence, sir.

COKES.

Two-pence! there's twelve-pence, friend: nay, I am a gallant, as simple as I look now;

if you see me with my man about me, and my artillery again.

LITTLEWIT.

Your man was in the stocks e'en now, sir.

COKES.

Who, Numps?

LITTLEWIT.

Yes, faith.

COKES.

For what, i'faith? I am glad o' that; remember to tell me on't anon; I have enough now. What manner of matter is this, master Littlewit? what kind of actors have you? are they good actors?

LITTLEWIT.

Pretty youths, sir, all children both old and young; here's the master of 'em——

Enter Leatherhead.

LEATHERHEAD.

[*aside to Littlewit.*] Call me not Leatherhead, but Lantern.

LITTLEWIT.

Master Lantern, that gives light to the business.

COKES.

In good time, sir! I would fain see them. I would be glad to drink with the young company; which is the tiring-house?

LEATHERHEAD.

Troth, sir, our tiring-house is somewhat little; we are but beginners yet, pray pardon us; you cannot go upright in't.

COKES.

No! not now my hat is off? what would you have done with me, if you had had me feather and all, as I was once to-day? Have you none of your pretty impudent boys now, to bring stools, fill tobacco, fetch ale, and beg money, as they have at other houses? Let me see some of your actors.

LITTLEWIT.

Shew him them, shew him them. Master Lantern, this is a gentleman that is a favorer of the quality.

[*Exit Leatherhead.*]

OVERDO.

Ay, the favoring of this licentious quality is the consumption of many a young gentleman; a pernicious enormity. [*Aside.*]

Re-enter Leatherhead, with a basket.

COKES.

What! do they live in baskets?

LEATHERHEAD.

They do lie in a basket, sir, they are o' the small players.

COKES.

These be players minors indeed. Do you call these players?

LEATHERHEAD.

They are actors, sir, and as good as any, none dispraised, for dumb shows: indeed, I am the mouth of them all.

COKES.

Thy mouth will hold them all. I think one tailor would go near to beat all this company with a hand bound behind him.

LITTLEWIT.

Ay, and eat them all too, an they were in cake-bread.

COKES.

I thank you for that, master Littlewit; a good jest! Which is your Burbage now?

LEATHERHEAD.

What mean you by that, sir?

COKES.

Your best actor, your Field?

LITTLEWIT.

Good, i'faith! you are even with me, sir.

LEATHERHEAD.

This is he, that acts young Leander, sir: he is extremely beloved of the womenkind, they do so affect his action, the green gamesters, that come here! and this is lovely Hero; this with the beard, Damon; and this pretty Pythias: this is the ghost of king Dionysius in the habit of a scrivener; as you shall see anon at large.

COKES.

Well, they are a civil company, I like 'em for that; they offer not to fleer, nor jeer, nor break jests, as the great players do: and then, there goes not so much charge to the feasting of them, or making them drunk, as to the other, by reason of their littleness. Do they use to play perfect? are they never fluster'd?

LEATHERHEAD.

No, sir, I thank my industry and policy for it; they are as well govern'd a company, though I say it——And here is young Leander, is as proper an actor of his inches, and shakes his head like an hostler.

COKES.

But do you play it according to the printed book? I have read that.

LEATHERHEAD.

By no means, sir.

COKES.

No! how then?

LEATHERHEAD.

A better way, sir; that is too learned and poetical for our audience: what do they know what *Hellespont* is, *guilty of true love's blood?* or what *Abydos* is? or *the other, Sestos hight?*

COKES.

Thou art in the right; I do not know myself.

LEATHERHEAD.

No, I have entreated master Littlewit to take a little pains to reduce it to a more familiar strain for our people.

COKES.

How, I pray thee, good master Littlewit?

LITTLEWIT.

It pleases him to make a matter of it, sir; but there is no such matter, I assure you: I have only made it a little easy, and modern for the times, sir, that's all. As for the Hellespont, I imagine our Thames here; and then Leander I make a dyer's son about Puddle-wharf: and Hero a wench o' the Bank-side, who going over one morning to Old Fish-street, Leander spies her land at Trig-stairs, and falls in love with her. Now do I introduce Cupid, having metamorphosed himself into a drawer, and he strikes Hero in love with a pint of sherry; and other pretty passages there are of the friendship, that will delight you, sir, and please you of judgment.

COKES.

I'll be sworn they shall: I am in love with the actors already, and I'll be allied to them presently.—They respect gentlemen, these fellows:—Hero shall be my fairing: but which of my fairings?—let me see—i'faith, my fiddle; and Leander my fiddle-stick: then Damon my drum, and Pythias my pipe, and the ghost of Dionysius my hobby-horse. All fitted.

Enter Winwife and Grace.

WINWIFE.

Look, yonder's your Cokes gotten in among his play-fellows; I thought we could not miss him at such a spectacle.

GRACE.

Let him alone, he is so busy he will never spy us.

LEATHERHEAD.

Nay, good sir!

[*To Cokes, who is handling the puppets.*]

COKES.

I warrant thee I will not hurt her, fellow; what, dost thou think me uncivil? I pray thee be not jealous; I am toward a wife.

LITTLEWIT.

Well, good master Lantern, make ready to begin that I may fetch my wife; and look you be perfect, you undo me else, in my reputation.

LEATHERHEAD.

I warrant you, sir, do not you breed too great an expectation of it among your friends; that's the hurter of these things.

LITTLEWIT.

No, no, no.

[*Exit.*]

COKES.

I'll stay here and see; pray thee let me see.

WINWIFE.

How diligent and troublesome he is!

GRACE.

The place becomes him, methinks.

OVERDO.

My ward, mistress Grace, in the company of a stranger! I doubt I shall be compell'd
to discover myself before my time.
[*Aside.*]

*Enter Knockem, Edgworth, and Mrs. Littlewit, followed by Whit supporting Mrs.
Overdo, masked.*

FILCHER.

Two-pence apiece, gentlemen, an excellent motion.

KNOCKEM.

Shall we have fine fire-works, and good vapors?

SHARKWELL.

Yes, captain, and water-works too.

WHIT.

I pree dee take care o' dy shmall lady there, Edgworth; I will look to dish tall lady
myself.

LEATHERHEAD.

Welcome, gentlemen, welcome, gentlemen.

WHIT.

Predee mashter o' the monshtersh, help a very sick lady here to a chair to shit in.

LEATHERHEAD.

Presently, sir.

[*A chair is brought in for Mrs. Overdo.*]

WHIT.

Good fait now, Ursula's ale and acquavitæ ish to blame for't; shit down, shweet-heart,
shit down and sleep a little.

EDGWORTH.

[*To Mrs. Littlewit.*] Madam, you are very welcome hither.

KNOCKEM.

Yes, and you shall see very good vapors.

OVERDO.

Here is my care come! I like to see him in so good company: and yet I wonder that
persons of such fashion should resort hither.
[*Aside.*]

EDGWORTH.

There is a very private house, madam.

LEATHERHEAD.

Will it please your ladyship sit, madam?

MRS. LITTLEWIT.

Yes, goodman. They do so all-to-be-madam me, I think they think me a very lady.

EDGWORTH.

What else, madam?

MRS. LITTLEWIT.
Must I put off my mask to him?

EDGWORTH.
O, by no means.

MRS. LITTLEWIT.
How should my husband know me then?

KNOCKEM.
Husband! an idle vapor; he must not know you, nor you him: there's the true vapor.

OVERDO.
Yea! I will observe more of this. [*Aside.*] Is this a lady, friend?

WHIT.
Ay, and dat is anoder lady, shweet-heart; if dou hasht a mind to 'em, give me twelve-
pence from tee, and dou shalt have eder oder on 'em.

OVERDO.
Ay, this will prove my chiefest enormity; I will follow this. [*Aside.*]

EDGWORTH.
Is not this a finer life, lady, than to be clogg'd with a husband?

MRS. LITTLEWIT.
Yes, a great deal. When will they begin, trow, in the name o' the motion?

EDGWORTH.
By and by, madam; they stay but for company.

KNOCKEM.
Do you hear, puppet-master, these are tedious vapors, when begin you?

LEATHERHEAD.
We stay but for master Littlewit, the author, who is gone for his wife: and we begin
presently.

MRS. LITTLEWIT.
That's I, that's I.

EDGWORTH.
That was you, lady; but now you are no such poor thing.

KNOCKEM.
Hang the author's wife, a running vapor! here be ladies will stay for ne'er a Delia of
them all.

WHIT.
But hear me now, here ish one o' de ladish ashleep, stay till shee but vake, man.

Enter Waspe.

WASPE.
How now, friends! what's here to do?

FILCHER.
Two-pence apiece, sir, the best motion in the Fair.

WASPE.
I believe you lie; if you do, I'll have my money again, and beat you.

MRS. LITTLEWIT.
Numps is come!

WASPE.

Did you see a master of mine come in here, a tall young 'squire of Harrow o' the Hill, master Bartholomew Cokes?

FILCHER.

I think there be such a one within.

WASPE.

Look he be, you were best: but it is very likely: I wonder I found him not at all the rest. I have been at the Eagle, and the Black Wolf, and the Bull with the five legs and two pizzles:—he was a calf at Uxbridge fair two years agone—and at the dogs that dance the morrice, and the hare of the Tabor; and mist him at all these! Sure this must needs be some fine sight that holds him so, if it have him.

COKES.

Come, come, are you ready now?

LEATHERHEAD.

Presently, sir.

WASPE.

Hoyday, he's at work in his doublet and hose! do you hear, sir, are you employ'd, that you are bare-headed and so busy?

COKES.

Hold your peace, Numps; you have been in the stocks, I hear.

WASPE.

Does he know that! nay, then the date of my authority is out; I must think no longer to reign, my government is at an end. He that will correct another must want fault in himself.

WINWIFE.

Sententious Numps! I never heard so much from him before.

LEATHERHEAD.

Sure master Littlewit will not come; please you take your place, sir; we'll begin.

COKES.

I pray thee do, mine ears long to be at it, and my eyes too. O Numps, in the stocks, Numps! where's your sword, Numps?

WASPE.

I pray you intend your game, sir, let me alone.

COKES.

Well then, we are quit for all. Come, sit down, Numps; I'll interpret to thee: did you see mistress Grace? It's no matter, neither, now I think on't, tell me anon.

WINWIFE.

A great deal of love and care he expresses!

GRACE.

Alas, would you have him to express more than he has? that were tyranny.

COKES.

Peace, ho! now, now.

LEATHERHEAD.

Gentles, that no longer your expectations may wander,
Behold our chief actor, amorous Leander.

With a great deal of cloth, lapp'd about him like a scarf,
For he yet serves his father, a dyer at Puddle-wharf;
Which place we'll make bold with, to call it our Abydus,
As the Bankside is our Sestos; and let it not be deny'd us.
Now as he is beating to make the dye take the fuller,
Who chances to come by, but fair Hero in a sculler;
And seeing Leander's naked leg and goodly calf,
Cast at him from the boat a sheep's eye and an half.
Now she is landed, and the sculler come back,
By and by you shall see what Leander doth lack.
LEANDER.
Cole, Cole, old Cole!
LEATHERHEAD.
That is the sculler's name without controul.
LEANDER.
Cole, Cole, I say, Cole!
LEATHERHEAD.
We do hear you.
LEANDER.
Old Cole.
LEATHERHEAD.
Old Cole! is the dyer turn'd collier? how do you sell?
LEANDER.
A pox o' your manners, kiss my hole here, and smell.
LEATHERHEAD.
Kiss your hole and smell! there's manners indeed.
LEANDER.
Why, Cole, I say, Cole!
LEATHERHEAD.
Is't the sculler you need?
LEANDER.
Ay, and be hang'd.
LEATHERHEAD.
Be hang'd! look you yonder.
Old Cole, you must go hang with master Leander.
COLE.
Where is he?
LEANDER.
Here, Cole: what fairest of fairs,
Was that fare that thou landedst but now at Trig-stairs?
COKES.
What was that, fellow? pray thee tell me, I scarce understand them.
LEATHERHEAD.
Leander does ask, sir, what fairest of fairs,
Was the fare he landed but now at Trig-stairs?

COLE.

It is lovely Hero.

LEANDER.

Nero?

COLE.

No, Hero.

LEATHERHEAD.

It is Hero
Of the Bankside, he saith, to tell you truth without erring,
Is come over into Fish-street to eat some fresh herring.
Leander says no more, but as fast as he can,
Gets on all his best clothes, and will after to the Swan.

COKES.

Most admirable good, is't not?

LEATHERHEAD.

Stay, sculler.

COLE.

What say you?

LEATHERHEAD.

You must stay for Leander,
And carry him to the wench.

COLE.

You rogue, I am no pander.

COKES.

He says he is no pander. 'Tis a fine language; I understand it now.

LEATHERHEAD.

Are you no pander, goodman Cole? here's no man says you are;
You'll grow a hot cole, it seems; pray you stay for your fare.

COLE.

Will he come away?

LEATHERHEAD.

What do you say?

COLE.

I'd have him come away.

LEATHERHEAD.

Would you have Leander come away? why, pray sir, stay.
You are angry, goodman Cole; I believe the fair maid
Come over with you a' trust: tell us, sculler, are you paid?

COLE.

Yes, goodman Hogrubber of Pickthatch.

LEATHERHEAD.

How, Hogrubber of Pickthatch.

COLE.

Ay, Hogrubber of Pickthatch. Take you that. [Strikes him over the pate.]

LEATHERHEAD.

O, my head!

COLE.
Harm watch, harm catch!
COKES.
Harm watch, harm catch, he says; very good, i'faith: the sculler had like to have knock'd you, sirrah.
LEATHERHEAD.
Yes, but that his fare call'd him away.
LEANDER.
Row apace, row apace, row, row, row, row, row.
LEATHERHEAD.
You are knavishly loaden, sculler, take heed where you go.
COLE.
Knave in your face, goodman rogue.
LEANDER.
Row, row, row, row, row.
COKES.
He said, knave in your face, friend.
LEATHERHEAD.
Ay, sir, I heard him; but there's no talking to these watermen, they will have the last word.
COKES.
Od's my life! I am not allied to the sculler yet; he shall be *Dauphin my boy.* But my fiddle-stick does fiddle in and out too much: I pray thee speak to him on't; tell him I would have him tarry in my sight more.
LEATHERHEAD.
I pray you be content; you'll have enough on him, sir.
Now, gentles, I take it, here is none of you so stupid,
But that you have heard of a little god of love call'd Cupid;
Who out of kindness to Leander, hearing he but saw her,
This present day and hour doth turn himself to a drawer.
And because he would have their first meeting to be merry,
He strikes Hero in love to him with a pint of sherry;
Which he tells her from amorous Leander is sent her,
Who after him into the room of Hero doth venture.

[*Leander goes into Mistress Hero's room.*]

JONAS.
A pint of sack, score a pint of sack in the Coney.
COKES.
Sack! you said but e'en now it should be sherry.
JONAS.
Why, so it is; sherry, sherry, sherry.
COKES.
Sherry, sherry, sherry! By my troth he makes me merry. I must have a name for Cupid too. Let me see, thou might'st help me, now, an thou would'st, Numps, at a dead lift:

but thou art dreaming of the stocks still.—Do not think on't, I have forgot it; 'tis but a nine days' wonder, man; let it not trouble thee.

WASPE.

I would the stocks were about your neck, sir; condition I hung by the heels in them till the wonder were off from you, with all my heart.

COKES.

Well said, resolute Numps! but hark you, friend, where's the friendship all this while between my drum Damon, and my pipe Pythias?

LEATHERHEAD.

You shall see by and by, sir.

COKES.

You think my hobby-horse is forgotten too; no, I'll see them all enact before I go; I shall not know which to love best else.

KNOCKEM.

This gallant has interrupting vapors, troublesome vapors; Whit, puff with him.

WHIT.

No, I pree dee, captain, let him alone; he is a child, i'faith, la.

LEATHERHEAD.

Now, gentles, to the friends, who in number are two,
And lodged in that ale-house in which fair Hero does do.
Damon, for some kindness done him the last week,
Is come, fair Hero, in Fish-Street, this morning to seek.
Pythias does smell the knavery of the meeting,
And now you shall see their true-friendly greeting.

PYTHIAS.

You whore-masterly slave, you.

COKES.

Whore-masterly slave you! very friendly and familiar, that.

DAMON.

Whore-master in thy face,
Thou hast lain with her thyself, I'll prove it in this place.

COKES.

Damon says, Pythias has lain with her himself, he'll prov't in this place.

LEATHERHEAD.

They are whore-masters both, sir, that's a plain case.

PYTHIAS.

You lie like a rogue.

LEATHERHEAD.

Do I lie like a rogue?

PYTHIAS.

A pimp and a scab.

LEATHERHEAD.

A pimp and a scab.
I say, between you, you have both but one drab.

DAMON.

You lie again.

LEATHERHEAD.
Do I lie again?
DAMON.
Like a rogue again.
LEATHERHEAD.
Like a rogue again?
PYTHIAS.
And you are a pimp again.
COKES.
And you are a pimp again, he says.
DAMON.
And a scab again.
COKES.
And a scab again, he says.
LEATHERHEAD.
And I say again, you are both whore-masters, again.
And you have both but one drab again.
DAMON *and* PYTHIAS.
Dost thou, dost thou, dost thou?

[They fall upon him.]

LEATHERHEAD.
What, both at once?
PYTHIAS.
Down with him, Damon.
DAMON.
Pink his guts, Pythias.
LEATHERHEAD.
What, so malicious?
Will ye murder me, masters both, in my own house?
COKES.
Ho! well acted, my drum, well acted, my pipe, well acted still!
WASPE.
Well acted, with all my heart.
LEATHERHEAD.
Hold, hold your hands.
COKES.
Ay, both your hands, for my sake! for you have both done well.
DAMON.
Gramercy, pure Pythias.
PYTHIAS.
Gramercy, dear Damon.
COKES.
Gramercy to you both, my pipe and my drum.

PYTHIAS *and* DAMON.

Come, now we'll together to breakfast to Hero.

LEATHERHEAD.

'Tis well you can now go to breakfast to Hero.
You have given me my breakfast, with a hone and honero.

COKES.

How is it, friend, have they hurt thee?

LEATHERHEAD.

O no:

Between you and I, sir, we do but make show.—

Thus, gentles, you perceive, without any denial,
'Twixt Damon and Pythias here, friendship's true trial.
Though hourly they quarrel thus, and roar each with other,
They fight you no more than does brother with brother;
But friendly together, at the next man they meet,
They let fly their anger, as here you might see't.

COKES.

Well, we have seen it, and thou hast felt it, whatsoe'er thou sayest. What's next, what's next?

LEATHERHEAD.

This while young Leander with fair Hero is drinking,
And Hero grown drunk to any man's thinking!
Yet was it not three pints of sherry could flaw her,
Till Cupid distinguished like Jonas the drawer,
From under his apron, where his lechery lurks,
Put love in her sack. Now mark how it works.

HERO.

O Leander, Leander, my dear, my dear Leander,
I'll for ever be thy goose, so thou'lt be my gander.

COKES.

Excellently well said, Fiddle, she'll ever be his goose, so he'll be her gander; was't not so?

LEATHERHEAD.

Yes, sir, but mark his answer now.

LEANDER.

And sweetest of geese, before I go to bed,
I'll swim over the Thames, my goose, thee to tread.

COKES.

Brave! he will swim over the Thames, and tread his goose to-night, he says.

LEATHERHEAD.

Ay, peace, sir, they'll be angry if they hear you eaves-dropping, now they are setting their match.

LEANDER.

But lest the Thames should be dark, my goose, my dear friend,
Let thy window be provided of a candle's end.

HERO.

Fear not, my gander, I protest I should handle

My matters very ill, if I had not a whole candle.
LEANDER.
Well then, look to't, and kiss me to boot.
LEATHERHEAD.
Now here come the friends again, Pythias and Damon,
And under their clokes they have of bacon a gammon.
PYTHIAS.
Drawer, fill some wine here.
LEATHERHEAD.
How, some wine there!
There's company already, sir, pray forbear.
DAMON.
'Tis Hero.
LEATHERHEAD.
Yes, but she will not be taken,
After sack and fresh herring, with your Dunmow-bacon.
PYTHIAS.
You lie, it's Westfabian.
LEATHERHEAD.
Westphalian, you should say.
DAMON.
If you hold not your peace, you are a coxcomb, I would say.

[*Leander and Hero kiss.*]

What's here, what's here? kiss, kiss, upon kiss!
LEATHERHEAD.
Ay, wherefore should they not? what harm is in this?
'Tis mistress Hero.
DAMON.
Mistress Hero's a whore.
LEATHERHEAD.
Is she a whore? keep you quiet, or, sir, knave, out of door.
DAMON.
Knave out of door?
HERO.
Yes, knave out of door.
DAMON.
Whore out of door.

[*They fall together by the ears.*]

HERO.
I say, knave out of door.
DAMON.
I say, whore out of door.

PYTHIAS.
Yea, so say I too.
HERO.
Kiss the whore o' the a—
LEATHERHEAD.
Now you have something to do:
You must kiss her o' the a—, she says.
DAMON *and* PYTHIAS.
So we will, so we will.

[*They kick her.*]

HERO.
O my haunches, O my haunches, hold, hold.
LEATHERHEAD.
Stand'st thou still!
Leander, where art thou? stand'st thou still like a sot,
And not offer'st to break both their heads with a pot?
See who's at thine elbow there! puppet Jonas and Cupid.
JONAS.
Upon'em, Leander, be not so stupid.
LEANDER.
You goat-bearded slave!
DAMON.
You whore-master knave!

[*They fight.*]

LEANDER.
Thou art a whore-master.
JONAS.
Whore-masters all.
LEATHERHEAD.
See, Cupid with a word has tane up the brawl.
KNOCKEM.
These be fine vapors!
COKES.
By this good day, they fight bravely; do they not, Numps?
WASPE.
Yes, they lack'd but you to be their second all this while.
LEATHERHEAD.
This tragical encounter falling out thus to busy us,
It raises up the ghost of their friend Dionysius;
Not like a monarch, but the master of a school,
In a scrivener's furr'd gown, which shews he is no fool:
For therein he hath wit enough to keep himself warm.

O Damon, he cries, and Pythias, what harm
Hath poor Dionysius done you in his grave,
That after his death you should fall out thus and rave,
And call amorous Leander whore-master knave?
DAMON.
I cannot, I will not, I promise you, endure it.

Rabbi Busy rushes in.

RABBI BUSY.
Down with Dagon! Down with Dagon! 'tis I, I will no longer endure your profanations.
LEATHERHEAD.
What mean you, sir?
RABBI BUSY.
I will remove Dagon there, I say, that idol, that heathenish idol, that remains, as I may say, a beam, a very beam,—not a beam of the sun, nor a beam of the moon, nor a beam of a balance, neither a house-beam, nor a weaver's beam, but a beam in the eye, in the eye of the brethren; a very great beam, an exceeding great beam; such as are your stage-players, rimers, and morrice-dancers, who have walked hand in hand, in contempt of the brethren, and the cause; and been born out by instruments of no mean countenance.
LEATHERHEAD.
Sir, I present nothing but what is licensed by authority.
RABBI BUSY.
Thou art all license, even licentiousness itself, Shimei!
LEATHERHEAD.
I have the master of the revels' hand for't, sir.
RABBI BUSY.
The master of the rebels' hand thou hast. Satan's! hold thy peace, thy scurrility, shut up thy mouth, thy profession is damnable, and in pleading for it thou dost plead for Baal. I have long opened my mouth wide, and gaped; I have gaped as the oyster for the tide, after thy destruction: but cannot compass it by suit or dispute; so that I look for a bickering, e'er long, and then a battle.
KNOCKEM.
Good Banbury vapors!
COKES.
Friend, you'd have an ill match on't, if you bicker with him here; though he be no man of the fist, he has friends that will to cuffs for him. Numps, will not you take our side?
EDGWORTH.
Sir, it shall not need; in my mind he offers him a fairer course, to end it by disputation: hast thou nothing to say for thyself, in defence of thy quality?
LEATHERHEAD.
Faith, sir, I am not well-studied in these controversies, between the hypocrites and us. But here's one of my motion, puppet Dionysius, shall undertake him, and I'll venture the cause on't.

COKES.

Who, my hobby-horse! will he dispute with him?

LEATHERHEAD.

Yes, sir, and make a hobby-ass of him, I hope.

COKES.

That's excellent! indeed he looks like the best scholar of them all. Come, sir, you must be as good as your word now.

RABBI BUSY.

I will not fear to make my spirit and gifts known: assist me zeal, fill me, fill me, that is, make me full!

WINWIFE.

What a desperate, profane wretch is this! is there any ignorance or impudence like his, to call his zeal to fill him against a puppet?

QUARLOUS.

I know no fitter match than a puppet to commit with an hypocrite!

RABBI BUSY.

First, I say unto thee, idol, thou hast no calling.

DIONYSIUS.

You lie, I am call'd Dionysius.

LEATHERHEAD.

The motion says, you lie, he is call'd Dionysius in the matter, and to that calling he answers.

RABBI BUSY.

I mean no vocation, idol, no present lawful calling.

DIONYSIUS.

Is yours a lawful calling?

LEATHERHEAD.

The motion asketh, if yours be a lawful calling.

RABBI BUSY.

Yes, mine is of the spirit.

DIONYSIUS.

Then idol is a lawful calling.

LEATHERHEAD.

He says, then idol is a lawful calling; for you call'd him idol, and your calling is of the spirit.

COKES.

Well disputed, hobby-horse.

RABBI BUSY.

Take not part with the wicked, young gallant: he neigheth and hinnieth; all is but hinnying sophistry. I call him idol again; yet, I say, his calling, his profession is profane, it is profane, idol.

DIONYSIUS.

It is not profane.

LEATHERHEAD.

It is not profane, he says.

RABBI BUSY.

It is profane.

DIONYSIUS.

It is not profane.

RABBI BUSY.

It is profane.

DIONYSIUS.

It is not profane.

LEATHERHEAD.

Well said, confute him with *Not,* still. You cannot bear him down with your base noise, sir.

RABBI BUSY.

Nor he me, with his treble creeking, though he creek like the chariot wheels of Satan; I am zealous for the cause——

LEATHERHEAD.

As a dog for a bone.

RABBI BUSY.

And I say, it is profane, as being the page of Pride, and the waiting-woman of Vanity.

DIONYSIUS.

Yea! what say you to your tire-women, then?

LEATHERHEAD.

Good.

DIONYSIUS.

Or feather-makers in the Friers, that are of your faction of faith? are not they with their perukes, and their puffs, their fans, and their huffs, as much pages of Pride, and waiters upon Vanity? What say you, what say you, what say you?

RABBI BUSY.

I will not answer for them.

DIONYSIUS.

Because you cannot, because you cannot. Is a bugle-maker a lawful calling? or the confect-makers? such you have there; or your French fashioner? you would have all the sin within yourselves, would you not, would you not?

RABBI BUSY.

No, Dagon.

DIONYSIUS.

What then, Dagonet? is a puppet worse than these?

RABBI BUSY.

Yes, and my main argument against you is, that you are an abomination; for the male, among you, putteth on the apparel of the female, and the female of the male.

DIONYSIUS.

You lie, you lie, you lie abominably.

COKES.

Good, by my troth, he has given him the lie thrice.

DIONYSIUS.

It is your old stale argument against the players, but it will not hold against the puppets;

for we have neither male nor female amongst us. And that thou may'st see, if thou
wilt, like a malicious purblind zeal as thou art.

[*Takes up his garment.*]

EDGWORTH.
By my faith, there he has answer'd you, friend, a plain demonstration.

DIONYSIUS.
Nay, I'll prove, against e'er a Rabbin of them all, that my standing is as lawful as his;
that I speak by inspiration, as well as he; that I have as little to do with learning as he;
and do scorn her helps as much as he.

RABBI BUSY.
I am confuted, the cause hath failed me.

DIONYSIUS.
Then be converted, be converted.

LEATHERHEAD.
Be converted, I pray you, and let the play go on!

RABBI BUSY.
Let it go on; for I am changed, and will become a beholder with you.

COKES.
That's brave, i'faith, thou hast carried it away, hobby-horse: on with the play.

Comus
A Mask
By JOHN MILTON

Sᴵɴᴄᴇ ᴛʜɪs ᴍᴀsᴋ *has never been treated as children's literature (except, perhaps, when it was first produced), I quote extensively from an article by Professor Lee Jacobus, who argues that it is, in fact, children's literature.*

Writing in the journal Children's Literature, *Temple University Press (Vol. 2, 1973), Jacobus notes that the leading role and two important supporting roles were played by children and written as children's parts:*

> Further *Comus* has a very specific didactic quality emphasizing problems of virtue and faith specifically pertinent to an adolescent girl. Then, the ambiguity of the genre, with a melodramatic quality more familiar to the mid-nineteenth-century stage than to the Stuart masquing ball, tends to put *Comus*—with its children threatened by a magician in a mazy wood—generically close to what we usually consider children's literature.

Commenting on the plot, he writes:

> A young lady is on her way home to her father's house for a celebration from an unknown whereabouts after an unknown length of time. These unknowns, as in most children's literature, pose no problem; they are not germane, so not developed.

Professor Jacobus concludes that surely, Milton, the master of so many genres—sonnet, pastoral elegy, ode, "twinned" poems, Christian epic, brief epic, tragedy—

> could surprise no one by inventing a new genre for the circle of his own acquaintance: the children's romance. The circumstances surrounding the masque would warrant it, as would his interest in specific literary genres. For one who loved and respected children as much as Milton did (see *Of Education*), it is only fitting and reasonable that he should make such a contribution for their enjoyment.

Comus *is reprinted from* A Mask . . . Presented at Ludlow-Castle *(1634) from* The Works of John Milton, *Vol. 1 (New York: Columbia University Press, 1931). This version reproduces the edition published by Humphrey Moseley in 1645. Following the text of* Comus *is an essay entitled "William Blake's Illustrations To* Comus*" by R. Loring Taylor.*

THE FIRST SCENE
Discovers a Wilde Wood.

The attendant Spirit descends or enters.

BEFORE THE STARRY threshold of *Joves* Court
My mansion is, where those immortal shapes
Of bright aereal Spirits live insphear'd
In Regions milde of calm and serene Ayr,
Above the smoak and stirr of this dim spot,
Which men call Earth, and with low-thoughted care
Confin'd, and pester'd in this pin-fold here,
Strive to keep up a frail, and Feaverish being
Unmindfull of the crown that Vertue gives
After this mortal change, to her true Servants
Amongst the enthron'd gods on Sainted seats.
Yet som there be that by due steps aspire
To lay their just hands on that Golden Key
That ope's the Palace of Eternity:
To such my errand is, and but for such,
I would not soil these pure Ambrosial weeds,
With the rank vapours of this Sin-worn mould.
   But to my task. *Neptune* besides the sway
Of every salt Flood, and each ebbing Stream,
Took in by lot 'twixt high, and neather *Jove*,
Imperial rule of all the Sea-girt Iles
That like to rich, and various gemms inlay
The unadorned boosom of the Deep,
Which he to grace his tributary gods
By course commits to severall government,
And gives them leave to wear their Saphire crowns,
And weild their little tridents, but this Ile
The greatest, and the best of all the main
He quarters to his blu-hair'd deities,
And all this tract that fronts the falling Sun
A noble Peer of mickle trust, and power
Has in his charge, with temper'd awe to guide
An old, and haughty Nation proud in Arms:
Where his fair off-spring nurs't in Princely lore,
Are coming to attend their Fathers state,
And new-entrusted Scepter, but their way
Lies through the perplex't paths of this drear Wood,
The nodding horror of whose shady brows

Threats the forlorn and wandring Passinger.
And here their tender age might suffer perill,
But that by quick command from Soveran *Jove*
I was dispatcht for their defence, and guard;
And listen why, for I will tell you now
What never yet was heard in Tale or Song
From old, or modern Bard in Hall, or Bowr.
   Bacchus that first from out the purple Grape,
Crush't the sweet poyson of mis-used Wine
After the *Tuscan* Mariners transform'd
Coasting the *Tyrrhene* shore, as the winds listed,
On *Circes* Iland fell (who knows not *Circe*
The daughter of the Sun? Whose charmed Cup
Whoever tasted, lost his upright shape,
And downward fell into a groveling Swine)
This Nymph that gaz'd upon his clustring locks,
With Ivy berries wreath'd, and his blithe youth,
Had by him, ere he parted thence, a Son
Much like his Father, but his Mother more,
Whom therfore she brought up and *Comus* nam'd,
Who ripe, and frolick of his full grown age,
Roaving the *Celtick*, and *Iberian* fields,
At last betakes him to this ominous Wood,
And in thick shelter of black shades imbowr'd,
Excells his Mother at her mighty Art,
Offring to every weary Travailer,
His orient Liquor in a Crystal Glasse,
To quench the drouth of *Phœbus*, which as they taste
(For most do taste through fond intemperate thirst)
Soon as the Potion works, their human count'nance,
Th' express resemblance of the gods, is chang'd
Into som brutish form of Woolf, or Bear,
Or Ounce, or Tiger, Hog, or bearded Goat,
All other parts remaining as they were,
And they, so perfect is their misery,
Not once perceive their foul disfigurement,
But boast themselves more comely then before
And all their friends, and native home forget
To roule with pleasure in a sensual stie.
Therefore when any favour'd of high *Jove*,
Chances to pass through this adventrous glade,
Swift as the Sparkle of a glancing Star,
I shoot from Heav'n to give him safe convoy,
As now I do: But first I must put off
These my skie robes spun out of *Iris* Wooff,

And take the Weeds and likenes of a Swain,
That to the service of this house belongs,
Who with his soft Pipe, and smooth dittied Song
Well knows to still the wilde winds when they roar,
And hush the waving Woods, nor of lesse faith,
And in this office of his Mountain watch,
Likeliest, and nearest to the present ayd
Of this occasion. But I hear the tread
Of hatefull steps, I must be viewles now.

COMUS *enters with a Charming Rod in one hand, his Glass
in the other, with him a rout of Monsters headed like
sundry sorts of wilde Beasts, but otherwise like Men and
Women, their Apparel glistring, they com in making a
riotous and unruly noise, with Torches in their hands.*

COMUS.
The Star that bids the Shepherd fold,
Now the top of Heav'n doth hold,
And the gilded Car of Day,
His glowing Axle doth allay
In the steep *Atlantick* stream,
And the slope Sun his upward beam
Shoots against the dusky Pole,
Pacing toward the other gole
Of his Chamber in the East.
Mean while welcom Joy, and Feast,
Midnight shout, and revelry,
Tipsie dance, and Jollity.
Braid your Locks with rosie Twine
Dropping odours, dropping Wine.
Rigor now is gon to bed,
And Advice with scrupulous head,
Strict Age, and sowre Severity,
With their grave Saws in slumber lie.
We that are of purer fire
Imitate the Starry Quire,
Who in their nightly watchfull Sphears,
Lead in swift round the Months and Years.
The Sounds, and Seas with all their finny drove
Now to the Moon in wavering Morrice move,
And on the Tawny Sands and Shelves,
Trip the pert Fairies and the dapper Elves;
By dimpled Brook, and Fountain brim,
The Wood-Nymphs deckt with Daisies trim,

Their merry wakes and pastimes keep:
What hath night to do with sleep?
Night hath better sweets to prove,
Venus now wakes, and wak'ns Love.
Com let us our rights begin,
'Tis onely day-light that makes Sin
Which these dun shades will ne're report.

Hail Goddess of Nocturnal sport
Dark vail'd *Cotytto*, t' whom the secret flame
Of mid-night Torches burns; mysterious Dame
That ne're art call'd, but when the Dragon woom
Of Stygian darkness spets her thickest gloom,
And makes one blot of all the ayr,
Stay thy cloudy Ebon chair,
Wherein thou rid'st with *Hecat'*, and befriend
Us thy vow'd Priests, till utmost end
Of all thy dues be done, and none left out,
Ere the blabbing Eastern scout,
The nice Morn on th' *Indian* steep
From her cabin'd loop-hole peep,
And to the tell-tale Sun discry
Our conceal'd Solemnity.
Com, knit hands, and beat the ground,
In a light fantastick round.

The Measure.

Break off, break off, I feel the different pace,
Of som chast footing near about this ground.
Run to your shrouds, within these Brakes and Trees,
Our number may affright: Some Virgin sure
(For so I can distinguish by mine Art)
Benighted in these Woods. Now to my charms,
And to my wily trains, I shall e're long
Be well stock't with as fair a herd as graz'd
About my Mother *Circe*. Thus I hurl
My dazling Spells into the spungy ayr,
Of power to cheat the eye with blear illusion,
And give it false presentments, lest the place
And my quaint habits breed astonishment,
And put the Damsel to suspicious flight,
Which must not be, for that's against my course;
I under fair pretence of friendly ends,
And well plac't words of glozing courtesie
Baited with reasons not unplausible
Wind me into the easie-hearted man,
And hug him into snares. When once her eye
Hath met the vertue of this Magick dust,
I shall appear som harmles Villager
Whom thrift keeps up about his Country gear,
But here she comes, I fairly step aside
And hearken, if I may, her busines here.

The Lady enters.

This way the noise was, if mine ear be true,
My best guide now, me thought it was the sound
Of Riot, and ill manag'd Merriment,
Such as the jocond Flute, or gamesom Pipe
Stirs up among the loose unleter'd Hinds,
When for their teeming Flocks, and granges full
In wanton dance they praise the bounteous *Pan*,
And thank the gods amiss. I should be loath
To meet the rudenesse, and swill'd insolence
Of such late Wassailers; yet O where els
Shall I inform my unacquainted feet
In the blind mazes of this tangl'd Wood?
My Brothers when they saw me wearied out
With this long way, resolving here to lodge
Under the spreading favour of these Pines,
Stept as they se'd to the next Thicket side
To bring me Berries, or such cooling fruit
As the kind hospitable Woods provide.
They left me then, when the gray-hooded Eev'n
Like a sad Votarist in Palmers weed
Rose from the hindmost wheels of *Phœbus* wain.
But where they are, and why they came not back,
Is now the labour of my thoughts, 'tis likeliest
They had ingag'd their wandring steps too far,
And envious darknes, e're they could return,
Had stole them from me, els O theevish Night
Why shouldst thou, but for som fellonious end,
In thy dark lantern thus close up the Stars,
That nature hung in Heav'n, and fill'd their Lamps
With everlasting oil, to give due light
To the misled and lonely Travailer?
This is the place, as well as I may guess,
Whence eev'n now the tumult of loud Mirth
Was rife, and perfet in my list'ning ear,
Yet nought but single darknes do I find.
What might this be? A thousand fantasies
Begin to throng into my memory
Of calling shapes, and beckning shadows dire,
And airy tongues, that syllable mens names
On Sands, and Shoars, and desert Wildernesses.
These thoughts may startle well, but not astound
The vertuous mind, that ever walks attended
By a strong siding champion Conscience.——

O welcom pure-ey'd Faith, white-handed Hope,
Thou hovering Angel girt with golden wings,
And thou unblemish't form of Chastity,
I see ye visibly, and now beleeve
That he, the Supreme good, t'whom all things ill
Are but as slavish officers of vengeance,
Would send a glistring Guardian if need were
To keep my life and honour unassail'd.
Was I deceiv'd, or did a sable cloud
Turn forth her silver lining on the night?
I did not err, there does a sable cloud
Turn forth her silver lining on the night,
And casts a gleam over this tufted Grove.
I cannot hallow to my Brothers, but
Such noise as I can make to be heard farthest
Ile venter, for my new enliv'nd spirits
Prompt me; and they perhaps are not far off.

SONG

Sweet Echo, sweetest Nymph that liv'st unseen
Within thy airy shell
By slow Meander's *margent green,*
And in the violet imbroider'd vale
Where the love-lorn Nightingale
Nightly to thee her sad Song mourneth well.
Canst thou not tell me of a gentle Pair
That likest thy Narcissus *are?*
O if thou have
Hid them in som flowry Cave,
Tell me but where
Sweet Queen of Parly, Daughter of the Sphear,
So maist thou be translated to the skies,
And give resounding grace to all Heav'ns Harmonies.

COM.
Can any mortal mixture of Earths mould
Breath such Divine inchanting ravishment?
Sure somthing holy lodges in that brest,
And with these raptures moves the vocal air
To testifie his hidd'n residence;
How sweetly did they float upon the wings
Of silence, through the empty-vaulted night
At every fall smoothing the Raven doune

Of darknes till it smil'd: I have oft heard
My Mother *Circe* with the Sirens three,
Amid'st the flowry-kirtl'd *Naiades*
Culling their Potent hearbs, and balefull drugs,
Who as they sung, would take the prison'd soul,
And lap it in *Elysium, Scylla* wept,
And chid her barking waves into attention,
And fell *Charybdis* murmur'd soft applause:
Yet they in pleasing slumber lull'd the sense,
And in sweet madnes rob'd it of it self,
But such a sacred, and home-felt delight,
Such sober certainty of waking bliss
I never heard till now. Ile speak to her
And she shall be my Queen. Hail forren wonder
Whom certain these rough shades did never breed
Unlesse the Goddes that in rurall shrine
Dwell'st here with *Pan*, or *Silvan*, by blest Song
Forbidding every bleak unkindly Fog
To touch the prosperous growth of this tall Wood.

LA.

Nay gentle Shepherd ill is lost that praise
That is addrest to unattending Ears,
Not any boast of skill, but extreme shift
How to regain my sever'd company
Compell'd me to awake the courteous Echo
To give me answer from her mossie Couch.

CO.

What chance good Lady hath bereft you thus?

LA.

Dim darknes, and this leavie Labyrinth.

CO.

Could that divide you from neer-ushering guides?

LA.

They left me weary on a grassie terf.

CO.

By falshood, or discourtesie, or why?

LA.

To seek i'th vally som cool friendly Spring.

CO.

And left your fair side all unguarded Lady?

LA.

They were but twain, and purpos'd quick return.

CO.

Perhaps fore-stalling night prevented them.

LA.

    How easie my misfortune is to hit!

CO.

    Imports their loss, beside the present need?

LA.

    No less then if I should my brothers loose.

CO.

Were they of manly prime, or youthful bloom?

LA.

As smooth as *Hebe*'s their unrazor'd lips.

CO.

Two such I saw, what time the labour'd Oxe
In his loose traces from the furrow came,
And the swink't hedger at his Supper sate;
I saw them under a green mantling vine
That crawls along the side of yon small hill,
Plucking ripe clusters from the tender shoots,
Their port was more then human, as they stood;
I took it for a faëry vision
Of som gay creatures of the element
That in the colours of the Rainbow live
And play i'th plighted clouds. I was aw-strook,
And as I past, I worshipt; if those you seek
It were a journey like the path to Heav'n,
To help you find them. LA. Gentle villager
What readiest way would bring me to that place?

CO.

Due west it rises from this shrubby point.

LA.

To find out that, good Shepherd, I suppose,
In such a scant allowance of Star-light,
Would overtask the best Land-Pilots art,
Without the sure guess of well-practiz'd feet.

CO.

I know each lane, and every alley green
Dingle, or bushy dell of this wilde Wood,
And every bosky bourn from side to side
My daily walks and ancient neighbourhood,
And if your stray attendance be yet lodg'd,
Or shroud within these limits, I shall know
Ere morrow wake, or the low roosted lark
From her thatch't pallat rowse, if otherwise
I can conduct you Lady to a low
But loyal cottage, where you may be safe
Till further quest'. LA. Shepherd I take thy word,
And trust thy honest offer'd courtesie,
Which oft is sooner found in lowly sheds
With smoaky rafters, then in tapstry Halls
And Courts of Princes, where it first was nam'd,

And yet is most pretended: In a place
Less warranted then this, or less secure
I cannot be, that I should fear to change it,
Eie me blest Providence, and square my triall
To my proportion'd strength. Shepherd lead on.

The two Brothers.

ELD. BRO.

   Unmuffle ye faint Stars, and thou fair Moon
That wontst to love the travellers benizon,
Stoop thy pale visage through an amber cloud,
And disinherit *Chaos,* that raigns here
In double night of darknes, and of shades;
Or if your influence be quite damm'd up
With black usurping mists, som gentle taper
Though a rush Candle from the wicker hole
Of som clay habitation visit us
With thy long levell'd rule of streaming light,
And thou shalt be our star of *Arcady,*
Or *Tyrian* Cynosure. 2. BRO. Or if our eyes
Be barr'd that happines, might we but hear
The folded flocks pen'd in their watled cotes,
Or sound of pastoral reed with oaten stops,
Or whistle from the Lodge, or village cock
Count the night watches to his feathery Dames,
'Twould be som solace yet, som little chearing
In this close dungeon of innumerous bowes.
But O that haples virgin our lost sister
Where may she wander now, whether betake her
From the chill dew, amongst rude burrs and thistles?
Perhaps som cold bank is her boulster now
Or 'gainst the rugged bark of som broad Elm
Leans her unpillow'd head fraught with sad fears,
What if in wild amazement, and affright,
Or while we speak within the direful grasp
Of Savage hunger, or of Savage heat?

ELD. BRO.

   Peace Brother, be not over-exquisite
To cast the fashion of uncertain evils;
For grant they be so, while they rest unknown,
What need a man forestall his date of grief,
And run to meet what he would most avoid?
Or if they be but false alarms of Fear,
How bitter is such self-delusion?
I do not think my sister so to seek,
Or so unprincipl'd in vertues book,
And the sweet peace that goodnes boosoms ever,
As that the single want of light and noise
(Not being in danger, as I trust she is not)
Could stir the constant mood of her calm thoughts,

And put them into mis-becoming plight.
Vertue could see to do what vertue would
By her own radiant light, though Sun and Moon
Were in the flat Sea sunk. And Wisdoms self
Oft seeks to sweet retired Solitude,
Where with her best nurse Contemplation
She plumes her feathers, and lets grow her wings
That in the various bustle of resort
Were all to ruffl'd, and somtimes impair'd.
He that has light within his own cleer brest
May sit i'th center, and enjoy bright day,
But he that hides a dark soul, and foul thoughts
Benighted walks under the mid-day Sun;
Himself is his own dungeon.
2. BRO.
   Tis most true
That musing meditation most affects
The pensive secrecy of desert cell,
Far from the cheerfull haunt of men, and herds,
And sits as safe as in a Senat house,
For who would rob a Hermit of his Weeds,
His few Books, or his Beads, or Maple Dish,
Or do his gray hairs any violence?
But beauty like the fair Hesperian Tree
Laden with blooming gold, had need the guard
Of dragon watch with uninchanted eye,
To save her blossoms, and defend her fruit
From the rash hand of bold Incontinence.
You may as well spred out the unsun'd heaps
Of Misers treasure by an out-laws den,
And tell me it is safe, as bid me hope
Danger will wink on Opportunity,
And let a single helpless maiden pass
Uninjur'd in this wilde surrounding wast.
Of night, or lonelines it recks me not,
I fear the dred events that dog them both,
Lest som ill greeting touch attempt the person
Of our unowned sister.
ELD. BRO.
   I do not, Brother,
Inferr, as if I thought my sisters state
Secure without all doubt, or controversie:
Yet where an equal poise of hope and fear
Does arbitrate th'event, my nature is
That I encline to hope, rather than fear,

And gladly banish squint suspicion.
My sister is not so defenceless left
As you imagine, she has a hidden strength
Which you remember not.
2. BRO.
    What hidden strength,
Unless the strength of Heav'n, if you mean that?
ELD. BRO.
    I mean that too, but yet a hidden strength
Which if Heav'n gave it, may be term'd her own:
'Tis chastity, my brother, chastity:
She that has that, is clad in compleat steel,
And like a quiver'd Nymph with Arrows keen
May trace huge Forests, and unharbour'd Heaths,
Infamous Hills, and sandy perilous wildes,
Where through the sacred rayes of Chastity,
No savage fierce, Bandite, or mountaneer
Will dare to soyl her Virgin purity,
Yea there, where very desolation dwels
By grots, and caverns shag'd with horrid shades,
She may pass on with unblench't majesty,
Be it not don in pride, or in presumption.
Som say no evil thing that walks by night
In fog, or fire, by lake, or moorish fen,
Blew meager Hag, or stubborn unlaid ghost,
That breaks his magick chains at *curfeu* time,
No Goblin, or swart Faëry of the mine,
Hath hurtfull power o're true virginity.
Do ye believe me yet, or shall I call
Antiquity from the old Schools of Greece
To testifie the arms of Chastity?
Hence had the huntress *Dian* her dred bow
Fair silver-shafted Queen for ever chaste,
Wherewith she tam'd the brinded lioness
And spotted mountain pard, but set at nought
The frivolous bolt of *Cupid,* gods and men
Fear'd her stern frown, and she was queen oth' Woods.
What was that snaky-headed *Gorgon* sheild
That wise *Minerva* wore, unconquer'd Virgin,
Wherwith she freez'd her foes to congeal'd stone?
But rigid looks of Chast austerity,
And noble grace that dash't brute violence
With sudden adoration, and blank aw.
So dear to Heav'n is Saintly chastity,
That when a soul is found sincerely so,

A thousand liveried Angels lacky her,
Driving far off each thing of sin and guilt,
And in cleer dream, and solemn vision
Tell her of things that no gross ear can hear,
Till oft convers with heav'nly habitants
Begin to cast a beam on th' outward shape,
The unpolluted temple of the mind,
And turns it by degrees to the souls essence,
Till all be made immortal: but when lust
By unchaste looks, loose gestures, and foul talk,
But most by leud and lavish act of sin,
Lets in defilement to the inward parts,
The soul grows clotted by contagion,
Imbodies, and imbrutes, till she quite loose
The divine property of her first being.
Such are those thick and gloomy shadows damp
Oft seen in Charnell vaults, and Sepulchers
Lingering, and sitting by a new made grave,
As loath to leave the Body that it lov'd,
And link't it self by carnal sensualty
To a degenerate and degraded state.
2. BRO.
   How charming is divine Philosophy!
Not harsh, and crabbed as dull fools suppose,
But musical as is *Apollo*'s lute,
And a perpetual feast of nectar'd sweets,
Where no crude surfet raigns. ELD. BRO. List, list, I hear
Som far off hallow break the silent Air.
2. BRO.
   Me thought so too; what should it be?
ELD. BRO.
   For certain
Either som one like us night-founder'd here,
Or els som neighbour Wood-man, or at worst.
Som roaving Robber calling to his fellows.
2. BRO.
   Heav'n keep my sister, agen agen and neer,
Best draw, and stand upon our guard.
ELD. BRO.
   Ile hallow,
If he be friendly he comes well, if not,
Defence is a good cause, and Heav'n be for us.

   The attendant Spirit habited like a Shepherd.

That hallow I should know, what are you? speak;
Com not too neer, you fall on iron stakes else.
SPIR.
 What voice is that, my young Lord? speak agen.
2. BRO.
 O brother, 'tis my father Shepherd sure.

ELD. BRO.

   Thyrsis? Whose artful strains have oft delaid
The huddling brook to hear his madrigal,
And sweeten'd every muskrose of the dale,
How cam'st thou here good Swain? hath any ram
Slip't from the fold, or young Kid lost his dam,
Or straggling weather the pen't flock forsook?
How couldst thou find this dark sequester'd nook?
SPIR.

   O my lov'd masters heir, and his next joy,
I came not here on such a trivial toy
As a stray'd Ewe, or to pursue the stealth
Of pilfering Woolf, not all the fleecy wealth
That doth enrich these Downs, is worth a thought
To this my errand, and the care it brought.
But O my Virgin Lady, where is she?
How chance she is not in your company?
ELD. BRO.

   To tell thee sadly Shepherd, without blame,
Or our neglect, we lost her as we came.
SPIR.

   Ay me unhappy then my fears are true.
ELD. BRO.

   What fears good *Thyrsis?* Prethee briefly shew.
SPIR.

   Ile tell ye, 'tis not vain or fabulous,
(Though so esteem'd by shallow ignorance)
What the sage Poets taught by th' heav'nly Muse,
Storied of old in high immortal vers
Of dire *Chimera*'s and inchanted Iles,
And rifted Rocks whose entrance leads to hell,
For such there be, but unbelief is blind.

   Within the navil of this hideous Wood,
Immur'd in cypress shades a Sorcerer dwels
Of *Bacchus,* and of *Circe* born, great *Comus,*
Deep skill'd in all his mothers witcheries,
And here to every thirsty wanderer,
By sly enticement gives his banefull cup,
With many murmurs mixt, whose pleasing poison
The visage quite transforms of him that drinks,
And the inglorious likenes of a beast
Fixes instead, unmoulding reasons mintage
Character'd in the face; this have I learn't
Tending my flocks hard by i'th hilly crofts,
That brow this bottom glade, whence night by night

He and his monstrous rout are heard to howl
Like stabl'd wolves, or tigers at their prey,
Doing abhorred rites to *Hecate*
In their obscured haunts of inmost bowres,
Yet have they many baits, and guileful spells
To inveigle and invite th' unwary sense
Of them that pass unweeting by the way.
This evening late by then the chewing flocks
Had ta'n their supper on the savoury Herb
Of Knot-grass dew-besprent, and were in fold,
I sate me down to watch upon a bank
With Ivy canopied, and interwove
With flaunting Hony-suckle, and began
Wrapt in a pleasing fit of melancholy
To meditate upon my rural minstrelsie,
Till fancy had her fill, but ere a close
The wonted roar was up amidst the Woods,
And fill'd the Air with barbarous dissonance,
At which I ceas't, and listen'd them a while,
Till an unusual stop of sudden silence
Gave respit to the drowsie frighted steeds
That draw the litter of close curtain'd sleep;
At last a soft and solemn breathing sound
Rose like a steam of rich distill'd Perfumes,
And stole upon the Air, that even Silence
Was took e're she was ware, and wisht she might
Deny her nature, and be never more
Still to be so displac't. I was all eare,
And took in strains that might create a soul
Under the ribs of Death, but O ere long
Too well I did perceive it was the voice
Of my most honour'd Lady, your dear sister.
Amaz'd I stood, harrow'd with grief and fear,
And O poor hapless Nightingale thought I,
How sweet thou sing'st, how neer the deadly snare!
Then down the Lawns I ran with headlong hast
Through paths, and turnings oft'n trod by day,
Till guided by mine ear I found the place
Where that damn'd wisard hid in sly disguise
(For so by certain signes I knew) had met
Already, ere my best speed could prevent,
The aidless innocent Lady his wish't prey,
Who gently ask't if he had seen such two,
Supposing him som neighbour villager;
Longer I durst not stay, but soon I guess't

Ye were the two she mean't, with that I sprung
Into swift flight, till I had found you here,
But furder know I not. 2. BRO. O night and shades,
How are ye joyn'd with Hell in triple knot
Against th' unarmed weakness of one Virgin
Alone, and helpless! is this the confidence
You gave me Brother? ELD. BRO. Yes, and keep it still,
Lean on it safely, not a period
Shall be unsaid for me: against the threats
Of malice or of sorcery, or that power
Which erring men call Chance, this I hold firm,
Vertue may be assail'd, but never hurt,
Surpriz'd by unjust force, but not enthrall'd,
Yea even that which mischief meant most harm,
Shall in the happy trial prove most glory.
But evil on it self shall back recoyl,
And mix no more with goodness, when at last
Gather'd like scum, and setl'd to it self
It shall be in eternal restless change
Self-fed, and self-consum'd, if this fail,
The pillar'd firmament is rott'nness,
And earths base built on stubble. But com let's on.
Against th' opposing will and arm of Heav'n
May never this just sword be lifted up,
But for that damn'd magician, let him be girt
With all the greisly legions that troop
Under the sooty flag of *Acheron*,
Harpyes and *Hydra*'s, or all the monstrous forms
'Twixt *Africa* and *Inde*, Ile find him out,
And force him to restore his purchase back,
Or drag him by the curls, to a foul death,
Curs'd as his life.

SPIR.

    Alas good ventrous youth,
I love thy courage yet, and bold Emprise,
But here thy sword can do thee little stead,
Farr other arms, and other weapons must
Be those that quell the might of hellish charms,
He with his bare wand can unthred thy joynts,
And crumble all thy sinews.

ELD. BRO.

    Why prethee Shepherd
How durst thou then thy self approach so neer
As to make this relation?

SPIR.

   Care and utmost shifts
How to secure the Lady from surprisal,
Brought to my mind a certain Shepherd Lad
Of small regard to see to, yet well skill'd
In every vertuous plant and healing herb
That spreds her verdant leaf to th' morning ray.
He lov'd me well, and oft would beg me sing,
Which when I did, he on the tender grass
Would sit, and hearken even to extasie,
And in requitall ope his leather'n scrip,
And shew me simples of a thousand names
Telling their strange and vigorous faculties;
Amongst the rest a small unsightly root,
But of divine effect, he cull'd me out;
The leaf was darkish, and had prickles on it,
But in another Countrey, as he said,
Bore a bright golden flowre, but not in this soyl:
Unknown, and like esteem'd, and the dull swain
Treads on it daily with his clouted shoon,
And yet more med'cinal is it then that *Moly*
That *Hermes* once to wise *Ulysses* gave;
He call'd it *Hæmony*, and gave it me,
And bad me keep it as of sovran use
'Gainst all inchantments, mildew blast, or damp
Or gastly furies apparition;
I purs't it up, but little reck'ning made,
Till now that this extremity compell'd,
But now I find it true; for by this means
I knew the foul inchanter though disguis'd,
Enter'd the very lime-twigs of his spells,
And yet came off: if you have this about you
(As I will give you when we go) you may
Boldly assault the necromancers hall;
Where if he be, with dauntless hardihood,
And brandish't blade rush on him, break his glass,
And shed the lushious liquor on the ground,
But sease his wand, though he and his curst crew
Feirce signe of battail make, and menace high,
Or like the Sons of *Vulcan* vomit smoak,
Yet will they soon retire, if he but shrink.

ELD. BRO.

   Thyrsis lead on apace, Ile follow thee,
And som good angel bear a sheild before us.

The Scene changes to a stately Palace, set out with all manner

of deliciousness: soft Musick, Tables spred with all dain-
ties. Comus *appears with his rabble, and the Lady set in*
an inchanted Chair, to whom he offers his Glass, which
she puts by, and goes about to rise.

COMUS.
　　Nay Lady sit; if I but wave this wand,

Your nerves are all chain'd up in Alablaster,
And you a statue, or as *Daphne* was
Root-bound, that fled *Apollo*.

LA.

    Fool do not boast,
Thou canst not touch the freedom of my minde
With all thy charms, although this corporal rinde
Thou haste immanacl'd, while Heav'n sees good.

CO.

    Why are you vext Lady? why do you frown?
Here dwell no frowns, nor anger, from these gates
Sorrow flies farr: See here be all the pleasures
That fancy can beget on youthfull thoughts,
When the fresh blood grows lively, and returns
Brisk as the *April* buds in Primrose-season.
And first behold this cordial Julep here
That flames, and dances in his crystal bounds
With spirits of balm, and fragrant Syrops mixt.
Not that *Nepenthes* which the wife of *Thone,*
In *Egypt* gave to *Jove*-born *Helena*
Is of such power to stir up joy as this,
To life so friendly, or so cool to thirst.
Why should you be so cruel to your self,
And to those dainty limms which nature lent
For gentle usage, and soft delicacy?
But you invert the cov'nants of her trust,
And harshly deal like an ill borrower
With that which you receiv'd on other terms,
Scorning the unexempt condition
By which all mortal frailty must subsist,
Refreshment after toil, ease after pain,
That have been tir'd all day without repast,
And timely rest have wanted, but fair Virgin
This will restore all soon.

LA.

    'Twill not false traitor,
'Twill not restore the truth and honesty
That thou hast banish't from thy tongue with lies,
Was this the cottage, and the safe abode
Thou told'st me of? What grim aspects are these,
These oughly-headed Monsters? Mercy guard me!
Hence with thy brew'd inchantments, foul deceiver,
Hast thou betrai'd my credulous innocence
With visor'd falshood, and base forgery,
And would'st thou seek again to trap me here

With lickerish baits fit to ensnare a brute?
Were it a draft for *Juno* when she banquets,
I would not taste thy treasonous offer; none
But such as are good men can give good things,
And that which is not good, is not delicious
To a well-govern'd and wise appetite.
co.
    O foolishnes of men! that lend their ears
To those budge doctors of the *Stoick* Furr,
And fetch their precepts from the *Cynick* Tub,
Praising the lean and sallow Abstinence.
Wherefore did Nature powre her bounties forth,
With such a full and unwithdrawing hand,
Covering the earth with odours, fruits, and flocks,
Thronging the Seas with spawn innumerable,
But all to please, and sate the curious taste?
And set to work millions of spinning Worms,
That in their green shops weave the smooth-hair'd silk
To deck her Sons, and that no corner might
Be vacant of her plenty, in her own loyns
She hutch't th' all-worshipt ore, and precious gems
To store her children with; if all the world
Should in a pet of temperance feed on Pulse,
Drink the clear stream, and nothing wear but Freize,
Th' all-giver would be unthank't, would be unprais'd,
Not half his riches known, and yet despis'd,
And we should serve him as a grudging master,
As a penurious niggard of his wealth,
And live like Natures bastards, not her sons,
Who would be quite surcharg'd with her own weight,
And strangl'd with her waste fertility;
Th' earth cumber'd, and the wing'd air dark't with plumes,
The herds would over-multitude their Lords,
The Sea o'refraught would swel, & th' unsought diamonds
Would so emblaze the forhead of the Deep,
And so bestudd with Stars, that they below
Would grow inur'd to light, and com at last
To gaze upon the Sun with shameles brows.
List Lady be not coy, and be not cosen'd
With that same vaunted name Virginity,
Beauty is natures coyn, must not be hoorded,
But must be currant, and the good thereof
Consists in mutual and partak'n bliss,
Unsavoury in th' injoyment of it self.
If you let slip time, like a neglected rose

It withers on the stalk with languish't head.
Beauty is natures brag, and must be shown
In courts, at feasts, and high solemnities
Where most may wonder at the workmanship;
It is for homely features to keep home,
They had their name thence; course complexions
And cheeks of sorry grain will serve to ply
The sampler, and to teize the huswifes wooll.
What need a vermeil-tinctur'd lip for that
Love-darting eyes, or tresses like the Morn?
There was another meaning in these gifts,
Think what, and be adviz'd, you are but young yet.
LA.
   I had not thought to have unlockt my lips
In this unhallow'd air, but that this Jugler
Would think to charm my judgement, as mine eyes
Obtruding false rules pranckt in reasons garb.
I hate when vice can bolt her arguments,
And vertue has no tongue to check her pride:
Impostor do not charge most innocent nature,
As if she would her children should be riotous
With her abundance, she good cateress
Means her provision only to the good
That live according to her sober laws,
And holy dictate of spare Temperance:
If every just man that now pines with want
Had but a moderate and beseeming share
Of that which lewdly-pamper'd Luxury
Now heaps upon som few with vast excess,
Natures full blessings would be well dispenc't
In unsuperfluous eeven proportion,
And she no whit encomber'd with her store,
And then the giver would be better thank't,
His praise due paid, for swinish gluttony
Ne're looks to Heav'n amidst his gorgeous feast,
But with besotted base ingratitude
Cramms, and blasphemes his feeder. Shall I go on?
Or have I said anow? To him that dares
Arm his profane tongue with contemptuous words
Against the Sun-clad power of Chastity;
Fain would I somthing say, yet to what end?
Thou hast nor Ear, nor Soul to apprehend
The sublime notion, and high mystery
That must be utter'd to unfold the sage
And serious doctrine of Virginity,

And thou art worthy that thou shouldst not know
More happiness then this thy present lot.
Enjoy your deer Wit, and gay Rhetorick
That hath so well been taught her dazling fence,
Thou art not fit to hear thy self convinc't;
Yet should I try, the uncontrouled worth
Of this pure cause would kindle my rap't spirits
To such a flame of sacred vehemence,
That dumb things would be mov'd to sympathize,
And the brute Earth would lend her nerves, and shake,
Till all thy magick structures rear'd so high,
Were shatter'd into heaps o're thy false head.
CO.
   She fables not, I feel that I do fear
Her words set off by som superior power;
And though not mortal, yet a cold shuddring dew
Dips me all o're, as when the wrath of *Jove*
Speaks thunder, and the chains of *Erebus*
To som of *Saturns* crew. I must dissemble,
And try her yet more strongly. Com, no more,
This is meer moral babble, and direct
Against the canon laws of our foundation;
I must not suffer this, yet 'tis but the lees
And setlings of a melancholy blood;
But this will cure all streight, one sip of this
Will bathe the drooping spirits in delight
Beyond the bliss of dreams. Be wise, and taste.—

*The Brothers rush in with Swords drawn, wrest his Glass
out of his hand, and break it against the ground; his rout
make sign of resistance, but are all driven in; The attendant Spirit comes in.*

SPIR.
   What, have you let the false enchanter scape?
O ye mistook, ye should have snatcht his wand
And bound him fast; without his rod revers't,
And backward mutters of dissevering power,
We cannot free the Lady that sits here
In stony fetters fixt, and motionless;
Yet stay, be not disturb'd, now I bethink me,
Som other means I have which may be us'd,
Which once of *Melibæus* old I learnt
The soothest Shepherd that ere pip't on plains.
   There is a gentle Nymph not farr from hence,
That with moist curb sways the smooth Severn stream,

Sabrina is her name, a Virgin pure,
Whilom she was the daughter of *Locrine*,
That had the Scepter from his Father *Brute*.
The guiltless damsel flying the mad pursuit
Of her enraged stepdam *Guendolen*,
Commended her fair innocence to the flood

That stay'd her flight with his cross-flowing course,
The water Nymphs that in the bottom plaid,
Held up their pearled wrists and took her in,
Bearing her straight to aged *Nereus* Hall,
Who piteous of her woes, rear'd her lank head,
And gave her to his daughters to imbathe
In nectar'd lavers strew'd with Asphodil,
And through the porch and inlet of each sense
Dropt in Ambrosial Oils till she reviv'd,
And underwent a quick immortal change
Made Goddess of the River; still she retains
Her maid'n gentlenes, and oft at Eeve
Visits the herds along the twilight meadows,
Helping all urchin blasts, and ill luck signes
That the shrewd medling Elfe delights to make,
Which she with pretious viold liquors heals.
For which the Shepherds at their festivals
Carrol her goodnes lowd in rustick layes,
And throw sweet garland wreaths into her stream
Of pancies, pinks, and gaudy Daffadils.
And, as the old Swain said, she can unlock
The clasping charm, and thaw the numming spell,
If she be right invok't in warbled Song,
For maid'nhood she loves, and will be swift
To aid a Virgin such as was her self
In hard besetting need, this will I try
And adde the power of som adjuring verse.

SONG

Sabrina fair
    Listen where thou art sitting
Under the glassie, cool, translucent wave,
    In twisted braids of Lillies knitting
The loose train of thy amber-dropping hair,
    Listen for dear honours sake,
    Goddess of the silver lake,
            Listen and save.

Listen and appear to us
In name of great *Oceanus*,
By the earth-shaking *Neptune*'s mace,
And *Tethys* grave majestick pace,
By hoary *Nereus* wrincled look,
And the *Carpathian* wisards hook,

By scaly *Tritons* winding shell,
And old sooth-saying *Glaucus* spell,
By *Leucothea*'s lovely hands,
And her son that rules the strands,
By *Thetis* tinsel-slipper'd feet,
And the Songs of *Sirens* sweet,
By dead *Parthenope*'s dear tomb,
And fair *Ligea*'s golden comb,
Wherwith she sits on diamond rocks
Sleeking her soft alluring locks,
By all the *Nymphs* that nightly dance
Upon thy streams with wily glance.
Rise, rise, and heave thy rosie head
From thy coral-pav'n bed,
And bridle in thy headlong wave,
Till thou our summons answer'd have.
                              Listen and save.

    Sabrina *rises, attended by water-Nymphes, & sings.*

        By the rushy-fringed bank,
Where grows the Willow and the Osier dank,
        My sliding Chariot stayes,
Thick set with Agat, and the azurn sheen
    Of Turkis blew, and Emrauld green
            That in the channel strayes,
        Whilst from off the waters fleet
        Thus I set my printless feet
        O're the Cowslips Velvet head,
            That bends not as I tread,
        Gentle swain at thy request
            I am here.
SPIR.
    Goddess dear
We implore thy powerful hand
To undo the charmed band
Of true Virgin here distrest,
Through the force, and through the wile
Of unblest inchanter vile.

SAB.
    Shepherd 'tis my office best
To help insnared chastity;
Brightest Lady look on me,
Thus I sprinkle on thy brest
Drops that from my fountain pure,

I have kept of pretious cure,
Thrice upon thy fingers tip,
Thrice upon thy rubied lip,
Next this marble venom'd seat
Smear'd with gumms of glutenous heat
I touch with chaste palms moist and cold,

Now the spell hath lost his hold;
And I must haste ere morning hour
To wait in *Amphitrite*'s bowr.

        Sabrina *descends, and the Lady rises out of her seat.*

SPIR.
    Virgin, daughter of *Locrine*
Sprung of old *Anchises* line
May thy brimmed waves for this
Their full tribute never miss
From a thousand petty rills,
That tumble down the snowy hills:
Summer drouth, or singed air
Never scorch thy tresses fair,
Nor wet *Octobers* torrent flood
Thy molten crystal fill with mudd,
May thy billows rowl ashoar
The beryl, and the golden ore,
May thy lofty head be crown'd
With many a tower and terras round,
And here and there thy banks upon
With Groves of myrrhe, and cinnamon.
Com Lady while Heaven lends us grace,
Let us fly this cursed place,
Lest the Sorcerer us intice
With som other new device.
Not a waste, or needless sound
Till we com to holier ground,
I shall be your faithfull guide
Through this gloomy covert wide,
And not many furlongs thence
Is your Fathers residence,
Where this night are met in state
Many a friend to gratulate
His wish't presence, and beside
All the Swains that there abide,
With Jiggs, and rural dance resort,
We shall catch them at their sport,
And our sudden coming there
Will double all their mirth and chere;
Com let us haste, the Stars grow high,
But night sits monarch yet in the mid sky.

The Scene changes, presenting Ludlow *Town and the* Presi-

dents Castle, then com in Countrey-Dancers, after them
the attendant Spirit, with the two Brothers and the Lady.

SONG

SPIR.

Back Shepherds, back, anough your play,
Till next Sun-shine holiday,
Here be without duck or nod
Other trippings to be trod
Of lighter toes, and such Court guise
As Mercury *did first devise*
With the mincing Dryades
On the Lawns, and on the Leas.

This second Song presents them to their Father and Mother.

Noble Lord, and Lady bright,
I have brought ye new delight,
Here behold so goodly grown
Three fair branches of your own,
Heav'n hath timely tri'd their youth,
Their faith, their patience, and their truth.
And sent them here through hard assays
With a crown of deathless Praise,
To triumph in victorious dance
O're sensual Folly, and Intemperance.

The dances ended, the Spirit Epiloguizes.

SPIR.

To the Ocean now I fly,
And those happy climes that ly
Where day never shuts his eye,
Up in the broad fields of the sky:
There I suck the liquid ayr
All amidst the Gardens fair
Of *Hesperus,* and his daughters three
That sing about the golden tree:
Along the crisped shades and bowres
Revels the spruce and jocond Spring,
The Graces, and the rosie-boosom'd Howres,
Thither all their bounties bring,
That there eternal Summer dwels,

And West winds, with musky wing
About the cedar'n alleys fling
Nard, and *Cassia*'s balmy smels.
Iris there with humid bow,
Waters the odorous banks that blow
Flowers of more mingled hew
Then her purfl'd scarf can shew,
And drenches with *Elysian* dew
(List mortals if your ears be true)
Beds of *Hyacinth,* and roses
Where young *Adonis* oft reposes,
Waxing well of his deep wound
In slumber soft, and on the ground
Sadly sits th' *Assyrian* Queen;
But far above in spangled sheen
Celestial *Cupid* her fam'd Son advanc't,
Holds his dear *Pysche* sweet intranc't
After her wandring labours long,
Till free consent the gods among
Make her his eternal Bride,
And from her fair unspotted side
Two blissful twins are to be born,
Youth and Joy; so *Jove* hath sworn.
    But now my task is smoothly don,
I can fly, or I can run
Quickly to the green earths end,
Where the bow'd welkin slow doth bend,
And from thence can soar as soon
To the corners of the Moon.
    Mortals that would follow me,
Love vertue, she alone is free,
She can teach ye how to clime
Higher then the Spheary chime;
Or if Vertue feeble were,
Heav'n it self would stoop to her.

WILLIAM BLAKE'S ILLUSTRATIONS
TO *COMUS*
By R. LORING TAYLOR

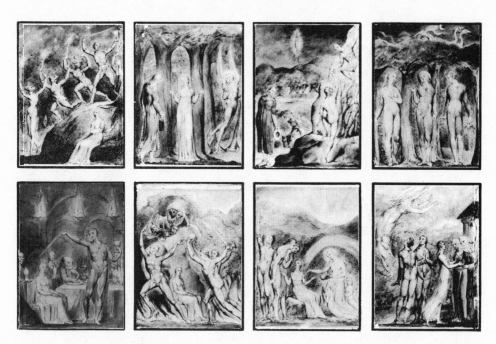

WILLIAM BLAKE *once commented, "Milton lov'd me in childhood & | shew'd me his face."*[1] *From childhood on, Blake lived with Milton, sharing, illustrating, interpreting and sometimes criticizing his visions. Blake's earliest poems, published as* Poetical Sketches *(1783), show the influence of Milton's diction and sentence structure.* The Marriage of Heaven and Hell *(1793) reverses the values of* Paradise Lost: *"But in Milton; the Father is Destiny, the Son, a Ratio of the five | senses. & the Holy-ghost, Vacuum! | Note. The reason Milton wrote in fetters when he wrote of Angels & | God, and at liberty when of Devils & Hell, is because he was a true Poet | and of the Devils party without knowing it."*[2] *Blake's contrary states of Innocence and Experience owe something to Milton's companion poems "L'Allegro" and "Il Penseroso" and, more generally, to the entire tradition of pastoral in Milton's early poems.*[3] *Blake's Thel, like the Lady in* Comus, *tentatively enters Experience, only to retreat apparently unscathed.*[4]

In 1800 Blake fell under the patronage of Hayley and moved to Felpham on the south coast of England. Here he was exposed to Hayley's theories about Milton;[5] *in having access to Hayley's extensive Milton library, he also became familiar with eighteenth-century fashions in illustrating Milton.*[6] *Encouraged partly by Fuseli's Milton Gallery and partly by patronage*[7] *followed by opposition*[8] *to Hayley, Blake commenced a burst of activity influenced by Milton. In Blake's epic* Milton *(1803–1808), a redeemed Milton, purged of his "puritanical" ideas, descends from Heaven and enters Blake's left foot, enabling Blake to stride forward through Eternity. Blake relies on Milton for inspiration and assistance in maintaining his Divine Vision in a fallen age. Shortly after arriving in Felpham Blake began illustrating Milton's major poems, a project which occupied him on and off for nearly twenty years. He completed two sets of designs for* Comus *(1801 and 1809); the* Nativity Ode *(both probably 1809);* Paradise Lost *(1807 and 1808); and one set of designs for "L'Allegro," "Il Penseroso," and* Paradise Regained *(probably 1816).*

Blake's first set of illustrations for Comus, *sold to the Reverend Joseph Thomas and now in the Huntington Library, emphasizes Blake's opposition to certain of Milton's ideas, particularly Milton's praise of chastity.[9] The illustrations depart from Milton in many details. The Attendant Spirit remains viewless throughout most of the masque, but Blake has him figure prominently in almost every scene. The midnight revels are not witnessed by the Lady in the masque itself, although Blake's Lady seems, in plate 1, painfully aware of them. Where Milton mentions the root of the haemony Blake pointedly illustrates the flower. The Lady's brothers appear as caricatures, engaging in actions and surrounded by phenomena whose sexual symbolism they do not comprehend. At the conclusion to* Comus *the Lady joins her noble parents in a formal public celebration; but in Blake's illustrations the Lady's parents are humble villagers, and there is no sign of any public festival. Blake's departures from the text are evidently intended as ironic counterstatements to Milton.*

Our appraisal of the commentary on Milton implied by Blake in his illustrations may depend on our interpretation of the meaning which Milton himself intended by the work. Irene Tayler claims that Milton's original intention was to portray a successful puberty ritual. The lady joining her parents in the final celebration takes her place in adult society. In the version presented at Ludlow castle the Lady's rejoinder to Comus was based on the mature virtues of temperance and the proper use of desire. However, in the 1637 version Milton added to the Lady's arguments "the sage / And serious doctrine of Virginity."[10] Whether one interprets such virginity narrowly as total abstinence or broadly as innocence, this additional doctrine threatens to alter the meaning of the masque. If the theme of the masque is temptation overcome, the return to the parents could signify a retreat from maturity.

According to Tayler, Blake's purpose in the illustrations was to take issue with the doctrine of chastity, which he may not have known was added later. In his illustrations the Lady does appear more chaste than wise. Comus and his revelers represent the sexual fears of a young virgin, which can be overcome by the golden flower of the haemony (an increase in sensual enjoyment). Blake would appear to be restoring the original function of the masque as successful puberty ritual.

While Tayler is undoubtedly correct in her interpretation of many details in Blake's illustrations, the issues are more complicated than she acknowledges. Blake would have no more enthusiasm for the kind of maturity Milton originally proposed than for a narrow doctrine of total abstinence. He had little respect for temperance, and he was utterly opposed to rational (or cold-blooded) use of desire to gain such goals as wealth or social position. Blake would consider a successful entry into a maturity based on such principles to be the fall itself. Blake's attitude toward chastity was, like Milton's, complex. Blake was sympathetic to virgin fears, which are based on the dread of a very real connection between sex and death, in the state Blake called Generation. What he opposed was manipulative chastity. Tayler claims that, in introducing the doctrine of chastity, Milton "very nearly cripple[d] the entire masque."[11] *However, this issue added an ambivalence to the key moments of the masque, which Blake apparently found congenial and analogous to his own complex polarities between Innocence and Experience, Thel and Oothoon.*

Joseph Wittreich has discussed the 1809 illustrations painted for Butts and now in the Boston Museum of Fine Arts (reproduced here). He points out that in many instances where Blake had departed from Milton in the earlier illustrations, he now returns to a more faithful rendering of the text. He restores the cup to Comus, sets the Lady apart from the revelers, curtails the presence of the Attendant Spirit, and alters many details of the Lady's awakening. Wittreich argues that the early illustrations to Comus were based on a spirit of contention, in which Blake sought to "correct" Milton. But the 1809 version, done after he had completed his own poem Milton, was based on a closer reading and deeper appreciation of the details in Milton. Now, according to Wittreich, Blake was less interested in quibbling with Milton's doctrine than in revealing Milton's "original vision," which had been blurred not only by Milton's subsequent commentators but by Milton himself, in his additions to the masque.[12]

The differences between the two versions which Wittreich points out are significant, but his distinction between doctrine and vision may beg interpretive questions. By the term "original vision" Wittreich clearly implies more than original version. A vision must have some content, but Wittreich does not make clear how Blake's interpretation of the content differs between the two sets of illustrations. Although Wittreich differs from Tayler in the interpretation of certain details (the fog, for example), he accepts her explanation of Blake's intention and therefore exaggerates the changes in Blake's purported intentions between the two series. It is likely that Blake was just as interested in the first as in the second set of illustrations in showing forth Milton's visionary potential, and it is unlikely that Blake had, by 1809, become a slavish follower of Milton.[13] *Wittreich and Tayler both assume that an entry into (sexual) experience is positive,*[14] *but Blake clearly regarded it as a mixed blessing. Sexual joy may commit one to the wheel of Generation. The symbolism in Blake's illustrations draws attention to both aspects of sexuality. Although the 1809 illustrations are more faithful to the details in Comus, it is likely that, in both versions, each of the eight scenes is ambivalent. The final scene may represent contraries embedded within contraries. The return to the parents may either be a breakthrough into maturity or a retreat back into innocence or chastity; either solution could be regarded as a triumph or a tragedy, and the tone could be euphoric or bitterly ironic. Blake's illustrations render the contraries in Milton fully explicit.*

FOOTNOTES

1. Sir Geoffrey Keynes, ed., *The Letters of William Blake* (London: Rupert Hart-Davis, 1968), p. 38.
2. David Erdman, ed., *The Poetry and Prose of William Blake* (New York: Doubleday, 1970), p. 35.

3. David Wagenknecht, in *Blake's Night* (Cambridge: Harvard University Press, 1973), explores Blake's relationship to Milton and the pastoral tradition.

4. S. Foster Damon, in "Blake and Milton," *The Divine Vision,* ed. by Vivian de Sola Pinto (London: Victor Gollancz, 1957), p. 92, states that *Thel* "is a reconsideration of the idea on which *Comus* is based."

5. Hayley published (1794–97) an expensive edition of Milton, for which he wrote an introductory biography. In 1800 he was preparing Cowper's translations of the Latin poems.

6. For a list of illustrated editions of *Comus* and a discussion of the significance of Hayley's Milton library see Joseph Anthony Wittreich, *Angel of Apocalypse* (Madison: University of Wisconsin, 1975), p. 86. Wittreich's discussion of the *Comus* illustrations covers pp. 79–90.

7. Hayley commissioned a series of "Heads of the Poets," including Milton's.

8. The manner in which Milton became involved in the quarrels between Blake and Hayley has been discussed frequently. See Northrop Frye, *Fearful Symmetry* (Princeton: Princeton University Press, 1972), pp. 313–55; and Evelyn Morchard Bishop, *Blake's Hayley* (London: Gollancz, 1951).

9. The illustrations now in the Huntington Library have been analyzed by Irene Tayler, in "Say First! What mov'd Blake? Blake's *Comus* Designs and Milton," *Blake's Sublime Allegory,* ed. by Curran and Wittreich (Madison: University of Wisconsin, 1973), pp. 233–58. The Boston series was lithographed in 1890 by William Griggs for Quaritch, and both sets of illustrations are reproduced in color in Angus Fletcher, *The Transcendental Masque: An Essay on Milton's Comus* (Ithaca: Cornell University Press, 1971), between pp. 256 and 257. The two sets of illustrations differ in size and style as well as content. The Huntington set (22 $\times$ 17.5 cm.) is darker, more painterly and more theatrical; the Boston set (15 $\times$ 12 cm.) has a greater emphasis on line, and the coloring is more delicate. Fletcher (pp. 253–56) argues that the second set is open and musical, emphasizing transcendental rather than dramatic features of the masque.

10. Merrit Hughes, ed., *John Milton: Complete Poems and Major Prose* (New York: The Odyssey Press, 1957), p. 108. Wittreich (p. 81) points out that passages emphasizing the sexual nature of the encounter were deleted from the original manuscript for the Ludlow performance and restored when the work was revised for publication. For a study of the variant forms of *Comus* and a review of critical positions on the argument of the masque see John G. Demaray, *Milton and the Masque Tradition* (Cambridge: Harvard University Press, 1968), pp. 173–80. Wittreich's position on this issue was anticipated by E. M. W. Tillyard ("The Action of *Comus*," *Essays and Studies* 28, 1942).

11. Tayler, p. 240.

12. Wittreich, p. 81, states, "Blake's designs spring from the understanding that Milton's vision has been darkened not only by his commentators but by his own spectral self. . . ."

13. Wittreich does point out that literal reproduction of detail may serve as exposé as well as praise. The more literal the illustrator becomes in his rendering of a text the more difficult it is to distinguish his intention.

14. Wittreich, p. 83, states, "For Blake, key and root alike symbolize the world of error and, ironically, the error of Milton, who, protecting the children from sexuality rather than exposing them to it, would harness them within the world of innocence rather than

usher them into the world of experience, whose trodden paths lead to eternity." It is questionable whether this statement does justice to either Blake or Milton. In the *Areopagitica* Milton argues for a position analogous to the one here attributed to Blake, and the assertion that the "trodden paths of experience lead to eternity" transforms the fallen world into the Garden of Eden. Although Blake reversed many traditional values, he relied too heavily on the conception of the fall to dilute its meaning in such a fashion.

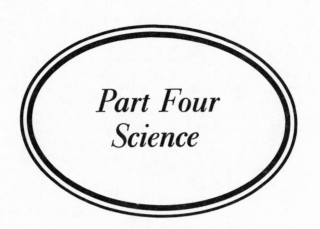

Part Four
Science

$$\boxed{10}$$

The Birth
of Mankinde
Otherwyse Named the Womans Booke

By THOMAS RAYNALDE

S E L E C T I O N S

AN OBSTETRICAL TEXT *by Eucharius Rösslin, the* Rosegarten, *was translated into English by Richard Jonas and published in London in 1540 as* The Byrthe of mankynde. *The book was so popular that it was revised and republished in 1565 by Thomas Raynalde (fl. 1550) and reprinted many times up through the early seventeenth century. Indeed, contrary to current belief that pregnant women were then disregarded, the text shows much concern for their welfare. There is even a depiction of a birth chair, and a suggestion of breathing exercises. The text clarifies the puzzling distinction between headfirst (natural) and headlong (not natural) birth—the latter referred to by John Donne in* The First Anniversary, *written as an elegy on the death of a friend's child.*

The end of Book Four contains beauty tips or "bellifying receptes," including information on controlling dandruff, getting rid of superfluous hair, removing freckles and warts, treatment for rough skin and pimples, mouth hygiene, halitosis, and underarm odor. Such material was available to children as well as to adults. The pictures of the child in the uterus of the mother are edifying, but of particular interest is advice on such problems as "the ranke savour of the arme-holes," which in print reads: "Aucthours do wryte, that the rootes of Artichautes . . . sodden in whyte wyne & so dronke, doth clense the stench of the armes-holes and other partes of the body by the urine." The treatment anticipates the use of chlorophyll tablets for the purpose. For dandruff, "oft washying shall puryfye the skyn of the headde, and stedfast the hayre from fallyng, leviate and lyghten the head, with all the sences therin conteyned, and greatly comfort the braynes."

The pages presented here are a transcription by Mark Boyer from the black-letter text of Raynalde's edition of 1598. The work is to be found in the Toner Collection, The Library of Congress. If words are unfamiliar, the reader is advised to consult the Oxford English Dictionary. Since this is a fresh transcription of a sixteenth-century edition, the original spelling and punctuation have been retained, so that the reader can experience the book in its original form.

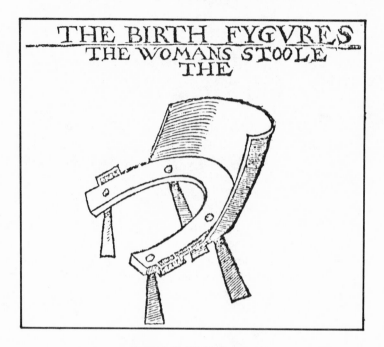

CHAPTER I

Of the time of byrth.
And which is called naturall,
or unnaturall.

IN THE FIRST booke we have sufficiently set foorth and described the manner, situation, and forme of the Matrix wherein man is conceyved, with divers other matters appending and concerning the better understanding of the same. And now here in this second Booke, we will declare the maner of the quiting and deliverance of the Infant out of the mothers wombe, with other things thereto appertaining. And first here in this Chapter we will declare the tokens and signes, whereby yee may perceive whether the time of labour be neere, or not: for when the houre of labour approcheth neere, these signes following evermore proceede and come before.

First certaine dolors and paines begin to growe about the guttes, the navill, and in the raynes of the back, and likewise about the thighes, and the other places being neere to the privie parts, which likewise then beginneth to swell and to burne, and to expell humors, so that it giveth a plaine and evident token that the labour is neere.

But yee shall note, that there is two manner of birthes, the one called naturall, the other not naturall. Naturall birth is, when the childe is borne both in due season, and also in due fashion.

The due season is most commonly after the ninth month, or about fortie weekes after the conception, although some be delivered sometimes in the seventh moneth, and the childe proveth very well. But such as are borne in the eyght moneth, other they be dead before the birth, or els live not long after.

The due fashion of byrth is this: first the head commeth forward, then followeth the necke and shoulders, the armes with the handes lying close to the body toward the feete, the face and the forepart of the child being towards the face and forepart of the mother, as it appeareth in the first of the byrth figures. For as hath been said alredy in the first Booke, before the time of deliverance, the childe lyeth in the mothers wombe the head upward, and the feete downeward, but when it should be delivered it is turned cleane contrarie, the head downeward, the feete upward, and the face towards the mothers belly, and that if the birth be naturall. Another thing also is this, that if the birth be naturall, the deliverance is earlie, without long tarying or looking for it.

The birth not naturall is, when the mother is delivered before her time, or out of due season, or after any other fashion then is here spoken of before: as when both the legges proceede first, or one alone, with both the hands up, or both downe, other els the one up and the other downe, and divers otherwise, as shalbe hereafter more cleerely declared.

CHAPTER II

*Of easie and uneasie, difficult, or dolorous deliverance,
and the causes of it: with the signes how to
know and forsee the same.*

V ERY MANY BE the perrils, dangers, and thronges, which chaunce to women in their labour, which also ensue and come in divers wayes, and for divers causes, such as I shall here declare.

First when the woman that laboureth is conceived over yong, as before xii. or xv. yeeres of age (which chaunceth sometime, though not very often) and that the passage be over angust, streate, or narrowe, other naturally, or els for some disease and infirmitie, which may happen about that part, as apostumes, pushes, pyles, or blisters, and such other. Through the which causes, nature cannot (but with great dolor and paine) open and dilate it selfe, to the expelling and deliverance of the childe. And sometime the vesicke or bladder, or other intrailes being about the Matrix or Wombe likewise for vicinitie and neighbourhead is greeved with them, and that hindereth greatly the deliverance. Also sometime in the fundement are hemoyrhodes, or pyles, and other pushes, chappings or chines, which cause great paine. Also hardnesse and difficultie or binding of the belly, which things for the greefe and paine that ensueth of them, couseth the woman to have little power to help herselfe in her labour.

Furthermore, if the partie be weake and of feeble complexion, or of nature very colde, or too young, or very aged, or exceeding grosse and fatt, or contrary-wise too spare and leane, or that shee never had childe before, or that she be over timorous and fearefull, divers, waywarde, or such one that will not bee ruled, remooving herselfe from one place to another, all such things causeth the labour to be much more painefull, cruell, and dolorous, then it would otherwise be. Also yee must understand, that generally the birth of the man child is easier than the byrth of the woman child.

Item, if the child be of a fuller and greater groweth, then that it may easily passe that narrowe passage, or contrarywise, if it bee so faint, weake and tender, that it cannot turne it selfe, or dooth it very slowlye, or if the woman have two children at once, other els that it with the which she laboureth bee a monster, as for example, if it hath but one body and two heads, as appeareth in the xviii. of the birth figures, such as of late was seene in the dominion of Werdenbergh.

Againe, when it proceedeth not in due time, or after due fashion, as when it commeth forth with both feet or both knees together, or els with one foote onely, or with both feete downewardes, and both hands upwards, otherels (the which is most perilous) sidelong, arselong, or backlong, other els (having two at a birth) both proceede with their feete first, or one with his feet, and the other with his head, by those and divers other wayes the woman sustaineth great dolor, paine, and anguish.

Item, if the woman suffer aborcement, that is to say, bring forth her childe in the iiii. or v. moneth after the conception, which is before the due tyme, in this case it shalbe great payne to her, for so much as in that tyme, the porte of the wombe is so firmely and strongly enclosed, that unneath the poynt of a needle may enter in at it.

To know whether the childe be weake in the mothers belly.

Also if the child be dead in the mothers belly, it is a very perrillous thing, forsomuch as it can not be easily turned, neither can it weld or helpe it selfe to come forth: or if the child be sicke or weakened, so that it can not for feeble-nesse helpe it selfe. The which thing may be foreseene and knowne by these tokens: if the woman with child have been long sicke before her labour, if she have ben sore tasked, if after her conception she have had daily and unwontly her flowes, if straight after one moneth upon the conception her breasts yeeld any milke, if the child stir not, ne move at such time as is convenient for it, these be argumentes and tokens that it should be very weake. By what tokens ye shall know it is dead, I shal shew you hereafter.

Perrill in the secundine.

Also there is great perrill in labouring, when the secundine or latter byrth is overfirme or strong, and will not soone rive or breake asunder, so that the child may have his earlie comming forth. And contrariwise when it is overweake, slender, or thinne, so that it breaketh asunder before that the childe bee turned, or apt to issue forth, for then the humors which are collect and gathered together about this secundine or secondbirth, passe away sooner then they should do, and the byrth shall lacke his due humidities and moystures which should cause it the easier to proceede, and with lesse payne.

The birth also is hindered by overmuch cold, overmuch heate: for in overmuch colde, the passage and all other pores of the labouring woman be coarcted and made more narower then they would otherwise be. Likewise overmuch heate debiliteth, weakeneth, and fainteth both the woman and the childe, so that neither of them in that case can well weeld or helpe themselves for faintnesse.

And further, if the woman have used to eate commonly such meate or fruites which doe exicate or drye, and constraine or binde, as Medlers, Chestnuts, and all sowre fruits, as Crabbes, Chokeperes, Quinces, and such other, with overmuch use of Vergeus, and such like sowre sauces, with Ryse, Mell, and many other things: all this shall greatly hinder the byrth.

Also the use of colde bathes after the fifth moneth folowing the conception, or to bathe in such waters where Alome is, Iron, or Salt, or any such things which do coarct and constraine, or if she have been oftentimes heavie and mourning, or ill at ease, or if she have been kept over hungrie and thurstie, or have used overmuch watch and walking, either if she used a little before her labour, things of great odour, smell or savour, for such things (in many mens opinions) attract and draw upward the mother or Matrix, the which is great hinderance to the byrth.

Also, if the woman feele paine onely in the backe, and above the navell, and not under, it is a signe of hard labour: like wise if she were wont in times passed to be delivered with great paine, is an evidence and likelyhood of great labour alwayes in the birth.

Tokens of easie de-liverance. Now signes and tokens of an expedite and easie deliverance, be such as be contrary to all those that have been rehearsed before. As for example, when the woman hath been wont in times passed easily to be deliveuered, and that in her labour she feele but little throng or dolor, or though she have great paines, yet they remaine not still in the upper parts, but descend alwayes downewardes to the neather partes, or bottom of the belly. And to be short, in all painefull and troublesome labours, these signes betoken and signifie good speede and lucke in the labour: unquietnesse, much stirring of the childe in the mothers belly, all the thronges and paines tombling in the forepart of the bottome of the belly, the woman strong and mightie of nature such as can well and strongly helpe her selfe to the deliverance of the byrth.

And againe, evill signes be those, when she sweateth colde sweate, and that her pulses beate and labour oversore, and that she her selfe in the labouring faint and sowne: these be unluckie and mortall signes.

CHAPTER III

How a Woman with childe shall use herselfe, and what remedyes be for them that have hard labour.

To succour and helpe them that are in such difficult perill of labour, as wee have spoken of before, ye must observe, keepe, and marke those things that we shall (by the grace of God) shewe you in this Chapter following.

First the woman with childe must keepe two dyets, the one a moneth before

How the
labour
may be
made more
easie. her labour, the other in the very labouring. And above all things she must eschue and forbeare all such occasions which may hinder the byrth, to the uttermost of her power, the which occasions we rehearsed in the Chapter before. But if there be any such thing which can not bee avoyded, forsomuch as it commeth by nature, or by long continuance and custome, in this case yet yee shall use some such remedies, the which may somewhat aswage it, molifie it, or make it more easie or tollerable, so that it hinder the byrth so much the lesse.

But if it so bee, that any infirmitie, or disease, swelling, or other apostumation chaunce about the mother or the privie parte, or about the vesicke or bladder, as the stone, the strangury, and such like, the which things may cause such straytnes and coarctation, that unneath without great and horrible payne the partie can bee delivered or discharged: In these cases it behoveth such things to be loked unto, and cured, before the time of labour commeth, by the advise of some expert Surgion.

Also if the woman be overmuch constipate or bound, most commonly she must use, the moneth before her labour, such things the which may lenifie, mollifie, dissolve, and lose the belly, as apples fryed with suger, taken fasting in the morning, and after that a draught of pure wine alone, or els tempered with the juice of sweete and very ripe apples.

Also to eate figges in the morning fasting, and at night, loseth well the belly. If these profit not, Cassia fistula taken iii. or iiii. drammes one halfe howre before dinner, shall lose the belly without perrill.

Agayne, in this case she must refrayne from all such thinges as doe harden, restrayne, and constipate, as meates broyled or roasted, and Rice, hard egges, beefe, chestnuttes, and all sowre fruites, and such like.

Also if farther necessitie require, she may receyve a glister, but it must be very gentle and easie, made of a pynte of the broath of a chickin, or other tender fleshe, thereto putting so much course suger, or hony, as may make it reasonably Things to
lose the
belly. sweet, and halfe a sponefull of white salt. Or for the poore woman may bee made a glister of a pynt of water, wherein hath been sod mallowes, or Holyoke, with Hony and Salt, as before. She may use also some other easie and temperate purgation, to molifie and lose her withall, as Mercurie sodden with fleshe in pottage, and divers such other, or els a suppositer tempered with Sope, Larde, or the yolkes of Egges.

And if it chaunce that (the labour drawing neere) she waxe faint or sickly, Wherewith
to com-
fort the
woman in
her la-
bour. then must yee comfort her with good comfortable meate, drincke, holesome and noble electuaries, and in this time must shee doe all such things the which can make her apte and sufficient to her labour, and to use such things the which may laxe, open, and mollifie the nature of the passage, so that the byrth may the more freely proceede, and that chiefly in the yonger women. The elder women, for that those partes in them be somewhat dryer, and harder, therefore they must use hoat and moyste things, which have propertie to lenifie and souple, and that both in meate and drincke, and also in outwarde fomentations, bathings, suppositories, and annoyntments.

Annointments wherewith ye may souple the privie place, be these, Hens grece,

Ointments to souple. Duckes grece, Goose grece, also oyle Olive, Linceede oyle, the oyle of the Fenegreke, or the viscosite of holioke, and such other: and for drinke, let her use good rype wyne, mixed with water. Also there must be a consideration in the dieting of the woman, that shee may use such thinges the which may moysten her, and not make her fat. Contrariwise, let her avoyde such thinges the which should exicate, drye, constrayne, or coarct her, and that all the moneth before

Bathes to lose and gentily to open the body. her labour. But about ten dayes before the time (if she feele any payne or greefe) let her use every day to wash or bath her with warme water, in the which also that she tary not over long in the bathing, for weakning of her, and therein let her stand, so that the water come above the navel a little, and also seeth in the water, Malowes, Holioke, Camomell, Mercurie, Maydenhayre, Lineseede, Fenegreeke seede, and such other thinges which have vertue to molifie and supple. And if it be so, that for weaknesse of the body she may not indure this bathing in warme water, then with a spunge or other cloth dipped in the forsayd bath, let her sokyngly wash her feete, her thighes, and her privie partes, the which thinges shall greatly profite her. But in such time beware ye come not in the common hotte houses, for they would cause you to bee feeble and faynt, which were yll in this case.

And when ye are thus bathed or washed, then shall it be very convenient for you to anoint with the foresaid greces and oyles, your backe, belly, navell, sydes, and such places as are neare to the privie partes. Furthermore it shalbe greatly

Annoint-ments to supple. profitable for her, to convey inward into the privie parte these foresayde oyles or greces, with a spunge, or other thing made for the purpose, she lying upright, the middest of her body most hiest, so that it may better remayne within her, and that cheefely if the Matrix be dry, other els the partie very leane and spare.

Sweete fumes. Also as I sayd before, she must take good heede to her dyet, that shee take things the which may comfort and strengthen the body, feeding not overmuch of any thing, and to drinke pleasant and well savouring wine, or other drinke, also moderately to exercise the body in doing some thing, stirring, mooving, going, or standing, more then otherwise she was wonte to do, these things further the byrth, and make it the easier. And this is the manner of dyet, the which we advise the woman to keepe the moneth before her labour, or longer.

Another dyet there is, the which she ought to observe in the time of labour, when the stormes and thronges beginne to come on, and the humours which yet hytherto have remayned about the Matrix or Mother collected, nowe be-

What is to be done when the time of labour is come. ginne to flowe foorth: and this manner of dyet consisteth in two sortes. First, that such thinges be procured and had in redinesse, which may cause the birth or labour to be very easie. Secondly, to withstande, defende, and to put away (so neare as may be) the instant and present dolours. And as touching this point, it shall be very profitable for her, for the space of an houre to sit still, then (rysing againe) to go up and downe a payre of stayres, crying and reaching so loud as she can, so to stir her selfe.

And also it shall be very good for a time, to retaine and keepe in her breath, for because that through that meanes, the guttes and entrayles be thrust together, and depressed downeward. And it shall be very good to receive some medecine to provoke the byrth, of the which we will speake more hereafter.

Now when the woman percyveth the Matrix or Mother to waxe laxe or lose, and to bee dissolved, and that the humors issue foorth in great plentie, then shall it bee meete for her to sit downe, leaning backeward, in manner upright: for which purpose in some regions (as in Fraunce and Germanie) the Midwives have stooles for the nonce, which being but lowe, and not high from the ground, be made so compasse wise and cave or hollowe in the middes, that that may be received from underneth which is looked for, and the backe of the stoole, leaning backward, receiveth the backe of the woman. The fashion of the which stoole, is set in the beginning of the birth figures hereafter.

And when the time of labour is come, in the same stoole ought to be put many clothes or cloutes in the backe of it, the which the Midwife may remove from one side to another, according as necessitie shall require. The Midwife her selfe shal sit before the labouring woman, and shall diligently observe and waite, how much and after what meanes the child stirreth it selfe: also shall with her handes, first anoynted with the oyle of Almondes, or the oyle of white Lillies, rule and direct every thing as shall seeme best.

Also the Midwife must instruct and comfort the partie, not onely refreshing her with good meate and drinke, but also with sweete wordes, giving her good hope of a speedefull deliveraunce, encouraging and enstomaking her to patience and tollerance, bidding her to hold in her breath so much as shee may, also striking gentlie with her handes her belly above the Navel, for that helpeth to depresse the byrth downeward.

But if the woman bee any thing grosse, fatt, or fleshie, it shalbe best for her to lye groveling, for by that meanes the Matrix is thrust and depressed downe-warde, anoynting also the privie partes with the oyle of white Lillies. And if necessitie require it, let not the Midwife be afrayde, ne ashamed to handle the places, and to relaxe and lose the straightes (for so much as shall lye in her) for that shall helpe well to the more expedite and and quicke labour.

But this must the Midwife above all thinges take heede of, that she compell not the woman to labour before the byrth come forwarde, and shew it selfe: For before that tyme, all labour is in vayne, labour as much as yee list. And in this case many times it commeth to passe, that the party hath labored so sore before the time, that when shee should labour indeede, her might and strength is spent before in vayne, so that she is not now able to helpe her selfe, and that is a perrillous case.

Furthermore, when the Secundine or second byrth (in the which the byrth is wrapped and contayned) dooth once appeare, then may yee know that the labour is at hand, wherefore if the same secundine breake not of his owne kinde, it shalbe the Midwives part and office, with her nayles easily and gentelly to breake and rent it, or if that may not conveniently be done, then rayse up betweene your fingers a peece of it, then cut it of with a payre of sheares, or sharpe knife, but so that ye hurt not the byrth with the cut. This done, by and by ensueth consequently the fluxe and flowe of the humours, of the which I spake before, and then next followeth immediately the byrth.

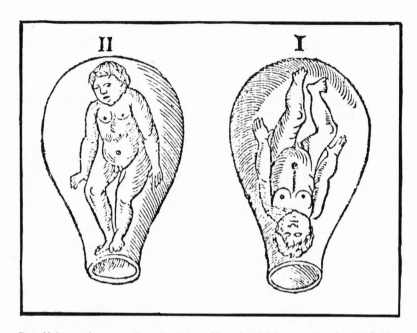

But if it so chaunce that the Secundine should be cut by the Midwife, and all the watery parte issued and spent before due tyme and necessitie should require it, so that the privie passage be left exicate and dry, the byrth not yet appearing, by this meanes the labour should be hindred and letted. In this case yee shall annoynt and molifie that privie passage with the oyle of white Lillies, or some of the greces spoken of before, first warmed and so conveyed into the privie partes, the which thinges will cause the waye to bee slippery, supple, and easie for the byrth to passe. But cheefly in these difficulties should profite the white of an egge, together with the yolke powred into the same place, which should cause it to be most slippery and slyding, and supplye the roome of the naturall humidities spent before.

The head proceed-ing first. And if it be so, that the byrth be of a great growth, and the heade sticke in the comming forth, then must the Midwife helpe all that shee may, with her hande first annoynted with some oyle, opening and enlarging the way, that the issue may be the freer. Likewise must be done if she beare two children at once. And all this is spoken of the naturall byrth, when that first proceedeth the head, and then the rest of the body ordinately, as yee may see in the first of the figures following.

The ii. figure. ii. But when the byrth commeth not naturally, then must the Midwife do all her diligence and payne (if it may be possible) to turne the byrth tenderly The legs and both handes downe, proceed-ing first. with her annoynted handes, so that it may bee reduced agayne to a naturall byrth. As for example: Sometyme it chaunceth the childe to come the legges and both armes and hands downward, close to the sides, first foorth, as appeareth in the second of the byrth figures. In this case the Midwife must do all her payne with tender handling and annoynting to receive forth the child, the legges being still close togeather, and the handes likewise remayning, as appeareth in the sayde second fygure.

Howbeit, it were far better (if it may be done by any possible wayes or meanes) that the Midwife should turne these legges comming first forth, upwardes agayne by the bellywarde, so that the head might descend downeward by the backe part of the wombe, for then naturally agayne and without perill might it proceede and come forth as the first.

The iii. figure. iii. Agayne sometyme the byrth commeth forth with both legs and feet first, the hands being lifted up above the head of the childe, and this is the periloust manner of byrth that is, as appeareth in the iii. of the byrth figures. And here must the Midwife do what she may to turne the byrth (if it may be possible) to the first figure, and if it will not be, then reduce the hands of it downe to the sides, and so to reduce it into the second figure. But if this also will not be, then receive the feete as they come forth and bind them with some fayre linnen cloth, and so tenderly and very softly lose out the byrth till all be come forth, and this is a very jeopardous labour.

The iiii. figure. iiii. Also sometime the byrth commeth foorth with one foote only, the other being lyft upward, as appereth in the fourth figure. And in this case it behooveth the labouring woman to lay her upright upon her backe, holding up her thighes and belly, so that her head bee the lower part of her body, then let the Midwife with her hand returne in againe the foote that commeth out first, in as tender manner as may be, and warne the woman that laboureth to stir and move herselfe, so that by the mooving and stirring, the birth may be turned the head downeward, and so to make a naturall birth of it, and then to set the woman in the stoole againe, and to do as yee did in the first figure. But if it be so that notwithstanding the mothers stirring and mooving, the byrth do not turne, then must the Midwife with her hand softly fetch out the other leg which remained behinde, evermore taking heed of this, that by handling of the childe she do not remoove ne set out of their place the two hands hanging downeward toward the feete.

The v. figure. v. Likewise sometime it commeth to passe, that the side of the child commeth forward as appeareth in the v. figure, and then must the Midwife do so, that it may be returned to his naturall fashion, and so to come forth.

The vi. figure. vi. Also sometime the child commeth foorth the feete forward, the legs being abroad, as in the vi. figure, and then must the Midwife see that the feete and legges maybe joyned together, and so come forth, evermore regarding the hands, as I warned you before.

The vii. figure. vii. If it come with one of the knees or both forward, as in the vii. figure, then must the Midwife put up the birth, till such time as the legges and feete come right foorth, and then do as afore.

The viii. figure. viii. When the child commeth headlong, one of the hands comming out and appearing before, as in the viii. figure, then let the birth proceed no farther, but let the Midwife put in her hand, and tenderly by the shoulders thrust in the

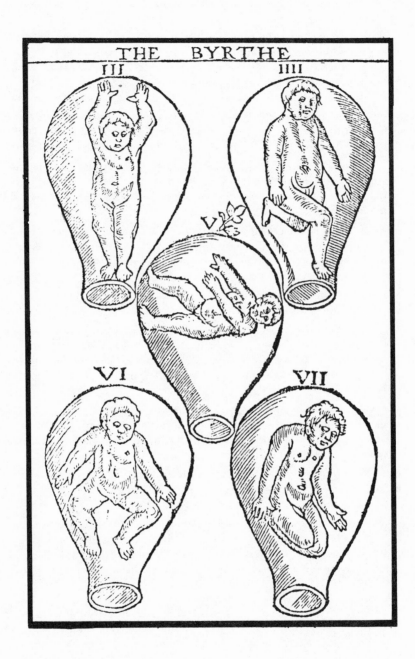

byrth againe, so that the hand may bee resetteled in his place, and the birth to come foorth ordinately and naturally, as in the first figure: But if by this meanes the hand come not to his convenient place, then let the woman lye upright with her thighes and belly upwards, and her head downewards, so that by that meanes it may be brought to passe, and then bring her to her seate againe.

The ix.
figure.   ix.   But if it proceede with both hands forward, then must ye likewise do as before, by the shoulders thrusting it back againe, untill such time as the hands lye close to the sides, & so to come forth, as appeareth in the ix. figure.

The x.
figure.   x.   But when it commeth arsward, as in the x. figure may be seene, then must the Midwife with her hands returne it againe, untill that time that the birth be turned, the legges and feete forward: other els, if it may be so, it were best that the head might come forwarde, and so naturally to proceed.

The xi.
figure.   xi.   But when the birth commeth forth with both the hands and both the feete at once, as in the xi. figure, then must the Midwife tenderly take the childe by the head, and returne the legs upward & so receive it forth.

The xii.
figure.   xii.   And if so be that it appeare and come foorth first with the shoulders, as in the xii. figure, then must ye fair and softly thrust it backe againe by the shoulders, till such time as the head come forward.

The xiii.
figure.   xiii.   And when it commeth brestward as in the xiii. figure, the legges and handes byding behinde, then let the Midwife take it by the feete, or by the head, which that shalbe most apt and commodious to come forward, returning the rest upward, and so to receive it foorth: but if it may be hedling, that shalbe best.

The xiiii.
figure.   xiiii.   Nowe sometime it chaunceth the woman to have two at a burthen, and that both proceede together headlong, as in the xiiii. figure, and then must the Midwife receive the one after the other, but so, that she let not slip the one, whylest she taketh the first.

The xv.
figure.   xv.   If both come foorth at once with their feete forward, then must the Midwife be very diligent to receive first the one, and then the other, as hath been shewed before.

The xvi.
figure.   xvi.   When the one commeth headlong, the other footewise, then must the Midwife helpe the birth that is most nearest the issue, and if that commeth footelong (if she can) to returne it upon the head, as is spoken of before, taking ever heed that the one be not noysome to the other in receiving foorth of either of them.

And to be shorte, let the Midwife often times annoynt and mollifie the way and passage with some of the foresayd oyntments, to make the womans labour so much the easier, and have the lesse travaile and paine. And if there chance to be any Apostume or disease about those places in this time, by such annoynting to alay and swage the paine, so that for that time it may be the lesse griefe to the partie, as I spake before also. And for them that be in this case, it shalbe best to lye groveling, as I said of the grosse, fat, and fleshie women.

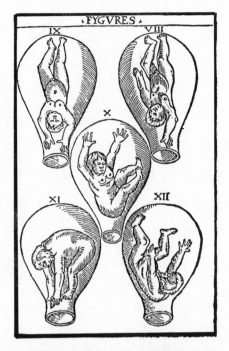

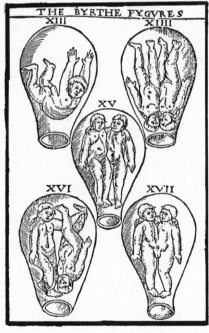

The Fourth Booke

CHAPTER VI

In this is entreated of divers
bellifying receptes, as ye may
hereafter reade.

THE EMBELLISHING OR bellifying medecines wherof I entend to speake here, be not to be understanden to be of that sort whereby any Adstiticious or outwarde forayne beautie or set colours should be acquired or gotten, the which far fet & dampnable curiositie, I doubt not but that all honest and vertuous sadde women do utterly abhorre and contempne: but here mine only meaning is, to shew how to remove certayne blemishes, & as it were weedes of the body, through the whiche many tymes, the naturall beautie therof is obscured and defaced. For as in a fayre Garden, be it never so beautifull, yet yf it be not regarded and looked unto, the weedes entermynglyng them selves among the good hearbes, wyll defourme and emperyshe the good grace of them. For in the earth, be it never so well diligented and pylied, yet alwayes therin will remayne some sparkes and seedes of unlooked for weedes, the whiche ever when time or season serveth, nature thrusteth forth.

Lykewyse in the body of man, among the good and necessary humours, is some sparke or qualitie of ill and not necessary humours, with the which nature being offended and cloyed, expelleth and dryveth them forth, sometymes into one place, and sometymes into another, accordyng to the aptitude or feblenesse in resistence of the place receyvyng it, and the force or violencie of nature (therwith greeved) sending it, so that the superfluities founde in the upper part and face or superficie of the skin, ensueth by the superfluitie and dominion of lyke matter contayned and commixed in the vaynes among the bloud, and is a great evidence and testimonie therof. But here I wyll not speake of all kindes of utter diseases springing of this inwardes corrupted humours, but onlye of suche thynges as commonly chaunce to men and woman without any imperishment of theyr health.

As for example, first I wyll briefly declare the fylthynesse of the head, called in laten *Perrigo*, in Englyshe, the Dandruffe of the head, the which is, when that in kembing and cratching of the head, certayne whyte scales, as it were bran, falleth of from the head, and lyeth verye thicke among and under the hayre.

Of the causes and remedies of Dandruffe of the head.

The cause of this Dandruffe commeth by aboundance of fleumatike humours, comixt with the bloud, the which dayly and hourely by unsessible sweatyng, evaporateth and issueth foorth of the poores, in the skinne that covereth the panbone, and as fast as it issueth forth, dryeth on the utter superficie of the skyn, and there remaynyng and gatheryng together, becommeth every day more and more, therto greatly helping the forest of hayre which covereth, harbereth and retayneth such superfluities, more in those places then in any other where no hayre groweth. And most commonly they that have blacke hayre, have more store of Dandruffe then other. This humour suffred overlong to raigne on the head, destroyeth and corrupteth the rootes of the hayres, makyng them to fall of in great plentie, and speciallye in kembing. And although this superfluitie be not clendly, yet not withstandyng it shall be no wysedome for me to teache, ne any other herewith encombred, to learne how to stoppe it, for feare of farther inconveniences, but onlye I counsell you once in ten dayes at the least to washe and scoure the head cleane with good lye wherin be steped in a lynne bagge of Annis seede, Cummin, dryed Rosemary, Fenugreke, and the ryndes of Pomegranate, of eche lyke much: and beware that after the washynge of your heade ye take no colde, before the heade be perfectly dryed.

And wheras some say, that they which use ofte washyng of theyr heades, shalbe very prone to head ache: that is not true, but only in such that after they have ben washed, roll up theyr hayre (beyng yet wet) about theyr heades, the colde wherof is daungerous to bryng them to Catarrhes and pooses, with other inconveniences. Wherfore all diligence must be had, that the head may be exactly well dryed with warm clothes, whylest the head is yet hotte of the washynge, and then never feare no inconveniences, but rather convenience and commoditie: & let this be done also fastyng in the mornyng, or els one houre before supper, or v. houres after supper: this oft washyng shall puryfye the skyn of the headde, and stedfast the hayre from fallyng, leviate and lyghten the head, with all the sences therin conteyned, and greatly comfort the braynes.

To take away hayre from places where it is unsemely.

Item, sometymes hayre groweth in places unsemely, and out of order: as in manye maydens and women the hayre groweth so lowe in the foreheades and the temples, that it disfigureth them: for this ye maye use three wayes to remove them, eyther to pluck up one after another with pincers, such as many women have for the nonce, eyther elles with this lye followyng. Take newe burnte Lyme foure ounces, of Arsenicke one ounce, stipe both these in a pynt of water the space of two dayes, and then boyle it from a pynt to the halfe.

And to prove whether it be perfecte, dyp a feather therin, and yf the plume of the feather depart of easely, then is it strong ynough, with this water then annoynt so farre the place that ye woulde have bare from hayre, as it lyketh you, and within a quarter of an houre plucke at the hayres, and they wyll folowe, and then washe that place muche with water wherin bran hath ben steped: and that done, annoynt the place with the whyte of a newe layde egge and oyle Olyfe, beaten and mixt together with the juice of Singrene or Purslayne, to alaye the heate engendred of the foresayde Lye. The thyrde way to remove hayre, is with a plaster made of a very drye pytche, and upon leather applyed to the place, the hayres beynge fyrste shaven, or cutte as neare as can be with a payre of Cysars.

Nowe when the hayres be up by the rootes, then to let them that they growe no more: take of Alome the wayght of a grote, and dissolve it in two sponefulles of the juice of Nyghtshade, or of Henbane, and therwithall annoynte the place two or three tymes every day, the space of ix. or x. dayes, and hayre will growe no more in that place.

To do away Frekens or other spottes in the face.

These Frekens and suche other spottes in the face or other where in the body, may be taken away by often annoyntyng them with the oyle of Tarter, to be founde alwayes at the Apothecaries, and suerly that oyle is soveraigne for that purpose.

Item, take Eleborus, and seeth of it an ounce in halfe a pynt of strong whyte Vinegre, tyll halfe be consumed, then myxte therwith Hony three sponefulles, and the wayght of a penye of Mercury sublimid, (to be had at the Apothecaries) and seeth these together agayne tyll it become thicke: with that annoynt the Frekens, and it wyl destroy them. This is also very good for the Morphewe, and other discoloration or staynyng of the skyn.

To destroy Wartes and such lyke excrescences
on the face or els where.

For this purpose nothyng is so excellent as every day once, the space of thre or four dayes, to droppe one droppe of strong water, called *Aqua fortis*, on them, for this destroyeth them in very short tyme.

Item the juice of a red Onion, and the juice of Marygoldes is very good for the same.

Item, dissolve a lyttle Mercury sublimid in fayre water, & therwith drop the Wartes, and they wyll sone wyther and consume away.

To cleare and claryfye the skin in the handes,
face or other part of the body.

For this is nothyng better then to take one sponefull of the oyle of Tarter, and sixe sponefulles of water, with these commixed together, washe the handes, face, and other partes, for it scoureth, clenseth and puryfyeth the skyn soveraignely, and wyll suffer no fylthynes to remayne in the poores of the flesh, and this oyle of Tarter is made on this wyse. Take wyne lyes dryed, the whiche the Goldesmythes do call Arguyl, and beate it into powder, and then fyll therof a Goldsmythes crudyble, and set it among hoate coales, tyll the Arguyll begyn to waxe blacke: then take it out of the fyre and lette it coole, and bynde it in a lynnen cloute, and hange it a lyttle over the vapour of hoate boylynge water: that done, hang this cloute with the Arguyll in a glasse, with a broade mouth, so that the bagge or clout touch not the bottome of the glasse, and the water or oyle called Tarter wyll droppe downe a lyttle and lyttle: and the sonei, yf it stands in a very colde and moyst sellar.

Item to scoure the handes and the bodye, some use to washe theyr handes with the powder of Ores, which is the roote of the blewe Flowredeluce, and some with Beane flowre.

Item, the yolke and whyte of egges is good for that purpose, and so is hony.

To souple and mollifie the ruggednesse
of the skine.

Annoynt the skinne with the oyle of sweet Almonds, the same is very good for chippinges of the lippes or handes.

Item, Deere suet is very proper for the same purpose, especially being well washed and tempered with Rosewater, wherein hath been dissolved two or three graynes of pure Muske.

Agaynst sodayne rysing of Pimples through unkinde
heate in the face, or els where.

Take the whyte of an egge, and beate it well with a spoone, and then therewith commixe two spoonefulles of Sallet oyle, one spoonefull of Rosewater, another of the juice of Sorell, and halfe a lytlle spoonefull of Vineger, herewith annoynt the pimples and risings.

To keepe and preserve the teeth cleane.

First, if they be very yellow and filthie, or blackish, let a Barber scoure, rub, and picke them cleane, and whyte, then after to maintaine them cleane, it shall be very good to rub them every day with the root of a Mallow, and to picke them cleane that no meate remaine and putrifie betweene the teeth.

Item, take of the small white pibble stones which bee found by the water sides, and beate them in a very small powder, hereof take an ounce, and of Masticke one dram, mingle them togeather, and with this powder once in xiii. days rub exactly your teeth, and this shall keepe your teeth fayre and white: but beware yee touch not, ne vexe the gummes therewithall.

Item, to stable and stedfast the teeth, and to keepe the gummes in good case, it shall be very good every day in the morning, to washe well the mouth with red Wine.

Of stinking breath.

Stinch of the breath commeth eyther by occasion bred in the mouth, or els in the stomacke. If it come from the stomacke, then the body must be purged by the further advise of a Phisition. If it be engendred in the mouth onely, then most commonly it commeth of some rotten and corrupted hollow teeth, which in this case must be plucked out and the gummes well scoured and washed with Vineger, wherein hath been sodden Cloves and Nutmegs. This cleanly keeping of the teeth dooth conferre much to the saveringes of the mouth.

Of the rank savour of the arme-holes.

This vice in many persons is very tedious and lothsome, the remedie whereof is, to purge first the chollericke and agre humours, originall causers of the same, and afterwardes to wash the arme-holes oftentimes with the water wherein Wormewoode hath been sodden, together with Camomell, and a little quantitie of Alome.

Item, Aucthours do wryte, that the rootes of Artichautes (the pyth pyked out) sodden in whyte wyne & so dronke, doth clense the stench of the armes-holes and other partes of the body by the urine. For (as Galen also doth testifie) he provoketh copy and plentie of stynkyng and unsavery urine from all partes of the body, the whiche propertie it hath by speciall gyfte, and not only by his hoate qualitie. And thus here I make an ende of this fourth and last booke.

FINIS

The Haven of Health

Chiefely Gathered for the Comfort
Of Students, and Consequently of all Those
That Have a Care of Their Health,
Amplified upon Five Words of Hippocrates

By THOMAS COGAN

SELECTIONS

Thomas Cogan (1545?–1607), noted physician of the Elizabethan period, introduces his work on health with two brief treatises on "labour," which he defines as exercise. The first treatise is on exercise of the body; the second, on exercise of the mind.

As the subtitle of this work indicates, it was "Chiefely gathered for the comfort of Students." (Students then, even at Oxford, were sometimes very young, not even in their teens.) The book suggests many exercises for all parts of the body, including wrestling, running, dancing, leaping, football and tennis. Work such as ploughing is good exercise, too. Cogan also recommends massage. Exercise should take place out in the fresh air. Wine is not good for students, but poached eggs washed down with Claret help those with weak heads. The smell of new-baked bread is wholesome. Don't exercise strenuously just after eating—"the same abuse is ripe among us here in Englande, both in universities and in the grammer Schooles." That exercise is good can be seen by observing little children: "Which thing may well be perceived even in little children: for as soone as they have gotten strength to goe of themselves, they are as busie as bees, and they devise a thousande toies to be occupied in. Which motions no doubt proceede from the minde . . . Idlenesse, therefore is not onely against nature, but also dulleth the minde." The best time to study is early in the morning, but once this has been done, don't be ashamed of honest play, for even "Socrates the Philosopher, who notwithstanding he was adjudged by the Oracle of Apollo, to bee the wisest man in the worlde, yet for recreation he blushed not to ride uppon a reede among his litle children: And when he was laughed to scorne of Alcibiades for so doing, he answered him verie pretily, tell no bodie (sayeth he) that thou sawest me, untill thou have children of thine owne. As who should say, such is the affection of parentes towardes their children, that they are not ashamed oftentimes to play the children with them." With respect to choice of foods, the doctrine of correspondences prevails—that is, there is a resemblance between the food and its effect on the human body. Trout, for example, is to be eaten with caution because "This fish of nature loveth flatterie: for being in the water it will suffer it selfe to be rubbed and clawed, and so to be taken. Whose example I would wish no maydes to folow, lest they repent after clappes."

Treacle, the one-gun materia medica or shotgun remedy first thought of by Mithridates, King of Pontus in 64 B.C., *is also strongly recommended. This medicine originally consisted of hundreds of drugs, some of them poisons, designed to build up a resistance to the poisons of disease. Eventually, they were embodied in a syrup or treacle to make them easier to take. Nero's physician is believed to have refined the medicine, which still appears in pharmacopoeias in the middle of the nineteenth century. A. E. Housman's poem, "A Shropshire Lad," relates the story of Mithridates, protected by his invention against all those who would put poison in his meat. "Mithridates, he died old." It is amusing to note that candies called treacle are still sold, but at most, the box they contain indicates that they are "good for health." So ends a mighty tradition.*

To make the text clearer but at the same time to keep the flavor of the original, the following transcription by Mark Boyer keeps the ancient irregular spelling. Since Elizabethans did not have dictionaries as we now know them, they were not obliged to regularize their spelling. In this respect, some students might consider them fortunate. As the extensive quotations from Greek and Latin authorities are generally translated and summarized by Cogan himself in the text, these are omitted.

The following selections from The Haven of Health *are reprinted from a 1584 edition, printed in London by Henrie Midleton for William Norton. It is to be found in the National Library of Medicine, Bethesda, Maryland. If meanings of words are unfamiliar, the reader should consult the* Oxford English Dictionary. *Since this is a fresh transcription of a sixteenth-century edition, the original spelling and punctuation have been retained so that the reader can experience the book in the original form.*

CHAPTER I

*What Labour Is, the commoditie thereof,
the difference of labours, the preparation to labour,
the time, the measure of labour.*

T HE FIRST WORDE in order of that golden sentence proposed by Hippocrates, is labour, which in this place signifieth exercise. For so is the word labour commonly taken of Hippocrates as Galen witnesseth. Labour then, or exercise, is a vehement moving, the end whereof is alteration of the breath or winde of man.

What labour is.

Of exercise do proceede many commodities, but especially thre. The first is hardnesse and strength of the members, whereby labour shall the lesse greeve, and

The benefit of exercise.

the body be more strong to labour. And that exercise or labour both strengthen the bodie, beside the witnes of Galen, it is prooved by experience in labourers, who for the more part be stronger than learned men, and can endure greater toyle. Whereof we have a notable example in Milo Crotoniates, who by the use of carying a Calfe every day certaine furlonges, was able to carie the same being a bull. The seconde commoditie of labour is encrease of heate. Whereby happeneth the more alteration of thinges to be digested, also more quicke alteration and better nourishing. The thirde is more violence of the

breath or winde, whereby the pores are cleansed, and the filth of the body naturally expelled. These thinges are so necessarie to the preservation of health, that
without them, no man may be long without sicknes. For as the flowing water
doeth not lightly corrupt, but that which standeth still: Even so bodies exercised
are for the more part more healthful, and such as be idle more subject to sick-

Difference
of exer-
cise.
nes. But there is great difference of exercises. For some are swift, as running,
playing with weapons, throwing of the ball. Some are strong or violent, as wrastling, casting the bar. Some are vehement, as dansing, leaping, footeball play.
Againe some are exercises onely, as those now rehearsed, and other mentioned of
Galen not used among us. Some are not onely exercises but workes also, as to
digge or delve, to care or plow land, or to doe any other worke appertaining to
husbandrie, or whatsoever Craftes men of any occupation are woont to doe for
the use and commoditie of mans life. For these as they are labours, so are they
exercises, and do make a good state or liking of the body as Galen declareth, and
is found true by common experience in England. For husbandmen and craftesmen, for the more parte doe live longer and in better health, than Gentlemen
and learned men, and such as live in bodily rest. Wherefore Galen him selfe sometime used rustical labours, especially in Winter: as to cleave wood, to punne

The prop-
er exer-
cises of
all parts
of the
bodie.
Barley and such like. Againe some exercises are appropried to the partes of the
body, as running, and going are the proper exercises of the legges. Moving of the
armes uppe and downe, or stretching them out as in shooting and playing with
weapons, serveth most for the armes and shoulders. Stowping and rising oftentimes, as playing at the bowles, as lifting great waightes, taking up of plummets
or other like poyses on the end of staves, these do exercise the backe and loynes.
Of the bulke and lungs the proper exercise is moving of the breath in singing,
reading, or crying. The musckles, and together with them the sinues, veines,
arteries, bones, are exercised consequently, by the moving of the partes aforesaide. The stomacke and entrals, and thighes, and reines of the backe are
chiefly exercised by ryding. As for sitting in a boate or barge which is rowed,
riding in a horse litter, Couche, or Waggen, is a kind of exercise which is called
gestation: and is mixte with mooving and rest, and is convenient for them that

Tenis play
is the
best ex-
ercise of
all other.
be weake and impotent, as in long and continuall sicknes. But above all other
kindes of exercises, Galen most commendeth the play with the litle ball, which
we call Tenise, in so much that he hath written a peculiar booke of this exercise,
and preferreth it before hunting, and all other pastimes. Because it may be
easily used of all estates, as being of little cost. But chiefly for that it both exercise all partes of the body alike, as the legges, armes, necke, head, eies, back and
loynes, and delighteth greatly the minde, making it lusty and cheerefull. All
which commodities may be found in none other kinde of exercise. For they
streine more one parte of the body than an other, as shooting the armes, running the legges, &c. wherefore those founders of Colleges are highly to be praysed,
that have erected Tenis courtes, for the exercise of their Scholers: and I counsaile
all studentes as much as they may to use that pastime.

The games
of Olim-
pus.
For in the Mount Olimpus in Greece, where the most principall playes and
exercises of all the worlde were solemlie kept and used everie fifth yeare, first or-

dayned by Hercules the Champion (as it is thought) all men did not practise one onelie kinde of activitie, but everie man as he was minded so he applyed himselfe. There was wrastling, running with horses and on foote, turning, leaping, coursing with Chariotes, contentions of Poetes, Rhetoricians, musicians, disputations of Philosophers and others. So I restraine no man from his naturall inclina-

The preparation to exercise.

tion, but I shewe what exercise is best by the judgement of Galen. But least that by the violence of heate kindled by exercise, anie of the excrementes shoulde hastilie be received into the habit of the bodie, also least some thing which is whole should by heavinesse of excrementes or violent motion be broken or pulled out of place, or that the excrements by violence of the breath should stoppe the

Fricacions.

pores or Cundites of the bodie, the olde Greekes and Romanes were wont to use fricacies or rubbings before exercise in this manner. First to rub the bodie with a course lynnen cloth softlie and easilie, and after to increase more & more to a hard and swift rubbing, untill the fleshe doe swell and bee somewhat ruddie: then to annoint it with sweete oyle, stroking it everie way gentlie with bare

Three sortes of rubbinges.

handes. And of fricacies they have made generallie three sortes, first hard rubbing to binde or consolidate, then soft rubbing to loose or mollifie, and lastlie mean rubbing to augment and increase flesh. But this kinde of preparation whereof Galen hath written abundantly in his seconde booke *De Sa. Tuen.* is not used in Englande, and therefore I will ende it with a merie tale of Augustus the

A merie tale of rubbing.

Emperour and an olde Souldier. On a time as the noble Emperour Augustus came to a bath, he behelde an olde man that had doone good service in the warres, rubbing himselfe against a Marble piller, for lack of one to helpe him. The Emperour mooved with pitie gave an annuitie, to finde him a servant to waite upon him. When this was knowen, a great host of old soldiers drewe them together and stoode where as the Emperour shoulde passe by, everie one of them rubbing his backe against the stones, the Emperour demaunded why they did so, because noble Emperour say they we be not able to keepe servantes to doe it. Why (quoth the Emperour) one of you might clawe and rubbe an others backe well enough. So wiselie did he delude the practise of Parasites.

Notwithstanding Maister Eliote reporteth of himselfe, that hee found great

A kinde of rubbing good for all men.

commoditie in one kind of fricacie, which is thus. In the morning after wee have beene at the stoole with our shirt sleves or bare handes (if our fleshe be tender) first softlie and afterwarde faster to rubbe the brestes and sides, downewarde and overtwharte, not touching the stomacke & bellie, and after to cause our servant semblably to rubbe overtwarte the shoulders and backe beginning at the necke bone, not touching the raines of the backe, except wee doe feele there much colde and winde, and afterwarde the legges from the knee to the anckle, last the armes from the elbowe to the hands & wrest. And for those that cannot exercise their bodies at convenient times, either because they are letted with necessarie businesses, or else by reason of utter weakenesse, this kinde of rubbing may well be used in steede of exercise. But leaving all kinde of fricacis to such as have leasure, I prescribe none other preparation to bee used before exercise, but onelie evacuation of excrementes from all such partes as nature hath appointed thereunto. That is, when you are risen from sleepe, to walke a litle up and downe, that so the superfluitie of the stomacke, guttes and liver, may the more speedily

descende, and the more easilie be expelled. That doone to wash your face and handes, with cleane colde water, and especiallie to bath and plunge the eyes therein. For that not onelie cleanseth away the filth, but also comforteth and greatlie preserveth the sight, (as Avicen writeth) whereof studentes shoulde have a speciall care, Moreover to extende and stretch out your handes, and feete and other limmes, that the vitall spirites may come to the utter partes of the bodie. Also to combe your heade that the pores may be opened to avoide such vapours as yet by sleepe are not consumed. Then to rubbe and cleanse the teeth. For the filthinesse of the teeth is noisome to the braine, to the breath, and to the stomacke.

They may bee clensed (as Cornelius Celsus teacheth) by washing the mouth with colde water, putting thereto a little vineger. And with the same (if you list) you may gargarize or guddle in your throte, and after rubbe them harde with a drie cloth. Some use to rubbe their teeth and gummes when they washe with a sage leafe or two, which is good to preserve them from corruption and abateth the ranke savour of the mouth. All these thinges (which are sixe in number) are briefely comprehended in *The School of Salerno*.

After this preparation, as occasion shall serve, you may fall to exercise, yet first you must diligently consider where and when (that is to say) the place, and time.

The place where exercise is to be used doeth chieflie concerne the aire, which among all thinges, not naturall, as in habitation, so in exercise is greatlie to be regarded, for as much as it doeth both enclose us about, and also enter into our bodies, especiallie the most noble member which is the heart, and we cannot bee separate one houre from it for the necessitie of breathing. Wherefore exercise must bee used in a good and wholesome aire, which consisteth in foure pointes, first that it be faire and cleare without vapours and mistes. Secondlie that it be lightsome and open, not darke, troublous and close. Thirdly that it be not infected with carrain lying long above ground. Fourthlie that it be not stinking or corrupted with ill vapours, as being neere to draughts, Sinckes, dunghils, gutters, chanels, kitchings, Churchyardes, or standing waters. For the aire so corrupted, being drawne into our bodies, must of necessitie corrupt our bodies also. These foure properties are brieflie conteined in two verses in *The School of Salerno*.

Nowe for the time when you shoulde exercise, that divine Phisician Hippocrates teacheth us plainely. We must begin the preservation of health with labour, after that take meate, drinke, and so foorth. The time then most convenient for exercise, is when both the firste and seconde digestion is complet as well in the stomacke as in the vaines, and that the time approcheth to eate againe. For if you doe exercise sooner or latter, you shall either fill the bodie with rawe

humours, or else augment yealowe choler. The knowledge of this time is perceaved by the colour of the urine, for that which resembleth unto cleare water, betokeneth that the juice which commeth from the stomacke is crude in the vaines, that which is well coloured not too high or base, betokeneth that the seconde digestion is nowe perfect. Where the colour is verie high or redde, it signifieth that the concoction is more than sufficient: wherefore when the urine appeareth in a temperate colour, not red nor pale, but as it were gilt, then shoulde exercise have his beginning. By this meanes doeth Galen trie out the time most fit for exercise. But because everie man hath not skill to judge of urine, or hath not leasure or oportunitie to viewe his water in a glasse as often as he woulde or shoulde exercise, for the time most convenient, it shall be sufficient to remember that golden sentence of Hippocrates *Labores cibos antecedant*. Let exercise be used before meate. Which rule (as that famous Phisicion Fuchsius noteth is unadvisedlie neglected in the Schooles of Germanie. For there the Scholers never exercise but foorthwith after meate, either leaping, or running, or playing at the ball, or koyting, or such like. And the same abuse is ripe emong us here in Englande, both in universities and in the grammer Schooles. Wherefore it is no mervaile if Scholers oftentimes be troubled with scabbes and other infirmities growing of corrupt humours: because by that meanes great store of raw humours are ingendred and brought foorth to the skinne: (according to the saying of Hippocrates). Wherefore I counsaile all studentes not to exercise immediately after meate, for by that meanes the meat is conveied into all the members before it be concocted or boyled sufficiently. Yet to rise up after meate, and to stande upright for a while, or to walke softly a little is verie wholesome: that so the meate may descend to the botome of the stomake, where (as Avicenna writeth) resteth the vertue of concoction, and is one of the first lessons in *The School of Salerno*. But hastie mooving driveth the natural heate from the inwarde parts, and causeth ill digestion. As for craftesmen, and labourers, if any demande the question howe they can have their health, and fal to worke straight after they have eaten, I answere with Vergil, *Labor omnia vincit improbus*. So I write not these preceptes for labouring men, but for students, and such as though they be no studentes, doe yet folowe the order and diet of studentes. Antoninus the Romane Emperour, who lived in Galens time, and had a speciall care of his health, was woont to come to the wrastling place about sunne setting when dayes were at the shortest, and about nine or ten of the clocke when they were at the longest. Whose example if anie list to folowe (as Georgius Pictorius doth interprete) hee shoulde exercise in Summer six hours before noone, and in the winter in the after noone at Sunne going downe, and in the spring time nere by noone. But I restrayne no man to the houre, so it be doone according to the rules afore saide, to brieflie conclude. Yet it is not sufficient in exercise to observe the time, the place, the thinges proceeding, except we keepe a measure therein: which also is taught by Hippocrates in the worde (*mediocria*) [the golden mean]. And although everie man doth know that measure is a merie meane, yet fewe can hit that meane, as well in other thinges as in this, unlesse they bee directed by a certayne rule. Wherefore Galen, who leaveth nothing unperfect, setteth downe foure notes, by the which wee may knowe howe long wee shoulde exercise, and when wee shoulde give over. The first is to exercise untill the fleshe doe swell: the second is untill the fleshe be somewhat ruddie: The third untill the bodie be

Rise up after meate.

The exercise of the Emperour Antonine.

The measure of exercise.

nimble, active, and readie to all motions: The fourth is, untill sweate and hot vapours burst foorth. For when anie of these doe alter, we must give over exercise. First if the swelling of the fleshe shall seeme to abate, we must give over foorthwith. For if wee shoulde procede, some of the good juyce also woulde be brought foorth and by that meanes the bodie shoulde become more slender and dryer, and lesse able to encrease. Secondlie if the lively colour stirred up by exercise shall vanishe away, we must leave of, for by continuance the bodie woulde waxe colder. Thirdlie when agilitie of the limmes shall beginne to faile, we must give over, least wearinesse and feeblenes doe ensue. Fourthly when the qualitie or quantitie of the sweate is changed, we must cease, least by continuance, the sweate be greater or hotter, and so the bodie become colder and dryer. But of these foure notes, as Hippocrates sheweth, sweat and swelling of the flesh, are the chiefest to be marked in exercise. As who should say, sweat and abating of the fleshe are two of the chiefest signes, to know when wee shoulde give over exercise. This measure Pythagorus, that was first named a Philosopher, though no Phisician, hath yet defined in his golden verses. And it was latined also by Vitus Amerbachius. The same in effect is uttered by the excellent greeke Orator Isocrates in his oration *ad Demonicum*, and latined by Vuolsius. Nowe as I have shewed what time we should give over exercise, so here I will ende my treatise of exercise if first I shall declare, what remedie is to be used against wearinesse which commeth by immoderate labour either voluntary or necessarie, for wee can not always keepe the meane, but we must doe as cause requireth. Wearinesse, as all other infirmities of the bodie, is cured by the contrarie: that is to say, by rest, according to the saying of Hippocrates. For when the bodie is tryed through over much labour, and the strength fayleth, and naturall moysture decayeth, then rest for a time recovereth the strength, reviveth the spirites, and maketh the limmes able to endure labour, whereas otherwise they woulde soone languish and pine away. Which thing Ovid well perceaved.

The remedie of immoderate exercise.

Where the Poet hath woorthilie added the worde (*Alterna*) that is to say (doone by course) for as it is not convenient alwayes to labour, so is it not good alwayes to rest. For that were idlenesse of slouthfulnesse, which corrupteth both the bodie and soule. For in the body through immoderate rest is ingendered cruditie, and great store of noysome humours. Wherefore Galen reckoneth Idlenesse or immoderate rest, among the causes of cold diseases. And what inconvenience doeth growe unto the soule thereby. Christ himselfe doeth teach in his Gospell where he saith, It is better for a man to rip his coate and sowe it againe than to be idle. But, as Ovid writeth, moderate rest doeth comfort both the bodie and minde.

Wherefore I will conclude with that notable sentence of Galen: As sluggish rest of the bodie is a verie great discommoditie to the preserving of health, so no doubt in moderate motion there is verie great commoditie.

CHAPTER II

*Of studie or exercise of the minde in what order
we may studie without hinderance of
our health.*

As man doeth consist of two partes, that is of bodie and soule, so exercise is of two sortes, that is to say of the bodie and of the minde. Hitherto I have spoken of exercise of the bodie, nowe I will entreat of exercise of the minde, which is Studie. This kinde of exercise (as Tullie writeth) is the naturall nourishment of the minde and wit. Which thing may well be perceived even in little children: for as soone as they have gotten strength to goe of themselves, they are as busie as bees, and they devise a thousande toies to be occupied in. Which motions no doubt proceede from the minde. For (as Tullie sayeth) idlenesse therefore is not onely against nature, but also dulleth the minde. Wherefore notable is that counsell of Isocrates *ad Demonicum*, latined by Volsius. Which lesson, Publius Scipio, who first was named Aphricanus, well followed as Tullie alleageth by the witnesse of Cato. Leasure then and solitarinesse are two of the chiefest thinges apperteyning to studie. Which two who so hath obteyned, let him observe these rules following.

Those thinges presupposed which I have spoken of in the preparation of exercise of the bodie, this golden lesson of Lilie is next to be observed. And if you go not to the Church, yet forget not *venerari Deum*. And for this purpose no time is more convenient than the morning. Which the Prophet David everie where witnesseth in his Psalmes, namely Psalm. 5. And for studie howe much better the morning is than other times of the day, the reasons following may declare. First of all there be three planetes (as the Astronomers teach) most favourable to learning. That is, *Sol, Venus,* and *Mercurie,* these three in a manner meeting together when night approcheth, depart from us, but when day draweth neere they returne and visite us againe. Wherefore the best time for studie is earlie in the morning, when the Planetes be favourable to our purpose. Againe, when the Sunne ariseth, the ayre is mooved, and made more cleare and subtill, and the blood and spirites of our bodies doe naturally followe the motion and inclination of the ayre. Wherefore the morning or sunne rising, is most fit for studie. Aristotle therefore in his Deconomikes, not without great cause biddeth us to rise before day, and sayeth, that it prevaileth greatly both to the health of the bodie, and to the studie of Philosophie. Whose counsell that famous Oratour of Greece Demosthenes, diligently followeth (as Tullie reporteth of him) whose good example I wish all studentes to folow, having always in mind this short sentence, *Aurora Musis amica:* and not to imitate the practise of Bonacius a young man of whom Poggius the Florentine maketh mention. This Bonacius was woont to lie long in bed, and when he was rebuked of his felowes for so doing, he ansered smyling, that he gave care to certaine persens who contended and disputed before him. For as soone as I wake (sayde he) there appeareth in the shape of women, *Solicitudo* and *Pigritia*. Carefullnesse and

Marginal notes:

What studie is.

Idlenesse is against nature.

How to beginne our studie.

The morning most fit for prayer.

The best time for studie is the morning.

A good counsell for studentes.

An example of a slothfull Scholar.

slouthfulnesse. Carefulnesse biddeth mee to rise, and fall to some worke, and not to spend the day in my bedde. Contrariwise slouthfulnesse biddeth me lie still, and take mine ease, and keepe me from colde in my warme coutch. Thus while they varie and wrangle, I like an indifferent judge inclining to neither part, lie hearkening and looking when they will agree. And by this meanes the day is over passed or I beware. This young mans practise I leave to loytering

How long we should studie without intermission. Lurdeines, and returne againe to diligent studentes, who having used the preparation aforesayde must applie themselves earnestlie to reading and meditation for the space of an houre: then to remitte a litle their cogitation, and in the meane time with an Kuorie combe to kembe their heade from the foreheade backewardes about fourtie times, and to rubbe their teeth with a course linnen cloth. Then to returne againe to meditation for two houres or one at the least, so continuing, but alwaies with some intermission, untill towarde noone. And sometimes two houres after noone, though seldome, except we be forced to eate in the meane season, for the sunne is of great power at the rising, and likewise being in the middes of the heavens. And in that part also which is next to the middes, which the Astronomers call the ninth part and the house of wisedome, the sunne is of great vertue.

Nowe because the Poetes doe account the sunne as captaine of the Muses and Sciences, if any thing be deeply to be considered, we must meditate thereon

Afternoone studie not verie good. especially the houres aforesaide. As for the residue of the day is convenient rather to revolve thinges reade before, than to reade or muse of newe. Alwaies remembred that everie houre once at the least wee remit a litle while the earnest consideration of the minde: neither should wee meditate anie longer than we have pleasure therein. For all wearinesse is hurtfull to health, wearinesse of the bodie is evill, but weariness of the minde is woorse: and wearinesse of both woorst of all. For contrarie motions draweth as it were a man in sunder and destroyeth life. But nothing is more hurtfull than studying in the night. For while the Sunne shineth over us, through the power thereof the pores of the bodie are opened, and the humours and spirites are drawen from the inner partes outwarde. And contrariwise, after the sunne setteth the bodie is closed uppe, and naturall heate fortified within. Wherefore to watch and to be occupied in minde or bodie in the day time, is agreeable to the motions of the

Why studie is better by day than night. humours and spirites: but to watch and to studie in the night, is to strive against nature, and by contrarie motions to impaire both the bodie, and minde. Againe by continuall operation of the ayre opening the pores, there followeth exhalation and consumption of the vitall spirites, whereby the stomacke is greatly weakened, and requireth a renewing and repayring of the Spirites: which may best be doone in the night season when naturall heate returneth from without to the inwarde partes. Wherefore whosoever at that time shall beginne long and difficult contemplation, shall of force drawe the spirites from the stomacke to the heade, and so leave the stomacke destitute: whereby the head shall be filled with vapours, and the meate in the stomacke for want of heate, shall be undigested or corrupted. Notwithstanding I knowe that such as be good studentes indeede, do spare no time, neither night nor day from their bookes. Whereof

Plinie himselfe hath given a goodly example, in that by his owne testimonie, he wrote that most excellent worke called the historie of nature, *Noctibus & succisivis temporibus.* Yea Galen in his olde age (as he writeth) was faine to eate lettuse boyled, of purpose to make him sleepe. As for poore studentes they must followe the example of Cleanthes, who in the night time by drawing of water, gate where withall to finde himselfe in the day to studie Philosophie under Chrisippus, or the example of that noble King Alured or Alfrede, the first founder of the universitie of Oxforde, who divided the day and the night into three partes, and spent eight houres in eating, drinking and sleeping, and eight houres in hearing and deciding of causes, and eight houres in studie. Or as that excellent Poet Plautus, who was faine for his living to serve a baker in turning a Querne or handmill, that he might yet sometime apply his studie. Wherefore let not poore studentes disdaine to doe service in the day, that they may yet imploy sometime in the night. And if they waxe pale with overmuch studie, it **Better** is not reproche but a verie commendable signe of a good student. Yet would **to be** I have none to studie so much, that thereby they should fall into sicknesse, or **pale with** become melancholicke, as Homere writeth of Ajax and Bellerophon. And if it **studie** happen that we be cloyed with studie, then must wee fall to recreation and use **than with** some honest playe or pastime, yet so as Tullie prescribeth. **love.**

How play Wherof we have a notable example in Valerius Maximus, of Scevola that **is to** learned lawyer, who being wearied with lawe matters, was woont to recreate his **be used.** mide with Tenise play, and therein is said to have excelled. Yet sometimes he played at Dice, and Tables, when he had beene long busied in well ordering the lawes of the Citizens, and ceremonies of the goddes. Likewise wee reade of Socrates the Philosopher, who notwithstanding he was adjudged by the Oracle of Apollo, to bee the wisest man in the worlde, yet for recreation he blushed **An wittie** not to ride upon a reede among his litle children: And when he was laughed **answere of** to scorne of Alcibiades for so doing, he answered him verie pretily, tell no bodie **Socrates** (sayeth he) that thou sawest me, untill thou have children of thine owne. As who **made to** should say, such is the affection of parentes towardes their children, that they **Alcibiades.** are not ashamed oftentimes to play the children with them. But of recreation of the bodie I have spoken sufficiently before, and nowe I will speake somewhat **Unlawfull** of recreation of the minde. For there bee some pastimes that exercise the minde **games.** onely as dise, tables, cardes, and such like, which because they are accounted unhonest games, and forbidden even by heathen writers, as by the sage Cato in his morall preceptes, I will omitte them: and if any student will use them he shall not doe it *me authore* [on my advice]: yet I will rehearse one example of dice playing because it is famous. Caligula the Emperour (as Erasmus reporteth) when he played at dice, gate more by lying and forswearing, than by true play. And uppon a time, yeelding his turne of casting unto his next fellowe, going foorth to the doore, he espied two rich gentlemen of Rome passing by, whom streightway hee commaunded to be taken, and their goods to bee seised to his use. And so returning againe into the house verie joyfull, he boasted, that hee never had a more luckie cast at the dice. As Caligula gate those gentlemens goods, so thinke I all is gotten that is wonne by dysing. Therefore I let it passe and returne to my purpose. There is an auncient game called the Chesse, which was invented

after Polidorus Virgilius, in the yeare of the worlde, 3635 by a certaine wise man called Xerxes, to mitigate the mindes or heartes of Tyrantes. For it declareth to a tyrant that maiestie or authoritie, without strength, helpe, and assistance of his men and subjects, is casuall, feeble and subiect to many calamities. This game is an earnest exercise of the minde, and verie commendable and convenient for studentes, & may easily be provided to be alwaies readie in their chambers. But for a mind wearied with studie, & for one that is melancholike, (as the most part of learned men are) especially those that bee excellent, as Arist., witnesseth, there is nothing more comfortable, or that more reviveth the spirites than Musicke, according to Hessus.

And because it is one of the liberall sciences it ought the more to be esteemed

of studentes. And that for good cause. For by the judgement of Aristotle, Musicke is one of those foure thinges that ought to be learned of youth in well governed common wealthes: and in the fourth chapter of the same booke, he declareth that Musicke is to be learned, not onely for solace and recreation, but also because it mooveth men to vertue & good maners, & prevaileth greatly to wisedome, quietnes of minde and contemplation. But what kind of Musicke everie student should use, I referre that to their owne inclination. Howbeit the examples

following may declare, that the harpe of all instrumentes is most auncient and hath bin in greatest price and estimation. Orpheus that auncient Poet and harper most excellent, (as the Poetes surmised) did with his Musicke delight wilde beastes, as Lyons & Tigres, and made them to folowe him, & with his sweete harmonie, drewe stones and woods after him, that is to say, mooved and qualified the rough heartes and rude mindes of men. The Prophet David, delighted in the harpe, and with the sweete melodie therof, delivered King Saul from the vexation of the evill spirite. And if everie student coulde playe upon instruments, it were the more commendable. And Socrates when hee was olde, so much esteemed of Musicke, that he was not ashamed beeing olde, to learne among boyes to play upon instrumentes. And howe comfortable Musicke is to all sortes of men, wee may plainely perceive by labourers, for the galieman, the ploughman, the carter, the carier, ease the tediousnesse of their labour and journey with singing and whisteling: yea the brute beastes be delighted with songs and noyses, as mules with belles, horses with trumpets and shalmes, are of a fiercer stomacke to their appointed ministerie. Wherefore I counsell all students oftentimes to refresh their wearied minds with some sort of melodie. For so shall they drive alway the dumpes of melancholie, and make their spirites more lively to learne. And so I ende this treatise of labour.

12

A Book of
Nymphs, Sylphs, Pygmies
and Salamanders

By THEOPHRASTUS VON HOHENHEIM
(Paracelsus)

SELECTIONS

ONE OF THE TOWERING figures of the Renaissance, Paracelsus (1493–1541) is now often called the father of biochemistry, father of the study of occupational diseases, and of modern psychoanalysis. Possibly other of Paracelsus' "farfetched" ideas will prove to be important and true. Paracelsans still collect, translate, and study his works, the center for such study being Switzerland, where he grew up. Instead of seeking for the secret of turning base metals into gold, which was the ambition of the alchemists, Paracelsus used his ovens and retorts to find the secrets to cure diseases. He advocated studying the patient at the bedside instead of indulging in remote study of symptoms in the Roman texts of Galen or Celsus. Indeed, he called himself "Paracelsus" because he believed himself to be above Celsus in common-sense seeking after the cause and cure of diseases. Throughout his adult life, he wandered from one university to another, ordering his students to make bonfires of the old Latin texts and telling them, in effect, to think for themselves. As a result he was driven from one place to another by either the authorities or his own dissatisfaction. During these wanderings, he wrote voluminously. An early work was published by Viator in Cracow, Poland, where Paracelsus was connected with Jagellonian University. Legend has it that the alchemical laboratory in the basement of the University was once used by Paracelsus and also by Faust, a minor figure compared with Paracelsus. In fact, in The Story of Paracelsus, Henry Pachter maintains that the Faust of Goethe was actually Paracelsus—Paracelsus being larger than any legend.

In the late sixteenth and early seventeenth centuries, doctors began to divide themselves into two groups: Galenists and Paracelsans. Early in the seventeenth century, John Donne, who had a copy of Paracelsus' Opera Omnia in his library, used Paracelsan imagery in some of his metaphysical poetry. The metaphysical concept is clear even in the excerpt from Paracelsus' writings below. Yet Donne, in his Ignatius his Conclave, put Paracelsus in the lowest place in hell. Throughout the seventeenth and on into the eighteenth centuries, Paracelsus was regarded by writers as someone who had sold his soul to the devil. Finally, in the nineteenth century, Robert Browning, in his early poem Paracelsus, depicted Paracelsus as a restless seeker after truth.

After a bitter life, in which his views were constantly attacked, Paracelsus died either of cancer or a blow on the head in Salzburg in 1541.

Though some of his works appeared in chapbooks in English, it was largely through the oral tradition that he was known to the people. He was like some great religious leaders, better known through what they say than what they write. Though many of his texts are scientifically penetrating and amazingly modern, others seem like fantasy. Paracelsus was actually a simple, deeply religious man, incapable of hypocrisy. This was part of his tragedy. The other part was his imagination, which extended so far beyond his own time that it left him universally homeless. The text reproduced here, translated by the eminent medical historian Henry Sigerist, illustrates the poetic, imaginative part of Paracelsus.

A Book of Nymphs, Sylphs, Pygmies and Salamanders *is reprinted from* Four Treatises of Theophrastus von Hohenheim, *ed. Henry Sigerist (Baltimore: Johns Hopkins University Press, 1942).*

Paracelsus' Talismans experienced popularity for many years and shows a somewhat lighter side of Paracelsus' nature. The reproductions shown below are from Volume I of Charles Nisard's Histoire des Livres Populaires ou de la Litterature de Colportage *(Paris: Librairie D'Amyot, Editeur, 1854), p. 200.*

TRACTATUS II

About Their Abode

THEIR ABODE IS OF four kinds, namely, according to the four elements: one in the water, one in the air, one in the earth, one in the fire. Those in the water are nymphs, those in the air are sylphs, those in the earth are pygmies, those in the fire salamanders. These are not good names, but I use them nevertheless. The names have been given them by people who did not understand them. But since they designate the things and since they can be recognized by the names, I shall leave it at that. The name of the water people is also undina, and of the air people sylvestres, and of the mountain people gnomi, and of the fire people vulcani rather than salamandri. Whatever it may be, and however the differentiation may be understood, let it stay. Now you must know that if their regions have to be described, they must be divided into their parts. For the water people have no intercourse with the mountain people, nor the mountain people with them, nor the salamanders. Each has his special abode, but they appear to man, as mentioned, so that he may recognize and see how marvellous God is in his works, that he does not leave any element void and empty, without having great wonders in them. And now follow the four regions, which explains the difference of abode; also of person, essence and kind, how far they differ from each, yet more similar to man than to each other, and yet all men, as was explained in the first treatise.

You know that there are four elements: air, water, earth and fire; and you also know that we, men from Adam, stand and walk in air and are surrounded by it as a fish by water, and we can just as little be without it as a fish without water. As the fish has its abode in water, where water takes for it the place of the air in which it lives, so air takes for man the place of water, in relation to the fish. Thus everything has been created in its element, to walk therein. From this example you understand that the undinae have their abode in water, and the water is given to them as to us the air, and just as we are astonished that they should live in water, they are astonished about our being in the air. The same applies to the gnomi in the mountains: the earth is their air and is their chaos. For everything lives in chaos, that is: everything has its abode in chaos, walks and stands therein. Now, the earth is not more than mere chaos to the mountain manikins. For they walk through solid walls, through rocks and stones, like a spirit; this is why these things are all mere chaos to them, that is, nothing. That amounts to: as little as we are hampered by the air, as little are they hampered by the mountain, by earth and rocks. And as it is easy for us to walk through air and air cannot stop us, so rocks and cliffs are easy to them. And so, things are all chaos to them which are not chaos to us. For a wall, a partition, stops us so that we cannot go through, but to them it is a chaos. That is why they walk through it; to them it is their air in which they live and walk, as man does in the air that is between heaven and earth. And the coarser the chaos, the more subtile is the creature; and the more subtile the chaos the coarser the creature. The mountain people have a coarse chaos; therefore, they must be the more subtile; and man has a subtile chaos; therefore he is all the coarser. And thus there are different kinds of chaos, and the inhabitants are adapted in nature and quality to live in them.

Thus one wonder is explained, that of their abode, and you know now that their

habitation in the four elements is their chaos, just as the air is for us, and there cannot
be such accidents to them as drowning, or suffocating or burning, for the elements are
nothing but air to the creatures who live in them. Since water is the fish's air, the fish
does not drown, and so the unda does not drown either. As in the water, so in the earth:
the earth is air to the gnomi; hence they do not suffocate. They do not require our air,
we do not theirs. Thus also with the salamanders: fire is their air, as our air our air is.
And the sylvestres are closest to us, for they too maintain themselves in our air, and they
are exposed to the same kind of death as we, namely: they burn in fire, and we too; they
drown in water, and we too; they suffocate in the earth, and we too. For, each remains
healthy in his chaos; in the others he dies.

Therefore, you must not be astonished about things that seem incredible to us; to God
everything is possible. He has created all things for us, not according to our thoughts and
intelligence, but above our thoughts and intelligence. For, he wants to be looked upon
as a God who is marvellous in his creations. Had nothing been created but merely what is
possible for man to believe, God would be all too weak, and man would be his equal. This
is why he has created things as a God, and let man marvel about them, and let his works
be so big, that no one can marvel enough about these beings also. God wants to have it
thus.

Let us philosophize further, about their food. Know that each chaos has its two spheres,
the heaven and the soil, just as we men walk on earth. Earth and heaven give us our food
and the chaos is in between the two. Thus we are nourished in between the two spheres
and the globules. Thus also, those who live in the water, have the earth at the bottom,
and the water as chaos, and the heaven down to the water; and so they are in between
heaven and earth and the water is their chaos. And their abode is according to their
kind. Thus also with the gnomi, whose soil is water, and whose chaos is terra, and the
heaven is their sphaera, that is, the earth stands in water. To them the earth is chaos and
the water the soil. Food grows to them in such a way. The sylphs are like men, nourish
themselves like men in the wilderness, on herbs in the woods. To the salamanders the
soil is earth, their heaven is the air, and fire their chaos. Thus food grows to them from
the earth and from fire, and the constellation from air is their heaven. Now, about the
things they eat and drink, you may understand so much. Water quenches our thirst, but
not that of the gnomi, nor of the nymphs, nor of the other two. Further: if water has
been created for us, to quench our thirst, then another water must have been created for
them, that we cannot see nor explore. Drink they must, but drink that which in their
world is a drink. Eat they must similarly, according to the content of their world. One
cannot find out more about these things, but only that their world has its own nature,
just as ours has.

About their clothing: they are clothed and cover their genitalia, but not in the way of
our world, in their own way. For they have modesty and similar qualities, as men must
have, have law and similar institutions, have their authorities, like the ants, which have
their king, and the wild geese, which have their leader, not according to the law of men,
but according to their inborn nature. The animals have their chief, and so have they too,
and more than all animals, because they are most similar to man. God has clothed all
beings and endowed them with modesty, to walk and stand before man. To the beasts
clothing is inborn by nature, but not to these people. To them nothing is inborn by
nature; they must work for it like man whom they resemble. Their work, like man's work,

is in the nature and kind of their own world and earth on which they live. For he who gave us wool from sheep, gives it to them also. For it is possible for God to create not only the sheep which are known to us, but also the same in fire, in water, in the earth. For he clothes not only us, but also the gnomi, the nymphs, the salamanders, the sylvestres. They are all under the protection of God and are all clothed and guided by him. For God has not only power to provide for man, but also for anything else, of which man knows nothing, and of which he becomes slowly aware. And when he sees and hears something, it is a miracle to him that bears no fruit, that is: he gives it no further thought, but remains obstinate and blind, like one who with good eyes has not the grace to see.

About their day, night, sleeping and waking, know that they rest, sleep and are awake like men, that is, in the same measure as man. With that, they have the sun and firmament as well as we. That is: the mountain manikins have the earth which is their chaos. To them it is only an air and no earth as we have it. From this we must conclude that they see through the earth, as we do through the air, and that the sun shines to them through the earth, as it does to us through the air, and that they have the sun, the moon and the whole firmament in front of their eyes, as we men. To the undinae the water is their chaos, and water does not keep them from the sun; and just as we have the sun through the air, they have it through the water, in the same measure. Thus also to the vulcans through the fire. And in the same way as the sun shines on us and fertilizes the earth, know that the same happens to them as to us. The consequence is, that they too have summer, winter, day and night, etc. But they do not need rain, snow, etc. They have it in a different way than we. These are the great miracles of God. From all this we must conclude that they have pestilence, fevers, pleurisies, and all diseases of the heaven, just as we do, and that they follow us in all these matters, since they are men. But in the judgment of God, in the resurrection, they will be beasts and not men.

About their figures, know that they are different. The water people look like men, both women and men. The sylvestres do not conform, but are cruder, coarser, longer and stronger than both. The mountain people are small, of about two spans. The salamanders are long, narrow and lean. Their place and abode are in their chaos, as was mentioned before. The nymphs live in water, in running brooks, etc., so close that they grasp the people who ride through or bathe therein. The mountain people are in the mountain chaos, and there they build their houses. This is why it often happens that one finds in the earth an attic, vaults, and similar structures, of the height of about a yard. They have been build by these people for their abode and dwellings. The water people do the same in their various places. Know also that the mountain people live in the caves of the mountains and this is why strange structures occur and are found in such places. These are their work. Know also about the fire people whose yelling, hammering and working can be heard in volcanic mountains. It can also be heard when the elements are incinerated. For all these things are the same as with us, but according to their secret quality. Those who travel through wild regions learn the reason for such beings and obtain information. There these beings are found. In the mines also, close to good ore, etc. they are found, and in waters the same also, and the vulcans near the Aetna. And there are many more marvellous things, about their coins, payments and customs, which would be too long in this connection, but will be described in their place.

13

The Herball, or
Generall
Historie of Plantes

By JOHN GERARD

SELECTIONS

POPULARLY KNOWN AS *Gerard's* Herball, *this work, originally published in 1597, preceded a long line of English Herbals, the best known of which is that of Nicholas Culpeper, much quoted by early American colonists.*

Herbals were very important to Elizabethans because they told them the properties of plants and when and how to plant. Since gardens were regarded, in accordance with the doctrine of correspondences, as small models of God's garden in Heaven, or Paradise, it was a sacred duty to have as splendid a garden as possible. Indeed the word sometimes used for garden was the Greek word παραδεισος, *for park, used in the Septuagint for the Garden of Eden, rather than the German word for a guarded place.*

Gardens had a beautifully established form, with special places for kitchen herbs, vegetables, flowers, and flowering shrubs. Meadows and tall trees often formed a background. Such gardens still can be seen on many parts of the European continent, in England, and in America, especially in colonial Williamsburg, where there are mazes or complicated arrangements of high shrubs in which lovers—or children—can lose themselves.

Gerard's Herball *is in beautiful Elizabethan prose. As Marcus Woodward suggests in his edition of 1927, it "continued for a long time to be the standard work for English students." This comment refers to Thomas Johnson's amended edition of 1636. One interesting aspect of seventeenth-century scientific works is their literary quality, which is often very high, as evidenced here. In modern times, it took scientists such as Sir William Osler, Sir James Jeans, and Alfred North Whitehead to show that scientific writing can be literature.*

The following excerpts are reprinted from a 1636 edition of Gerard's Herball, or Generall Historie of Plantes.

CHAPTER 11

Of Tarragon.

The description.

Tarragon the sallade herbe hath long and narrow leaves of a deepe greene colour, greater and longer than those of common Hyssope, with slender brittle round stalkes two cubits high: about the branches whereof hang little round flowers, never perfectly opened, of a yellow colour mixed with blacke, like those of common Wormewood. The root is long and fibrous, creeping farre abroad under the earth, as doe the rootes of Couch-grasse, by which sprouting forth it increaseth, yeelding no seede at all, but as it were a certaine chaffie or dustie matter that flieth away with the winde.

The place.

Tarragon is cherished in gardens, and is encreased by the young shootes: *Ruellius* and such others have reported many strange tales hereof scarse worth the noting, saying, that the seed of flaxe put into a radish roote or sea Onion, and so set, doth bring forth this herbe Tarragon.

The time.

It is greene all Summer long, and a great part of Autumne, and floureth in July.

The names.

It is called in Latine, *Draco, Dracunculus hortensis,* and *Tragum vulgare* by *Clusius;* Of the Italians, *Dragoncellum;* in French, *Dragon;* in English, Tarragon.

It is thought to be that *Tarchon* which Avicen mentioneth in his 686. chapter: but he writeth so little thereof, as that nothing can certainly be affirmed of it. *Simeon Sethi* the Greeke also maketh mention of *Tarchon*.

Tarragon.

The temperature and vertues.

Tarragon is hot and drie in the third degree, and not to be eaten alone in sallades, but joyned with other herbes, as Lettuce, Purslain, and such like, that it may also temper the coldness of them, like as Rocket doth, neither doe we know what other use this herbe hath.

CHAPTER 67

Of yellow Henbane, or English Tabaco.

The Description.

Yellow Henbane groweth to the height of two cubits: the stalke is thicke, fat, and greene of colour, full of a spongeous pith, and is divided into sundry branches set with smooth and even leaves, thick and ful of juice. The floures grow at the tops of the branches, orderly placed, of a pale yellow colour, something lesser than those of the blacke Henbane. The cups wherein the floures do stand are like, but lesser, tenderer, and without sharpe points, wherein is set the husk or cod somewhat round, full of very small seed like the seed of Marjerome. The root is small and thready.

The Place.

Yellow Henbane is sowen in gardens, where it doth prosper exceedingly, insomuch that it cannot be destroyed where it hath once sowen it selfe, and it is dispersed into the most parts of England.

The Time.

It floureth in the Sommer moneths, and oftentimes till Autumne be farre spent, in which time the seed commeth to perfection.

Hyoscyamus luteus.
Yellow Henbane.

The Names.

Yellow Henbane is called *Hyoscyamus luteus:* of some, *Petum,* and *Petun:* of others, *Nicosiana,* of *Nicot* a Frenchman that brought the seeds from the Indies, as also the seeds of the true Tabaco, whereof this hath beene taken for a kinde; insomuch that *Lobel* hath called it *Dubius Hyoscyamus,* or doubtfull Henbane, as a plant participating of Henbane and Tabaco: and it is used of divers in stead of Tabaco, and called by the same name, for that it hath beene brought from Trinidada, a place so called in the Indies, as also from Virginia and Norembega, for Tabaco; which doubtlesse taken in smoke worketh the same kinde of drunkennesse that the right Tabaco doth.

Some use to call this Nicotian, in English, being a name taken from the Latine.

The Nature.

This kinde of Henbane is thought of some to be cold and moist, but after *Lobel* it rather heateth than cooles at all, because of the biting taste, as also that rosenninesse or gummines it is possessed of; which is evidently perceived both in handling and chewing it in the mouth.

The Vertues.

This herbe availeth against all apostumes, tumors, inveterate ulcers, botches, and such like, being made into an unguent or salve as followeth: Take of the greene leaves three pounds and an halfe, stampe them very small in a stone morter; of Oyle Olive one quart; set them to boyle in a brasse pan or such like, upon a gentle fire, continually stirring it untill the herbes seem blacke, and will not boyle or bubble any more: then shall you have an excellent greene oyle; which being strained from the feces or drosse, put the cleare and strained oyle to the fire againe; adding thereto of wax halfe a pound, of rosen foure ounces, and of good Turpentine two ounces: melt them all together, and keepe it in pots for your use, to cure inveterate ulcers, apostumes, burnings, greene wounds, and all cuts and hurts in the head; wherewith I have gotten both crownes and credit.

It is used of some in stead of Tabaco, but to small purpose or profit, although it do stupifie and dull the sences, and cause that kind of giddinesse that Tabaco doth, and likewise spitting; which any other herbe of hot temperature will do, as Rosemary, Time, winter Savorie, sweet Marjerome, and such like: any of the which I like better to be taken in smoke than this kinde of doubtfull henbane.

1 *Piper nigrum.*
Blacke Pepper.

2 *Piper album.*
White Pepper.

CHAPTER 152

Of the Pepper Plant.

The Kindes.

T HERE BE DIVERS sorts of Pepper, that is to say, white, blacke, and long Pepper, one greater and longer than the other; and also a kinde of Ethiopian Pepper.

The Description.

The Plant that beareth the blacke Pepper groweth up like a vine among bushes and brambles where it naturally groweth; but where it is manured it is sowne at the bottome of the tree Faufel and the Date trees, whereon it taketh hold, and clymbeth up even to the top, as doth the Vine, ramping and taking hold with his clasping tendrels of any other thing it meeteth withall. The leaves are few in number, growing at each joint one, first on one side of the stalke, then on the other, like in shape to the long undivided leaves of Iuy, but thinner, sharpe pointed, and sometimes so broad, that they are four inches over, but most commonly two inches broad, and foure long, having alwaies five pretty large nerves running alongst them. The fruit grow clustering together upon long stalks, which come forth at the joints against the leaves, as you may see in the figure: the root (as one may conjecture) is creeping; for the branches that lie on the ground do at their joint put forth new fibres or roots. We are beholden to *Clusius* for this exact figure and description, which he made by certaine branches which were brought home by the Hollanders from the East Indies. The curious may see more hereof in his Exotickes and notes upon *Garcias*.

3 *Piper longum.*
Long Pepper.

4 *Piper Aethiopicum, sive Vitalonga.*
Pepper of Ethiopia.

2 The Plant that brings white Pepper is not to be distinguished from the other plant, but only by the colour of the fruit, no more than a Vine that beareth blacke Grapes, from that which bringeth white: and of some it is thought, that the selfe same plant doth sometimes change it selfe from black to white, as divers other plants do. Neither *Clusius*, nor any other else that I have yet met with, have delivered us any thing of certaine, of the plant whereon white Pepper growes: *Clusius* only hath given us the manner how it growes upon the stalkes, as you may see it here exprest.

There is also another kinde of Pepper, seldome brought into these parts of Europe, called *Piper Canarium*: it is hollow within, light, and empty, but good to draw flegme from the head, to helpe the tooth-ache and cholericke affects.

3 The tree that beareth long Pepper hath no similitude at all with the plant that brings black and white Pepper: some have demmed them to grow all on one tree, which is not consonant to truth, for they grow in countries far distant one from another, and also that countrey where there is blacke Pepper hath not any of the long Pepper; and therefore *Galen* following *Dioscorides*, were together both overseen in this point. This tree, saith *Monardes*, is not great, yet of a wooddy substance, dispersing here and there his clasping tendrels, wherewith it taketh hold of other trees and such other things as do grow neere unto it. The branches are many and twiggie, whereon growes the fruit, consisting of many graines growing upon a slender foot-stalke, thrust or compact close together, greene at the first, and afterward blackish; in taste sharper and hotter than common blacke Pepper, yet sweeter, and of better taste.

For this figure also I acknowledge my selfe beholden to the learned and diligent *Clusius*, who caused it to be drawne from a branch of some foot in length, that he

5   *Piper Caudatum.*
Tailed Pepper.

received from Dr. *Lambert Hortensius*, who brought it from the Indies. The order of growing of the leaves, and fruit is like that of the blacke; but the joints stand somewhat thicker together, the leafe also doth little differ from that of the blacke, onely it is thinner, of a lighter greene, and (as *Clusius* thought) hath a shorter foot-stalke, the veines or nerves also were lesse imminent, more in number, and run from the middle rib to the sides, rather than alongst the leafe.

4   This other kinde of Pepper brought unto us from Æthiopia, called of the country where it groweth, *Piper Æthiopicum:* in shops *Amomum,* and also *Longa Vita.* It groweth upon a small tree, in manner of an hedge bush, whereupon grow long cods in bunches, a finger long, of a browne colour, uneven, and bunched or puft up in divers places, divided into five or six lockers or cels, each whereof containeth a round seed somewhat long, lesser than the seeds of Paeony, in taste like common Pepper, or *Carda-momum,* whose facultie and temperature it is thought to have, whereof we hold it a kinde.

5   Another kinde of Pepper is sometimes brought, which the Spaniards to call *Pimenta de rabo,* that is, Pepper with a taile: it is like unto Cubebes, round, full, somewhat rough, blacke of colour, and of a sharpe quicke taste, like the common Pepper, of a good smell: it groweth by clusters upon small stems or stalkes, which some have un-advisedly taken for *Amomum.* The King of Portingal forbad this kinde of Pepper to be brought over, for feare least the right Pepper should be the lesse esteemed, and so himselfe hindered in the sale thereof.

The Place.

Blacke and white Pepper grow in the kingdome of Malavar, and that very good; in Malaca also, but not so good; and also in the Islands Sunde and Cude: there is great store growing in the kingdome of China, and some in Cananor, but not much.

Pepper of Æthiopia groweth in Africa, in all the tract of the country where Nata and Carthago are situated. The rest hath been spoken of in their severall descriptions. The white Pepper is not so common as the blacke, and is used there in stead of salt.

The Time.
The plant riseth up in the first of the spring; the fruit is gathered in August.

The Names.
The Grecians, who had best knowledge of Pepper, do call it the Latines, *Piper:* The Arabians, *Fulfel* and *Fulful:* in Italian, *Pepe:* in Spanish, *Pimenta:* in French, *Poivre:* in high-Dutch, Pfeffer: in English, Pepper.

That of Æthiopia is called, *Piper Æthiopicum, Amomum, Vita longa,* and of some, *Cardamomum,* whereof we hold it to be a kinde. I received a branch hereof at the hands of a learned Physition of London, called Mr. *Steven Bredwell,* with his fruit also.

The Temperature.
The Arabians and Persian Physitians judge, that Pepper is hot in the third degree.

But the Indian Physitians which for the most part are Emperickes, hold that Pepper is cold, as almost all other spice, which are hot indeed: the long Pepper is hot also in the third degree, and as we have said, is thought to be the best of all the kindes.

The Vertues.
Dioscorides and others agreeing with him, affirme, that Pepper resisteth poison, and is good to be put in medicaments for the eies.

CHAPTER 350

Of Potatoes of Virginia.

The Description.

VIRGINIA POTATO HATH many hollow flexible branches trailing upon the ground, three square, uneven, knotted or Kneed in sundry places at certaine distances: from the which knots commeth forth one great leafe made of divers leaves, some smaller, and other greater, set together upon a fat middle rib by couples, of a swart greene colour tending to rednesse; the whole leafe resembling those of the Winter-Cresses, but much larger; in taste at the first like grasse, but afterward sharpe and nipping the tongue. From the bosome of which leaves come forth long round slender foot-stalkes, whereon do grow very faire and pleasant floures, made of one entire whole leafe, which is folded or plaited in such strange sort, that it seemeth to be a floure made of five sundry small leaves, which cannot easily be perceived except the same be pulled open. The whole floure is of a light purple colour, striped downe the middle of every fold or welt with a light shew of yellownesse, as if purple and yellow were mixed together. In the middle of the floure thrusteth forth a thicke flat point all yellow as gold, with a small sharpe

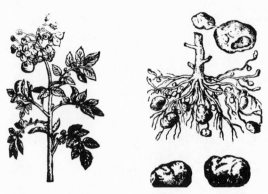

Battata Virginiana, sive Virginianorum, & Pappus
Virginian Potatoes

greene pricke or point in the middest thereof. The fruit succeedeth the floures, round as a ball, of the bignesse of a little Bullesse or wilde plum, greene at the first, and blacke when it is ripe; wherein is contained small white seed lesser than those of Mustard. The root is thicke, fat, and tuberous, not much differing either in shape, colour, or taste from the common Potatoes, saving that the roots hereof are not so great nor long; some of them are as round as a ball, some ovall or egge-fashion; some longer, and others shorter: the which knobby roots are fastened unto the stalkes with an infinite number of threddie strings.

The Place.

It groweth naturall in America, where it was first discovered, as reports *C. Clusius*, since which time I have received roots hereof from Virginia, otherwise called Norembega, which grow and prosper in my garden as in their owne native countrey.

The Time.

The leaves thrust forth of the ground in the beginning of May: the floures bud forth in August. The fruit is ripe in September.

The Names.

The Indians do call this plant Pappus, meaning the roots: by which name also the common Potatoes are called in those Indian countries. We have the name proper unto it mentioned in the title. Because it hath not onely the shape and proportion of Potatoes, but also the pleasant taste and vertues of the same, we may call it in English, Potatoes of America or Virginia.

Clusius questions whether it be not the *Arachidna* of *Theophrastus. Bauhinė* hath referred it to the Nightshades, and calleth it *Solanum tuberosum Esculentum*, and largely figures and describes it in his *Prodromus, pag.* 89.

The Temperature and Vertues.

A The temperature and vertues be referred unto the common Potatoes, being likewise a food, as also a meate for pleasure, equall in goodnesse and wholesomenesse unto the same, being either rosted in the embers, or boyled and eaten with oyle, vinegar, and pepper, or dressed any other way by the hand of some cunning in cookerie.

B *Bauhine* saith, That he heard that the use of these roots was forbidden in Bourgondy (where they call them Indian Artichokes) for that they were persuaded the too frequent use of them caused the leprosie.

1   *Fragaria & Fraga.*
    Red Straw-berries.

2   *Fragaria & Fraga subalba.*
    White Straw-berries.

CHAPTER 386

Of Straw-berries.

The Kindes.

THERE BE DIVERS sorts of Strawberries; one red, another white, a third sort greene, and likewise a wilde Straw-berrie, which is altogether barren of fruit.

The Description.

The Straw-berry hath leaves spred upon the ground, somewhat snipt about the edges, three set together upon one slender foot-stalke like the Trefoile, greene on the upper side, and on the nether side more white: among which rise up slender stems, whereon do grow small floures, consisting of five little white leaves, the middle part somewhat yellow, after which commeth the fruit, not unlike to the Mulberrie, or rather the Raspis, red of colour, having the taste of wine, the inner pulpe or substance whereof is moist and white, in which is contained little seeds: the root is threddy, of long continuance, sending forth many strings, which disperse themselves far abroad, whereby it greatly increaseth.

2   Of these there is also a second kinde, which is like to the former in stems, strings, leaves, and floures. The fruit is something greater, and of a whitish colour, wherein is the difference.

There is another sort, which brings forth leaves, floures, and strings like the other of his kinde. The fruit is green when it is ripe, tending to rednesse upon that side that lieth to the Sun, cleaving faster to the steemes, and is of a sweeter taste, wherein onely consisteth the difference.

There is also kept in our gardens (onely for varietie) another Strawberrie which in leaves and growing is like the common kinde; but the floure is greenish, and the fruit is harsh, rough and prickely, being of a greenish colour, with some shew of rednesse. Mr. *John Tradescant* hath told me that he was the first that tooke notice of this Straw-berry, and that in a womans garden at Plimouth, whose daughter had gathered and set the roots in her garden in stead of the common Straw-berry: but she finding the fruit not to answer her expectation, intended to throw it away: which labor he spared her, in taking it and bestowing it among the lovers of such varieties, in whose gardens it is yet preserved. This may be called in Latine, *Fragaria fructu hispido,* The prickly Straw-berry.

3 This wild Strawberry hath leaves like the other Straw-berry, but somewhat lesse, and softer, slightly indented about the edges, and of a light greene colour: among which rise up slender stems bearing such floures as the common Straw-berries doe, but lesser, which doe wither away, leaving behinde a barren or chaffie head, in shape like a Straw-berrie, but of no worth or value: the root is like the others.

3 *Fragaria minime vesca, sive sterilis.*
Wilde or barren Straw-berry.

The Place.

Straw-berries do grow upon hills and vallies, likewise in woods and other such places that be somewhat shadowie: they prosper well in Gardens, the first every where, the other two more rare, and are not to be found save only in gardens.

The barren one growes in divers places, as upon Black heath, in Greenwich parke, &c.

The Time.

The leaves continue greene all the yeare: in the Spring they spred further with their strings, and floure afterward: the berries are ripe in June and July. The barren one floures in April and May, but never carries any berries.

The Names.

The fruit or berries are called in Latine by *Virgil* and *Ovid, Fraga:* neither have they any other name commonly knowne: they are called in high-Dutch *Erdbeeren:* in low-Dutch, *Eertbessen:* in French, *Fraises:* in English, Strawberries.

The Temperature.

The leaves and roots do coole and dry, with an astriction or binding quality: but the berries be cold and moist.

The Vertues.

A   The leaves boyled and applied in manner of a pultis taketh away the burning heate in wounds: the decoction thereof strengthneth the gummes, fastneth the teeth, and is good to be held in the mouth, both against the inflammation or burning heate thereof, and also of the almonds of the throat: they stay the overmuch flowing of the bloudy flix, and other issues of blood.

B   The berries quench thirst, and do allay the inflammation or heate of the stomach: the nourishment which they yeeld is little, thin, and waterish, and if they happen to putrifie in the stomacke, their nourishment is naught.

C   The distilled water drunke with white Wine is good against the passion of the heart, reviving the spirits, and making the heart merry.

D   The distilled water is reported to scoure the face, to take away spots, and to make the face faire and smooth: and is likewise drunke with good successe against the stone in the kidnies.

E   The leaves are good to be put into Lotions or washing waters, for the mouth and the privie parts.

The ripe Straw-berries quench thirst, coole heat of the stomack, and inflammation of the liver, take away (if they be often used) the rednesse and heate of the face.

CHAPTER 510

Of Peason.

The Kindes.

THERE BE DIVERS sorts of Peason, differing very notably in many respects, some of the garden, and others of the field, and yet both counted tame: some with tough skinnes or membranes in the cods, and others have none at all, whose cods are to be eaten with the Pease when they be young, as those of the young Kidney Beane: others carrying their fruit in the tops of the branches, are esteemed and taken for Scottish Peason, which is not very common. There be divers sorts growing wild, as shall be declared.

1   *Pisum maius.*
    Rowncivall Pease.

2   *Pisum minus.*
    Garden and field Pease.

The Description.

The great Pease hath long stalks, hollow, brickle, of a whitish green colour, branched, and spread upon the ground, unlesse they be held up with proppes set neere unto them: the leafe thereof is wide and long, made up of many little leaves which be smooth, white, growing upon one little stalke or stem, and set one right against another: it hath also in the upper part long clasping tendrels, wherewith it foldeth it selfe upon props and staies standing next unto it: the floure is white and hath about the middle of it a purple spot: the cods be long, round, *Cilindriforma:* in which are contained seeds greater than *Ochri*, or little Peason, which being drie are cornered, and that unequall, of colour some-times white and sometimes gray: the roots are small.

2   The field Pease is so very well knowne to all, that it were a needlesse labour to spend time about the description.

3   Tufted Pease are like unto those of the field, or of the garden in each respect, the difference consisteth onely in that, that this plant carrieth his floures and fruit in the tops of the branches in a round tuft or umbel, contrary to all other of his kinde, which bring forth their fruit in the midst, and alongst the stalks: the root is thick and fibrous.

4   Pease without skins, in the cods differ not from the precedent, saving that the cods hereof want that tough skinny membrane in the same, which the hogs cannot eat by reason of the toughnesse; whereas the other may be eaten cods and all the rest, even as Kidney beanes are: which being so dressed are exceeding delicate meat.

5   The wilde Pease differeth not from the common field Pease in stalke and leaves, saving that this wilde kind is somewhat lesser: the floures are of a yellow colour, and the fruit is much lesser.

6   The Pease whose root never dies differeth not from the wilde Pease, only his con-tinuing without sowing, being once sowne or planted, setteth forth the difference.

3 *Pisum umbellatum.*
Tufted or Scottish Pease.

4 *Pisum excorticatum.*
Pease without skins in the cod.

5 *Pisum sylvestre.*
Wilde Pease.

6 *Pisum perenne sylvestre.*
Everlasting wilde Pease.

The Place.

Pease are set and sown in gardens, as also in the fields in all places of England. The tufted Pease are in reasonable plenty in the West part of Kent, about Sennocke or Sevenock; in other places not so common.

The wilde Pease do grow in pastures and earable fields in divers places, specially about the field belonging unto Bishops Hatfield in Hartfordshire.

The Time.

They be sowne in the Springtime, like as be also other pulses, which are ripe in Summer: they prosper best in warme weather, and easily take harme by cold, especially when they floure.

The Names.

The great Pease is called in Latine *Pisum Romanum,* or *Pisum maius:* in English, Roman Pease, or the greater Pease, also garden Pease: of some, Branch Pease, French Pease, and Rouncivals. *Theophrastus* and other old writers do call it in Greeke πισος in Latine also *Pisum:* in low Dutch, *Roomsche erwiten:* in French, *des Pois.* The little Pease is called of the Apothecaries everywhere *Pisum,* and *Pisum minus:* it is called in English, little Pease, or the common Pease.

The Temperature and Vertues.

The Pease, as *Hippocrates* saith, is lesse windie than Beans, but it passeth sooner through the belly. *Galen* writeth, that Peason are in their whole substance like unto Beanes, and be eaten after the same manner that Beans are, notwithstanding they differ from them in these two things, both because they are not so windie as be the beanes, and also for that they have not a clensing faculty, and therefore they do more slowly descend through the belly. They have no effectuall qualitie manifest, and are in a meane between those things which are of good and bad juice, that nourish much and little, that be windie and without winde, as *Galen* in his booke of the Faculties of Nourishments hath written of these and of beans.

14

A Briefe and True Report
of the New Found
Land of Virginia

By THOMAS HARIOT

SELECTIONS

MEN, WOMEN, AND *children in the early seventeenth century were not only interested in exploring past civilizations but were eagerly searching out the mysteries of the new world. Theodor de Bry, in 1590, published an account of Virginia, with John White's illustrations to Thomas Hariot's notes. (White's grandchild was Virginia Dare, the first white child born in America.) The portrait of the Indian woman shows her with her little daughter, who is playing with a rattle and a doll in Elizabethan costume. The note indicates that children also liked English puppets. Both the picture and the prose are simple and straightforward, and bound to appeal to children. Another intriguing illustration is that of Indians hollowing out a log to make a boat.*

The following two pages from "The True Pictures and Fashions of the People in That Part of America Now Called Virginia, Discoverd by Englishmen" are reproduced from a 1972 facsimile of the complete 1590 Theodor de Bry edition of Thomas Hariot's A Briefe and True Report of the New Found Land of Virginia.

A bout 20. milles from that Iland, neere the lake of Paquippe, ther is another towne called Pomeioock hard by the ſea. The apparell of the cheefe ladyes of dat towne differeth but litle from the attyre of thoſe which lyue in Roanaac. For they weare their haire truſſed opp in a knott, as the maiden doe which we ſpake of before, and haue their ſkinnes powncedin theſame manner, yet they wear a chaine of great pearles, or beades of copper, or ſmoothe bones 5. or 6. fold obout their necks, bearinge one arme in the ſame, in the other hand they carye a gourde full of ſome kinde of pleaſant liquor. They tye deers ſkinne doubled about them crochinge hygher about their breaſts, which hange downe before almoſt to their knees, and are almoſt altogither naked behinde. Commonlye their yonge daugters of 7. or 8. yeares olde do waigt vpon them wearinge abowt them a girdle of ſkinne, which hangeth downe behinde, and is drawen vnder neath betwene their twiſte, and bownde aboue their nauel with moſe of trees betwene that and thier ſkinnes to couer their priuiliers withall. After they be once paſt 10. yeares of age, they wear deer ſkinnes as the older ſorte do. They are greatlye Diligted with puppetts, and babes which wear brought oute of England.

THe manner of makinge their boates in Virginia is verye wonderfull. For wheras they want Inftruments of yron, or other like vnto ours, yet they knowe howe to make them as handfomelye, to faile with whear they lifte in their Riuers, and to fifhe with all, as ours. Firft they choofe fome longe, and thicke tree, accordinge to the bignes of the boate which they would frame, and make a fyre on the grovnd abowt the Roote therof, kindlinge the fame by little, and little with drie moffe of trees, and chipps of woode that the flame fhould not mounte opp to highe, and burne to muche of the lengte of the tree· When yt is almoft burnt thorough, and readye to fall they make a new fyre, which they fuffer to burne vntill the tree fall of yt owne accord. Then burninge of the topp, and bowghs of the tree in fuche wyfe that the bodie of thefame may Retayne his iuft lengthe, they raife yt vppon potes laid ouer croffwife vppon forked pofts, at fuche a reafonable heighte as rhey may handfomlye worke vp-po yt. Then take they of the barke with certayne fhells: thy referue the, innermoft parte of the lenn-ke, for the nethermoft parte of the boate. On the other fide they make a fyre accordinge to the lengthe of the bodye of the tree, fauinge at both the endes. That which they thinke is fufficientlye burned they quenche and fcrape away with fhells, and makinge a new fyre they burne yt agayne, and foe they continne fomtymes burninge and fometymes fcrapinge, vntill the boate haue fufficient bothowmes. This god indueth thife fauage people with fufficient reafon to make thinges neceffarie to ferue their turnes.

A Perfit Description
of the Caelestiall Orbes

According To The Most Aunciente
Doctrine Of The Pythagoreans.

Latelye Revived By Copernicus And
By Geometricall Demonstrations Approved

By THOMAS DIGGES

SELECTIONS

THROUGH HIS SMALL *treatise on the Copernican universe (Copernicus'* De revolutionibus *was published in 1543), Thomas Digges (d. 1595) did much to introduce this new world view to England. There were seven separate editions of Digges' work between 1576 and 1605. A distinguished mathematician and astronomer, Digges was, like Thomas Huxley in the nineteenth century, also a popularizer of science. He did not talk down to his readers but wrote in simple, clear Elizabethan English, so that any intelligent person, old or young, could understand him. His study, originally only a few pages added to* Prognostication everlasting, *a book by his father, Leonard Digges, is a fusion of a phrase-by-phrase translation from Copernicus combined with Digges' own far-seeing views on the universe. According to Francis R. Johnson, "He was the first modern astronomer of note to portray an infinite, heliocentric universe, with the stars scattered at varying distances throughout infinite space."*

Digges spent his youngest years, even from his cradle, in the study of the natural sciences. Similarly, Copernicus, as a young student at Jagellonian University, Cracow, Poland, already was, through his scientific studies, beginning the process of making fantasy into reality, and relegating the old Ptolemaic idea of the world to fantasy. Instead of a stable universe of concentric circles with the earth at the center, Copernicus had drawn a small circle at the center and labeled it "sol" (sun). This one act had changed both science and philosophy and brought us into the modern world. Among active young minds, he had introduced a restless seeking after still more knowledge. One can readily imagine how exciting the new findings must have been to boys, some of whom entered universities when they were twelve years old or thereabouts. Small wonder there was "uncumly Hemminge & hauking" at class lectures still conducted by staid scholars in the medieval tradition who were not keeping up with the times.

The following excerpt is from Digges' treatise, which was republished in the Huntington Library Bulletin, *no. 5 (April 1934).*

WORKS CONSULTED:

Dictionary of National Biography

Charles M. Coffin, John Donne and the New Philosophy *(New York: Humanities Press, 1958).*

William T. Costello, S.J., The Scholastic Curriculum at Early Seventeenth-Century Cambridge *(Cambridge, Mass.: Harvard Univ. Press, 1958).*

Francis R. Johnson, Astronomical Thought in Renaissance England *(Baltimore: The Johns Hopkins Press, 1937).*

Basil Willey, The Seventeenth Century Background *(New York, 1955).*

James Winny, The Frame of Order: An Outline of Elizabethan Belief taken from Treatises of the Late Sixteenth Century *(London: Allen & Unwin, 1957).*

H EEREIN CAN WEE never sufficiently admire thys wonderfull & incomprehensible huge frame of goddes woorke proponed to our senses, seinge fyrst thys baull of the earth wherein we move, to the common sorte seemeth greate, and yet in respecte of the Moones Orbe is very small, but compared with *Orbis magnus* wherein it is caried, it scarcely retayneth any sensible proportion, so merveilously is that Orbe of Annuall motion greatèr then this litle darcke starre wherein we live. But that *Orbis magnus* beinge as is before declared but as a poynct in respect of the immensity of that immoveable heaven, we may easily consider what litle portion of gods frame, our Elementare corruptible worlde is, but never sufficiently be able to admire the immensity of the Rest. Especially of that fixed Orbe garnished with lightes innumerable and reaching up in *Sphaericall altitude* without ende. Of whiche lightes Celestiall it is to bee thoughte that we onely behoulde sutch as are in the inferioure partes of the same Orbe, and as they are hygher, so seeme they of lesse and lesser quantity, even tyll our sighte beinge not able farder to reache or conceyve, the greatest part rest by reason of their wonderfull distance invisible unto us. And this may wel be thought of us to be the gloriouse court of the great god, whose unserchable worcks invisible we may partly by these his visible conjecture, to whose infinit power and majesty such an infinit place surmountinge all other both in quantity and quality only is conveniente. But because the world hath so longe a tyme bin carryed with an opinion of the earths stabilitye, as the contrary cannot but be nowe very imperswasible, I have thought good out of *Copernicus* also to geve a taste of the reasons philosophicall alledged for the earthes stabilitye, and their solutions, that sutch as are not able with *Geometricall* eyes to beehoulde the secrete perfection of *Copernicus Theoricke*, maye yet by these familiar, naturall reasons be induced to serche farther, and not rashly to condempne for phantasticall, so auncient doctrine revived, and by *Copernicus* so demonstratively approved.

What reasons moved Aristotle and others that followed him to thincke the earth to rest immoveable as a Centre to the whole worlde.

T HE MOST EFFECTUALL reasons that they produce to prove the earthes stability in the middle or lowest part of the world, is that of Gravitye and Levitye. For of all other the Elemente of the earth say they is most heavy, and all ponderous thinges are carryed unto it, stryvinge as it were to sway even downe to the inmoste part thereof. For the earthe being rounde into the which all waighty thinges on every side fall, makinge ryghte angles on the superficies, muste neades if they were not stayde on the superficies passe to the Center, seinge every right line that falleth perpendicularly upon the *Horizon* in that place where it toucheth the earth muste neades passe by the Centre. And those thinges that are carried towarde that *Medium*, it is likely that there also they woulde reste. So mutche therefore, the rather shall the Earth rest in the middle, and (receyvinge all things into yt selfe that fall) by hys owne wayghte shall be moste immoveable: Agayne they seeke to prove it by reason of motion and his nature, for of one and the same a simple body the motion must also be simple saith *Aristotle*. Of simple motions there are two kyndes right and circulare, Right are either up or downe: so that every simple motion is eyther downewarde towarde the Center, or upwarde from the Center, or circular about the Centre. Nowe unto the earth and water in respect of their waight the motion downwarde is convenient to seeke the Center. To ayre and fyer in regarde of their lightnes, upwarde and from the Center. So it is meete to these elementes to attribute the right or streyghte motion, and to the heavens only it is proper circularly aboute this meane or Center to be turned rownde. Thus much *Aristotle.* Yf therefore saith *Ptolomy* of *Alexandria* the earth should turne but only by the dayly motion, thinges quite contrary to these should happen. For his motion should be most swift and violent that in 24 howres should let passe the whole circuite of the earth, and those things whiche by sodaine toorninge are stirred, are altogether unmeete to collecte but rather to disperse thinges united, onelesse they shoulde by some firme fasteninge be kept toogether. And longe ere this the Earthe being dissolved in peeces should have been scattered through the heavens, which were a mockery to thincke of, and mutch more beastes and all other waights that are loose could not remayne unshaken. And also thinges fallinge should not light on the places perpendiculare under theym, neyther shoulde they fall directly thereto, the same beinge violentlye in the meane carryed awaye. Cloudes also and other thynges hanginge in the ayre shoulde alwayes seeme to us to bee carried towarde the West.

The Solution of these Reasons
with their insufficiencye.

THESE ARE THE causes and sutch other wherwith they approve the Earthe to reste in the middle of the worlde and that out of all question: But hee that will mainteyne the Earthes mobility may say that this motion is not violent but naturall. And these thinges whyche are naturally mooved have effectes contrary to sutch as are violentlye carried. For sutche motions wherein force and vyolence is used, muste needes bee dissolved and cannot be of longe continuance, but those which by nature are caused, remayne stil in their perfit estate and are conserved and kepte in their moste excellent constitution. Without cause therefore did *Ptolomey* feare least the Earth and all earthelye thynges shoulde bee torne in peeces by thys revolution of the Earthe caused by the woorkinge of nature, whose operations are farre different from those of Arte or sutche as humayne intelligence may reache unto. But whye shoulde hee not mutch more thincke and mis-dought the same of the worlde, whose motion muste of necessity be so mutche more swift and vehemente then this of the Earth, as the Heaven is greater then the Earth. Is therefore the Heaven made so huyge in quantitye that yt might wyth unspeakable vehemencye of motion bee severed from the Centre, least happily restinge it should fall, as some Philosophers have affirmed: Surelye yf this reason shoulde take place, the Magni-tude of the Heaven shoulde infinitely extende. For the more this motion shoulde vio-lentlye bee carryed higher, the greater should the swiftnes be, by reason of the increasing of the circumference which must of necessity in 24 houers bee paste over, and in lyke manner by increase of the motion the Magnitude muste also necessarilye bee augmented. Thus shoulde the swiftnes increase the Magnitude and the Magnitude the swiftnes in-finitely: But according to that grounde of nature whatsoever is infinite canne never be passed over. The Heaven therefore of necessity must stande and rest fixed. But say they without the Heaven there is no body, no place, no emptynes, no not any thinge at all whether heaven should or could farther extende. But this surelye is verye straunge that nothinge shoulde have sutche efficiente power to restrayne some thinge the same havinge a very essence and beinge. Yet yf wee would thus confesse that the Heaven were indeede infinite upwarde, and onely fynyte downewarde in respecte of his sphericall concavitye, Mutch more perhappes might that sayinge be verified, that without the Heaven is nothinge, seeinge everye thinge in respect of the infiniteness thereof had place sufficient withing the same. But then must it of necessity remaine immoveable. For the cheefest reason that hath mooved some to thincke the Heaven limited was Motion, whiche they thoughte without controversie to bee in deede in it. But whether the worlde have his ͵boundes or bee in deede infinite and without boundes, let us leave that to be discussed of Philosophers, sure we are that the Earthe is not infinite but hath a circumference lymitted, seinge therefore all Philosophers consent that lymitted bodyes maye have Motion, and infinyte cannot have anye. Whye dooe we yet stagger to confesse motion in the Earth beinge most agreeable to hys forme and nature, whose boundes also and circumference wee knowe, rather than to imagyne that the whole world should sway and turne, whose ende we know not, ne possibly can of any mortal man be knowne. And therefore the true Motion in deede to be in the Earth, and the apparance only in the Heaven: And that these apparances are no otherwise then yf the *Virgilian Aeneas* shoulde say.

Provehimur portu, terraeque urbesque recedunt

For a shippe carryed in a smoothe Sea with sutch tranquility dooth passe away, that al thinges on the shores and the Seas to the saylers seeme to moove and themselves onely quietly to rest with all sutche thinges as are aboorde them, so surely may it bee in the Earth whose Motion beinge naturall and not forcible of all other is most uniforme and unperceaveable, whereby too us that sayle therein the whole worlde maye seeme too roull about. But what shall wee then saye of Cloudes and other thinges hanginge or restinge in the ayre or tendinge upward, but that not only the Earth and Sea makinge one globe but also no small part of the ayre is likewyse circularly carried and in like sort all sutche thinges as are derived from them or have any maner of aliance with them.

Either for that the lower Region of the ayre beinge mixte with Earthlye and watrye vapours folowe the same nature of the Earth. Eyther that it be gayned and gotten from the Earth by reason of *Vicinity* or *Contiguity*. Which if any man merveyle at, let him consider howe the olde Philosophers did yeelde the same reason for the revolution of the highest Region of the ayre, wherein we may sometime behoulde Comets carryed circularly no otherwise then the bodies Celestial seeme to bee, and yet hath that Region of the ayre lesse convenience with the Orbes Celestiall, then this lower part with the earthe. But we affyrme that parte of the aire in respect of his great distance to be destitut of this Motion *Terrestriall*, and that this part of the ayre that is next to the Earthe dooth appeare moste still and quiet by reason of hys uniforme naturall accompanyinge of the Earth, and lykewyse thinges that hange therein, onelesse by windes or other violent accident they be tossed to and fro. For the wynde in the ayre is nothing els but as the wave in the Sea: And of thinges ascendinge and descendinge in respect of the worlde we must confesse them to have a mixt motion of right & circulare, albeit it seeme to us right & streight, No otherwise then if in a shippe under sayle a man should softly let a plummet downe from the toppe alonge by the maste even to the decke: This plummet passing alwayes by the streight maste, seemeth also too fall in a righte line, but beinge by discours of reason wayed his Motion is found mixt of right and circulare. For sutch thinges as naturally fall douneward beinge of earthly nature there is no doubt but as partes they retayne the nature of the whole. No otherwise is it of these things that by fiery force are carried upward. For the earthly fyer is cheefly nourished wyth earthly matter, and flame is defined to be nought els but a burninge fume or smoke and the propertye of fyer is to extende the subject whereunto it entereth, the whiche it doth with so great violence as by no meanes or engines it canne be constrayned but that with breache of bandes it will perfourme his nature. This motion extensive is from the Centre to the circumference, so that if any earthly part be fiered, it is carryed violently upward. Therefore whereas they say that of simple bodyes the motion is altogether simple, of the circulare it is cheefely verified, so longe as the simple bodye remayneth in his naturall place and perfit unity of composition, for in the same place there can bee no other motion but circulare, whiche remayninge wholye in it selfe is most like to rest and immobility. But right or streight motion only happen to those things that stray and wander or by anye meanes are thrust out of their natural place. But nothing can bee more Repugnaunte to the fourme and Ordinance of the world, then that thinges, naturally should be out of their naturall place. This kinde of motion therefore that is by right line is only accident to those things that are not in their right state or perfection naturall, while partes are disjoyned from their whole bodie, and covet to retourne to the unity thereof againe. Neither do these thinges which are carryed upwarde or downwarde besides this circular movinge make anye simple, uniforme, or equall motion, for with their levity or ponderositye of their body they cannot be tempered but alwaies as they fall (beginning slowly) they increase their motion, and the farder the more swiftly, wheras contrariwise this our earthly fier (for other wee cannot see) we may behould as it is carryed upwarde to vanish and decay as it were confessinge the cause of violence to proceede only from his matter *Terrestriall*. The circulare motion alwaye contynueth unyforme and equall by reason of his cause whiche is indeficient and alway continuinge. But the other hasteneth to ende and to attayne that place where they leave lenger to be heyve or lighte, and having attayned that place, theyr motion ceaseth. Seinge therefore this circulare motion is proper to the whole as streighte is only unto partes, we may say that circulare doth rest with streighte as *Animall cum Aegro*. And whereas *Aristotle* hath dystrybuted *Simplicem motum* into these thre kyndes *A medio*, *medium*, and *Circa medium*, it must be onely in reason and imagination, as wee likewise sever in consideration Geometricall a poincte, line, and a superficies, whereas in deede neither can stand without other, ne any of them without a bodye.

Heereto we may adjoyne that the condition of immobilitye is more noble and divine then that of chandge, alteration or instabilitye, therefore more agreeable to Heaven then to this Earth where thinges are subject to continual mutability. And seeinge by evident proofe of Geometricall mensuration wee finde that the Planets are sometimes nigher to us and sometimes more remote, and that therefore even the mainteyners of the Earthes stability are enforced to confesse that the Earth is not their Orbes Centre, this motion *Circ medium* must in more generall sort bee taken and that it maie bee understande that every Orbe hath his peculiare *Medium* and Centre, in regarde whereof this simple and uniforme motion is to bee considered. Seinge therefore that these Orbes have severall Centres, it may be doughted whether the Centre of this earthly Gravity be also the Centre of the worlde. For Gravity is nothing els but a certaine proclivitye or naturall covetinge of partes to be coupled with the whole, whiche by divine providence of the Creater of al is given & impressed into the partes, that they should restore themselves into their unity and integritie concurringe in sphericall fourme, which kinde of propriety or affection it is likelye also that the Moone and other glorious bodyes wante not to knit & combine their partes together, and to mainteyne them in their round shape, which bodies notwithstandinge are by sundrye motions, sundry wayes conveighed. Thus as it is apparant by these natural reasons that the mobility of the Earth is more probable and likelye then the stabilitye. So if it bee Mathematically considered and wyth Geometricall Mensurations every part of every *Theoricke* examined: the discreet Student shall fynde that *Copernicus* not without greate reason did propone this grounde of the Earthes Mobility.

The Historie of Foure-Footed Beastes

Describing The True and Lively Figure Of Every Beast, With A Discourse Of Their Severall Names, Conditions, Kindes, Vertues.

By EDWARD TOPSELL

SELECTIONS

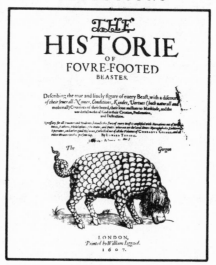

EVEN IN THE *Old English period (to the twelfth century* A.D.*), beasts were not regarded simply as beasts by writers about animals, but as symbolic creatures having mysterious relationships with God and man. By the time Topsell (1572–1625) took over Conrad Gesner's sixteenth-century volumes for translation and elaboration, descriptions of animals had become more realistic, but far from completely so, as the following excerpts and Topsell's complete title for his work will reveal:*

The Historie of Foure-Footed Beastes. Describing the true and lively figure of every Beast, with a discourse of their severall Names, Conditions, Kindes, Vertues (both naturall and medicinall) Countries of their breed, their love and hate to Mankinde, and the wonderfull worke of God in their Creation, Preservation, and Destruction. Necessary for all Divines and Students, because the story of every Beast is amplified with

Narrations out of Scripture, Fathers, Phylosophers, Physitians, and Poets: wherein are declared divers Hyerogliphicks, Emblems, Epigrams, and other good Histories, Collected out of all the Volumes of Conradus Gesner, and all other Writers to this present day.

This anthology was printed by the eminent Elizabethan printer William Jaggard, who in 1599 printed The Passionate Pilgrim, *containing two sonnets by Shakespeare and parts of Love's Labor's Lost. Indeed, the First Folio of Shakespeare's plays was printed by William Jaggard's son, Isaac, as William had died shortly before the printing of the book was completed, after which Isaac took over the firm. The Jaggards were printer-publishers, selling and distributing work as well as printing it.*

The book contains a wild mixture of descriptions of animals, often wholly or at least partly imaginary, together with medical advice in the form of remedies recommended by the pharmacologist Dioscorides, who lived the first century after Christ, and remedies suggested by his contemporary, the elder Pliny, with whom he was in substantial agreement, as both writers apparently borrowed from the same older sources. Advice is also drawn from Galen, who in the second century after Christ, came from Asia Minor to Rome, where he wrote prolifically on medicine and served as physician to powerful Romans, including the Emperor Aurelius Antoninus. Galen was extremely influential even up to the period of this book, and was frequently quoted by writers in various fields. Many physicians were Galenists, in fact, though a growing number of followers of the father of biochemistry, Paracelsus (1493–1541), were questioning his authority. Albertus Magnus (1193–1280) is also quoted. The brilliant and influential teacher of St. Thomas Aquinas, Albertus Magnus is remembered now chiefly through apocrypha attributed to him, such as The 6th and 7th Books of Moses or Moses' Magical Spirit Art, *a book of magical signs and remedies believed to have first appeared in manuscript in the thirteenth century and to have been published continuously ever since the invention of printing. In fact, it still can be procured, generally in slum districts, where people with little realistic hope for the future employ the suggested incantations and signs in an effort to control their environment. The publisher of the work is seldom specified.*

Physiognomy was an attractive science at this period, and in Foure-Footed Beastes *one gets a sense of the physical similarities in the animal and human world, as well as a suggestion that the kinds of transformations that are objectified in the* Odyssey *when Circe changes men to beasts are altogether possible. Men do descend the Chain of Being until they resemble animals. Milton's* Comus, *in this volume, suggests these occurrences. One also finds the old allegorical treatments familiar from classical times. Even five hundred years earlier, a writer described the phoenix and then went on to compare its supposed rising from its ashes to the redemption of Adam's descendants and to the resurrection of Christ. About the same period,* The Bestiary or Physiologus *describes the panther and compares it to Christ; the whale and compares it to the Devil. (One is reminded of the lamb and tiger symbolism of William Blake.)*

Topsell's work is pivotal, standing between the old imaginary bestiaries and the emerging scientific investigations of the Renaissance. Now that new interest in animals is developing among scientists, perhaps findings will emerge in time almost as strange as Topsell's recorded "facts."

The following selections from The Historie of Foure-Footed Beastes *are reprinted from a 1608 edition, published in London, England.*

OF THE UNICORNE

WE ARE NOW come to the history of a beast, whereof divers people in every age of the worlde have made great question, because of the rare Vertues thereof; therefore it behooveth us to use some dilligence in comparing to-gither the severall testimonies that are spoken of this beast, for the better satisfaction of such as are now alive, and clearing of the point for them that shall be borne heereafter, whether there bee a Unicorne; for that is the maine question to be resolved.

Now the vertues of the horne, of which we will make a particular discourse by itselfe, have bin the occasion of this question, and that which doeth give the most evident testimony unto all men that have ever seene it or used it, hath bred all the contention; and if there had not bin disclosed in it any extraordinary powers and vertues, we should as easily beleeve that there was a Unicorne in the worlde, as we do beleeve there is an Elephant although not bred in Europe. To begin therefore with this discourse, by the Unicorne wee doe understand a peculiar beast, which hath naturally but one horne, and that a very rich one, that groweth out of the middle of the foreheade, for wee have shewed in other parts of the history, that there are divers beasts, that have but one horne, and namely some Oxen in *India* have but one horne, and some have three, and whole hooves. Likewise the Buls of Aonia, are saide to have whole hooves and one horne, growing out of the middle of their foreheads.

Likewise in the Citty Zeila of *Ethopia*, there are Kine of a purple colour, as *Ludovicus Romanus* writeth, which have but one horne growing out of their heads, and that turneth up towards their backes. *Cæsar* was of opinion that the Elke hadde but one horne, but we have shewed the contrary. It is said that *Pericles* had a ram with one horn, but that was bred by way of prodegy,

Many beasts with hornes, improperly called Uni-cornes.

Solinus. Aelianus. Oppianus.

and not naturally. *Simeon Sethi* writeth, that the Muskcat hath also one horne growing out of the forehead, but we have shewed already that no man is of that opinion beside himselfe. *Aelianus* writeth, that there be Birds in *Ethiopia* having one horn on their foreheads, and therefore are cald *Unicornus:* and *Albertus* saith, there is a fish cald *Monoceros,* and hath also one horne. Now our discourse of the Unicorne is of none of these beasts, for there is not any vertue attributed to their hornes, and therefore the vulgar sort of infidell people which scarcely beleeve any hearbe but such as they see in their own Gardens, or any beast but such as is in their own flocks, or any knowledge but such as is bred in their owne braines, or any birds which are not hatched in their owne Nestes, have never made question of these, but of the true Unicorne, whereof ther were more proofes in the world, because of the noblenesses of his horn, they have ever bin in doubt: by which distraction, it appeareth unto me that there is some secret enemy in the inward degenerate nature of man, which continually blindeth the eyes of God his people, from beholding and beleeving the greatnesse of God his workes.

Whether there be any Uni-cornes in the World

But to the purpose that there is such a beast, the Scripture it selfe witnesseth, for *David* thus speaketh in the 92. Psalme: *Et erigetur cornu meum tanquam Monocerotis.* That is my horne shall be lifted up like the horne of a Unicorne; whereupon all Divines that ever wrote have not onely collected that there is a Unicorne, but also affirme the similitude to be betwixt the kingdome of *David* and the horne of the Unicorne, that as the horne of the Unicorne is wholesome to all beasts and creatures, so should the kingdome of *David* be in the generation of Christ; And do we think that David would compare the vertue of his kingdom, & the powerful redemption of the world unto a thing that is not, or is uncertain and fantastical, God forbid that ever any wise man should so dispight the holy ghost. For this cause also we read in *Suidas,* that good men which worship God and follow his lawes, are compared to Unicornes, whose greater parts as their whole bodies are unprofitable and untamable, yet their horne maketh them excellent: so in good men, although their fleshly partes be good for nothing, and fall downe to the earth, yet their grace and piety exalteth their soules to the heavens.

The hebrew names in script prove Unicornes

We have shewed already in the story of the Rhinocerot, that *Reem* in Hebrew signifieth a Unicorne, although *Munster* be of another opinion, yet the Septuagints in the translation of Deut. 33. do translate it a Unicorn, for the Rhinocerot hath not one horne, but two. *Rabbi Solamon, David Kimbi,* and *Saadius* do alwayes take *Reem & Karas* for a Unicorn, and they derive *Reem* from *Rom,* which signifieth *Altitudinem* height, because the Horn of the Unicorne is lifted upon high. Hereunto the Arabians agree which call it *Barkeron,* and the Persians *Bark.* The Chaldeans *Remana.* In the 39. of *Job,* the Lord speaketh in this manner to Job: *Numquid acquiesset Monoceros ut serviat tibi, aut ut moretur juxta praesepia tua? Numquid ligabis Monocerotem sune suo pro sulco faciendo aut complanabit glevas vallium post te?* That is to say, will the Unicorne rest and serve thee, or tarry beside thy cratches? canst thou bind the Unicorn with a halter to thy plough to make furrows, or will he make plaine the clots of the vallies? Likewise in the prophecy of Esau the 34. chap. and in many other places of Scripture, whereby God himselfe must needs be traduced, if there be no Unicorne in the world.

Besides the Arabians, as *And Bellum,* writeth, call this beast *Alcherceden,* and say that it hath one horne in the forehead which is good against poisons. The Grætians call it *Monokeros,* from whence *Pliny* and all the ancient *Grammarians* doe call it *Monoceros,* yet the devines both elder and later do name it by a more learned proper Latin word *Unicornis.* The Italians

The
kinds of
Unicornes

Alicorno, Unicorno, Liocorno, Leocorno, the French *Licorne,* the Spaniards *Unicornio,* the Germans *Einborne,* and the Illirians *Gednorozecz:* And thus much for the name. All our *Eropean* Authors which write of beastes, do make of the Unicorne divers kindes, especially *Pliny, Ludovicus Romanus, Paulus Venetus, Nicholaus Venetus, Aeneas Sylvius, Albertus Magnus,* out of whose words we must gather the best description that we can of the Unicorne. The *Arcean* Indians (saith Pliny) do hunt a certaine wild beast which is very curst untamable, having one horne, which in the head resembleth a Hart, in the feet an Elephant, in the taile a Bore, and in the residue of the body

Countries of
Unicorns.

a Horse: the horne he saith, is about two cubits long, and the voice like the lowing of an Oxe, somewhat more shrill, and they deny that this beast is ever taken alive. *Aelianus* writeth herof in this manner, there are (saith he) certaine Mountaines in the middest of India, unto the which the passage is very difficult, where are abundance of wild beasts, & among other Unicornes, which the Indians call *Cartazonons,* who in their ripe age are as big as a Horsse, and their mane and haires are yellow, excelling in the celerity of their feet and bodies, having feet cloven like an Elephants, the taile of a Boare, and one blacke horne growing out betwixt their eye-browes, not smooth, but rough all over with wrinkles, and the same groweth to a most sharp point, these thinges (saith *Aelianus*) by comparing of whose wordes with Pliny, it is apparant they describe in these words but one and the same beast, and so also doth *Phyles;* wherby I gather, that is no other beast then the wilde Asse, or at the least the wilde Asse commeth nearest to the Unicorne of all others, for they agree in these thinges, first, in that both of them have one horn in the middle of the forehead, secondly, in that both of them are bred in India, thirdly, in that they are both about the bignesse of a Horsse, fourthly in their celerity and solitary life, fiftly and lastly in their exceeding strength and untamable natures; but herein they differ both in their feet and colours, for the feet of the wilde Asses are whole and not cloven like the Unicornes, and their colour white in their body, and purple on their head; and *Aelianus* saith, that the horne also differeth in colour from the Unicornes, for the middle of it is onely blacke, the roote of it white, and the top of it purple, which *Bellonius* doth interpret, that the superificies or upper face of the Horne is all purple, the inner parte white, and the inward part or middle blacke; but of this Indian wilde Asse we have spoken already, and therefore I will adde nothing in this place but the words of *Philostratus* in the life of *Apolonius*, who writeth in this manner.

There are many wilde Asses which are taken in the Fens, neare the river *Hiphasis*, in whose forehead there is one horne, wherewith they fight like Buls, and the Indians of that horne make pots, affirming that whatsoever drinketh in one of those pots, shall never take disease that day, and if they bee wounded shall feele no paine, or safely passe through the fire without burning, nor yet be poisoned in their drinke, and therefore such cuppes are only in the possession of their Kings, neither is it lawful for any man except the King, to hunt that beast, and therefore they say that *Appollonius* looked upon one of those beastes, and considered his nature with singular admiration.

OF THE SPHINGA OR SPHINX

THE *Sphinx* or *Sphinga* is of the kind of Apes, having his body rough like Apes, but his breast up to his neck, pilde and smooth without hair: the face is very round yet sharp and piked, having the breasts of women, and their favour or visage much like them: In that part of their body which is bare without hair, there is a certain red thing rising in a round circle like Millet seed, which giveth great grace and comliness to their colour, which in the middle parte is humane. Their voice is very like a mans but not articulate, sounding as if one did speak hastily with indignation or sorrow. Their hair brown or swarthy colour. They are bred in *India* and *Ethiopia*. In the Promontory of the farthest *Arabia* neer *Dira*, are *Sphinges*, and certain Lions called *Formice*, so likewise they are to be found amongst the

Pliny.
Calisthius
The description

Aelianus.
Countrey of breed.

Lions-
formicae.
Pliny.

Their nature.

Albertus.
Manner of
carrying
their meat.

Trogladitae. As the *Babouns* and *Cinocephals* are more wild then other Apes, so the Satyres and *Sphinges* are more meek and gentle, for they are not so wilde that they will not be tamed, nor yet so tame but they will revenge their own harms; as appeared by that which was slain in a publick spectacle among the *Thebanes.* They carry their meat in the storehouses of their own chaps or cheeks, taking it forth when they are hungry, and so eat it: not being like the *Formice,* for that which is annual in them, is daily and hourly amongst these.

Of the
name and
notation
thereof.
*Hermolaus.
*Varrianus.

Hesiod.
Ausonius.

The name of this *Sphinx* is taken from binding, as appeareth by the Greek notation, or else of delicacie and dainty nice loosnesse, (wherefore there were certain common strumpets called *Sphinctæ,* and the *Megarian Sphingas,* was a very popular phrase for notorious harlots) hath given occasion to the Poets, to saigne a certain monster called *Sphinx,* which they say was thus derived. *Hydra* brought forth the *Chymæra, Chymæra* by *Orthus* the *Sphinx,* and the *Nemean* Lion: now this *Orthus* was one of *Geryons* Dogges. This *Sphinx* they make a treble formed monster, a Maidens

The descrip-
tion of the
Poets Sphinx.

face, a Lions legs, and the wings of a Fowl; or as *Ausonius* and *Varinus* say, the face and hand of a Maid, the body of a Dog, the wings of a Bird, the voice of a man, the claws of a Lion, and the tail of a Dragon: and that she kept continually in the *Sphincian* mountain; propounding to all travellers

The Riddle
of the
Sphinx.

that came that way, an *Aenigma* or Riddle, *which was this, What was the creature that first of all goeth on four legs, afterwards on two, and lastly on three:* and all of them that could not dissolve that Riddle, she presently slew, by taking them and throwing them down headlong from the top of a Rocke. At last *Oedipus* came that way and declared the secret, that it was

The solution
of the
Riddle by
Oedipus.

(a Man) *who in his infancy creepeth on all four,* afterward *in youth, goeth upright upon two legs,* and last of all *in old age, taketh unto him a staffe which* maketh him to go as it were on three legs; which the monster hearing, she presently threwe downe her selfe from the former rock, and so she ended. Whereupon *Oedipus* is taken for a subtle and wise opener of mysteries.

Palaephatus.
The true
History of
Sphinx.

But the truth is, that when *Cadmus* had married an Amazonian woman called *Sphinx,* and with her came to *Thebes* and there slew *Draco* their King, and possessed his Kingdom; afterward there was a sister unto *Draco* called *Harmonia,* whom *Cadmus* maried, *Sphinx* being yet alive: she in revenge (being assisted by many followers) departed with great store of wealth into the Mountaine SPHINCIUS, taking with her a great Dog which *Cadmus* held in great account, and there made daily incursions or spoils upon his people: Now *Aenigma* in the Theban language, signifieth an inrode or warlike incursion, wherefore the people complained in this sort, *This* Grecian Sphinx *robbeth us, in setting upon with an* Aenigma, *but no man knoweth after what manner she maketh this* Aenigma.

Cadmus hereupon made Proclamation, that he would give a very bountiful reward unto him that would kill *Sphinx,* upon which occasion the CORINTHIAN *Oedipus* came unto her, being mounted on swift Courser, and accompanied with some *Thebans* in the night season, slew her. Others say, that *Oedipus* by counterfeiting friendship, slew her, making shew to be of her faction; and *Pausanias* saith, that the former Riddle was not a riddle, but an Oracle of *Apollo*, which *Cadmus* had received, whereby his posterity should be inheritors of the *Theban* Kingdom; and whereas *Oedipus*, being the Son of *Laius* a former King of the Countrey, was taught the Oracle in his sleep, he recovered the Kingdom usurped by *Sphinx* his Sister, and afterward unknowne, married his own Mother *Jocasta*. But the true moral of this poetical fiction, is by that learned *Alciatus* in one of his emblems deciphered, that her monstrous treble-formed-shape, signified her lustful pleasure under a Virgins face, her cruel pride under the Lions claws, her winde-driven levity under the Eagles, or birds feathers, and I will conclude with the words of *Suidas* concerning such Monsters, that the *Tritons*, *Sphinges*, and *Centaures*, are the images of those things, which are not to be found within the compass of the whole world.

Suidas.
Meaning this
Poetical
Sphinx.

The true *Sphinx* first described, is of a fierce though a tameable nature, and if a man do first of all perceive or discern these natural *Sphinges*, before the beast discern or perceive the man, he shall be safe; but if the beast first descry the man, then is it mortal to the man. These *Sphinges* were of great account for their strangeness: with their image did *Augustus* sign all his Grants, Libels, and Epistles: afterward he left that, and signed with the image of *Alexander* the great, and last of all with his own. *Syclis* the King in the City of the *Boristhenites*, had a fair house, about which there were *Sphinges* and *Gryphins* wrought out of white stone. At *Athens*, in the Temple *Parthenona*, there is described the contention betwixt *Pallas* and *Neptune*, about the earth, and the image of *Pallas* made of Ivory and gold, hath in the midst of her shield the picture of a *Sphinx*. *Amasis* the King of *Egypt*, built in the porch of Pallas, an admirable work called *Sai:* where he placed such great *Colosses* and *Andro-Sphinges*, that it was afterward supposed he was buried therein, and was likely to be seen imputrible. To conclude, the *Egyptians* in the porches of their Temples painted a *Sphinx*, whereby they insinuated that their divine wisdom was but dark and uncertain, and so covered with fables, that there scarce appeared in it any sparkles or footsteps of verity.

The nature
of the
Sphinx.

Suetonius.
The use of
Sphinges.

Herodotus.
Pausanias.

Herodotus.

OF THE LAMIA

The significa-
tion of the
word Lamia.

THIS WORD *Lamia* hath many significations, being taken sometime for a Beast of *Lybia*, sometimes for a fish, and sometimes for a Spectre or apparition of women called *Phairies*. And from hence some have ignorantly affirmed, that either there were no such Beasts at all, or else that it was a compounded monster of a Beast and a Fish, whose opinions I will briefly set down. *Aristophanes* affirmeth, that he heard one say, that he saw a great wilde Beast having several parts resembling outwardly an Ox, and inwardly a

Mule, and a beautiful Woman, which he called afterwards *Empusa*.

Visions of Phairies.

When *Appollonius* and his companions travelled in a bright Moon-shine-night, they saw a certain apparition of *Phairies*, in *Latine* called *Lamiæ*, and in Greek, *Empusa*, changing themselves from one shape into another, being also sometimes visible, and presently vanishing out of sight again: as soon as he perceived it, he knew what it was, and did rate it with very contumelious and despiteful words, exhorting his fellows to do the like, for that is the best remedie against the invasion of Phairies. And when his companions did

Philostratus. likewise rail at them, presently the vision departed away.

The Poetical Lamia.

The Poets say, that *Lamia* was a beautiful woman, the daughter of *Bellus* and *Lybia*, which *Jupiter* loved, bringing out of *Lybia* into *Italy*, where he begot upon her many sons, but *Juno* jealous of her husband, destroyed them as soon as they were born, punishing *Lamia* also with a restless estate, that she should never be able to sleep, but live night and day in continual

Varinus. mourning, for which occasion she also stealeth away and killeth the children of others, whereupon came the fable of changing of children: *Jupiter* having pity upon her, gave her exemptile eyes that might be taken in and out at her own pleasure, and likewise power to be transformed into what shape she would: And from hence also came the saigned name of *Acho*, and *Alphito*, wherewithal women were wont to make their children afraid, according to these verses of *Lucilius*.

> *Terricolas Lamias, Fauni quas Pompiliiq:*
> *Instituere Numa, tremit has,*

Old Wives tails of Phairies.

Of these *Angelus Politianus* relateth this old wives story, in his preface upon *Aristotles* first book of *Analyticks*, that his Grand-mother told him when he was a childe, there were certain *Lamia* in the Wilderness, which like Bug-bears would eat up crying boys, and that there was a little Well near to *Jesulanum*, being very bright, yet in continual shadow, never seeing Sun, where these Phairy women have their habitation, which are to be seen of them which come thither for water.

Plutarch also affirmeth, that they have exemptile eyes as aforesaid, and that as often as they go from home, they put in their eyes, wandring abroad by habitations, streets, and cross ways, entring into the assemblies of men, and prying so perfectly into every thing, that nothing can escape them, be it never so well covered: you will think (saith he) that they have the eyes of Kites, for there is no small mote but they espy it, nor any hole so secret but they find it out, and when they come home again, at the very entrance of their house they pull out their eyes, and cast them aside, so being blinde at home, but seeing abroad.

OF THE MANTICHORA

THIS BEAST OR rather Monster (as *Ctesias* writeth) is bred among the Indians having a treble rowe of teeth beneath and above, whose greatnesse, roughnesse, and feete are like a Lions, his face and eares like unto a mans, his eyes gray, and collour red, his taile like the taile of a Scorpion of the earth, armed with a sting, casting forth sharp pointed quils, his voice like the voice of a small trumpet or pipe, being in course as swift as a Hart; His wildnes such as can never be tamed, and his appetite is especially to the flesh of man. His body like the body of a Lion, being very apt both to leape and to run, so as no distance or space doth hinder him, and I take it to bee the same Beast which *Auicen* calleth *Marion*, and *Maricomorion*, with her taile she woundeth her Hunters whether they come before her or behind her, and presently when the quils are cast forth, new ones grow up in their roome, wherewithal she overcommeth all the hunters: and although India

Philes

be full of divers ravening beastes, yet none of them are stiled with a title of *Andropophagi*, that is to say, Men-eaters; except only this *Mantichora*. When the Indians take a Whelp of this beast, they all to bruise the buttockes and taile thereof, that so it may never be fit to bring sharp quils, afterwards it is tamed without peril. This also is the same beast which is called *Leucrocuta* about the bignesse of a wilde Asse, being in legs and hoofes like a Hart, having his mouth reaching on both sides to his eares, and the head & face of a female like unto a Badgers. It is called also *Martiora*, which in the Persian tongue signifieth a devourer of men, and thus we conclude the story of the Hyaena for her description, and her severall kindes now followeth the medicines arising out of her severall partes.

THE MEDICINES OF THE HYAENA

THE OILE IN which a Fox is baked either alive or dead, doth either altogether cure and make whole those which are troubled with the gout, if so be that the disease or sicknesse be greene or new, or at the least not of to longe continuance, it doeth so cure them, that although it may happen to returne againe: yet it will be much more milde and gentle then before it had beene. But the oile which proceedeth from Foxes doth nothing more drive away the forenamed disease, then that which likewise is got or prepared out of the Hyaena; for that hath an excellent and eminent quallity of dissolving & dispersing. The flesh of the *Alzabo* is both hot and cold, and being baked with oile, doth very much help either men or women which have their feet gouty, or have any paine in their joints, which may happen or come by the occasion of colde: for it is of a slender and dissolute substance.

The vanity of the *Magi* or Wise-men which is witty in nothing but in circumstance of words, doth say that the best time to take Hyaenaes is when

(marginal notes:)
The medicinal properties

Galen

Rasis

Pliny.

the Moone passeth over the signe called *Gemini,* and that for the most part the haires bee all kept and preserved. The Magi do also affirme that the skinne of an Hyaena being spread upon a sore which was bitten by a mad Dogge, doth presently and without any paine cure the same. The same also being bound to that part of the head, which doth ake, will imediately drive away the pain and griefe thereof.

The same doth very effectually and speedily helpe them which are troubled with the gout, or swelling in the jointes. The flower of Barly being mingled with the blood of an Hyaena, and fryed or baked over the fire and so taken, doth very much asswage the wringings and wrinchings either in the guts or belly of a man or woman. If the blood of an Hyaena being whot be annointed on them which are infected with the Leprosie, it will without delay very effectually cure them.

The Hyaenes flesh being eaten doeth much availe against the bitings of ravenous Dogs: but some are of opinion that the liver only being eaten is of more force and power to cure or heale them. The Nerves or sinnewes of an Hyaena being beaten to small powder and dried and mingled with the Frankincence, together and so drunke, doth restore fertility and plenty of seede in that women which before was barren.

There is also for the biting of a ravenous dog another excellent remedy, which is that first to annoint the place so bitten with the fat or greace of a Sea-calfe, or else to give it in drinke, and then to make the operation more effectuall mingle the marrow of an Hyaena, and oile that commeth from the Masticke tree and waxe together, and being so applyed and annointed upon the sore it will presently cure the same. The same marrow of the Hyaena is very good and effectuall against the paine and griefe in the sinnewes, as also for the loosenesse and weakenesse of the raines.

The marrow which proceedeth from the Chine-bone of an Hyaena, being mixed with his gall and old Oile altogether, and so boiled untill they come unto a soft temperance, and mollifying medicine, being annointed upon the sinnewes, doth expell and force away all paine of griefe thereof whatsoever. The same marrow being bound unto the backe of either man or woman who are troubled with vaine fantasies or dreams in their sleep, doth very speedily and very effectually help them. The fat or greace of an Hyaena being burnt, doth drive away all venemous Serpentes from the place where it is so used.

The same being mingled with leaven and so being wrought into a plaister is a very good cure or remedy for the falling of the haire, or the disease called the Foxes evill. The left part of the braine of an Hyaena being annointed upon the nostrils of either men or beasts is of such vertue that it will cure diseases upon them which are in maner mortall. For the sterility or barrennesse of women, the eye of an Hyaena being mixed with Lycoras, and the hearb called Dill, and so taken in drinke, is of such force and power, that in three dayes it will make them fit for conception.

The teeth of an Hyaena either touched or bound in order unto the teeth of any man or woman who are troubled with the tooth-ach, will presently

Pliny.

Albertus

Rasis

Plinius

Democritus.

Mirepsus

ease the paine and vexation thereof. One of the great teeth of an Hyaena being bound with a string unto any that are troubled in the night tims with shadowes and fantasies, and which are frayed out of their sleepe with feareful visions, doth very speedily and effectually procure them ease and rest. The tooth of an Hyaena (called *Alzabo*) being bound uppon the right arme of any one which is either oblivious or forgetfull, and hanging downe from the arme unto the middle finger or wrist, doth renew and refresh their decayed memory.

The pallat of an Hyaena being dryed and beaten to powder, and then mingled with Egyptian Allum, and so made whot and mixed altogether, being three times turned in any ones mouth which hath either sore or ulcer in it, will in smal time procure them remedy and help of their vexation and trouble. The flesh which groweth upon the hinder part of the necke being burned and then eaten or taken in drinke, doth very speedily helpe and cure the griefe and aches of the loines.

The shoulders likewise being used in the aforesaid maner, doth profit much for the healing of any who are vexed with any anguish or paine in their shoulders or sides. The lungs being dryed and taken in drinke, do ease any either man or woman which is troubled with the Collick or stone. But being dryed into powder and mingled with Oile and so annointed upon the belly, it killeth the wormes and expelleth all aches away from the belly. The Hart being used in the aforesaid manner and taken in drinke, doth ease and help all aches, paines, or griefe in the body whatsoever. The white flesh being taken from the breast of an Hyaena, and seven haires, and the genitall of a Hart, being bound altogether in the skin or hide of a buck or a Doe, and afterwards hanged about the neck of a woman which is in travell, will greatly hinder her for bringing forth her child.

If ther shal be any flesh or bones of men found in the body of a dead Hyaena, being dried and beaten to powder, and then mixed with a certaine perfume, they will bee very excellent to help the gout, or drive away the convulsion of the sinewes. The kell or caule wherein the bowels are contained, being used in the aforesaid manner and also mixed with oile will be a present remedy against the burnings and imflamations of sores, botches, and ulcers.

The chine bone of an Hyaena being brused and beaten into small powder, and so dried, and then mingled with the tongue and the right foot of a Sea-calfe, the gall of an Oxe being added thereunto, and all of them boiled or baked togither, and annointed uppon the hide or skinne of an Hyaena, and so lapped about the legges or jointes of them which are troubled with the gout, will in short time ease the paine, and ridde them altogether of the greefe thereof.

The chine-bone being also beaten to powder and given in wine to drinke, is very profitable and necessary for those which are in sore travaile or paine of childe-birth. The firste or eighth rib of the same beast, being beaten and mingled with a certaine perfume, is very good and medicinable for sores and botches which do breake thorough the flesh.

Their flesh also being eaten, doth quickly cure and heal the bitings or tearings of a ravenous Dogge, but the liver being so used is more effectuall and speedy, for the curinge thereof. The liver of the aforesaide beast is also very curable for Agues or Quarterne feavers being beaten to powder and drunke in Wine, before the augmentation of second assaults thereof. The same also is an excellent and speedy remedy for the wringings & aches of the

Dioscorides. belly, as also for that grievous and painefull disease called the collicke and stone. For the same diseases, the gall of a Sea Scorpion, and of a fish called *Halops*, and of a sea crabbe and of an Hyaena, being beaten to powder, and mixed together, and so drunke in Wine, is a very good and effectual cure

Marcellus and help. The gall of an Hyaena, by itself alone being rubd or anointed upon the head of either man or woman whose haires are fallen off, doth presently procure the haire to renew and grow againe, it will also bring haire upon the eye-lids, being rubbed thereupon.

The gal of an Hyaena being mingled with hony, and annointed upon the eyes; doth sharpen and cleare the eye sight, and expell and drive away al blemishes and smal skins which cover the sight of the eye, as also the paine in the eyes called the pinne and the webbe. But *Apollonius Pitanaus* doth

Galen say, that the gal of a Dog being used in the aforesaide manner is better to cure the sight of the eyes then the gal of an Hyaena. But Pliny whom I thinke best to follow, and worthiest to be believed, doth best allow of the Hyaenaes gal for the aforesaid purpose, and also for the expelling of certaine

Marcellus. white spottes in the eye which doe hinder the sight thereof.

The gall of a Beare and of a Hyaena, being dried and beaten to powder, and so mixed with the best hony which is possible to bee had, and then stirred up and downe a long time together, doth helpe them unto their eye-sight which are starke blinde, if that it bee dailye annointed and spred uppon the eyes for a reasonable space together: The gall of a Hyaena being baked in a cruse of Athenian hony, and mingled with the crooked hearbe *Crocis*, and so annointed upon the browes or forehead of them which are purblind doth

Pliny. speedily helpe them; it doth also ease them which are troubled with the water or rheum which falleth in the eyes. *Democritus* doth also affirme that if the brow of either man or woman be annointed with the gall of an Hyaena onely, it will drive away all darkeninges, and blemishes, in the eyes, and expell the Water or rheume thereof, and also asswage the paine or griefe which may come or happen in them whatsoever it be.

The marrow which proceedeth from the chine-bone of an Hyaena, being mixed with his owne gall, and with old oile, and then baked or boiled in a

Marcellus cruse untill it come unto a temperate and mollifying medicine, and then being hid or annointed uppon the sinnewes or Nerves who is in those parts troubled, wil thoroughly heale and cure any default or paine which may hapen thereunto. The gal of a male Hyaena being pounded or beaten and bound about the left thigh of any woman that is barren, doth help for conception. The gal of the same beast being drunke in wine to the value of a dram, with the decoction or liquor which commeth from Spike-Lavender called oile of spike, is a very good remedy and helpe against the timpany or swelling of the belly. The gall also being beaten and mixed with the stone called Eat-flesh, is very good & profitable for them which are trobled with the gout. The milt of an Hyaena is very effectual to cure and heale any paine or griefe in the milt of either man or woman. The lunges being dryed and beaten to powder, and mingled with oile, and annointed upon the loines of any one who is grieved or troubled in those places, will speedily cure the Aches or griefes thereof.

Pliny.

The bladder of an Hyaena being drunke in wine, is a very good and effectuall remedy against the incontinency of man or womans urin, or the running of the raines. But if there be any urine in the blader of the Hyaena found when he be taken, let it be poured forth into some cleane vessell, and mixed with oile which proceedeth from the pulse or corne of India, and so drunke up, and it will much ease and help them who are troubled in mind, and are full of care and griefe. The secret partes of a femal Hyaena beaten and mixed with the rind or skin of a Pomgranate and taken in drinke is very profitable to cure the inconveniences or paine of a womans secret parts.

Marcellus

The genitall of a male Hyaena dryed and beaten to powder, being mingled with a certaine perfume, doth cure and help those which are troubled with the crampe, and convulsion of the sinnewes. The feete of an Hyaena being taken doth heale and cure those which are sand-blind, and such as have botches and sores breaking through the skin and flesh, and also such as are troubled with inflamations or breedings of winde in their bodies, only by touching and rubbing them over.

Dioscorides

The durt or dung which is found in the interior partes of an Hyaena, being burned, and dryed into powder and so taken in drinke is very medicinable and curable for those which are grieved with painful excoriations and wringings of the belly, and also for those which are troubled with the bloody-slixe. And the same being mingled with Goose-grease and annointed over all the body of either man or woman, wil ease them of any paine or griefe which they have upon their body whatsoever. The dung or filth of an Hyaena also being mingled with certaine other medicins, is very excellent to cure and heale the bites and stingings of crocodiles and other venemous Serpents. The dung of selfe is also very good to purge and heale rotten wounds; and sores which are full of matter, and filthy corruption.

Checklist

An Annotated Bibliography of Works Believed to Have Been Shared by Children and Adults of the Late Sixteenth, Seventeenth, and Early Eighteenth Centuries

By CHARITY CHANG

*I am almost inclined to set it up as a
canon that a children's story which is
enjoyed only by children is a bad
children's story.*
—C. S. LEWIS

Items included in any bibliography compiled by one person will understandably reflect the personal judgment and preferences of the compiler. While stated definitions and scope should generally govern inclusions, compilers are tempted upon occasion to give notice to some fascinating item outside stated boundaries. The compiler of this checklist has perhaps yielded to such temptation. The checklist is admittedly uneven in quality and by no means either complete or comprehensive. It is simply the unrefined by-product of research done for the volume in hand. Although refinement and expansion are planned for a later date, much time and considerably more research will be necessary to make the checklist of greatest value to the more advanced scholar of children's literature. It is hoped, nonetheless, that readers will find this working list of interest. Where shortened references are given, full citations appear in the bibliography that follows the checklist.

The checklist includes works believed to have been shared and enjoyed by both children and adults from 1550 to 1750. There were then, as there are now, books of fiction, biography, poetry, history, fables, and fairy tales. There were travel books, courtesy books, picture books, and religious books. There is evidence, moreover, that children and adults of all classes and at all times have enjoyed many of the same books, regardless of type or purpose.

Eric Quayle reminds us that young people until almost the middle of the eighteenth century had little to read except adult books they had adopted as their own (*Collector's Book of Children's Books,* p. 19). These personal possessions, according to Quayle, "were nearly always in the form of debased, chap-book versions of well-known prose-tales, or doggerel verses with a moral to swallow." As might be expected, there was strong Puritan resistance, both in England and in America, to the reading of chapbooks. Cotton Mather of America comes to mind as one who strenuously objected to chapbooks. In his introduction to *Early American Children's Books,* however, A. S. W. Rosenbach observes that the "chapbooks which were such a source of consternation to Mr. Mather were probably popular with both parents and children" (p. x1). According to Louis B. Wright, even though the middle-class reader and to a certain extent his aristocratic contemporary had "a holy fear of vain and idle works ... some stories frankly amusing, and sometimes impiously coarse, got into print and doubtless were read with equal avidity by the apprentice and his master, each being careful to prevent the other from catching him wasting time with such lewd and idle toys." But as a rule, "authors, editors, translators, or printers attempted to give the stories they set forth a coat of moral varnish" by glossing them "with assurances of virtue-provoking qualities" (*Middle-Class Culture in Elizabethan England,* pp. 376–77).

What specifically did children read and enjoy during the late sixteenth, seventeenth, and early eighteenth centuries? A partial answer can be found in *The Unlucky Citizen* (1673) by Francis Kirkman and *A Tale of a Tub* (1710) by Jonathan Swift. In Kirkman's tale (pp. 10–13) the son of a London merchant declares:

> ... Once I happened upon a Six Pence, and having lately read that famous Book, of the *Fryar and the Boy,* and being hugely pleased with that, as also the excellent History of the *Seven Wise Masters of Rome,* and having heard great Commendation of *Fortunatus,* I laid out all my mony for that, and thought I had a great bargain. ... now having read this Book, and being desirous of reading more of that nature; one of my School-fellows lent me *Dr. Faustus,* which also pleased me, especially when he travelled in the Air, saw all the World, and did what he listed. ... The next Book I met with was *Fryar Bacon,* whose pleasant stories much delighted me: But when I came to Knight Errantry, and reading *Montelion Knight of the Oracle,* and *Ornatus* and *Artesia,* and the Famous *Parismus:* I was contented beyond measure, and (believing all I read to be true) wished my self Squire to one of these Knights: I proceeded on to *Palmerin of England,* and *Amadis de Gaul:* and borrowing one Book of one person, when I read it my self, I lent it to another, who lent me one of their Books; and thus robbing Peter to pay Paul, borrowing and lending from one to another, I in time had read most of these Histories. All the time I had from School, as Thursdays in the afternoon, and Saturdays, I spent in reading these Books; so that I being wholy affected to them, and reading how that Amadis and other Knights not knowing their Parents, did in time prove to be Sons of Kings and great Personages; I had such a fond and idle Opinion, that I might in time prove to be some great Person, or at leastwise be Squire to some Knight.

Whether or not the son in *The Unlucky Citizen* is real or fictional, Kirkman has given an interesting picture of some of the stories seventeenth-century children are likely to have read.

Swift's introduction to *A Tale of a Tub* tells the reader:

> This great work was entred upon some years ago by one of our most eminent members. He began with the *History of Reynard the Fox,* but neither lived to publish his essay nor to proceed farther in so useful an attempt, which is very much to be lamented because the discovery he made and communicated with his friends is now universally received: nor do I think any of the learned will dispute that famous treatise to be a compleat body of civil knowledge and the Revelation, or rather the Apocalyps, of all state-arcana. [The author seems here to be mistaken, for I have seen a Latin edition of *Reynard the Fox* above an hundred years old, which I have taken to be the original: for the rest, it has been thought by many people to contain some satyrical design in it.] But the progress I have made is much greater, having already finished my annotations upon

several dozens; from some of which I shall impart a few hints to the candid reader, as far as will be necessary to the conclusion at which I aim.

The first piece I have handled is that of *Tom Thumb,* whose author was a Pythagorean philosopher. This dark treatise contains the whole scheme of the metempsycosis, deducing the progress of the soul thro' all her stages.

The next is *Dr. Faustus,* penn'd by Artephius, an author *bonae notae* [of good repute] and an *adeptus* [successful alchemist]. He published it in the nine hundred eighty fourth year of his age. [He lived a thousand.] This writer proceeds wholly by reincrudation [chemical reduction], or in the *via humida* [humid way], and the marriage between Faustus and Helen does most conspicuously dilucidate the fermenting of the male and female dragon [in alchemy, sulphur and mercury].

Whittington and his Cat is the work of that mysterious rabbi, Jehuda Hannasi, containing a defense of the *Gemara* of the Jerusalem *Misna* and its just preference to that of Babylon, contrary to the vulgar opinion. [The *Gemara* and the *Mishna* make up the *Talmud.*]

The Hind and Panther. This is the master-piece of a famous writer Dryden now living [viz., in the year 1698], intended for a compleat abstract of sixteen thousand schoolmen from Scotus to Bellarmin.

Tommy Potts. Another piece supposed by the same hand, by way of supplement to the former.

The Wise Men of Goatham, cum appendice. This is a treatise of immense erudition, being the great original and fountain of those arguments bandied about both France and England for a just defense of the moderns learning and wit, against the presumption, the pride, and the ignorance of the antients. This unknown author hath so exhausted the subject that a penetrating reader will easily discover whatever hath been written since upon that dispute to be little more than repetition.

The checklist that follows includes several of the titles mentioned by Kirkman and Swift. It is hoped that the notes will provide users with "a taste of what the whole work is likely to produce, wherein I have now altogether circumscribed my thoughts and my studies, and, if I can bring it to a perfection before I die, I shall reckon I have well employ'd the poor remains of an unfortunate life" (borrowed from the introduction to Swift's *A Tale of a Tub*).

ADAM BELL, CLIM OF THE CLOUGH, AND WILLIAM OF CLOUDESLIE

The story of the outlaw Adam Bell and his two outlaw friends is one of those popular stories that delighted the common people in general and at the same time was especially suited to the taste of children (Louise F. Field, *The Child and His Book,* p. 50).

In his discussion of feudal and forest legends, William Carew Hazlitt characterizes the legend of Adam Bell as "perhaps the latest picture of old forest life remaining to us in this class of composition" (*Tales and Legends of National Origin,* p. 324). Hazlitt indicates that the writer of *Adam Bell* is unknown and that this tale was, in part at least, derived from the then surviving North-country oral tradition. The first known edition is dated 1536.

The British Museum has an undated copy of *Adam Bell* in ballad form (black letter, published in quarto). Copies of the 1605 and 1616 reprint editions are preserved in the Bodleian Library (Robert Bell, *Early Ballads Illustrative of History, Traditions, and Customs,* pp. 20–21).

John Ashton (*Chap-Books of the Eighteenth Century*, p. 354) refers to a Wyllyam Copland edition of the poem in black letter, printed in 1550, entitled *Adam bel Clym of the cloughe and wyllyym of cloudesle*. Harry B. Weiss (*A Book about Chapbooks*, p. 69) states that chapbook versions of *Adam Bell, Clim of the Clough, and William of Cloudeslie* follow the old poem closely.

AESOP'S FABLES

Percy Muir (*English Children's Books, 1600–1900*, p. 23) tells us that Caxton's 1484 edition of *Aesop* was "read to pieces," so much so that only one perfect and two imperfect copies of that edition have survived. Ogilby's translation in 1651, with illustrations by Hollar and Fairthorne, was too large to be handled easily by children. A 1666 edition by Robert Codrington in three languages (English, French, and Latin), entitled *Aesop's Fables with his Life*, was illustrated with one hundred and twelve sculptures by Francis Barlow. The sculptures in all probability were enjoyed by children of the time.

In 1692, however, appeared Sir Roger L'Estrange's *Fables of Aesop . . . with morals and reflections*. The L'Estrange edition was adopted by children, and "it was almost certainly his version, which was continuously reprinted, that was read by Steele's young godson" (Muir, p. 44).

Richard Evelyn, the diarist's son, had read Aesop by the age of five (William Sloane, *Children's Books in England and America in the Seventeenth Century*, p. 8). Biographers of Lincoln indicate that two of his favorite books were the Bible and *Aesop's Fables* (Edna Johnson et al., *Anthology of Children's Literature*, pp. 794, 796).

A copy of the 1666 Codrington edition of the fables is in the David McCandless McKell Collection of the Ross County Historical Society, Chillicothe, Ohio (Frank Fieler, *The David McCandless McKell Collection: A Descriptive Catalog*, item 57). A copy of the 1692 L'Estrange edition of the fables is in the British Museum.

For additional editions and locations of copies see Arundell Esdaile, *A List of English Tales and Prose Romances Printed Before 1740*, pp. 2–8.

BEVIS OF SOUTHAMPTON

The popular old story "Bevis of Southampton" belongs to Crusading days and can be attributed to Walter of Exeter (Field, p. 51). Wright (p. 391) states that Bevis was almost as great a champion as Guy of Warwick. There were French editions of the Bevis story as early as 1502, and an Italian edition as early as 1497. The Bodleian Library contains a very early copy of an English edition with the Richard Pynson imprint (Ashton, p. 157).

Esdaile shows copies of three seventeenth-century editions in the British Museum. The first of these is entitled *The Famous and Renowned History of Bevis of Southampton*, etc., for W. Thackeray and J. Deacon, 1689, black letter (see Esdaile, p. 163, for the other seventeenth-century titles).

John Bunyan was one of the "countless readers who was as a lad instructed by Bevis's heroic deeds" (Wright, p. 391), as were Steele's godson and Robert Ashley (Sloane, p. 6).

BIBLE: THE HOLY BIBLE IN VERSE

Apparently the earliest English edition of the Bible in verse is the 1698 edition entitled *The Holy Bible; Containing, the Old and New Testaments, with the Apocrypha. Done into Verse by B. H. for the benefit of weak Memories* (London, Benja. Harris, Senior, 1698). Wilbur Macey Stone, an American collector, at one time owned the "only known copy of an issue printed in London in 1698," a volume three inches high. Writing in *Library Journal* in 1938, Stone commented:

> *The Holy Bible in Verse* compiled by Benjamin Harris, the reputed author and publisher of the first *New England Primer,* is an elusive title. About ten copies are known, ranging in date from 1698 to 1754, in England and America. For many years an advertisement in the *London Post* of July, 1699, was the earliest record, but no copy of that year has yet been found. It was my good fortune, about a year ago, to acquire the only known copy of an issue printed in London in 1698. This volume is three inches high and the subtitle is amusing, to wit: "For the Benefit of Weak Memories; The whole containing about one thousand Lines, with Cuts."

The comments of the late D'Alté Welch concerning *The Holy Bible in Verse* ("A Bibliography of American Children's Books Printed Prior to 1821," pp. 135–37) are also helpful.

There is a copy of a 1698 London edition of *The Holy Bible in Verse* in the David McCandless McKell Collection (Fieler, item 74). It is not known to the compiler whether this copy, which contains three woodcuts, has any connection with the copy formerly owned by Wilbur Macey Stone.

A Benjamin Harris edition of *The Holy Bible in Verse* was issued in Boston in 1717. This edition is of particular note because it contains ten cuts from an unknown edition of the *New England Primer.* The American Antiquarian Society has the copy of the 1717 edition originally owned by the late D'Alté Welch. The Connecticut Historical Society owns copies of the 1717 and 1729 editions. The McKell Collection has a copy of the 1717 edition (Fieler, item 1020).

Commenting on thumb Bibles, Sloane mentions Benjamin Harris's *The Holy Bible in Verse* (pp. 49, 99) and gives dates slightly different from those in other sources concerning first publication and earliest known copy (p. 99, n. 10).

BIBLE: VERBUM SEMPITERNUM

The first edition of John Taylor's summary of the Bible, less than two inches square, was published in Aberdeen, Scotland, in 1614. Only one copy of the 1614 *Verbum Sempiternae* (sic) seems to have survived. It was reissued in 1616 with the title corrected (Wright, p. 238, n. 12). American collector Wilbur Macey Stone owned a copy of a 1670 edition, also published in Aberdeen. Only four copies of the 1670 edition are known. The present location of the copy formerly belonging to Mr. Stone is not known to the compiler at this writing.

An updated *Verbum Sempiternum* was printed in New York around 1760 by Samuel Parker. The earliest dated *Verbum Sempiternum* was printed in Boston. Harvard University, Yale University, the Philadelphia Free Library, and the Essex Institute each own copies of fine early editions of *Verbum Sempiternum.* The American Antiquarian Society owns the D'Alté Welch copy printed in Boston in 1786. *Verbum Sempiternum* was constantly reprinted throughout the seventeenth and eighteenth centuries.

It was the eighteenth- and not the seventeenth-century condensations of the Bible that were especially prepared for children; children shared the seventeenth-century condensations with adults (Sloane, p. 49). Perhaps Ned Harley, father of Robert Harley, Earl of Oxford and minister to Queen Anne, was one such child. It may well have been a copy of

Verbum Sempiternum that little Ned received from his father, Sir Robert Harley. At any rate, Lady Brilliana Harley, Ned's mother, wrote her husband on December 4, 1629, and asked him to buy a little bible for their son (Sloane, p. 48).

Bibles were apparently considered usual reading fare for young children during the period under consideration. At least in one noble household, "each child, when it was three or four years old, was given two Bibles, one in Latin and one in English, together with a Catechism and a Book of Common Prayer" (Gladys Scott Thomson, *Life in a Noble Household, 1641–1700,* p. 74). Jonathan Swift is reputed to have been able to read any chapter in the Bible when only three (*Prose Works,* vol. 1, Introduction). In America in 1756—somewhat later than the period we are considering—Timothy Dwight reputedly could read the Bible before he was four years old (Rosenbach, p. xxxii).

BOOK FOR BOYS AND GIRLS (John Bunyan)

First published in 1686, this work was titled *A Book for Boys and Girls: or, Country Rhymes for Children.* By 1724 the ninth edition was titled *Divine Emblems: or Temporal Things Spiritualized.* From the title of the first edition, the work would appear to have been written specifically for children, and William Sloane includes it in the invaluable checklist of children's books that appears in his study of seventeenth-century children's books in England and America.

Muir, however, makes two observations that lead to some doubt as to Bunyan's intended audience. In the first place, the preface of the work contains a "curious sidelight on the relations between adult and child readers, where Bunyan admits that the young have not been exclusively regarded in its writing, for 'childish Motions' make children of some greybeards and 'Girls big as old Women' " (p. 29). In a footnote Muir states that *A Book for Boys and Girls* "was severely cut down" in later reprint editions. The "cutting down" suggests that Bunyan may have attempted to design his work specifically for children at a later time rather than with the first edition.

A copy of the 1686 first edition is in the Harvard University library, and a copy of the 1701 second edition is in the Bodleian (Sloane, p. 198). J. Harvey Darton (*Children's Books in England,* p. 66) indicates a copy of the 1686 edition in the British Museum and gives further details in a footnote.

BOOK OF MARTYRS (John Foxe)

Foxe's *Book of Martyrs* "was so popular in England that with the Bible and the Catechism it was included in the library of all households that could afford it" (Rosalie V. Halsey, *Forgotten Books of the American Nursery,* p. 10). Discussing the history and progress of children's literature of the seventeenth century, Field (p. 193) states that "the *Book of Martyrs* was considered a most desirable book for children at that time." D'Alté Welch comments that while "such detailed descriptions of martyrdom are disconcerting to a modern reader . . . such tortures probably did not faze the Puritan children who devoured Foxe's book" (*A Bibliography of American Children's Books Printed Prior to 1821,* p. xxi).

In his *A Little Book for Little Children,* the English Puritan Thomas White recommended that children read from the *Book of Martyrs.* White further encouraged children to "mark in the margins or underline passages they found most pleasure in," provided the copies were their own (Sloane, p. 56). Since White died in 1672 (Muir, p. 44) and since *A Little Book for Little Children* was in its twelfth edition in 1702, we know that many seventeenth-century children were exposed to his advice. Although the *Book of Martyrs* was first published in the latter half of the sixteenth century under the title *Actes and Monuments,* there is substantial evidence that it was read by both children and adults throughout the seventeenth century.

John Taylor, the water poet, issued a thumb-book version in verse in 1617, just as he had done with the Bible in 1614. The British Museum has a copy of the 1639 edition of Taylor's thumb book entitled *The booke of martyrs.*

Thomas Fuller loved to look at pictures in the *Book of Martyrs* (Sloane, p. 50), and Samuel Sewall, in a 1671 letter to a friend, spoke of "'little Betty, who though Reading passing well, took three Moneths to Read the first Volume of the *Book of Martyrs,'* as she sat by the fire-light at night after her daily task of spinning was done" (Halsey, p. 10). In the second part of Janeway's *A Token for Children* (p. 64), Janeway describes the young John Sudlow, age six or seven perhaps, as "hugely taken with the reading of the Book of *Martyrs*" and as one who "would be ready to leave his Dinner to go to his Book." This same lad is also described by Janeway as "reading by himself from *Draiton's* [sic] Poems about *Noah's* Flood and the Ark" (p. 66).

CAWWOOD THE ROOKE

The Pleasant History of Cawwood the Rooke, or the Assembly of Birds, with the Severall Speeches which the Birds made to the Eagle, in hope to have the Government in his absence: and lastly how the Rooke was banished; with the reason why crafty Fellowes are called Rookes. As also fit Morrals and expositions added to every chapter was published in 1640 by T. C. for F. Grove.

This is a case in which title explains content. Esdaile (pp. 28–29) lists several editions, showing a copy of the 1640 edition in the British Museum. Harvard University also has a copy of the 1640 edition. Esdaile (p. 117) shows that the sixth (1735) edition of *The History of Cawwood the Rooke* was published with an edition of *Reynard the Fox.* The two stories appeared at least five or six times between the same covers.

It is reasonably certain, both from its own content and from its having been published with *Reynard the Fox,* that *Cawwood the Rooke* was a work of dual interest. Wright (pp. 400–401) states that this moralized tale of the fable type was much liked by the general public and that it went through at least five separate editions of its own.

CROWN GARLAND OF GOLDEN ROSES (Richard Johnson)

The British Museum has a 1631 edition in black letter entitled *The Crowne Garland of Golden Roses: Gathered out of England's Royall Garden. Set forth in many new Songs and Sonets: with new additions . . . divided into two Parts* (for J. Wright, London). Three other seventeenth-century editions in black letter are held by the British Museum.

ELIZABETH AND ESSEX

"No ballads on Essex's death could be registered until after the death of Elizabeth because of censorship by the government against anything which could be construed to be a matter of state" (Sir Charles Harding Firth, "Ballads and Broadsides," in *Shakespeare's England,* ed. Raleigh et al., vol. 2, p. 522). Certainly the same stance would have governed the issuing of chapbooks or other publications that might have been harmful during Elizabeth's lifetime.

By 1650, however, the subject of Elizabeth's love for Essex could be more safely handled, and that year a romance, *The History of the most Renowned Queen Elizabeth and her great Favourite the Earl of Essex,* was published. In 1680 there appeared *The Secret History of the Most Renowned Q. Elizabeth and the E. of Essex. By a Person of Quality.* There were at least two other editions of this work by 1700 (one in 1695, another in 1700), and numerous editions appeared throughout the eighteenth century. A chapbook version drawn mainly from the 1695 edition is "taken up with an elaborate confession by Elizabeth, to the Countess of Nottingham, of her love for the unfortunate Earl of Essex" (Ashton, p. 397). The British Museum has at least one copy each of the 1650, 1695, and 1700 editions.

For other editions and copy locations see Esdaile (pp. 215–16) and the British Museum's *Catalogue of Printed Books,* vol. 15 (1946).

EMBLEMS (Francis Quarles)

First published in 1635, the *Emblems* of Francis Quarles appeared in twelve editions before 1700. This work was extremely popular during the seventeenth century and remained so for many years. Gordon S. Haight furnishes valuable information concerning both the sources and the popularity of the *Emblems* in "The Sources of Quarles's *Emblems.*"

According to Haight (p. 188), the engravings used by Quarles for his *Emblems* were in part responsible for the work's popularity, especially with children: "Children's hands, pawing over the engravings at a time when picture-books were rare, undoubtedly helped to wear the editions of the *Emblems* to rags. But their parents were also delighted with it, as many bits of practical morality copied into commonplace books bear witness, and used it in teaching difficult Christian doctrines to the young." Haight goes on to say that "it was the generation brought up on Quarles's *Emblems* that welcomed *The Pilgrim's Progress* so heartily in later years."

The British Museum has a 1635 edition entitled *Emblemes,* printed by G. M. and sold at I. Marriot's Shop, and a later seventeenth-century edition as well as numerous eighteenth- and nineteenth-century editions.

FAMILY WELL-ORDERED (Cotton Mather)

A Family Well-Ordered; or, an Essay to render Parents and Children Happy in one another was first published in 1699 in Boston, Massachusetts. Although it is perhaps properly regarded as the earliest American juvenile work, and a good example of the type of reading Puritan parents urged on their children, the book's title indicates the dual nature of its content.

A copy of the first edition is in the Rosenbach Collection of the Philadelphia Free Public Library. The British Museum also has a copy.

FAUSTUS

The Historie of the damnable life, and deserved death of Doctor John Faustus was first translated into English in 1592 from the first German edition of 1587. This English translation became one of the most popular books of seventeenth-century England, as well as a favorite in Puritan New England (Wright, p. 394). Victor E. Neuberg (*Penny Histories,* p. 12) suggests that the "many-sided fascination of the Faust theme ensured its popularity" and that "as a story of magic it could hardly have failed to appeal to children."

The Faustus tale belongs in the category of demonology and witchcraft tales, which became ready subjects for chapbooks and other forms of popular street literature. There is a ballad entry, for example, in the Register of the Stationers' Company for 1588. Hazlitt provides interesting insights into the Faustus history in the section on supernatural legends in his critical introduction to *Faustus* in *Tales and Legends* (pp. 97–107). He refers to *Faustus* as pseudo-biography and suggests that under the name of Faustus we find at least four impersonations: the Faustus of real life, the Faustus of German prose fiction, the Faustus of Marlowe, and the Faustus of Goethe. Hazlitt warns that "we have always to recollect that the school of biography to which the old account of Faustus appertains considered it a legitimate, or at least a safe and advantageous, feature in their work to heighten the colour or shadow of the portraiture which they presented to view by a free use of borrowed accessories." There was undoubtedly a real Faustus who lived from 1491 to 1538, "a philosopher whose precise views will never be accurately known" because of the fusion of fact with thirteenth- and fourteenth-century folklore.

Esdaile (pp. 46–48) provides a useful listing of editions of *Faustus* prior to 1740, indicating locations when known.

FORTUNATUS

Fortunatus was first published in Augsburg, Germany, in 1509 and in time had many German successors. It first appeared in England in 1600. There Dekker adapted it as a play, and many chapbook reprints followed (Neuberg, pp. 12–13). The earliest English chapbook edition with an absolute date appears to be the Thomas Churchyarde edition of 1676. A copy of a 1682 edition in the British Museum bears the title *The right, pleasant and variable trachical history of Fortunatus, whereby a young man may learn how to behave himself in all worldly affairs and casual chances. First penned in the Dutch tongue; there hence abstracted and now published in English by T. C.* (Ashton, p. 124).

Fortunatus is a supernatural legend with possible kinship to supernatural elements of the Arabian nights (Hazlitt, pp. 156–57). This legend remained extremely popular in England and as late as 1900 was included by Andrew Lang in his *Grey Book of Fairy Tales*.

Further details of editions and locations appear in Esdaile (pp. 156–57).

FRIAR AND THE BOY

According to D'Alté Welch (*Bibliography*, p. xxvii), popular chapbooks printed in England prior to John Newbery were sometimes "coarse, ribald, and even obscene." It is not surprising, therefore, that *The Friar and the Boy* went through many editions. It was undoubtedly read by both children and adults. Muir (p. 27) reminds us that "all the chapbooks had a family likeness, so that the children, at any rate [whether or not the content was suited to juvenile consumption], would not find it easy to choose between one and another." He also points out that "there is abundant evidence of the buying and reading of these cheap little books by children."

The first English version of this humorous metrical tale was printed by Wynkyn de Worde, but Hazlitt (p. 17) says that the tale itself is probably of German origin and that it may have reached England via a French text. He includes it among supernatural legends and places it as fifteenth-sixteenth century (p. iii).

The earliest chapbook version located is an edition of around 1750 in two parts and in verse. A copy is in the British Museum.

FRIAR BACON (Robert Greene)

Greene's play in the 1594 edition, entitled *The Honourable Historie of frier Bacon, and frier*

Bongay: As it was plaid by her Majesties servants in verse and prose, has survived in only three copies, two of which are imperfect. The perfect copy is in the Huntington Library, and one of the two imperfect copies is in the British Museum. The earliest known chapbook version of the play is a 1627 edition, *The Famous Historie of Fryer Bacon.* There were also editions in 1629 and 1630. The Bodleian Library and the British Museum each have a copy of the 1630 edition (Malone Society Reprints, vol. 67, pp. v–x).

Hazlitt (pp. 74–96) considers the tale of Friar Bacon a supernatural legend.

GULLIVER'S TRAVELS (Jonathan Swift)

Although Swift did not intend *Gulliver's Travels* for children, many generations of children have delighted in the predicaments of Gulliver in Brobdingnag. "To them it is a story, as alive today as when it first appeared in 1726" (Lillian Smith, *The Unreluctant Years,* p. 23). An unauthorized abridgement by J. Stone and R. King appeared in 1727.

One of the most appealing elements in *Gulliver's Travels* is its "topsy-turvydom." According to Darton (p. 107), seeing things turned topsy-turvy has permanent appeal, and "it would be interesting to study topsy-turvydom with *Gulliver* as a text." The complete title of *Gulliver* as first published in 1726 was *Travels into several Remote Nations of the World. In Four Parts. By Lemuel Gulliver, First a Surgeon, and then a Captain of Several Ships, etc.* (for B. Motte).

For various editions and their locations, see Esdaile (pp. 314–15).

GUY OF WARWICK

Guy of Warwick is perhaps the most typical of the medieval metrical romances whose popularity survived the sixteenth and seventeenth centuries. The exact origin of the story is not clear, but it was almost certainly told to children and sung by minstrels from very early times (Field, p. 55). An early version appears in a Wynkyn de Worde edition of *Gesta Romanorum.* Ashton (p. 138) says the earliest known printed edition of this romance is the French edition of 1525, but Ronald S. Crane says that editions began to appear shortly before 1500 ("The Vogue of Guy of Warwick from the Close of the Middle Ages to the Romantic Revival," p. 128).

In any case, there were several reprintings of English editions of *Guy* during the sixteenth century, most, if not all, in black letter. In 1592 this old romance appeared as a ballad printed on a single sheet (Neuberg, p. 9). Many editions, most of them on broadsides illustrated with rude woodcuts, were printed during the seventeenth and eighteenth centuries (Crane, p. 150). The British Museum has a few of these, chiefly editions of the late seventeenth and early eighteenth centuries. The earliest copy (1560?) in the British Museum, indicated as an imperfect copy printed by William Copland, is entitled *The Booke of the Most Victoryous Prince, Guy of Warwick.*

The British Museum also owns a 1632 edition of Rowland's poem "The Famous History of Guy Earle of Warwick." The best-known chapbook edition, assumed to be the first, is the edition of 1607. A copy is in the British Museum (Crane, p. 153). For prose versions and their locations see Esdaile (pp. 233–34).

Many literary men were acquainted with the Guy legend, including Skelton, Udall, Puttenham, Drayton, and Shakespeare. Both Puttenham and Drayton made use of the legend in works of their own (Crane, pp. 131, 149). Robert Ashley, a miscellaneous writer, recalled in 1614 that he had as a boy read *Guy of Warwick* (Crane, "The Reading of an

Elizabethan Youth," pp. 269–71). Indeed *Guy of Warwick* remained for the mass of readers "a sort of popular classic, familiar to them from boyhood, a pleasant tale to beguile the long winter evenings in the country" (Crane, "The Vogue of Guy of Warwick," p. 131).

HISTORIE OF FOURE-FOOTED BEASTES (Edward Topsell)

In the latter third of the sixteenth century, interest in natural history was such that writers of prose and poetry "found in the habits of animals and the qualities of plants and stones material from which literary style might be enriched" (Wright, p. 572). Hence it was to be expected that some of the seventeenth-century zoological and plant treatises would provide not only useful but pleasurable reading. According to Wright, the massive folios of Edward Topsell "united zoology and morality to the complete satisfaction of Puritan readers."

In 1607 appeared Topsell's *The Historie of Foure-Footed Beastes. Describing the true and lively figure of every Beast, with a discourse of their severall Names, Conditions, Kindes, Vertues (both naturall and medicinall) Countries of their breed, their love and hate to Mankinde, and the wonderfull worke of God in their Creation, Preservation, and Destruction. Necessary for all Divines and Students, because the story of every Beast is amplified with Narrations out of Scripture, Fathers, Phylosophers, Physitians, and Poets: wherein are declared divers Hyerogliphicks, Emblems, Epigrams, and other good Histories, Collected out of all the Volumes of Conradus Gesner, and all other Writers to this present day.* The title is obviously descriptive of the content. Topsell's work is largely a translation of Conrad Gesner's *Historiae Animalium.* The McKell Collection has a copy of *The Historie of Foure-Footed Beastes* bound with Topsell's 1608 *Historie of Serpents* (Fieler, item 48).

It is possible that William Penn had such a work as *Foure-Footed Beastes* in mind in *Some Fruits of Solitude* (I, "Reflections and Maxims," no. 15):

It is a pity therefore that books have not been composed for youth by some curious careful naturalists, and also mechanics, in the Latin tongue, to be used in schools that they might learn things with words, things obvious and familiar to them, and which would make the tongue easier to be attained by them.

Walter de la Mare is said to have used for his *Animal Stories* (1939) illustrations from the 1658 edition of Topsell's *Foure-Footed Beastes.*

HUON OF BOURDEAUX

The first seventeenth-century edition of the tale of Huon of Bourdeaux is the 1601 black-letter edition entitled *The Ancient, Honorable, Famous and delightfull Historie of Huon of Bourdeaux, one of the Peeres of France, and Duke of Guyenne . . . Being now the Third time imprinted, and the rude English corrected and amended* (T. Purfoot, and are to be sould by E. White).

Esdaile (p. 79) indicates that the Bodleian and the British Museum each have a copy of the 1601 edition, and lists a Haigh Hall copy of a Wynkyn de Worde edition of around 1594, although publisher and date are both uncertain.

There were undoubtedly earlier versions, for "Montaigne, who was born in 1533, tells us that the favorite reading of his youthful companions" included *Huon of Bourdeaux* (Muir, p. 25, n. 1).

JACK THE GIANT KILLER

George Orwell has referred to *Jack the Giant Killer* as the "basic myth of the Western World"

(Neuberg, p. 17). The 1711 edition in two parts appears to be the earliest (Weiss, p. 58). The tale was known much earlier, however, for Shakespeare made use of it in *King Lear* around 1605. According to Weiss (p. 60), the earliest version may have appeared between 1140 and 1160 in an old Scandinavian folk tale known as "Thor's Journey to the Land of Giants," although there are similar themes in the tales of Germany and India. Weiss concludes, "One may make the somewhat indefinite statement that 'Jack the Giant Killer' is apparently of Indo-European origin and was probably introduced into England during the Saxon invasion" (p. 61).

There have been numerous English editions of this old tale. A copy of the second part of the 1711 edition, titled *The History of Jack and the Giants,* is located in the British Museum (Esdaile, p. 251).

Weiss (*Chapbooks,* p.141) states:

No less a person than James Boswell collected chapbooks, and his collection, bound in three small volumes with the title "Curious Productions," is housed in the Library of Harvard University. . . . About his chapbooks, James Bowell inserted a little auto-graphed note in one of the volumes saying, "Having, when a boy, been much interested with 'Jack the Giant Killer' and such little story books, I have always retained a kind of affection for them, as they recall my early days. I went to the printing office in Bow Churchyard and bought this collection and had it bound up with the title of 'Curious Productions.' I shall certainly, some time or other, write a little story book in the style of these. It will not be an easy task for me. It will require much nature and simplicity and a great acquaintance with the humours and traditions of the English common people. I shall be happy to succeed, for he who pleases children will be remembered with pleasure by men.

Among other well-known writers who are likely to have read *Jack the Giant Killer* are Wordsworth, Coleridge, and Crabbe. The lesser-known Samuel Bradford, a weaver and poet, described how "every farthing he could scrape together was spent in purchasing *Jack the Giant Killer, Saint George and the Dragon, Tom Hickathrift,* and *The Seven Champions of Christendom*" (Neuberg, p. 1). According to Iona and Peter Opie (*The Classic Fairy Tales,* p. 50), Dr. Johnson, James Boswell, and William Cowper admitted having read *Jack the Giant Killer,* and both Boswell and Cowper were entertained by it.

JOE MILLER'S JESTS

Jest books were carried by the chapmen along with other cheap books, and we may assume that *Joe Miller's Jests* was popular with both children and adults. As late as 1781 American newspapers were advertising various "Little Histories for Children" and other works "just imported and to be sold by Thomas Bradford." Among the assortment of penny-dreadfuls was *Joe Miller's Jests* (Halsey, p. 90). According to Weiss (*Chapbooks,* p. 82), the Joe Miller books are the best known of the jest books.

Apparently the earliest edition of a Joe Miller jest book was published by the dramatist John Mottley in London in 1739. The complete title is *Joe Miller's Jests: or Wits Vade-Mecum. Being a collection of the most brilliant jests, the politest repartees, the most elegant bon mots, and the most pleasant short stories in the English language. First carefully collected in the company, and many of them transcribed from the mouth, of the facetious gentlemen whose name they bear, and now set forth and published by his lamentable friend and former companion, Elijah Jenkins, Esq. (or rather compiled by J. Mottley).*

The British Museum has a copy of this first edition and of three other editions published in 1739. By 1755 *Joe Miller's Jests* was in its fifteenth edition. For additional information on the origin of *Joe Miller's Jests,* see Ashton (p. 289) and Weiss (*Chapbooks,* p. 82).

JOHN BARLEYCORN

In his 1877 collection *Early Ballads Illustrative of History, Traditions and Customs* (p. 230), editor Robert Bell described his work as follows:

> The value of this volume consists in the genuineness of its contents, and the healthiness of its tone. While fashionable life was masquerading in imaginary Arcadias, and deluging theatres and concert rooms with shams, the English peasant remained true to the realities of his own experience, and produced and sang songs which faithfully reflected the actual life around him. Whatever these songs describe is true to that life. There are fictitious raptures in them. Love here never dresses its emotions in artificial images, nor disguises itself in the mask of a Strephon or a Daphne. It is in this particular aspect that the poetry of the country posseses a permanent and moral interest.

In his volume Bell includes the West-country ballad of Sir John Barleycorn, stating that it is very ancient (p. 300). Ashton includes two versions in his work, the second reprinted from a black-letter ballad (c. 1640) that "was stolen wholesale by Robert Burns" for his version of *John Barleycorn* (p. 318n).

The British Museum has a copy of one of the ballads described and included by Ashton (pp. 318–22). See British Museum *Catalogue,* vol. 4, under Barleycorn, Sir John.

JOSEPH AND HIS BRETHREN

According to Ashton (p. 1), the first printed metrical version of this obviously Biblical episode was the Wynkyn de Worde edition of fourteen pages. The British Museum *Catalogue,* vol. 28, lists copies of various editions under Joseph, the Patriarch. *The History of Joseph and his brethren* (1750?), a chapbook edition in verse and illustrated with cuts, is in the British Museum.

KEY OF KNOWLEDG (Thomas Willis)

The Key of Knowledg, Opening The Principles of Religion . . . Design'd For the Conduct of Children and Servants, in the right way to Heaven and Happiness was published in 1682. The last section of this work, called "Apples of Gold in Pictures of Silver," contains poetry by several writers of note.

A copy of the 1682 edition is in the British Museum.

KING AND COBLER

The earliest work on this subject appears to be *Cobler turned Courtier, being a Pleasant Humour between K. Henry 8th and a Cobler,* 1680 (Ashton, p. 236). There are many later editions with variations in title, such as *The History of the King and Cobler,* etc. The British Museum has a copy of the 1680 edition, as well as copies of many later editions.

Welch ("Bibliography," p. 132) says that *The King and the Cobler* was probably written in chapbook form for adults but was undoubtedly read by children.

LONG MEG

Ashton (p. 323) says there can be little doubt that this virago, Long Meg of Westminster, was a real person who must have lived during the reign of Henry VIII. The British Museum has an imperfect copy of a 1582 black-letter edition entitled *The Life and Pranks of Long Meg of Westminster.* Esdaile (p. 101) cites several other editions, most of which are also in black letter.

A play about Long Meg was a favorite during much of the seventeenth century.

MAN IN THE MOONE

According to a brief preface by James O. Halliwell to the Percy Society's reprint of the 1609 edition of *The Man in the Moone Telling Strange Fortunes; or, The English Fortune Teller,* copies of the 1609 edition are very rare, the only copy known to Halliwell being that preserved in the Bodleian. However, the British Museum also has a copy of the 1609 edition. A later rifacimento edition appeared as *The Wandering Jew.* For additional comments on the Wandering Jew legend, see below under that title.

MARTYRS IN FLAMES (Nathaniel Crouch)

Martyrs in Flames was one of many chapbooks published by Nathaniel Crouch. Muir (p. 35) states that "although possibly not intended primarily for children, this will amost invariably have been seized upon by them."

One can imagine that *Martyrs in Flames; The English Hero, or Sir Frances Drake reviv'd; The History of the Nine Worthies of the World;* and *The Kingdom of Darkness, or the History of daemons* were four of the Crouch histories Benjamin Franklin read as a boy (see Halsey, p. 36).

The British Museum has a copy of the 1729 third edition entitled *Martyrs in Flames; or, the History of Popery. Displaying the . . . cruelties exercised upon Protestants by Papists . . . by Richard Burton* (pseudonym of N. Crouch).

MILK FOR BABES AND MEAT FOR MEN (Hugh Peters)

When Hugh Peters was in exile in Rotterdam, he was for a time minister to an English congregation. One of his first acts was to publish in 1630 *Milk for Babes, and Meat for Men. Or Principles necessary, to bee known and learned, of such as would know Christ here, or be known of him hereafter.*

Milk for Babes is included in this listing because it is representative of numerous catechisms considered essential for children and adults of the time. In the case of this particular catechism, the title suggests its dual purpose.

The Houghton Library of Harvard University has a copy of the 1630 edition of *Milk for Babes, and Meat for Men.* A copy of the 1641 edition is in the British Museum.

MOTHER BUNCH'S CLOSET

Mother Bunch's Closet Newly Broke Open, and the History of Mother Bunch of the West is the exact title of a 1685 version in the Pepysian Library at Cambridge (G. L. Gomme and H. B. Wheatley, eds., *Chap-books and Folk-Lore Tracts,* vol. 3, p. i).

Versions of *Mother Bunch* are similar in some respects to *Mother Shipton's Prophecy* and *Nixon's Cheshire Prophecy,* and such fortune-telling books appeal to children of almost every generation. Certainly children of the seventeenth century found delight in them, and as late as 1850 there is evidence that *Mother Bunch* continued to be recommended.

MOTHER SHIPTON'S PROPHECY (Richard Head)

Ashton (p. 90) indicates that a small quarto tract called *The Prophesie of Mother Shipton in the raigne of Henry the eighth* . . . was printed in 1641. The earliest edition cited by Esdaile is a 1667 edition called *The Life and Death of Mother Shipton,* reprinted in Manchester in 1881. The British Museum has a 1684 edition. The Bodleian has a 1687 edition, and the McKell Collection has a 1687 edition bearing the book plates of Howard Pyle (Fieler, item 67).

See Esdaile (pp. 242–43, 305) for other editions and their locations.

NATURAL HISTORY (Thomas Boreman)

A quaint little volume appeared in 1730 bearing the title *A Description of Three Hundred Animals; viz. Beasts, Birds, Fishes, Serpents and Insects. With a Particular Account of Whale Fishery. Extracted out of the Best Authors, and adapted to the Use of all Capacities; especially to allure Children to Read* (illustrated with Copper Plates. [Etc.] London. Printed by J. T. Jos. Rich. Ware at the Bible and Sun in Amen Corner, Thomas Boreman the Corner of St. Clements Lane without Temple Bar, etc. MDCCXXX). This work is now often referred to simply as *Natural History* or *Three Hundred Animals.*

According to Hugh S. Gladstone, who owns an edition dated 1797, editions subsequent to that of 1730 vary slightly "in pagination, title page, etc." Gladstone points out that the *Times Telescope* in 1817 suggested one Mr. McQuin as author of the work in question (*Notes and Queries,* June 19, 1946, p. 446).

In any case, the person responsible for *A Description of Three Hundred Animals* acknowledges in a preliminary note "To the Reader" that he has extracted "from some of the most considerable Authors" this "short Account of Beasts, Birds, Fishes, Serpents, and Insects." He clearly indicates that the work is "for the Entertainment of Children," but, as with the various sources from which the compiler undoubtedly drew, such as Edward Topsell's *Historie of Foure-Footed Beastes,* it is relatively certain that adults as well as children were entertained by *A Description of Three Hundred Animals.*

The Osborne Collection of the Toronto Public Library has a 1786 edition of the original 1730 edition, and a 1744 second edition of a supplement to the 1730 edition, entitled *A Description of a Great Variety of Animals and Vegetables; viz. Beasts, Birds, Fishes, Insects, Plants, Fruits, and Flowers. Extracted from the most considerable writers of natural history; and adapted to the use of all capacities, but more particularly to the entertainment of youth. Being a supplement to The Description of Three Hundred Animals* . . . (illustrated with above ninety copper plates, whereon is curiously engraven every animal and vegetable described in the whole book).

The British Museum has a 1730 original edition, several later editions, and a 1736 edition of the supplement.

NIXON'S CHESHIRE PROPHECY

According to Ashton (p. 94), the first printed book relating to Nixon was *The Cheshire*

Prophesy; with Historical and Political Remarks, by John Oldmixon, published in London in 1714. By 1750 there had been at least twenty-one editions or versions of Nixon and his prophesying. The British Museum has a 1715 third edition and several other editions published prior to 1750.

OLD WIVES TALE (George Peele)

The Malone Society reprinted the 1595 edition of *The Old Wives Tale* in 1909. Extant copies of the original quarto are in the British Museum and the Dyce Collection, according to the preface of the reprint.

Sloane (p. 65) draws attention to a scene from *The Old Wives Tale* in which one of the characters asks an old woman for a story. "Though he was no longer a little one," says Sloane, "he still wanted to hear the kind of story he had liked as a child."

ORBIS PICTUS

Although the *Orbis Pictus* of Comenius is not of English origin, it must be considered in even the slightest study of books available to children during the period we are considering. According to John E. Sadler's introduction to the facsimile reproduction of the first (1659) English *Orbis Pictus* (London: Oxford University Press, 1968), Comenius did not intend it as an isolated work but as a part of a larger series. "In fact," Sadler adds, "we might go further and say it was part of a pansophic education which must extend throughout the whole of life" (pp. 46–47). Sadler places the *Orbis Pictus* among books suitable for both children and adults: "Comenius did not draw a sharp distinction between school textbooks and books for adults since he believed that the whole of life was a school" (pp. 55–56).

Whatever the author's intent, Charles Hoole, who translated *Orbis Pictus* into English in 1659 from the German edition of 1658, felt that Comenius had a tendency to "somewhat overshoot the capacities of children" (*A New Discovery of the Art of Teaching Schoole,* p. 58).

Thomson (pp. 75–76) states that John Thornton, chaplain to the Earl of Bedford and tutor of his children, bought a *Pictus Orbis Comenii* for Mr. Robert for five shillings. In fact, when the *Orbis Pictus* "was published in Nuremberg in 1658, Thornton immediately ordered not one, but several copies for his pupils and continued to repeat the order in subsequent years."

Copies of various editions of *Orbis Pictus* are in the British Museum, including Hoole's translation: *Joh. Amos Commenii Orbis Sensualium Pictus. . . . A Work newly written by the Author in Latine, and High-Dutch . . . & translated into English, By Charles Hoole . . .* (London, 1659). The McKell Collection has a 1666 edition of *Orbis Pictus* (Fieler, item 58).

PATIENT GRISELDA

The Griselda legend has a long and variegated history. Wirt Armistead Cate suggests that it has appeared in more forms than any other short narrative in world literature ("The Problem of the Origin of the Griselda Story," p. 389). Indeed, the "legend has appeared in practically every literary form from ballad to play" (Wright, p. 415). *Patient Griselda* appeared in ballad form in 1566 and may have appeared as early as 1557 (Gomme and Wheatley, vol. 4, p. vii). In France the Griselda story dates at least as far back as 1025, under the title *Parement des Dames* (Ashton, p. 171n.). The 1619 English edition entitled *The Ancient True and Admirable History of Patient Grisel,* purportedly translated from the French, is obviously of English making (Gomme and Wheatley, vol. 4, p. ix). Another English edition, probably printed around 1630, is entitled *The Pleasant Sweet History of Patient Grissel.* This edition purports to be translated from the Italian, but like the 1619 edition, it too is patently English.

Certainly, like many other stories appearing in print in seventeenth-century England, *Patient Griselda* has come down to us from the Middle Ages, having been previously used by Boccaccio, Petrarch, and Chaucer, according to the introduction to the reprint of the 1619 edition in *Chap-Books and Folk-Lore Tracts,* vol. 4. "Its earliest appearance in English was in Chaucer's *Canterbury Tales* where it is assigned to the Clerk of Oxenford" (Percy Society's Publications, vol. 3, p. x).

The British Museum has copies of the 1619 edition and a later (1630?) edition of the Patient Griselda tracts. From these editions come the two Griselda tracts in the Percy Society's Publications, vol. 3. Both the British Museum and the Bodleian have copies of the 1603 edition of a play believed to have been authored by Thomas Dekker, Henry Chettle, and William Haughton (Gomme and Wheatley, vol. 4, pp. x–xi; see also Esdaile, pp. 72–73).

Oliver Goldsmith in *The Vicar of Wakefield* (chapter 6), first published in 1766, provides this interesting reference to Patient Grissel:

> As I spoke, poor Mr. Burchell entered the house, and was welcomed by the family, who shook him heartily by the hand, while little Dick officiously reached him a chair.
>
> I was pleased with the poor man's friendship for two reasons; because I knew that he wanted mine, and I knew him to be friendly as far as he was able. He was known in our neighbourhood by the character of the poor Gentleman that would do no good when he was young, though he was not yet thirty. He would at intervals talk with great good sense; but in general he was fondest of the company of children, whom he used to call harmless little men. He was famous, I found, for singing them ballads, and telling them stories; and seldom went out without something in his pockets for them, a piece of ginger-bread, or an halfpenny whistle. He generally came for a few days into our neighbourhood once a year, and lived upon the neighbours hospitality. He sate down to supper among us, and my wife was not sparing of her gooseberry wine. The tale went round; he sung us old songs, and gave the children the story of the Buck of Beverland, with the history of Patient Grissel, the adventures of Catskin, and then Fair Rosamond's bower.

PILGRIM'S PROGRESS (John Bunyan)

According to Muir (p. 28), Bunyan's *Pilgrim's Progress* was used by the Puritans somewhat as fairy tales are used, and the work does have some characteristics of the classic fairy tale:

> The Puritans were fully aware of the importance of indoctrinating the young, and Marxist versions of classical fairy-tales, such as used to decorate the pages of the *Daily Worker,* have their exemplars in the catchpenny titles with which the Puritans hoped to amuse their infants.
>
> Bunyan was the best of them by a very long way. The *Pilgrim's Progress,* while not expressly written for children, has long been annexed by them. It is, in outline, an adventure story, complete with giants and fabulous monsters, sword contests, ill fortune

from which the hero is regularly delivered, and the happiest of all endings. Hallam called it the most perfect and complex of fairy tales.

Part I of *Pilgrim's Progress* was published in England in 1678, and Part II in 1684. In 1681 *Pilgrim's Progress* was first printed in Boston by Samuel Green, and according to Halsey (p. 10), it superseded Foxe's *Book of Martyrs* as a household treasure. Halsey (p. 36) also quotes from Benjamin Franklin's autobiography to show that Franklin read *Pilgrim's Progress* as a boy: "All the little money that came into my hands was laid out in books. Pleased with *Pilgrim's Progress,* my collection was of John Bunyan's works in separate volumes. I afterwards sold them to buy R. Burton's Historical Collections; they were Chapmen's books, and cheap. 40 or 50 in all." *Pilgrim's Progress* was one of Abraham Lincoln's favorite books when he was a boy (Johnson et al., p. 796).

For a comprehensive listing of seventeenth-century editions and locations of copies, see Esdaile (pp. 173–77).

REYNARD THE FOX

Animal stories have enjoyed wide popularity in the literature of many cultures. The best-known older collections of animal stories are perhaps the *Panchatantra* and *Aesop's Fables.* From the latter, the French *Roman de Renart* is said to have originated around 1175. The Reynard fable was a favorite in France and the Low Countries long before becoming popular in England. However, Caxton's 1481 translation of the Gouda edition from Dutch into English was the first of a long series of broadly popular English editions. "For almost five centuries *The History of Reynard the Fox* has remained the most popular of Caxton's translations" (N. F. Blake, ed., *History of Reynard the Fox,* 1970 preface). According to Blake (p. iii), Caxton regarded *Reynard the Fox* as primarily a moral fable, and his translation was one of his own favorites. There are apparently six extant copies of Caxton's 1481 edition (for description and location of these, see Blake, pp. lx–lxii). Seventeenth- and eighteenth-century versions differ enough from their Caxton forerunners to suggest a continuous process of "modernization, adaptation, and interpolation, and the last hundred years has seen the appearance of a host of modernized versions, metrical adaptations, and renderings for children" (Blake, p. lxiii).

Esdaile (p. xii) states that Caxton's 1481 edition was followed by a 1489 reprint, by two Pynson editions, probably around the turn of the century, and "then, after one surviving edition and two appearances in the licenses of the Stationer's Company, it reappears in 1620 . . . and was constantly reprinted." See Esdaile (pp. 115–17) for various editions up to 1740 and for location of copies.

The McKell Collection has an unusual copy of all three parts of John Shirley's version of *Reynard the Fox* bound together. The first part is entitled *The Most Delectable History of Reynard the Fox*. . . (printed by T. Ilive for Edward Brewster at the Sign of the Crane in St. Paul's Church-Yard, 1681). The second part is called *The Most Pleasant and Delightful History of Reynard the Fox*. . . (printed by A. M. and R. R. for Edward Brewster at the Sign of the Crane in St. Paul's Church-Yard, 1681), and the third, *The Shifts of Reynardine the Son of Reynard the Fox*. . . (printed by T. F. for Edward Brewster at the Crane in St. Paul's Church-Yard, and Thomas Passenger at the Three Bibles in London Bridge, 1684).

A distinguished early German poet, J. W. Lawrenberg, is said to have called *Reynard the Fox* the "best book in the world, next to the Bible," and Francis Douce avowed that he read

Reynard the Fox "regularly every Christmas to Mrs. Douce" (William J. Thoms, ed., *History of Reynard the Fox,* pp. v, lxxixn.). That John Locke considered *Reynard the Fox* a good book for children is well known.

ROBINSON CRUSOE

Defoe's story of Robinson Crusoe was no more intended for children than was Bunyan's *Pilgrim's Progress* or Swift's *Gulliver's Travels,* but it was annexed by children with the same unerring instinct that "has led succeeding generations to endorse their choice" of all three (Quayle, pp. 15–16). Jonathan Cott has drawn attention to the fact that *Robinson Crusoe* was "the *only* book Rousseau approved of for children" (*Beyond the Looking Glass,* p. xliii), and Louise Field has called it "one of the best of storybooks" (p. 230).

Robinson Crusoe was published in three parts as follows: Part 1, *The Life and Strange Surprizing Adventures of Robinson Crusoe, of York, Mariner: Who lived Eight and Twenty Years, all alone in an uninhabited Island on the Coast of America, near the Mouth of the Great River Oroonoque; Having been cast on Shore by Ship-wreck, wherein all the men perished but himself. With an Account how he was at last strangely deliver'd by Pyrates. Written by Himself* (for W. Taylor. April 25, 1719); Part 2, *The Farther Adventures of Robinson Crusoe; Being the Second and Last Part of His Life, and the Strange Surprising Accounts of his Travels Round three Parts of the Globe. Written by Himself. To which is added a Map of the World, in which is Delineated the Voyages of Robinson Crusoe* (for W. Taylor. August 20, 1719); Part 3, *Serious Reflections during the Life and Surprising Adventures of Robinson Crusoe: With his Vision of the Angelic World. Written by Himself,* published by Taylor in 1720.

The British Museum has first editions of Parts 1 and 2. For other editions and copy locations, see Esdaile (pp. 206–7).

Robinson Crusoe was one of the books Abraham Lincoln enjoyed as a boy (Johnson et al., p. 796).

ROYAL MARTYR

The earliest chapbook version of the Royal Martyr appears to be that entitled *The History of the Royal Martyr, King Charles the First with the Effigies of those Worthy Persons that Suffered; and the Time and Places where they lost their Lives in his Majesties Cause, during the Usurpation of Oliver Cromwell* (London, W. & C. Dicey, 1750?). There was, however, an edition of 1660 entitled *The Royall Martyr. Or, King Charles the First no man of blood but a martyr for his people. Being a brief account of his actions from the beginnings of the late unhappy warrs, untill he was basely butchered . . . To which is added, a short history of His Royal Majesty Charles the Second, etc. The epistle dedicatory signed: W. H. B. By Fabian Philipps. With a portrait of Charles I* (for Henry Bell, London).

The British Museum owns copies of both editions.

SEVEN CHAMPIONS OF CHRISTENDOM

Sloane (p. 70) says that the 1608 edition of *The Seven Champions* is the first known edition. There were, however, editions in 1596 and 1597 (first and second parts respectively) of Richard Johnson's prose romance, and both parts went through six editions before 1640 (Wright, p. 391). Esdaile (pp. 82–85) lists a great many other editions, with locations of copies where known.

Some of the seventeenth-century English editions of *The Seven Champions* are available in America, among them an edition (1620?) in the McKell Collection, to name only one location. The British Museum has copies of some of the more important editions, for example, a black-letter edition entitled *The Famous Historie of the Seaven Champions of Christendome . . . 2 pt.* (Thomas Snodham, London, 1616).

The ninety-fifth number of the *Tatler* (1709) indicates that Steele's godson was acquainted with *The Seven Champions,* as many other youngsters of the period undoubtedly were (Muir, p. 23).

SEVEN WISE MASTERS OF ROME

Field (p. 50) reminds us that during the seventeenth century there were

> a number of popular stories in circulation, the delight of the common people generally, and especially suited to the children's taste. Some of these were very early printed, and afterwards constantly brought out afresh, chiefly in the tract, "ballett," or chapbook form, but also as bound and illustrated volumes. An interesting collection of these exists in the Pepysian Library at Cambridge, four quarto volumes in black letter, entitled "Vulgaria," and consisting of "the most noted pieces of chivalry and wit, pastime and devotion, in vogue with the English populace." Among the contents are "Bevis of Southampton," "Adam Bell," "Fortunatis," "Bellianis and Flores of Greece," "Patient Grisel," "Reynard the Fox," "The Seven Wise Masters," "Guy of Warwick," "Fryer Bacon," "Robin Hood," "King Arthur," "William of Cloudesley," "Canwood the Cook," "The Seven Champions," "Dr. Faustus," "Clim of the Clough," and others less familiar to us.

For other particularly useful comments see Sloane (p. 67, p. 105, n. 9, n. 10) and Wright (pp. 87–88).

The 1520 Wynkyn de Worde edition of a translation from Latin to English of *The Seven Wise Masters of Rome* is preserved in a fine copy in the British Museum (Gomme and Wheatley, vol. 2, pp. ii–iii). After that date there were many chapbook versions, reaching far into the nineteenth century.

Upon translating *The Seven Wise Masters* from the French in 1674, Francis Kirkman observed that in Ireland, "next to the horn-book and knowledge of letters, children are in general put to read in it, and I know only that by that book severall have learned to read well, so great is the pleasure that young and old take in reading thereof" (quoted in J. O. Halliwell, "Descriptive Notices of Popular English Histories," Percy Society's Publications, vol. 23, p. 5).

Esdaile (pp. 124–26) shows a number of seventeenth-century editions and their locations.

SQUIRE OF LOW DEGREE

Wynkyn de Worde printed many of the older metrical romances, among them *The Squire of Low Degree* (Wright, p. 376). According to Hazlitt (p. 377), this romantic legend is of distinctly English origin although its scene is laid elsewhere. Hazlitt places its composition in the fifteenth century, after the date of *Guy of Warwick.*

The British Museum has a copy published in London (1550?) by W. Copland, entitled *The Squyr of lowe degree.*

TAFFY

The British Museum *Catalogue* lists a copy of *The Pleasant History of Taffy's Progress to London; with the Welchman's Catechism* (London, 1709?).

TALE OF A TUB (Jonathan Swift)

The compiler wavers over including *A Tale of a Tub* in this checklist but yields to the temptation to do so largely because Field (p. 232) suggests that Swift's story might well have been found amusing by children too, so far as concerns the adventures of Peter, Martin, and Jack, their conflicts with giants and monsters, and their different fulfillment of their father's commands. Field adds this qualification: "We may suppose, however, that it would, as a rule, be carefully kept out of their way, on account of its bitter satire on religious teachers." It is tempting to reply that sometimes the books "kept out of their way" are the ones children determine to examine.

In the edition of *A Tale of a Tub* published by Columbia University in 1930, the following quotes from the foreword by Edward Hodnett seem relevant:

> *A Tale of a Tub* is a grand idle tale. It is fantasy of the highest order. It is clear, brilliant intellectual play. It moves with a burly animation. Yet it is shot through with an intensity of feeling—a passionate honesty and a supreme hatred of pretense—that is close to the heart of poetry.
>
> Allegory is out of fashion these days. It usually leaves the modern reader bored and irritated. *Pilgrim's Progress* for generations shared with the Bible the simple man's reading hours, then it became an illustrated gift book for children, and now it is read indulgently by the bookish.

According to Hodnett, *A Tale of a Tub* was first published anonymously in 1704, and by 1710 there had been five editions, the 1710 fifth edition being the best. For copies of various editions in the British Museum, see the British Museum *Catalogue*, vol. 53.

"[William] Cobbett tells us that at eleven years old he spent the threepence intended for his supper on the *Tale of a Tub* and could 'relish nothing else'" (Field, pp. 232–33). We may surmise that though some children, like Cobbett, read and enjoyed *A Tale of a Tub*, others may have found Swift's pedantic digressions somewhat disconcerting.

TOKEN FOR CHILDREN (James Janeway)

In 1879 the American Antiquarian Society bought a unique copy of *A Token for Children. Being An Exact Account of the Conversion, Holy and Exemplary Lives and Joyful Deaths of several Young Children. By James Janeway, Minister of the Gospel. To which is Added, A Token, for the Children of New-England. Or, Some Examples of Children, in whom the Fear of God was Remarkably Budding before they Dyed; in several parts of New-England. Preserved and Published for the Encouragement of Piety in other Children* (Boston in NE Printed for Nicholas Boone, at his shop over against the Meeting House 1700). According to the 1933 annual report of the Librarian of the American Antiquarian Society, "The title of the Cotton Mather appendix, which is separately paged, has the imprint 'Boston, in N.E. Printed by Timothy Green, for Benjamin Eliot at his shop, under the west-end of the Town House. 1700.'"

D'Alté Welch has pointed out that in America "there were few narrative books, but the earliest is *A Token for Children.*" It was in two parts by Janeway, with an American contribution by Cotton Mather. Janeway's portion of the 1700 Boston edition had appeared in England in two parts, in 1671 and 1672. This compilation of "stories of overpious preaching children, who died at an early age of some unpleasant disease," was popular and was repeatedly issued in America. It is represented by twenty-nine editions prior to 1816 (*Bibliography*, p. xxi).

In addition to the unique 1700 Boston edition, the American Antiquarian Society has at least five other American editions printed in the early nineteenth century. Seventeenth-century English editions of Janeway's strange work, which was undoubtedly read by children and adults, are in the British Museum.

THOMAS HICKATHRIFT

In his introduction to *The History of Thomas Hickathrift*, G. L. Gomme states that "there seems to be some considerable reason to believe that the hero of this story was a reality." Sir Francis Palgrave, however, suggests that the tale of Thomas Hickathrift is "among those grand mythic tales which belong to the study of comparative mythology" (Gomme and Wheatley, vol. 1, pp. i, xii). Palgrave demonstrates that there are similarities between the story of Thomas Hickathrift and the Scandinavian "Grettir the Strong" (p. xiv). In any case, although the story may have folk origins reaching back beyond the seventeenth century, it has existed in chapbook or literary form since the seventeenth century. The prose version printed in *Chap-Books and Folk-Lore Tracts*, vol. 1, is divided into two parts. The first part, obviously the earliest, is taken from an edition printed between 1660 and 1690, located in the Pepysian Library at Magdalene College, and titled *The Pleasant History of Thomas Hic-Ka-Thrift*. Part 2 is taken from a copy of the 1780 edition located in the British Museum.

The British Museum has a number of eighteenth-century editions, but apparently no earlier editions. See Esdaile (pp. 72–73) for various other editions and locations.

TOM THUMB

With the publication in 1621 of *The History of Tom Thumbe, the Little, for his small stature surnamed, King Arthurs Dwarfe*, Richard Johnson brought to a close his career as the common folk's fiction maker (Wright, pp. 392–93). In his preface (quoted in Wright, p. 393, n. 36) Johnson states:

> The Ancient Tales of Tom Thumbe in the Olde Time, have beene the only revivers of drouzy age at midnight; old and young have with his tales chim'd Mattens till the cocks crow in the morning; Batchelors and Maides with his Tales have compassed the Christmas fire-blocke, till the Curfew-Bell rings candle out; the old Shepheard and the young Plow boy after their dayes labour, have carold out a Tale of Tom Thumbe to make them merry with: and who but little Tom, hath made long nights seem short and heavy toyles easie?

Tom Thumb is a humorous metrical tale that belongs to one of the groups or divisions of the so-called Swallow Cycle, in which a hero is usually swallowed once or more and miraculously escapes (Weiss, *Chapbooks*, p. 90). Almost every man, woman, and child of the seventeenth century was familiar with the story of Tom Thumb. Says Weiss (pp. 94–95),

> Ever since the story has been current, Tom's thrilling adventures have been told and retold, with modifications by each generation, and many variations occur in the numerous editions within a generation. Although the coarseness of the seventeenth century would not be allowed to circulate in the nurseries of today, it should be remembered that in the seventeenth century Tom Thumb was as popular with adults as with children, and no doubt some of the allusions in the early accounts were not intended for childish understanding.

A copy of the 1630 edition of *Tom Thumb* was bequeathed to the Bodleian by Robert Burton, author of *The Anatomy of Melancholy.* John Dunton is said to have sold copies of *Tom Thumb* in 1686 from his Boston, Massachusetts, warehouse. The Pierpont Morgan Library has a unique copy of the 1621 edition.

In his introduction to *Early American Children's Books* (p. xlvii), Rosenbach makes a fascinating comment: "The great Dr. Johnson was a firm upholder of fairy tales for chldren. He relates how he 'withdrew his attention' from the celebrity who was boring him, and 'thought about Tom Thumb' and believed that 'babies do not want to hear about babies, they like to be told of giants and castles, and of somewhat which can stretch and stimulate their little minds.' "

TWO CHILDREN IN THE WOOD

Ashton (p. 371) indicates a 1700 chapbook titled *The Most Lamentable and Deplorable History of the Two Children in the Wood . . . to which is annex'd The Old Song Upon The Same* (London: Printed by and for W. O.). It is likely that earlier ballads preceded the 1700 chapbook version.

Esdaile (p. 186) shows a copy of the 1700 chapbook edition in the British Museum. A copy of a black-letter edition entitled *The History of the Children in the Wood,* etc., is in the Bodleian. The Esdaile listing shows only one other edition, undated, of which a copy is in the British Museum.

VALENTINE AND ORSON

Tales of children reared by animals have always held a certain fascination; hence the great popularity of the Valentine and Orson legend. According to Neuberg (p. 13), the legend has French origins and was popular as a chapbook for well over one hundred years. It was one of the works read by Robert Ashley as a boy (Sloane, p. 5). It may also have been read by Rudyard Kipling, who wrote about a child raised by animals in his *Jungle Book.*

For exact titles and location of copies of the several English editions published prior to 1740, see Esdaile (pp. 133–35).

The library of the University of Connecticut in Storrs has a 1736 edition entitled *The Famous History of Valentine and Orson, the Two Sons of the Emperor of Greece* (16th ed. London: Printed for A. Bettesworth . . . 1736).

THE WANDERING JEW

Although Ashton (pp. 28–29) provides a facsimile title page and a few helpful comments on *The Wandering Jew,* material on this particular romance seems elusive. Ashton says that the myth probably originated in the Gospel of St. John (21:22) and was in existence before the thirteenth century. *The Wandering Jew* was first known in England from a German version of unknown origin (Neuberg, p. 13).

The British Museum has a copy of a ballad edition presumed to have been printed in London (1700?) by and for W. O. and sold by the Booksellers of Pye-Corner and London-Bridge. The copy is entitled *The Wandering Jew; or the Shoemaker of Jerusalem, who lived when our Lord and Saviour Jesus Christ was Crucified, and appointed by him to live until his coming again.*

WHITTINGTON AND HIS CAT

The legend now known as *Whittington and His Cat* arose from the intermingling of fact and folk tale. One Sir Richard Whittington was in actual life Lord Mayor of London during the late fourteenth and early fifteenth centuries. After his death some facts of his life were intermingled with a widespread Persian folk tale. Various accounts of Sir Richard's history were prevalent in one literary form or another throughout the entire seventeenth century, and it is not entirely clear just when the factual became substantially subordinate to the folk-tale characteristics.

In his introduction to *The History of Sir Richard Whittington,* reprinted from the edition entitled *The Famous and Remarkable History of Sir Richard Whittington* (1670?), Henry B. Wheatley states that the reason for grafting the life of Whittington on to a folk tale is still unexplained (Gomme and Wheatley, vol. 5, p. v).

The History of Richard Whittington was licensed as a play in 1604 and as a ballad in 1605. In 1612 Richard Johnson's *Crowne Garland of Golden Roses* contained a song about Whittington, and in 1641 the Roxburghe ballad of Whittington appeared. Esdaile (p. 326) lists various editions and locations. A copy of the 1670 *Famous and Remarkable History* referred to earlier is in the Pepysian Library. The British Museum has a copy of the later edition of 1678. A copy of a 1730 chapbook edition entitled *Sir Richard Whittington, Thrice Lord Mayor of London* can also be found in the British Museum.

Samuel Pepys reportedly saw a puppet show about Whittington in 1668 at the Southwark Fair (Weiss, *Chapbooks,* p. 64).

WINTER EVENING'S ENTERTAINMENTS (Nathaniel Crouch)

"*Winter Evening's Entertainments* consists of 'Ten pleasant and delightful relations of many rare and notable actions and occurrences, fifty ingenious riddles,' and has sixty illustrations. It is, according to R. B. ["Richard Burton," pseudonym of Nathaniel Crouch], 'excellently accommodated to the fancies of old or young, and exceedingly useful to advance chearful society and conversations'" (Field, p. 195).

A copy of the sixth edition (1737) is in the British Museum (Esdaile, p. 197). Muir's comments (pp. 34–35) are worth notice:

"R. B." was also responsible for *Winter Evening's Entertainments,* divided into two parts, the first comprising short stories slightly revamped from previous borrowings, the second of fifty riddles, each illustrated with cuts. Ingenuity of design enables the use of only twenty-seven different cuts to illustrate all the riddles. The same cut, of a man searching his clothing, serves for riddles on the louse and the flea; a miser watching an hour-glass does duty for two subjects; and a ship on the water also does a double stint. The use of cuts in this connection shows a poor grasp of the purpose of illustration, for the illustrations give away the answers.

WISE MEN OF GOTHAM

The Merry Tales of the Wise Men of Gotham, supposedly the work of Andrew Borde, who lived during the fifteenth and sixteenth centuries, was a popular and much-printed chapbook (Weiss, p. 88).

The British Museum has a seventeenth-century (1690?) black-letter edition published in London by J. R. for G. Coniers and J. Dacon, bearing the title *The Merry Tales of the Mad-Men of Gotam. By A. B., Doctor of Physick* [Andrew Borde].

WORLD TURNED UPSIDE DOWN

There have been numerous chapbook versions of *The World Turned Upside Down*. The ox turned farmer, the horse turned groom, the soldier turned nurse, the child turned parent— these and other topsy-turvy situations have delighted young and old for centuries.

Muir (p. 99) suggests that this "topsy-turvydom" may have inspired Swift, particularly his *Gulliver,* and that it most certainly influenced Lewis Carroll's *Alice.* Weiss (*Chapbooks,* pp. 87–88) states that such popular drolleries as appear in English chapbook versions of *The World Turned Upside Down* are found in the literature and popular imagery of all European countries. Weiss notes that the pictures in the earlier chapbook versions were often more amusing than the text, which consisted of "dreary moral essays in verse." Muir (p. 91) feels that "by far the best treatment of this ancient theme" of topsy-turvydom is to be found in the 1810 edition by the Taylor sisters, Ann and Jane, illustrated by their brother Isaac. This nineteenth-century edition is entitled *Signor Topsy Turvy's Wonderful Magic Lantern, or the World Turned Upside Down.*

The British Museum has a 1750 chapbook version of *The World Turned Upside Down.*

Bibliography of Helpful Sources

BOOKS

Aesop. *Aesop: Five Centuries of Illustrated Fables.* Edited by John J. McKendry. New York: Metropolitan Museum of Art, 1964.

———. *Caxton's Aesop.* Edited by R. T. Lenaghan. Cambridge: Harvard University Press, 1967.

Armin, Robert. *Fools and Jesters; with a reprint of Robert Armin's Nest of Ninnies.* Shakespeare Society Publications, vol. 5. London: Shakespeare Society, 1842.

Ashton, John. *Chap-Books of the Eighteenth Century.* 1882. Reprint. New York: Benjamin Blom, 1966.

Ballad Society. *The Roxburghe Ballads.* 9 vols. 1871–99. Reprint (9 vols. in 8). New York: AMS Press, 1966.

Baring-Gould, William S., and Baring-Gould, Ceil, eds. *The Annotated Mother Goose: Nursery Rhymes Old and New.* Illustrated by Walter Crane, Randolph Caldecott, Kate Greenaway, Arthur Rackham. New York: Clarkson N. Potter, 1962.

Bell, Robert, ed. *Early Ballads Illustrative of History, Traditions, and Customs; also Ballads and Songs of the Peasantry of England.* 1887. Reprint. Detroit: Singing Tree Press, 1968.

Bennett, Joan. *Four Metaphysical Poets: Donne, Herbert, Vaughan, Crashaw.* New York: Vintage Books, 1953.

Bingham, Jane, and Scholt, Grace. *Fifteen Centuries of Children's Literature: An Annotated Chronology of British and American Works in Historical Context.* Westport, Ct.: Greenwood Press, 1980.

Blake, N. F., ed. *The History of Reynard the Fox.* Translated by William Caxton. 1481. Reprinted in Early English Text Society Original Series, no. 263. London and New York: Oxford University Press, 1970.

Boas, George. *The Cult of Childhood.* London: Warburg Institute, 1966.

Bradbook, Muriel Clara. *The Rise of the Common Player: A Study of Actor and Society in Shakespeare's England.* Cambridge: Harvard University Press, 1962.

Bunyan, John. *A Book for Boys and Girls; or, Country Rhymes for Children.* Facsimile of the 1686 first edition. London: Elliot Stock, 1890.

Cary, Elizabeth Luther. *The Art of William Blake.* New York: Moffatt, Yard & Co., 1907.

Chambers, Edmund Kercheyer. *The English Folk-play.* Oxford: Clarendon Press, 1933.

Cogan, Thomas. *The Haven of Health . . . Amplified upon Five Words of Hippocrates.* London: Printed by Henry Midleton for William Norton, 1584.

Collection of Old Ballads, A. Corrected from the best and most ancient copies extant. With introductions historical, critical, or humourous. 3 vols. London: J. Roberts, 1723–25.

Cooper, William Durrant, ed. *Ralph Roister Doister, a Comedy by Nicholas Udall, and The Tragedie of Gorboduc, by Thomas Norton and Thomas Sackville.* London: Shakespeare Society, 1847.

Cott, Jonathan, ed. *Beyond the Looking Glass: Extraordinary Works of Fantasy and Fairy Tale*. New York: Stonehill, 1973.

Daiken, Leslie H. *Children's Games Throughout the Year*. London and New York: B. T. Batsford, 1949.

Darton, Frederick Joseph Harvey. *Children's Books in England: Five Centuries of Social Life*. 2d ed. Cambridge: At the University Press, 1929.

Dickson, Arthur. *Valentine and Orson: A Study in Late Medieval Romance*. New York: Columbia University Press, 1929.

Digges, Thomas. *A Perfit Description of the Caelestiall Orbes as contained in Leonard Digges' Prognostication Everlastinge*. London: Thomas Marsh, 1576. Reprinted in "Thomas Digges, the Copernican System, and the Idea of the Infinity of the Universe in 1576," by Francis R. Johnson and Sanford V. Larkey. *Huntington Library Bulletin* 5 (April 1934): 69–117.

Earle, John, Bishop of Salisbury. *Micro-cosmographie. Or, A Peece of the World Discovered; in essays and characters*. Edited by Edward Blount. London: Printed by W. Stansby for R. Allot, 1628.

Egoff, Sheila A. *The Republic of Childhood: A Critical Guide to Canadian Children's Literature in English*. Toronto: Oxford University Press, 1969.

Egoff, Sheila; Stubbs, G. T.; and Ashley, L. F., eds. *Only Connect: Readings on Children's Literature*. Toronto and New York: Oxford University Press, 1969.

Esdaile, Arundell. *A List of English Tales and Prose Romances Printed Before 1740*. 1912. Reprint. New York: Burt Franklin, 1971.

Famous History of Valentine and Orson, the Two Sons of the Emperor of Greece, The. 16th ed. London: A. Bettesworth, 1736.

Favorite Fairy Tales: The Childhood Choice of Representative Men and Women. Illustrated by Peter Newell. New York and London: Harper & Brothers, 1907.

Field, Louise Francis (Story). *The Child and His Book: Some Accounts of the History and Progress of Children's Literature in England*. 2d ed. 1892. Reprint. Detroit: Singing Tree Press, 1968.

Fieler, Frank B. *The David McCandless McKell Collection: A Descriptive Catalog of Manuscripts, Early Printed Books and Children's Books*. Boston: G. K. Hall, 1973.

Fox, Levi. *Shakespeare's England*. London: Wayland, 1972.

Foxe, John. *Actes and Monuments of these latter and perilous dayes . . . from the year of our Lorde a thousande, unto the tyme nowe present*. 8 vols. 4th ed. Revised and corrected by the Rev. Josiah Pratt. London: Religious Tract Society, 1877.

Freeman, Rosemary. *English Emblem Books*. New York: Octagon Books, 1966.

Gailey, Alan. *Irish Folk Drama*. Cork, Ireland: Mercier Press, 1969.

Gerard, John. *The Herball; or Generall Historie of Plantes*. 2d ed. Enlarged and amended by Thomas Johnson. London: Printed by A. Islip, J. Norton and R. Whitakers, 1636.

Gomme, Alice Bertha, ed. *The Traditional Games of England, Scotland, and Ireland; with tunes, singing-rhymes, and methods of playing according to the variants extant and recorded in different parts of the Kingdom*. 2 vols. 1894–98. Reprint. New York: Dover Publications, 1964.

Gomme, G. L., and Wheatley, H. B., eds. *Chap-Books and Folk-Lore Tracts*. First Series. 5 vols. London: Villon Society, 1885.

Greene, Robert. *Friar Bacon and Friar Bungay*. 1594. Malone Society Reprints, vol. 67. London: Printed by John Johnson at the Oxford University Press, 1926.

Griffith, Dudley David. *The Origin of the Griselda Story.* University of Washington Publications in Language and Literature, vol. 8, no. 1. Seattle: University of Washington Press, 1931.

Halliwell, James Orchard, ed. *The Man in the Moone Telling Strange Fortunes; or, The English Fortune Teller.* 1609. Reprinted in Percy Society's Publications, vol. 29. London: Percy Society, 1849.

Halsey, Rosalie V. *Forgotten Books of the American Nursery: A History of the Development of the American Story-Book.* 1911. Reprint. Detroit: Singing Tree Press, 1969.

Hariot, Thomas. *A Briefe and True Report of the New Found Land of Virginia.* Facsimile edition of the 1588 quarto. New York: History Book Club, 1951.

Harris, J. Henry. *Robert Raikes: The Man Who Founded the Sunday School.* Rev. ed. London: National Sunday School Union, n.d.

————. *Robert Raikes: The Man and His Work.* Bristol: J. W. Arrowsmith; London: Simpkin, Marshall, Hamilton, Kent & Co., 1899.

Hazlitt, William Carew, ed. *Tales and Legends of National Origin or Widely Current in England from Early Times.* London: Swann Sonnenschein & Co., 1892.

Helm, Alex. *The Chapbook Mummers' Plays: A Study of the Printed Versions of the North-West of England.* Leicester, England: Guizer Press, 1969.

————, ed. *Five Mumming Plays.* London: English Folk Dance and Song Society and the Folklore Society, 1965.

Hoole, Charles. *A New Discovery of the Art of Teaching Schoole.* Introduced and annotated by T. Mark. Syracuse, N.Y.: C. W. Bardeen, 1912.

Janeway, James. *A Token for Children . . . to which is added A Token, for the Children of New-England* [by Cotton Mather]. Boston: Nicholas Boone, 1700.

Johnson, Edna; Sickels, Evelyn R.; and Sayers, Francis Clarke. *Anthology of Children's Literature.* 3d ed. Boston: Houghton Mifflin Co., 1959.

Kendall, Guy. *Robert Raikes: A Critical Study.* London: Nicholson & Watson, 1939.

Key, Ellen. *The Century of the Child.* New York and London: G. P. Putnam's Sons, 1909.

Kirkman, Francis. *The Unlucky Citizen.* London: Printed by A. Johnson for F. Kirkman, 1673.

Lewis, C. S. *English Literature of the Sixteenth Century.* Oxford: Clarendon Press, 1954.

Lloyd, W. F. *Sketch of the Life of Robert Raikes, Esq.* New York: n.p., 1891.

Mac Donald, Ruth K. *Literature for Children in England and America from 1646 to 1774.* Troy, N.Y.: Whitston Publishing Co., 1982.

Mad Pranks and Merry Jests of Robin Goodfellow, The. 1628. Reprinted in Percy Society's Publications, vol. 2. London: Percy Society, 1841.

Martz, Louis Lohr. *The Poetry of Meditation: A Study in English Religious Literature of the Seventeenth Century.* Yale Studies in English, vol. 125. New Haven: Yale University Press, 1954.

Mish, Charles Carroll, ed. *Short Fiction of the Seventeenth Century.* New York: New York University Press, 1963.

Motter, Thomas Hubbard Vail. *The School Drama in England.* 1929. Reprint. Port Washington, N.Y.: Kennikat Press, 1968.

Muir, Percy. *English Children's Books, 1600–1900.* London: B. T. Batsford, 1954.

Neuberg, Victor E. *The Penny Histories: A Study of Chapbooks for Young Readers over Two*

Centuries. 1st American ed. New York: Harcourt, Brace & World, 1969.

Opie, Iona, and Opie, Peter, eds. *The Classic Fairy Tales.* London: Oxford University Press, 1974.

―――. *Oxford Dictionary of Nursery Rhymes.* Oxford: Clarendon Press, 1951.

Paracelsus. *Four Treatises of Theophrastus von Hohenheim, called Paracelsus.* Edited by Henry E. Sigerist. Baltimore: Johns Hopkins Press, 1941.

Peele, George. *The Old Wives Tale.* 1595. Malone Society Reprints, vol. 32. London: Oxford University Press, 1909.

Penn, William. *The Peace of Europe, Some Fruits of Solitude and Other Writings.* London and Toronto: J. M. Dent & Sons; New York: E. P. Dutton & Co., 1915.

Percy Society. *Early English Poetry, Ballads, and Popular Literature of the Middle Ages.* Percy Society's Publications, 30 vols. London: Percy Society, 1840–52.

Quarles, Francis. *Emblems, Divine and Moral; The School of the Heart; and The Hieroglyphics of the Life of Man.* Rev. ed. London: William Tegg, 1866.

Quayle, Eric. *The Collector's Book of Children's Books.* New York: Clarkson N. Potter, 1971.

Raleigh, Sir Walter Alexander; Lee, Sir Sidney Lazarus; and Onions, Charles Talbut, eds. *Shakespeare's England: An Account of the Life and Manners of His Age.* 2 vols. Oxford: Clarendon Press, 1916.

Raynalde, Thomas. *The Birth of Mankynde, otherwyse named The Womans Booke.* Rev. ed. London: T. Raynalde, 1565.

Rimbault, Edward F. *Maroccus Extaticus; or, Bankes' Bay Horse in a Trance.* 1595. Reprinted in Percy Society's Publications, vol. 9. London: Percy Society, 1843.

Ritson, Joseph, ed. *Ancient Popular Poetry, from Authentic Manuscripts and Old Printed Copies.* Revised by Edmund Goldsmid. Edinburgh: n.p., 1884.

―――, comp. *Ancient Songs and Ballads, from the Reign of King Henry the Second to the Revolution.* 1877. 3d ed. Revised by W. Carew Hazlitt. Reprint. Detroit: Singing Tree Press, 1968.

Rosenbach, A. S. W. *Early American Children's Books.* Portland, Me.: Southworth Press, 1933.

Sands, Donald B., ed. *The History of Reynard the Fox.* Translated by William Caxton. 1481. Reprint. Cambridge: Harvard University Press, 1960.

Scottish Text Society. *The Bannatyne Manuscript.* Vol. 4. Edinburgh: Blackwood, 1930.

Shepard, Leslie. *The Broadside Ballad: A Study in Origins and Meanings.* London: Herbert Jenkins, 1962.

Sloane, William. *Children's Books in England and America in the Seventeenth Century: A History and Checklist; Together with The Young Christian's Library.* New York: Columbia University, King's Crown Press, 1955.

Smith, Lillian. *The Unreluctant Years: A Critical Approach to Children's Literature.* Chicago: American Library Association, 1953.

Southern, Richard. *The Seven Ages of the Theatre.* London: Faber and Faber, 1962.

Stafford, Margaret. *Small Books and Pleasant Histories: Popular Fiction and Its Readership in Seventeenth-Century England.* Athens: University of Georgia Press, 1981.

Swift, Jonathan. *The Prose Works of Jonathan Swift.* Edited by Herbert Davis. Vol. 1. Oxford: Blackwell, 1939.

―――. *A Tale of a Tub, written for the universal improvement of mankind.* Edited by Edward Hodnett. New York, Columbia University Press, 1930.

Thoms, William J., ed. *Early English Prose Romances.* London: George Routledge and Sons; New York: E. P. Dutton and Co., 1906.

———. *The History of Reynard the Fox.* Translated by William Caxton. 1481. Reprinted in Percy Society's Publications, vol. 12. London: Percy Society, 1844.

Thomson, Gladys Scott. *Life in a Noble Household, 1641–1700.* 1937. Reprint. Ann Arbor: University of Michigan Press, 1959.

Tillyard, E. M. W. *The Elizabethan World Picture.* New York: Random House, 1959.

Topsell, Edward. *The Historie of Foure-footed Beastes.* London: William Jaggard, 1607.

Weiss, Harry B. *A Book about Chapbooks: The People's Literature of Bygone Times.* 1942. Facsimile reprint. Hatboro, Pa.: Folklore Associates, 1969.

Welch, D'Alté Aldridge. *A Bibliography of American Children's Books Printed Prior to 1821.* Worcester, Mass.: American Antiquarian Society, 1972.

Willey, Basil. *The Seventeenth Century Background: Studies in the Thought of the Age in Relation to Poetry and Religion.* New York: Columbia University Press, 1950.

Wright, Louis B. *Middle-Class Culture in Elizabethan England.* 1935. Reprint. Ithaca, N.Y.: Cornell University Press, 1958.

Zall, Paul M., ed. *A Nest of Ninnies and Other English Jestbooks of the Seventeenth Century.* Lincoln: University of Nebraska Press, 1970.

ARTICLES

Brockman, Bennett. "Robin Hood and the Invention of Children's Literature." *Children's Literature* 10 (1982): 1–18.

———. "Children and the Audiences of Robin Hood." *South Atlantic Review* 46 (1983): 67–83.

Brown, Arthur C. "The Source of a Guy of Warwick Chap-book." *Journal of Germanic Philology* 3 (1901): 14–23.

Burns, Lee. "Red Riding Hood." *Children's Literature* 1 (1972): 30–36.

Cate, Wirt Armistead. "The Problem of the Origin of the Griselda Story." *Studies in Philology* 29 (July 1932): 389–405.

Crane, Ronald S. "The Reading of an Elizabethan Youth." *Modern Philology* 11 (1913–14): 269–71.

———. "The Vogue of Guy of Warwick from the Close of the Middle Ages to the Romantic Revival." *PMLA* 30 (1915): 125–94.

Haight, Gordon S. "The Publication of Quarles's *Emblems.*" *Library* 15 (1934–35): 97–109.

———. "The Sources of Quarles's *Emblems.*" *Library* 16 (1935): 188–209.

Hanks, Carole, and Hanks, D. T., Jr. "Perrault's 'Little Red Riding Hood'; Victim of the Reviewers." *Children's Literature* 7 (1978): 68–77.

Jacobus, Lee A. "Milton's *Comus* as Children's Literature." *Children's Literature* 2 (1973): 67–72.

Miner, Robert G., Jr. "Aesop as Litmus: The Acid Test of Children's Literature." *Children's Literature* 1 (1972): 9–15.

Mish, Charles C. "Reynard the Fox in the Seventeenth Century." *Huntington Library Quarterly* 27 (1953–54): 327–44.

Queenan, Bernard. "The Evolution of the Pied Piper." *Children's Literature* 7 (1978): 104–14.

Rollins, Hyder E. "An Analytical Index to the Ballad Entries, 1557–1709, in the Registers of the Company of Stationers in London." *Studies in Philology* 21 (1924).

Scott, Dorothea Hayward. "Perrault and Aesop's Fables." *Children's Literature* 10 (1982): 218-25.

Stone, Harry. "Dark Corners of the Mind: Dickens' Childhood Reading." *Horn Book* 39 (June 1963): 306-21.

Stone, Wilbur Macey. "Collections of Rare Children's Books—A Symposium, Part III." *Library Journal* 63 (March 1, 1938): 192-93.

Weiss, Harry B. "American Editions of 'Sir Richard Whittington and His Cat.' " *New York Public Library Bulletin* 42 (June 1938): 477-85.

_____. "The Autochthonal Tale of Jack the Giant Killer." *Scientific Monthly* 28 (February 1929): 126-33.

_____. "Three Hundred Years of Tom Thumbe." *Scientific Monthly* 34 (February 1932): 157-66.

Welch, D'Alté A. "A Bibliography of American Children's Books Printed Prior to 1821." *Proceedings of the American Antiquarian Society* 73 (April 17, 1963): 121-324.

White Allison. "Pilgrim's Progress as Fairy Tale." *Children's Literature* 1 (1972): 42-45.

Wooden, Warren W. "Childermass Ceremonies in Late Medieval England: The Literary Legacy." *Fifteenth-Century Studies* 4 (1981): 195-205.

_____. "Childhood and Death: A Reading of John Skelton's *Phillip Sparrow.*" *Journal of Psychohistory* 7 (Spring 1980): 403-14.

_____. "A Child's Garden of Sprites: English Renaissance Fairy Poetry." In *Perspectives on Children's Literature,* edited by Anita Moss. Knoxville: University of Tennessee Press, in press.

_____. "From Caxton to Comenius: The Origins of Children's Literature." *Fifteenth-Century Studies* (1983).

_____. "John Foxe's *Book of Martyrs* and the Child Reader." *Proceedings of the Children's Literature Association* (1982).

_____. "Michael Drayton's *Nymphidia:* A Renaissance Children's Classic?" *Children's Literature* 6 (1977): 34-41.

_____. "Recent Studies in John Foxe." *English Literary Renaissance* 11 (Spring 1981): 224-32.

_____. "The Topos of Childhood in Marian England." *Journal of Medieval and Renaissance Studies* 12 (1982): 179-94.

DISSERTATIONS OF NOTE:

Mac Donald, Ruth K. "Literature for Children in England, 1659-1774." Ph.D. dissertation, Rutgers University, 1977. 38:6744A.

Wahlquist, Dennis John. "The Best Copy of Adam: Seventeenth-Century Attitudes Toward Childhood in the Poetry of Donne, Herbert, Vaughan, and Traherne." Ph.D. dissertation, University of Southern California, 1979. DAI 39:6785A.

Charity Chang has an M.A. in English from the University of Tennessee and an M.S. in Library Science from the University of Illinois. She continued advanced study in English at Baylor University, the University of Nebraska, and the University of Connecticut, where she did graduate study in children's literature under Francelia Butler.